PRIZE WINNING RECIPES
FROM AROUND THE WORLD

If additional copies of this book are desired, please send

$10.00

for each book ordered to:

BECKER PUBLICATIONS, INC.
Dept. PWR
23450 Kidder St.
Hayward, CA 94545

California residents please add appropriate sales tax.

Recipe for Cover Photo can be found on page 119.

Printed in the United States of America.

MAIN DISHES

SUKIYAKI

1 Chuck Steak (about 1½ lbs.)
¼ Cup Vegetable Oil
2 Medium Sweet Potatoes, pared
    and thinly sliced
½ Lb. Green Beans, tipped and cut
    into 1" pieces
1 Small Green Pepper, halved, seeded
    and cut into thin strips
1 Small Sweet Red Pepper, halved,
    seeded and cut into thin strips
1 Cup Thinly-sliced Celery
½ Cup Soy Sauce
1 Cup Water
1 Small Head Chinese Cabbage,
    shredded
1 Bunch Green Onions, trimmed and
    cut into 2" pieces
4 Large Mushrooms, washed, trimmed
    and sliced

Trim all fat from steak. Partially freeze the meat for 1 hour so it is firm, then cut meat into very thin strips. Heat oil in a large skillet with a cover. Add the steak strips and saute', stirring occasionally, for 2 to 3 minutes, or until brown. Remove with a slotted spoon and keep warm. Add potatoes, green beans, green and red peppers and celery; saute' 2 to 3 minutes, or until vegetables start to soften. Combine soy sauce and water in a cup; pour over vegetables. Cover and simmer for 5 minutes. Stir in shredded cabbage, green onions and mushrooms. Cover and cook 5 minutes longer, or until cabbage wilts and vegetables are tender-crisp. Return cooked steak strips to pan and heat until piping hot. Serve with hot cooked rice and more soy sauce. Makes 6 servings.

BELGIAN BEEF CASSEROLE

1½ Lbs. Beef Round, sliced 1" thick
    and cut into 1" cubes
4 Tbs. Butter
2 Cups Beef Stock
1¼ Cups Dried Apricots
1 Tsp. Sugar
4 or 5 Onions, white parts only
Salt and Pepper to taste
1 Tsp. Grated Lemon Peel

In a flameproof casserole over fairly high heat, brown the beef quickly in the butter. Add the stock, apricots and sugar & reduce the heat to low; simmer for 15 min. Blanch the onions by putting them into cold water and gradually bringing them to a boil; drain. Add the onions to the casserole; season to taste. Cover and simmer gently for 2 hours, until the beef is fork-tender. Check the seasoning; add the lemon peel. Stir and simmer for 5 min. Makes 4 servings.

THREE-MEAT GOULASH
(From Prague)

1½ Lbs. Onions, coarsely chopped
    (about 4 cups)
¼ Cup Shortening
1½ Lbs. Beef Chuck, cubed
2 Tsp. Salt
1 - 6 Oz. Can Tomato Paste
½ Lb. Veal Shoulder, cubed
½ Lb. Fresh Pork Shoulder, cubed
1 Cup Dry White Wine
1 Cup Dairy Sour Cream

In a heavy three-quart saucepan or Dutch oven, saute' the onions in the fat until they are golden. Add the beef and cook over medium heat until it loses its bright redness. Add the salt and tomato paste; reduce heat, cover and simmer slowly 30 minutes. Add the veal and pork and continue to simmer slowly, covered, for 1 hour; add the wine and continue to simmer, covered, for 30 minutes more, or until the meats are tender. Stir in the sour cream and heat for a few minutes, but do not boil. Makes 8 servings.

BARBECUED BEEF FOR A CROWD

4½ Lbs. Boneless Beef
3 Tbs. Melted Shortening (more
   if needed)
3 Cups Water
¼ Cup Worcestershire Sauce
1 Cup Tomato Sauce
1 Cup Ketchup
4 Cups Chopped Onions
1½ Tsp. Salt, or to taste
¼ Tsp. Pepper, or to taste

Cut beef into 4" pieces; brown well in hot shortening. Add to 3 cups of water and simmer until tender, about 2 hours. Remove beef from cooking liquid and put through a food chopper, using coarse blade. While the meat is cooking, saute' the onions in melted shortening until tender. Combine onions & remaining ingredients with the ground meat and add enough of the cooking liquid to make the filling moist but spreadable (you will need about 2 cups of the liquid). Heat the filling and serve on hamburger buns or small French rolls. Makes enough filling for 50 sandwiches.

STEAK PIZZAIOLA

1 Cup Chopped Onion (1 large)
2 Cloves Garlic, minced
3 Tbs. Olive Oil or Vegetable Oil
1 - 1 Lb. Can Italian Tomatoes
1 Tsp. Salt
¼ Tsp. Seasoned Pepper
Dash of Sugar
1 - 2 Lb. Chuck Steak
Unseasoned Instant Meat Tenderizer

Saute' the onion and garlic in oil until soft in a large saucepan. Stir in tomatoes, salt, pepper and sugar. Simmer sauce, uncovered, for 10 minutes. Set aside. While sauce is simmering, trim any excess fat from steak & score remaining fat edge every inch. Sprinkle meat with tenderizer, following directions on label. Heat a large skillet. Pan-broil the steak in skillet, turning once, for 5 minutes on each side, or until steak is as done as you like it. Place steak on cutting board; carve into thin slices. Return to skillet. Stir in reserved tomato mixture and simmer for 3 minutes to blend flavors. Makes 6 servings.

SWEDISH MEATBALLS

4 Eggs, slightly beaten
2 Cups Milk
1 Cup Packaged Dry Bread Crumbs
4 Tbs. Butter or Margarine
1 Cup Finely-chopped Onion
2 Lbs. Ground Chuck
½ Lb. Ground Pork
Salt
Dill Weed
¼ Tsp. Allspice
¼ Tsp. Nutmeg
¼ Tsp. Ground Cardamom
1/3 Cup Flour
¼ Tsp. Pepper
2 - 10½ Oz. Cans Condensed Beef
   Broth, undiluted
1 Cup Light Cream

In a large bowl combine eggs, milk and dry bread crumbs. In 2 tablespoons of hot butter in large skillet, saute' chopped onion until soft--about 5 minutes. Lift out with a slotted spoon. Add to bread-crumb mixture along with ground meats, 3 teaspoons salt, ½ tsp. dill weed, the allspice, nutmeg and cardamom. Mix well with a wooden spoon or with your hands. Refrigerate for 1 hour, covered. Shape meat mixture into 60 meatballs. Preheat oven to 325°F. In remaining hot butter, saute' the meatballs, about one-third at a time, until browned all over. Remove as browned to two 2-quart casseroles. Remove skillet from heat and pour off all but ¼ cup drippings; stir in flour, ½ teaspoon salt, and the pepper. Gradually stir in beef broth. Bring to a boil, stirring constantly. Add cream and 1 teaspoon dill weed. Pour over meatballs in casseroles. Bake, covered, for 30 minutes. Garnish top of meatballs with fresh dill sprigs, if desired. Makes 20 servings.

SOMBRERO CHILI

2 Lbs. Lean Boneless Beef Chuck,
   cut in 1" cubes
¼ Cup Sifted All-purpose Flour
2 Tbs. Chili Powder
2 Tsp. Salt
¼ Tsp. Pepper
¼ Cup Shortening
1 Large Onion, chopped (1 cup)
2 - 1 Lb. Cans Red Kidney Beans
2 - 1 Lb. Cans Tomatoes
1 - 12 or 16 Oz. Can Whole-kernel Corn
2 Tbs. Butter or Margarine
2 Cups Hot Cooked Rice
1 Cup Grated Cheddar Cheese
   (4 ounces)
1 - 4 Oz. Can Pimientos, sliced
1 - 4 Oz. Can Hot Chili Peppers

Combine flour, chili powder, salt and pepper in a paper bag. Add beef cubes and shake to coat well with flour mixture. Brown the pieces of meat, a few at a time, in shortening in a kettle or Dutch oven. Return all meat to the kettle. Stir in onion and saute' for 5 minutes, or until onion is soft. Spoon off any excess drippings and stir any remaining flour-seasoning mixture into pan. Drain the liquid from the kidney beans and add to beef mixture; stir in tomatoes. Cover and simmer for 1½ hours, or until beef is tender. Stir several times during the 1½ hours. Stir in kidney beans; heat just to boiling.

To serve, drain the corn and heat in butter or margarine in a small saucepan. Spoon hot chili into a heated 12-cup deep serving bowl or tureen. Spoon corn in a layer in center; top with a cone of hot rice. If you prefer, the corn can simply be heated in the chili mixture. Serve the rice separately, doubling the amount to 4 cups so that guests can spoon chili over generous servings of rice. Serve with grated cheese, sliced pimientos and chili peppers to put over top. Makes 8 servings.

SUMMER MEAT LOAF

1 Lb. Lean Beef, ground
½ Lb. Ground Pork
½ Lb. Ground Veal
½ Cup Wheat Germ
2 Eggs
1 Medium Onion
1 Garlic Clove
1 Tsp. Salt
1/8 Tsp. Ground Pepper
2 Tbs. Catchup
1 Tsp. Worcestershire Sauce
Dash of Hot Pepper Sauce
1 Bay Leaf
¼ Tsp. Thyme
6 Strips Bacon

Combine ground meats in large mixing bowl. Stir in wheat germ. Place all other ingredients, except bacon, in electric blender and liquify. Pour liquid over meat; knead with fingers until well blended. Place 3 strips of bacon in bottom of a lightly-greased loaf pan (8½x4½x2-5/8"). Put meat loaf mixture in pan, patting down. Place 3 strips of bacon lengthwise across top. Bake at 350°F. for 1½ to 1¾ hours, or until meat is cooked through. Makes 6 to 8 servings.

BRAISED BEEF ROAST

1 - 2½ Lb. Beef Eye of Round
1 Tbs. Olive Oil or Vegetable Oil
1 Tbs. Butter
1 Slice Bacon, chopped
Salt and Pepper to taste
1/8 Tsp. Grated Nutmeg
3 or 4 Anchovy Fillets, soaked in
   water for 10 minutes, patted dry
   and finely chopped
2 Tsp. Chopped Fresh Parsley
1 Cup Beef Stock or Water

Put meat into a large saucepan with the oil, butter, bacon, salt, pepper & nutmeg; brown the meat slowly but thoroughly. When it is well browned, add the anchovies, parsley & stock or water. Reduce the heat, cover the pan and cook slowly for about 1¼ hours, or until the meat is tender. Slice the meat and serve it covered with its gravy. Add a little water to the gravy if necessary. Makes 6 servings.

KOREAN MEATBALLS

2 Tbs. Sesame Seed
1 Green Onion, minced
1 Clove Garlic, minced
2 Tsp. Soy Sauce
½ Tsp. Accent
1 Tbs. Salad Oil
1 Lb. Ground Beef

Toast sesame seed in frying pan. Add all ingredients, except oil, to the ground beef. Mix well. Form into balls the size of walnuts. Fry until brown in oil. Makes 4 servings.

CHEDDAR STEAK

1 Chuck Beef Steak, about 3½ lbs.
Instant Unseasoned Meat Tenderizer
3 Tbs. Bottled Steak Sauce
¼ Cup Chopped Pecans
½ Cup Grated Cheddar Cheese

Remove the steak from the refrigerator 1 hour before cooking. When ready to cook, sprinkle with meat tenderizer, following label directions. Brush both sides with steak sauce; place on rack in broiler pan. Bake in very hot oven, 450°F, for 25 min., for rare, or until done as you like it. Remove from oven; turn off heat. Sprinkle pecans, then cheese, over steak; return to heated oven just until cheese melts. Carve into ¼-inch-thick slices; spoon juices over. Makes 6 servings.

VIENNESE BEEFSTEAKS

4 Fillet Steaks, ½" thick
1 Tbs. Lard
4 Tbs. Chopped Onion
1 Tbs. Butter
1 Cup Beef Broth

Beat the steaks well and fry quickly in the lard on both sides. Add the onions and continue cooking on lower heat until the meat is done. Remove the meat and keep it hot. Fry the onions until golden, adding butter to the pan. Pour in the broth and bring to a boil. Pour over the meat and serve with boiled potatoes.

CANTONESE SLIPPERY BEEF

1 Lb. Beef Flank Steak (or sirloin tip) cut 1" thick
1 Egg White, lightly beaten
3 Tbs. Cornstarch
2 Tbs. Soy Sauce
3 Medium Tomatoes
4 Thin Slices Fresh Gingerroot
3 Tbs. Peanut Oil

Soy Glaze:
1 Tbs. Soy Sauce
1 Tbs. Oyster Sauce
1 Tsp. Sugar

Cut the beef diagonally and across the grain into slices ¼" thick, then cut the slices into pieces 1½" long, to make about 2 cups. Put the beef into a bowl. Add the egg white, cornstarch and soy sauce. Mix well with your hands and set beef aside for 30 min.

Dip the tomatoes into boiling water for 10 seconds. Peel and cut each tomato into 6 to 8 wedges. Remove the seeds and set the tomatoes aside on a plate.

In a large pot bring 1 quart of water to a rolling boil. Add the marinated beef, stirring gently to separate the pieces. Turn off the heat and drain the meat immediately. Cool the meat in 1 quart of cold water. Drain well again. The meat can sit for several hours at this stage. Heat a wok over medium heat until very hot. Add the oil, tomatoes and ginger, and stir-fry for 1 min. Turn the heat to high and add the drained beef. Stir for 30 seconds. Add the mixed sauce ingredients to the beef. Keep over high heat and stir until the sauce coats everything well, about 30 seconds more. Serve immediately. Makes 4 servings.

BEEF ROLLS

3 Lbs. Ground Beef
1 Tsp. Salt
1 Tsp. Dired Vegetable Flakes
1 - 8 Oz. Pkg. Sliced Swiss Cheese
1 - 6 Oz. Pkg. Sliced Canadian Bacon
2 Eggs
¼ Cup Water
1 Cup Seasoned Bread Crumbs
1/3 Cup Butter or Margarine
1 - 10½ Oz. Can Condensed Golden
   Mushroom Soup
1 Cup Milk
1 Medium Tomato, cut into 8 wedges

Mix ground beef lightly with salt and vege-table flakes in a large bowl. Shape into 8 patties about ¼" thick. Cut slices of Swiss cheese in half crosswise. Top each pattie with a slice of cheese and Canadian bacon and roll up, jelly-roll fashion. Beat eggs with water in a pie plate; place bread crumbs in a second pie plate. Dip meat rolls into egg mixture, then into bread crumbs to coat well. Saute', turning often, in butter or mar-garine in a large frying pan for 25 minutes, or until beef is done as you like it. Remove to a heated serving platter; keep warm while making gravy. Pour all drippings from fry-ing pan, then stir soup and milk into pan. Heat slowly, stirring constantly and scraping brown bits from bottom of pan, until bub-bly hot. Taste and season with salt and pep-per, if needed. Garnish meat rolls with to-mato wedges; serve with gravy. Makes 8 servings.

HAMBURGER GUACAMOLE

1 Lb. Beef Chuck, ground
1 Avocado
1 Tomato, chopped
1 Medium Onion, chopped
¼ Tsp. Hot Pepper Sauce
1 Tbs. Fresh Lemon Juice
4 Slices of Toast

Shape meat into 4 good-size patties and cook to desired doneness. Mash avocado and add next four ingredients. Put meat on toasted rounds of bread. Spoon some of the mixture over each and put under broiler or heat in oven for a few minutes. Serve with remaining sauce. Serves 4.

BEEF BIRMINGHAM

1 Garlic Clove, sliced
1 Lb. Beef for Stew, cut into
   thin strips
1 Cup Sliced Onion (3 medium)
1 Cup Sliced Celery
2 Tbs. Cooking Oil
2 Tbs. Peanut Butter
2 Tbs. Soy Sauce
½ Tsp. Sugar
1 Cup Beef Bouillon
Dash of Pepper
Hot Cooked Rice or Noodles

Saute' garlic, beef, onions and celery in hot oil until lightly browned. Add remaining in-gredients except for rice; bring to a boil, cover and simmer for 1 hour, or until meat is tender. Add additional liquid during cooking if needed. Serve on rice. Makes 4 servings.

SPICY SHORT RIBS

3 to 4 Lbs. Beef Short Ribs
1 Cup Catsup
1 Cup Water
1 Tbs. Cider Vinegar
1 Tbs. Worcestershire Sauce
1 Tbs. Prepared Horseradish
1 Tbs. Sugar
1 Tbs. Dry Mustard
1 Tsp. Salt
¼ Tsp. Pepper
1 Bay Leaf
2 Medium Onions, sliced

Combine short ribs with remaining ingre-dients, except onions, in large saucepan. Cover and simmer for 2 hours, or until meat is tender. Cool, then chill until 1¼ hours before serving time. Skim off all fat and remove any loose bones from ribs; remove bay leaf. Place meat in a 6-cup baking dish; pour sauce over and top with onion slices. Cover and bake in 350°F. oven for 30 minutes; uncover; baste on-ions with sauce in dish. Bake 30 minutes longer, or until meat is very tender. Makes 4 servings.

BARBECUED BEEF BRISKET

2 Tbs. Liquid Smoke
6 to 7 Lb. Boneless Brisket,
   well trimmed
2/3 Cup Vegetable Oil
1/3 Cup White Wine Vinegar
2 Tsp. Hickory-smoked Salt
   (charcoal-flavored)
1 Tsp. Garlic Salt
1 Tsp. Black Pepper, freshly
   ground
3 Cups Hickory-flavored
   Barbecue Sauce

Rub liquid smoke over entire surface of
brisket. Place meat in a shallow pan and
pour combined oil and vinegar over it.
Refrigerate for 4 to 5 hours, turning occasionally. Just before cooking, remove
the brisket from the marinade and pat dry.
Rub the salts and pepper into both sides
of the beef. Brush with ¼ cup of barbecue
sauce.

Have coals hot in barbecue (it is best to
use a covered grill). Toss on a layer of
dampened hickory chips and position the
grill 5 inches above the coals. Sear meat
5 to 6 minutes on each side. Remove the
brisket from the grill and place it on two
layers of heavy-duty aluminum foil. Coat
with additional ½ cup barbecue sauce. Seal
foil carefully to prevent the juices from es-
caping. Place sealed brisket back on grill &
roast 45 minutes on each side, or until done
as desired. Renew coals as necessary. The
time given is for an open grill; keep in mind
that if you are using a covered grill, the
brisket will cook faster, thus shortening the
length of time the meat stays on the grill.

When meat is done, remove it carefully from
the foil, saving any juices to add to remaining barbecue sauce. Serve brisket, thinly
sliced against the grain, with warmed barbecue sauce. Any leftover brisket is excellent
served cold. Makes 10 to 12 servings.

JAPANESE-STYLE SKEWERED BEEF

1 Can Pineapple Chunks
1/3 Cup Soy Sauce
1 Garlic Clove, minced
¾ Tsp. Ground Ginger
1 Lb. Sirloin of Beef, cut
   into ¾" slices
1 Small Jar Stuffed Olives
   (small olives)

Drain the juice from the pineapple and
mix with the soy sauce, garlic & ginger.
Add the beef and let it marinate for 1
hour. Cut the beef into ¾" cubes.
Place alternate pieces of beef and pineapple on wooden skewers and put an
olive at the end of each skewer. Grill,
turning once, for 10 to 12 minutes.
Makes about 2 dozen, allowing 2 to 3
per person.

HAWAIIAN MEAT ROLLS

1 Lb. Ground Beef
½ Cup Shredded Pineapple
1 Tsp. Minced Onion
1 Tbs. Tomato Sauce
Salt and Pepper
1 Lb. Potatoes
1 Tsp. Butter
½ Cup Self-rising Flour
1 Tbs. Chopped Parsley
1 Egg

Combine meat, pineapple, onion and
tomato sauce. Season with salt and pepper and cook over low heat until the
meat is no longer red. Cook the potatoes in a separate pot; drain, mash and
mix with the butter, flour, parsley and
beaten egg. Turn onto a floured board
and roll out ¼" thick and cut into 3"
squares. Place a spoonful of meat mixture on each square; moisten the edges
and fold over. Press the edges lightly
with a fork. Place on a greased baking
tray and brush with the remaining egg
mixture. Bake in a moderate oven
(425°F.) for 15 to 20 minutes. Serve
piping hot.

CALCUTTA BEEF CURRY

1 Lb. Lean Beef
2 Cups Water
1 Tbs. Ground Coriander Seed
1 Tsp. Ground Turmeric
1 Tsp. Ground Chili Peppers
Pinch of Ginger
Pinch of Black Pepper
2 Tbs. Butter
1 Cup Thick Coconut Milk
1 Onion, sliced
1 Clove Garlic, crushed
Salt to taste
Lemon Juice

Remove any fat from the meat. Cut it into pieces and simmer in water until just tender. Mix together the seasonings and pepper and make a paste with a little of the coconut milk. Fry the onion and garlic until tender and add the paste, then continue to fry for an additional 3 to 4 minutes. Add the meat and a little stock; bring slowly to a boil and add the coconut milk, salt and lemon juice. Serve with rice.

BEEF-MACARONI LOAF

Macaroni Layers:
1 - 8 Oz. Pkg. Elbow Macaroni
2 Tbs. Butter or Margarine
2 Tbs. Flour
1 Tsp. Salt
¼ Tsp. Pepper
1 Egg
2 Cups Milk
½ Cup Grated Parmesan Cheese

Meat Layer:
1 Small Onion, chopped (¼ cup)
1 Tbs. Butter or Margarine
1½ Lbs. Ground Beef
1 Egg
1 - 10¾ Oz. Can Condensed Tomato
   Soup
1 Tsp. Salt
¼ Tsp. Pepper

Sauce:
1 - 8 Oz. Can Tomato Sauce
1 Tsp. Sugar
¼ Tsp. Leaf Basil, crumbled

Grease a loaf pan, 9x5x3"; line bottom and ends with a double-thick strip of foil, leaving a 1-inch overhang; grease foil. Make the macaroni layers. Cook macaroni, following directions on label. Drain and return to kettle. Stir in butter or margarine; sprinkle the flour, salt and pepper over; toss to mix well. Beat egg; stir in milk and pour over macaroni mixture. Cook, stirring constantly, over medium heat until thickened. Remove from heat and stir in Parmesan cheese.

To make meat layer, saute' onion in butter or margarine until soft; add ground beef & brown, breaking up meat with a fork as it cooks. Beat egg; stir in ½ can of tomato soup, salt, and pepper. Stir into cooked meat mixture. Spoon half of the macaroni mixture in an even layer in prepared pan and top with all of the meat mixture, then remaining macaroni mixture. Bake in 350º F. oven for 1 hour, or until firm and brown on top.

While loaf bakes, prepare the sauce. Heat tomato sauce with the remaining ½ can of tomato soup, sugar and basil. Bring to a boil; reduce heat and simmer 2 to 3 minutes to blend flavors. Cool loaf in pan 10 minutes; loosen from sides with knife, then lift up ends of foil and set loaf on a heated serving platter. Slide out foil. Slice loaf and serve sauce separately to spoon over the slices. Makes 6 to 8 servings.

BEEF STEW

2 Lbs. Lean Beef for Stew
Cooking Oil
2 Lbs. Small White Onions, peeled
1 Bay Leaf
2 Tsp. Salt
½ Tsp. Cloves
¼ Tsp. Allspice
¼ Tsp. Pepper
1 - 8 Oz. Can Tomato Sauce
½ Cup Dry Red Wine
2 Garlic Cloves, crushed

Brown meat in oil in a large skillet. Combine meat and remaining ingredients in an electric cooker. Cover and cook on low for 8 to 10 hours, or until meat is tender. Serve with noodles, if desired. Makes 8 servings.

MOUNTAIN PASS CHILI

½ Lb. Ground Beef
4 Green Onions, chopped
1 Tbs. Salad Oil
1 No. 2 Can Pinto Beans
1 - 8 Oz. Can Tomatoes
1 - 4 Oz. Can Chopped Green
   Chili Peppers
1 Tsp. Salt
1 Tsp. Pepper
1 Tbs. Chili Powder

Cook meat and onions in salad oil in a
heavy skillet, stirring with a fork, until
meat loses its pink color. Add remaining
ingredients with 1 cup water. Bring to
a boil. Serve immediately, or simmer
until serving time. Makes 4 servings.

LONDON BROIL

2½ Lbs. Top-quality Steak,
   cut 1½ to 2" thick
3 Tbs. Butter or Margarine
1 - 6 Oz. Can Sliced Mushrooms
3 Tbs. Lemon Juice
½ Tsp. Salt
Freshly-ground Pepper
¼ Cup Consomme'
¼ Cup Dry Red Wine
1 Tsp. Cornstarch
2 Tbs. Grated Lemon Peel

Place steak on greased grill about 4 inches
above hot glowing coals. Broil 4 to 5 min.
on each side, longer if you prefer medium
or well-done meat. While steak cooks, melt
butter or margarine in saucepan. Stir in
mushrooms and liquid and saute' for 1 to
2 minutes. Add lemon juice. Stir & cook
for 2 minutes. Add salt, pepper, consomme'
and wine. Bring to a boil. Remove from
heat. Stir cornstarch into about 1 tablespoon of cold water until smooth, then
stir into hot sauce. Return to heat and
bring to a boil, stirring constantly. Boil
1 or 2 minutes, or until clean and
thickened. Use a sharp, thin knife and
cut steak diagonally into thin slices onto
a warm platter, overlapping the slices.
Pour hot sauce over. Serve at once (the
sauce may be made ahead of time and
reheated at the barbecue). Makes 6
servings.

JAPANESE BEEF DINNER

1 Cup Shoyu Sauce
½ Cup Dry Sherry or Sake
½ Cup Olive Oil
¼ Cup Cider Vinegar
¼ Tsp. Chili Powder
Beef Fat, for skillet
1 Lb. Sirloin Steak, cut into
   thin strips
2 or 3 Cubes Bean Curd (Tofu)
2 Green Peppers, cut into strips
   and parboiled
1 Small Eggplant, cut into thin
   slices
6 Carrots, scraped, boiled and
   cut into strips

Mix shoyu sauce, sherry or sake, oil and
vinegar. Season with chili powder to
taste. Pour about half of mixture into a
shallow dish. Pour remaining mixture into
4 small dishes for guests. Add just enough
fat to skillet to sizzle evenly all over the
cooking surface. Dip strips of steak into
shoyu mixture. Lay on hot cooking surface. Cook at high heat, turning meat
once, until beef is done. Serve at once
or push to one side in skillet. Add the
vegetables. Cook in very little fat until
tender and brown. Serve all at once on
warm dinner plates. Guests use fork or
chopsticks to dip meat into sauce. Makes
4 servings.

GINGERED POT ROAST

4 Lbs. Beef for Pot Roast
1 Tsp. Ground Turmeric
2 Tsp. Ground Ginger
2 Tsp. Salt
2 Tbs. Fat
2 Onions, chopped
2 Garlic Cloves, minced
1 Cup Canned Tomatoes
1 Cup Beef Bouillon
2 Dried Red Peppers, crushed

Rub meat with turmeric, ginger and salt.
Brown on all sides in fat in a heavy kettle. Put meat on a rack in the kettle;
add remaining ingredients. Cover and
simmer over low heat for 3½ hours, or
until meat is tender. Makes 6 servings.

CALIFORNIA STYLE SWISS STEAK

1 Cup Dry White Table Wine
3 Tbs. Wine Vinegar
1 Can Green Chili, finely chopped
1 Tbs. Brown Sugar
1 Tsp. Salt
¼ Tsp. Garlic Powder
2 Lbs. Beef Round Steak, cut
   1½ to 2 inches thick
2 Tbs. Shortening

Sauce:

1 Cup Drained Marinade
½ Cup Bouillon
¼ Cup Chili Sauce
2 Tbs. Chopped Onion
2 Tsp. Cornstarch
2 Tsp. Water

Garnish:

3 Medium-size Tomatoes, quartered
½ Cup Pitted Ripe Olives
1 - 4 Oz. Can Artichoke Hearts,
   drained

Mix first 6 ingredients for marinade. Trim any excess fat from meat. Place meat in pan or bowl, and marinate in refrigerator overnight. The next day, drain meat well, saving marinade. In a large pan with cover, brown meat on both sides in heated shortening. Add marinade, bouillon, chili sauce, and chopped onion. Cover pan and simmer the meat until tender, about 1¼ hours. Skim any fat from liquid. Blend cornstarch with water and stir into liquid. Cook until thickened. Add tomatoes, olives, artichoke hearts. Heat.

Place meat on heated serving platter. Arrange garnish around and on top of meat. Spoon a little of the sauce over the top. Serve the remainder of the sauce separately. Makes 6 servings.

NUTTY MEAT LOAF

1½ Lbs. Lean Ground Beef
½ Cup Chopped Walnuts
¼ Cup Chopped Onion
1 Tbs. Chopped Parsley
1 Egg, lightly beaten
1 Tsp. Salt
¼ Tsp. Paprika
¼ Tsp. Marjoram Leaves, crushed
1/8 Tsp. Pepper
½ Cup Dry Red Wine
¼ Cup Milk
1 Tbs. Butter
1½ Tbs. Flour

Combine all ingredients except butter and flour. Mix together lightly. Shape into a round loaf. Put into a greased electric cooker. Cover and cook on low for 4 hrs. Remove loaf from cooker. Turn cooker control to high. Mix butter and flour; add to liquid in cooker and mix well. Cook & stir until thickened. Serve gravy over meat loaf. Makes 8 servings.

COUNTRY BEEF LOAF

2 Tbs. Butter or Margarine
½ Lb. Mushrooms, trimmed and sliced
1 Large Onion, diced (about 1 cup)
1 Cup Thinly-sliced Celery
1 Cup Shredded, Pared Carrots
2 Tbs. Water
2 Lbs. Ground Beef
½ Cup Sifted All-purpose Flour
2 Tsp. Salt
1 Tsp. Seasoned Salt
1 Tsp. Fines Herbes
2 Tbs. Soy Sauce

Combine butter or margarine, mushrooms, onion, celery, carrots and water in a medium-size frying pan; heat to boiling. Cover and cook for 10 minutes, or until vegetables are tender-crisp. Combine ground beef, flour, salt, seasoned salt, fines herbes, soy sauce & cooked vegetable mixture in a large bowl. Mix lightly until well blended. Shape into a rectangular loaf, 8x6'', in a greased jelly-roll pan. Bake in moderate oven (350°F.) for 1 hour, or until crusty brown. Sprinkle with chopped parsley before serving, if you wish. Makes 8 servings.

OYSTER-STUFFED STEAKS

4 Beef Tenderloin Steaks (fillets
  preferred), cut 2" thick
8 Live Oysters, shucked
¼ Tsp. Salt
Black Pepper
2 Tbs. Butter
1 Tbs. Vegetable Oil
4 Tbs. Butter, melted
1 Tbs. Finely-chopped Fresh Parsley

Have butcher cut a pocket in each of the
steaks. Sprinkle the oysters with the salt
and a little pepper, then insert 2 oysters
into each steak. Close the pockets with
small skewers or sew them shut with cot-
ton thread and a large needle. Pat steaks
completely dry with paper towels and
season with as much pepper as you like.

Melt the butter with the oil over high
heat in a heavy skillet. Add the steaks
and brown them quickly for 1 to 2 minutes on each side, turning them with tongs
to avoid piercing the meat. Reduce heat
to moderate. Saute' the steaks--turning
them every minute or two, so that the
pepper does not form a crust on either
side--for about 8 minutes (rare), or about
10 minutes (medium rare). Remove the
steaks immediately to a warmed platter
and pour the melted butter, combined
with the chopped parsley, over them.
Makes 4 servings.

SALISBURY PIE

1 Lb. Ground Beef
1 Tsp. Salt
¼ Cup Milk
2 Cups Soft Bread Crumbs
½ Cup Grated Carrots
¼ Cup Chopped Celery
1 Onion, minced
¾ Tsp. Poultry Seasoning
2 Tbs. Melted Butter

Mix ground beef with salt and milk; press
half of mixture into a greased 9" pie plate.
Combine bread crumbs, carrot, celery, onion, poultry seasoning and melted butter
and place on top of meat in pie plate. Top
with remaining meat mixture. Bake at 400°
F. for 30 minutes.

BEEF WITH PIQUANT SAUCE

1 - 2 to 2½ Lb. Beef Rib Eye,
  Boneless Sirloin, Strip or
  Tenderloin Steak, cut into
  4 thick slices

Piquant Sauce:
2 Shallots
2 Tbs. Olive Oil
2 Anchovy Fillets, soaked in water
  for 10 minutes, patted dry and
  chopped
½ Cup Red Wine Vinegar
3 or 4 Cloves Garlic
1 Bay Leaf
½ Tsp. Thyme
1 Whole Clove
1 or 2 Small Red Chilies, stemmed
  and seeded
Salt and Pepper
1 Tbs. Flour
2 Cups Beef Stock
1 Tbs. Finely-chopped Gherkins
1 Tbs. Capers, rinsed in cold water,
  drained well and finely chopped

Brown the shallots in the oil in a stainless-
steel saucepan. Add the anchovies, then
pour the vinegar into the pan. Add the garlic, bay leaf, thyme, clove and chilies. Season with salt and pepper. As soon as the
vinegar has evaporated, add the flour and
brown it. Add the stock, a little at a time,
stirring constantly to achieve a completely
smooth sauce. Stir until all of the stock is
added and well mixed. Simmer on very low
heat for about 30 minutes. Ten minutes before serving, add the gherkins and capers to
the sauce. Cover the pan to keep the sauce
warm while you broil the beef, then serve
the sauce with the meat. Makes 4 servings.

BEEF LOAF

3 Lbs. Lean Ground Beef
3 Tbs. Finely-chopped Beef Suet
2 Medium Onions, finely chopped
2 Large Tomatoes, peeled and seeded
½ Lb. Fresh Mushrooms, coarsely
   chopped
4 Tbs. Butter
1 Lb. Green Beans, halved lengthwise
   and roughly chopped
6 Small, Tender Celery Stalks, with
   some leaves, thinly sliced
2 Small Carrots, coarsely grated
1 Small Garlic Clove, crushed
2 Tbs. Finely-chopped Fresh Parsley
1 Tbs. Finely-cut Fresh Chives
Salt
Freshly-ground Black Pepper
Thyme Leaves
½ Tsp. Dry Mustard
¼ Cup Worcestershire Sauce or
   Steak Sauce
1/3 Cup Soy Sauce
2 Large Eggs, separated
½ Cup Milk
5 or 6 Thin Slices Bacon
1 Tbs. Flour
1 Bunch Watercress

Melt the suet in an iron pan and lightly brown the onions in it. Add the tomatoes, breaking up the pulp. In a separate pan, saute' the mushrooms in 3 tablespoons of butter for 4 to 5 minutes over low heat, stirring constantly. Place the onions, tomatoes, mushrooms, beans, celery and carrots in a mixing bowl. Add the garlic, parsley, chives and beef and stir lightly, tossing all of the ingredients over and over until they are thoroughly mixed. Season with salt, pepper and a good pinch of thyme leaves. Also add dry mustard, Worcestershire sauce or steak sauce, and soy sauce; toss again. Set mixture aside.

Beat the yolks of the eggs lightly with cold milk, then add to the meat mixture. Prepare a glass baking dish, or any pan having a tight-fitting cover, by lining it on the bottom and sides with the bacon. Beat the egg whites until stiff but not dry and fold them gently into the mixture. Shape the mixture into a loaf.

Put the baking dish into a large cast-iron casserole with a cover. If this is not avail-able, cover the baking dish and place it in a pan of boiling water in a preheated 400° F. oven, replenishing the water as it boils away. Bake for about 2 hours, reducing the heat to moderate, 350°F., after 20 minutes.

While loaf is baking, prepare a roux by blending the flour and the remaining butter over gentle heat until lightly browned. When you uncover the baking dish, you will find that the loaf has shrunk from the sides and is surrounded by a rich, delicious sauce. Carefully drain off the sauce into a saucepan; skim off all but 2 tablespoons of the fat and thicken with the roux. Turn the loaf onto an ovenproof serving dish and peel off any bacon strips sticking to the sides of the dish, replacing them on the loaf. Put the serving dish in a very hot oven, 425°F., or under the broiler and brown the surface quickly without drying it. The bacon will dry off and crisp at the same time. Serve in the hot dish, garnishing the loaf with the sauce. Pass the remaining sauce in a heated gravy boat. Makes 8 servings.

PAKISTANI KIMA

1 Lb. Ground Beef
1 Cup Chopped Onion
1 Clove Garlic, minced
2 Tomatoes, peeled and cubed
2 Raw Potatoes, peeled and
   cubed
1 - 10 Oz. Pkg. Frozen Peas,
   broken apart
2 Tsp. Curry Powder
1½ Tsp. Salt
Dash of Pepper
Flaked Coconut
Hot Cooked Rice

In a skillet cook beef, onion and garlic until meat is browned. Pour off fat. Stir in remaining ingredients, except coconut and rice. Cover and simmer for 20 to 25 minutes, or until vegetables are tender. Sprinkle with coconut. Serve with hot cooked rice. Makes 6 servings.

DEVILED FLANK STEAK

1½ Lbs. Flank Steak
All-purpose Flour
1 Onion, minced
3 Tbs. Fat
2 Tsp. Salt
¼ Tsp. Pepper
¼ Tsp. Paprika
1 Tsp. Prepared Mustard
1 Tsp. Vinegar
½ Cup Tomato Sauce
1½ Cups Hot Water

Cut the flank steak into strips across the grain. Roll in flour; brown meat and onion in hot fat. Stir in 2 tablespoons of flour and seasonings. Add remaining ingredients; cover and simmer for 1 hour, or until meat is tender. Makes 4 servings.

CORNED BEEF AND NOODLES

1 - 8 or 9 Oz. Pkg. Noodles
1 Onion
1 Green Pepper
2 Tbs. Butter or Margarine
1 - 1 Lb. Can Corned Beef
1 - 8 Oz. Can Tomato Sauce
¼ Cup Chili Sauce
¼ Cup Water or Bouillon
1 Tsp. Prepared Mustard
1 Tsp. Worcestershire Sauce
¼ Cup Grated Cheddar Cheese

Preheat oven to 350°F. Grease a 1½-quart casserole or baking dish.

Cook the noodles until tender, following directions on the package. Peel and dice the onion. Cut green pepper fine. Cook onion and green pepper in butter or margarine about 5 minutes, or until tender.

Break corned beef into small chunks with a fork. Add to onion mixture. Stir and add tomato sauce, chili sauce, water or bouillon, mustard, and Worcestershire sauce. Stir and heat 1 minute. Pour the noodles into prepared baking dish. Make a depression or well in center and fill with meat combination. Sprinkle top with cheese. Bake for 30 minutes. Makes 4 or more servings.

STEAKETTES with STUFFING

6 Slices Bottom Round (½" thick each)
1 Cup Chopped Onion (1 large)
6 Tbs. Vegetable Oil
3 Cups Soft Bread Crumbs (about 6 slices)
½ Cup Grated Parmesan Cheese
½ Cup Chopped Parsley
1 Tsp. Salt
2 Tbs. Hot Water (for stuffing)
4 Tbs. All-purpose Flour
2 Tsp. Granulated Beef Bouillon
1 Tsp. Leaf Thyme, crumbled
2½ Cups Water (for gravy)
Chopped Parsley

Pound the beef slices with a wooden or metal meat mallet, to ¼-inch thickness. Saute' onion in 4 tablespoons of the oil until soft (use a large skillet with a cover). Add bread crumbs, Parmesan cheese, parsley, salt and the 2 tablespoons of hot water; toss lightly to mix. Spread ¼ cup of the stuffing on each beef slice. Roll up, jelly-roll fashion; secure with wooden picks. Heat remaining 2 tablespoons of oil in same skillet. Add beef rolls; turn to brown on all sides. Remove to a hot platter; keep warm while making sauce.

Stir flour, granulated beef bouillon and the thyme into drippings in skillet; cook, stirring constantly, just until bubbly. Stir in the 2½ cups of water; continue cooking and stirring, scraping to loosen cooked-on juices in skillet, until gravy thickens and boils for 1 min. Return beef rolls to skillet; cover and simmer for 1½ hours, or until tender when pierced with a fork. Place on a heated serving platter; spoon a little of the sauce over the beef rolls and sprinkle with parsley. Serve remaining sauce separately. Makes 6 servings.

SPICY BEEF TONGUE

2 Tbs. Fat or Salad Oil
1 Small Onion, minced
1 Cup Diced Celery
1 - 8 Oz. Can Tomato Sauce
½ Cup Water
½ Tsp. Salt
1 Tsp. Worcestershire Sauce
1/8 Tsp. Pepper
Dash of Ground Cloves
1 Tbs. Vinegar
1 - 6 Oz. Can Beef Tongue

Heat fat in saucepan. Add onion and celery and saute' until golden. Add remaining ingredients, except the tongue; simmer for 15 minutes. Cut tongue into ½" cubes; add to the sauce and heat thoroughly. Serve over cooked spaghetti, noodles or potatoes. Makes 4 servings.

MEATBALLS WITH EGG-LEMON SAUCE (From Greece)

1 Lb. Lean Ground Beef
1/3 Cup Chopped Onion
1 Tsp. Finely-chopped Fresh Mint
1 Tbs. Chopped Fresh Parsley
2 Tbs. Raw Unprocessed Rice
Salt and Pepper
1½ Cups Beef Stock
1 Cup Water
2 Egg Yolks
1 to 2 Tbs. Fresh Lemon Juice

Mix together the beef, onion, mint, parsley and rice. Season with salt and pepper to taste and add ¼ cup beef stock. Mix well and form into walnut-sized balls. In a large pot, bring the remaining stock and water to a boil and drop meatballs into it. Lower the heat and simmer for 45 minutes. In a bowl, beat the egg yolks and add the lemon juice. Still beating, slowly add a few tablespoons of the hot stock to the egg yolks. Then stir the egg-yolk mixture into the stock and meatballs in the pot. Cover; remove from the heat and let stand for 5 minutes. Makes 4 servings.

BEEF BOURGEOIS

¼ Cup Butter
½ Lb. Chicken Livers
1 Bay Leaf
¼ Tsp. Thyme
1 Truffle, finely chopped
2 Lbs. Beef Tenderloin Tips
Salt to taste
Freshly-ground Black Pepper
   to taste
¼ Cup Cognac, heated

In a skillet, heat half the butter; add the chicken livers, bay leaf and thyme and saute' quickly, shaking the pan occasionally, until the livers are barely cooked. Remove the bay leaf. Place the chicken livers and chopped truffle in the container of an electric blender.

Cut the beef into very thin strips across the grain. Sprinkle with salt and pepper and sear quickly in the remaining butter to seal in the juices (1 minute or less). Pour the warm cognac over the meat and ignite it. Remove the meat to a warm serving platter. Add the beef juices to the container of the blender and blend until smooth, about 30 seconds. If necessary, add canned beef broth to aid the blending. Reheat the sauce and pour over the beef. Serve immediately. Makes 4 to 6 servings.

MEATBALLS AND FRANKS

1 Lb. Ground Beef
1 Egg, slightly beaten
¼ Cup Dry Bread Crumbs
1 Medium Onion, grated
1 Tsp. Salt
¾ Cup Chili Sauce
¼ Cup Grape Jelly
2 Tbs. Lemon Juice
2/3 Cup Water
1 Lb. Frankfurters, cut diagonally
   into ½" slices

Combine beef, egg, crumbs, onion and salt. Shape into small balls. Combine chili sauce, grape jelly, lemon juice and water in a large skillet. Heat; add meatballs and simmer until meat cooks through. Just before serving, add the frankfurters and heat through. Makes 6 servings.

SAUERBRATEN

4 Lb. Beef Pot Roast
2 Tsp. Salt
1 Tsp. Ground Ginger
2 Cups Cider Vinegar
2½ Cups Water
2 Medium Onions, sliced
2 Tbs. Mixed Whole Pickling Spice
2 Bay Leaves
1 Tsp. Peppercorns
8 Whole Cloves
1/3 Cup Sugar
2 Tbs. Fat
Flour or Gingersnaps

Rub meat with salt and ginger; put in a large bowl. Combine remaining ingredients except fat and flour; bring to a boil and pour over meat. Cool. Cover and put in the refrigerator for 3 days. Turn meat once each day. Remove meat from pickling liquid; reserve liquid.

Dry the meat with paper towels; brown the meat on all sides in fat in a heavy kettle. Put on rack; add 1 cup reserved pickling liquid and half the onions and spices from liquid. Cover tightly and simmer very slowly for 3½ hours, or until tender, adding more liquid as needed. Remove meat to hot platter.

Strain liquid in pan and return to heat; strain in additional pickling liquid to make about 2 cups. Skim off excess fat. Thicken gravy with a little flour mixed with cold water, or thicken with 6 crumbled gingersnaps. Serve with sliced meat, mashed potatoes, rice, or potato dumplings. Makes about 6 servings.

DICED MEAT ROAST

¾ Lb. Boned Beef Chuck or
   Shoulder Arm
¾ Lb. Boned Lean Fresh Pork
½ Cup Hot Water
½ Tsp. Salt
1 Egg, beaten
¾ Cup Cracker Crumbs
1 Tbs. Lemon Juice
¼ Lb. Salt Pork
Parsley

Dice beef and pork into ½" cubes. Add hot water. Combine all ingredients except for salt pork, mixing thoroughly. Pack firmly into a loaf pan (8x4½x2½"). Slice salt pork thin and lay over top of loaf. Bake in a moderate oven (350°F.) for 1 hour. Turn out onto a platter, turn right-side-up and garnish with parsley. Serve hot. Makes 5 servings.

CANTONESE BEEF, TOMATO, AND GREEN PEPPER

1 Lb. Beef Round or Sirloin
¼ Cup Soy Sauce
1 Tsp. Sugar
2 Large Firm Tomatoes
2 Large Green Peppers
2 Ginger Roots, or ½ Tsp. Ground
   Ginger
¼ Cup Salad Oil
1 Clove Garlic, sliced fine
2 Tsp. Cornstarch
1 Tbs. Soy Sauce
Hot Boiled Rice, or Noodles

The beef will be easier to slice if it is frozen and then partially thawed before slicing. Slice beef in strips ½" wide and as thin as possible. Pour the ¼ cup soy sauce and the sugar over meat and marinate for ½ hour. In the meantime, cut tomatoes and green peppers into 1" cubes. Pulverize the ginger roots by hammering between folds of wax paper to a fine powder, then sift to remove coarse particles and measure 1 teaspoonful.

Heat oil in a large skillet and add garlic & ginger. After a minute, remove garlic and add green pepper. Saute' for 3 minutes; stir occasionally during entire remaining cooking period so ingredients will cook evenly. Add beef and its liquid and saute' for 3 minutes. Add tomatoes and immediately blend cornstarch and remaining soy sauce and gently stir it into the entire mixture. Cook, stirring gently, for another minute. Entire cooking period is over medium heat and takes 9 to 10 minutes. Ingredients should only be cooked long enough to heat through completely; do not overcook. Serve with fluffy rice or crisp noodles. Makes 4 servings.

LASAGNA WITH MEATBALLS
(Mexican)

¾ Lb. Lean Beef, ground
½ Tsp. Salt
¼ Tsp. Pepper
1 Tsp. Grated Lemon Rind
2 Tbs. Olive Oil
3 Cups Favorite Tomato Sauce
1 Lb. Lasagna, cooked and drained
1 Lb. Ricotta or Cottage Cheese
1 Lb. Mozzarella Cheese, cubed
1½ Cups Grated Parmesan Cheese

Season beef with salt and pepper, add lemon rind and shape into balls the size of a large marble. Brown in hot oil. Cover bottom of a large 2 to 3" deep baking dish sparingly with tomato sauce. Line with lasagna. Dot with half of cheeses. Spread with half of remaining sauce; top with meat. Cover with remaining lasagna, sauce and cheeses. Bake in preheated slow oven (325°F.) for about 45 minutes. Cool slightly. Makes 10 to 12 servings.

BAKED BARBECUED CORNED BEEF

5 to 6 Lb. Corned Brisket of Beef
1 Tbs. Whole Mixed Pickling Spice
Whole Cloves
2 Tbs. Butter or Margarine,
   melted
1/3 Cup Packed Brown Sugar
1 Tbs. Prepared Mustard
1/3 Cup Ketchup
2 Tbs. Sweet Pickle Juice, or
   Vinegar

Wash the corned beef and put into a large kettle. Cover with cold water. Add the pickling spice. Bring to boil; cover and simmer for 4 hours, or until tender. Cool beef in broth. Put into shallow roasting pan and score fat layer. Insert whole cloves in fat. Mix butter, sugar, mustard, ketchup, and pickle juice. Pat on beef. Bake in preheated 350°F. oven for about 30 minutes. Serve warm, sliced thin for sandwiches. Makes 10 to 12 servings.

PASTA with BEEF AND EGGPLANT

2 Lbs. Top Round of Beef
8 Tbs. Olive Oil
4 Slices Prosciutto, finely chopped
2 Onions, chopped
1 Cup Dry White Wine
2½ Lbs. Tomatoes, peeled,
   seeded and diced
1¼ Tsp. Salt
Freshly-ground Black Pepper
2 Tbs. Butter
5 Fresh Mushrooms, sliced
3 Chicken Livers, chopped
1 Lb. Mostaccioli or Rigatoni
1½ Lbs. Eggplant, peeled and cut
   into small strips
¼ Cup Parmesan Cheese, grated

Heat 2 tablespoons of oil in a large, deep fireproof casserole. Stir in the prosciutto and onions and saute' until soft. Add the beef to the casserole and brown it on both sides over high heat. Lower the heat, add the wine and cook, uncovered, stirring and turning the meat until the wine has evaporated. Stir in the tomatoes and season with 1 teaspoon of salt and some freshly-ground pepper. Cover the casserole and simmer, stirring often and basting the meat frequently, for 2 hours, or until the meat is tender.

In a large saucepan, melt the butter and saute' the mushrooms and livers for 5 min. Sprinkle with ¼ teaspoon of salt; stir. Remove from the heat and keep warm. Remove the meat from the casserole; pour the sauce through a sieve into a bowl and degrease it. Dice the beef and add it to the liver and mushroom mixture. Add the sauce from the meat to the mixture and blend well. Cook the mostaccioli or rigatoni al dente. Drain the pasta and place it in a heated bowl.

Saute' the eggplant strips in the remaining olive oil until tender and lightly browned. Sprinkle Parmesan on the pasta; toss. Add half of the sauce and toss again--well but gently. Serve in hot soup bowls, with strips of eggplant on top. Pass the remaining sauce and grated cheese at the table. Makes 6 servings.

BEEF STROGANOFF

1½ Lbs. Top Sirloin of Beef
1 Tsp. Salt
1 Tsp. Pepper
3 Tbs. Butter or Margarine
1 Tbs. All-purpose Flour
1 Cup Beef Bouillon
1 Scant Tsp. Hot Prepared Mustard
2 Small Onions, sliced
3 Tbs. Dairy Sour Cream, at
    room temperature

Remove all fat and gristle from the meat.
Cut it into narrow strips, 2" long and ½"
thick. Sprinkle meat strips with salt and
pepper. Melt 1½ tablespoons of the butter. Blend in flour. Stir in bouillon and
bring to a boil. Stir in mustard. Cook,
stirring constantly, until thick and smooth.
Heat remaining butter in another saucepan.
The butter must be very hot. Brown meat
and onions quickly on all sides. Add sour
cream to mustard sauce. Bring to a boil.
Add meat and onions to sauce. Cover the
saucepan and keep hot for 20 minutes.
The mixture must be kept hot, but must
not simmer. Before serving, heat through
over high heat for about 3 minutes. Makes
3 to 4 servings.

SPICED STRIPS-OF-BEEF

1½ Lbs. Beef Round Steak,
    cut ¼" thick
2 Tbs. Butter or Margarine
1 Small Clove Garlic, crushed in
    a garlic press
2 Tsp. Instant Minced Onion
½ Tsp. Salt
Cayenne Pepper, to taste
1/8 Tsp. Chili Powder
1/8 Tsp. Cinnamon
1 /8 Tsp. Ground Celery Seed
1 Tbs. Prepared Mustard
1 Beef Bouillon Cube, dissolved
    in ½ cup boiling water

Cut steak into 2x½-inch strips. Brown in
butter in a large skillet. Turn the browned
meat into an electric cooker and add remaining ingredients. Stir well. Cover and
cook on low for 6 to 8 hours. Serve over
hot fluffy rice. Makes 6 servings.

POT ROAST with
SESAME-SOY SAUCE

2 Tbs. Sesame Seeds
1 Cup Water
¼ Cup Soy Sauce
2 Tbs. Molasses
2 Tbs. Wine Vinegar or
    Cider Vinegar
2 Green Onions, chopped
1 Tsp. Garlic Powder
1/8 Tsp. Cayenne
1 Boneless Chuck Beef Roast
    (about 4 lbs.)
2 Tbs. Cornstarch
2 Tbs. Water

Toast sesame seeds in a small frying pan
over low heat, shaking pan often, just until golden brown. Combine the sesame
seeds with 1 cup water, soy sauce, molasses,
vinegar, green onions, garlic powder and
cayenne in a bowl. Pour over meat in a
large bowl; cover and chill, turning meat
several times to season evenly, for 3 to 4
hours, or overnight.

When ready to cook, remove meat from the
marinade. Pat meat dry with paper towels.
Brown in fat in Dutch oven over medium
heat (or use an electric skillet). Pour marinade over; cover and simmer for 3 hours,
turning meat once or twice. Meat should
be very tender. Remove to a heated platter and keep hot while making gravy.

Pour pan liquid into a measuring cup or
bowl and let stand for about 1 minute,
or until fat rises to the top. Skim off the
fat and add water, if needed, to remaining
liquid to make 2 cups. Return to pan and
heat to boiling. Blend cornstarch with 2
tablespoons of water; stir into hot liquid.
Cook, stirring constantly, until gravy is
thick; boil for 3 minutes. Carve meat into
thin slices and serve with gravy. Makes 6
servings.

BROILED SLICED BEEF WITH SOY-SEASONED GLAZE
(From Japan)

1½ Lbs. Lean Boneless Beef,
  preferably tenderloin or
  boneless sirloin, cut in 12 slices,
  ¼" thick

Teriyaki Sauce:
1 Cup Sweet Sake, or 1 Cup, less
  2 Tbs. Pale Dry Sherry
1 Cup All-purpose Soy Sauce
1 Cup Chicken Stock, fresh or
  canned

Teriyaki Glaze:
¼ Cup Teriyaki Sauce
1 Tbs. Sugar
2 Tsp. Cornstarch mixed with
  1 Tbs. Cold Water

Garnish:
4 Tsp. Powdered Mustard, mixed
  with just enough hot water to
  make a thick paste and set aside
  to rest for 15 minutes
12 Sprigs Fresh Parsley

To make the sauce, warm the sake or sherry in a 1½ to 2-quart stainless-steel saucepan over moderate heat. Off the heat, ignite the liquid with a match and shake the pan back and forth until the flame dies out. Now stir in the soy sauce and chicken stock, and bring to a boil. Pour the sauce into a bowl and cool to room temperature.

To make the glaze, combine ¼ cup of the teriyaki sauce and 1 tablespoon of sugar in a stainless-steel saucepan. Bring almost to a boil over moderate heat, then reduce heat to low. Stir the combined cornstarch and water into the sauce. Cook, stirring constantly, until it thickens to a clear syrupy glaze. Immediately pour into a dish and set aside.

Preheat broiler to its highest point, or use a hibachi or charcoal grill. Dip the beef, one slice at a time, into the teriyaki sauce. Broil 2" from heat for 1 minute on each side, or until lightly brown. For well-done meat, broil for an additional minute.

Slice the meat into 1" wide strips and place them on individual serving plates. Spoon a little of the glaze over each serving, and garnish each plate with a dab of the mustard and a sprig of parsley. This will serve 4 as a main course, or 6 if other dishes are served with it. Any leftover teriyaki sauce can be stored in a tightly closed jar and refrigerated for as long as 1 month. Before using, bring to a boil and skim the surface of any residue.

MEATBALL, TOMATO and EGG STEW (From Morocco)

1 Lb. Beef or Lamb, finely ground
2 Tbs. Chopped Fresh Parsley
1 Tbs. Chopped Coriander Leaves
  (or ½ Tbs. Ground Coriander)
½ Tsp. Ground Cumin Seed
1 Small Onion, grated
¼ Tsp. Cayenne Pepper
Salt
2 Tbs. Vegetable Oil
6 Eggs

Tomato Sauce:
2 Medium Onions, chopped
1 Small Bunch Fresh Parsley,
  chopped
2 to 2½ Lbs. Ripe Tomatoes,
  peeled, seeded and chopped
1 Tsp. Ground Cumin
1 Tsp. Freshly-ground Black Pepper
2 Garlic Cloves, chopped
½ Tsp. Ground Cinnamon
¼ Tsp. Cayenne Pepper

In a large bowl, combine all meatball ingredients except eggs and oil. Wet your hands to prevent the mixture from sticking and form 1" balls. Heat the oil in a frying pan and brown the meatballs on all sides. Remove them from the pan and set them aside, covered. Add all sauce ingredients to the frying pan. Cook, uncovered, for 30 min., or until the sauce has reduced to a thick gravy. Return the meatballs to the sauce and cook together for 10 minutes. Carefully break the eggs into the sauce and poach them until set. Serve this dish immediately, directly from the pan. Makes 6 servings.

CHINESE BEEF WITH BROCCOLI

1 Lb. Flank Steak
2 Tbs. Soy Sauce
1 Tbs. Sherry or Dry Vermouth
1 Tbs. Cornstarch
1 Tsp. Sugar
½ Bunch Broccoli
4 Tbs. Peanut Oil
1 Tsp. Salt
¼ Cup Chopped Onion

Cut steak across grain into thin bite-sized pieces. Pour soy sauce and sherry over steak. Sprinkle with cornstarch and sugar; mix well. Cut broccoli into thin slices. Peel stem; slice into 2" pieces. Pour half the oil into a skillet or Dutch oven. Add salt and broccoli. Cook over high heat, stirring constantly, for 2 minutes. Remove from skillet. Add remaining oil and onion, stir well and add the steak; cook for 2 minutes. Add broccoli; mix thoroughly and serve. Makes 4 servings.

MOUSSAKA
(Baked Meat Custard)

1½ Lbs. Potatoes
Fat for Deep Frying
2 Medium Onions, finely chopped
¼ Cup Olive Oil
1 Lb. Ground Lean Beef
2 Garlic Cloves, minced or put
   through garlic press
1 - 8 Oz. Can Tomato Sauce
1 Tsp. Ground Cinnamon
Salt and Pepper
2 Eggs
1 Cup Milk
1/3 Cup Grated Kefaloteri Cheese

Peel potatoes and cut into ¼" slices. Deep fry in hot fat until golden brown and drain. Arrange half of potatoes in an even layer on the bottom of a pan (7x11"). Saute' onions in olive oil until soft. Set aside. In oil remaining in pan, cook beef, stirring with a fork, until redness disappears. Add onions, garlic, tomato sauce, cinnamon and salt & pepper to taste. Pour over potatoes. Arrange remaining potato slices over meat. Beat eggs and add milk. Pour mixture over meat and potatoes. Sprinkle with cheese. Bake in preheated 350°F. oven for 45 min. Cut into squares to serve. Makes 4 servings.

BAVARIAN BEEF DINNER

1 Boneless Chuck Beef Roast
   (4 to 5 lbs.)
2 Tbs. Vegetable Shortening
1 Tbs. Sugar
3 Tsp. Salt
2 Tsp. Caraway Seeds
½ Tsp. Ground Cardamom
1 Large Onion, chopped (1 cup)
1 Large Carrot, pared and chopped
   (1 cup)
1 Cup Sliced Celery
½ Cup Chopped Parsley
1 Cup Dry Red Wine

Brown roast slowly in shortening in a Dutch oven or electric skillet. Stir in sugar, salt, caraway seeds, cardamom, onion, carrot, celery, parsley, and wine; heat to boiling. Cover and simmer, turning meat once or twice, for 3 hours, or until very tender. Remove to a heated serving platter; keep warm while making gravy. Spoon liquid from Dutch oven into an electric-blender container; cover and blend until smooth. Return liquid to Dutch oven and reheat just to boiling. Carve part of the meat into ¼" thick slices. Top with several spoonfuls of gravy. Serve with remaining gravy. Makes 8 servings.

OVEN-BARBECUED SWISS STEAK

2 Lbs. Round or Chuck Steak,
   1" thick
2 - 8 Oz. Cans Seasoned Tomato
   Sauce (2 cups)
1 Tbs. Sugar
1 Tbs. Vinegar
1 Tbs. Worcestershire Sauce
2 Dashes Bottled Hot Pepper Sauce
1 Medium Onion, sliced

Combine 1/3 cup all-purpose flour, 1 tsp. salt and ¼ tsp. pepper. Coat meat with mixture. Brown slowly on both sides in hot fat. Spoon off excess fat. Combine tomato sauce, sugar, vinegar, Worcestershire sauce, and pepper sauce in small bowl; pour over the meat. Add salt and pepper to taste. Simmer, uncovered, for 5 minutes. Add onion slices. Cover and bake in oven-proof skillet or Dutch oven at 350°F. for 1 to 1¼ hours, or until fork tender. Makes 6 servings.

BEEF POT ROAST with ALMONDS AND BACON

1 - 3 Lb. Beef Brisket, trimmed
 of excess fat
¼ Lb. Bacon or Ham
1½ Tbs. Slivered, Blanched Almonds
3 Large Dried Ancho Chilies (available
 where Latin American foods are
 sold)
3 Whole Cloves
½" Stick Cinnamon
1/8 Tsp. Dried Thyme
1/8 Tsp. Dried Marjoram
1/8 Tsp. Dried Oregano
4 Peppercorns
3 Garlic Cloves
2 Tsp. Salt
1½ Tbs. Vinegar
¾ Cup Water
3 Tbs. Lard or Rendered Bacon Fat
8 New Potatoes, unpeeled

Cut the bacon or ham into small pieces; gash the beef all over with a knife point and insert the bacon or ham and the almonds into the gashes. Set the meat aside while the sauce is prepared.

Toast the chilies lightly for 3 to 4 minutes on a griddle or in a heavy skillet, turning them from time to time so that they do not burn. Slit them open and remove the seeds. Put the chilies into a bowl of hot water & leave them to soak for about 20 minutes. Transfer them with a slotted spoon to the jar of an electric blender. Add the rest of the ingredients (except lard, potatoes and meat) and blend to a smooth puree. If you do not have a blender, pound the ingredients to a paste in a mortar.

Melt the lard in a heavy casserole and, when the lard is very hot, brown the meat well all over. Remove the meat and set it aside. Drain off the fat, leaving 3 tbs. Add the chili mixture and let it simmer briskly for about 5 minutes, stirring it all the time. Return the meat to the casserole and baste it with the sauce. Cover with a tight-fitting lid and cook in preheated 325°F. oven for 2 hours. Meanwhile, put the potatoes into a saucepan; cover them with boiling water and boil for 5 minutes. Drain the potatoes and set aside; when cool enough to handle, skin them. Remove the casserole from the oven, turn the meat over and baste it well with the sauce. Scrape the sauce from the sides and bottom of the casserole; add a little water if the sauce has thickened too much. Put the potatoes into the sauce around the meat, replace the lid of the casserole and let the meat cook until it is very tender but not falling apart--test after about 1 hour and 10 minutes. Slice the meat fairly thick and arrange it on a warm platter with the potatoes around it. Pour the sauce over it. Makes 6 servings.

PARMESAN BROILED STEAK

3½ Lbs. Sirloin or Porterhouse Steak
2 Garlic Cloves, mashed
½ Cup Olive Oil
1 Cup Grated Parmesan Cheese
½ Cup Bread Crumbs
1 Tsp. Salt
½ Tsp. Pepper
½ Tsp. Dried Oregano
¼ Tsp. Rosemary

Place steak in shallow dish. Add garlic to oil and pour over steak. Let stand, covered, in cold place (not necessarily in refrigerator) for 1 hour. Turn steak a few times during the hour. Make a mixture of cheese, crumbs, salt, pepper and herbs. Lay drained steak on preheated broiler pan. Broil about 5 min. Quickly spread with half of cheese mixture. Return to heat. Broil slowly, until browned. Turn steak. Pour a little of garlic oil over it. Broil 5 minutes. Spread quickly with remaining cheese mixture. Broil slowly to desired doneness. Serve on hot platter. Makes 4 to 6 servings.

NEW ENGLAND BOILED DINNER

4 to 5 Lb. Corned Beef Brisket
1 Clove Garlic
2 Whole Cloves
10 Whole Black Peppercorns
2 Bay Leaves
8 Medium carrots, peeled
8 Medium Potatoes, peeled
8 Medium Yellow Onions, peeled
1 Medium Head Cabbage, cut into
    8 wedges
2 Tbs. Butter or Margarine
Chopped Parsley

Wipe corned beef with damp paper towels. Place in large kettle. Cover with cold water and add garlic, cloves, peppercorns and bay leaves. Bring to a boil; reduce heat and simmer 5 minutes. Skim surface, then simmer, covered, for 3 to 4 hours, or until meat is fork-tender. Add carrots, potatoes and onions during last 25 minutes. Add cabbage during last 20 minutes. Cook just until vegetables are tender. To serve, slice corned beef thinly across the grain. Arrange on one side of serving platter. Place cabbage wedges beside meat. Brush the potatoes with butter and place in serving dish; sprinkle with parsley. Arrange carrots and onions in another dish. Serve with mustard. Makes 8 servings.

ALMOND-MUSHROOM NOODLES
with MEATBALLS

1 - 10½ Oz. Can Condensed Tomato
    Soup
1 Cup Dairy Sour Cream
1 Lb. Ground Beef Chuck
2 Parsley Sprigs, chopped
1 Tsp. Salt
1/8 Tsp. Pepper
1/3 Cup Fine, Dry Bread Crumbs
1 Egg
3 Tbs. Butter or Margarine
1 Medium Onion, minced
1 Garlic Clove, minced
1 Bay Leaf
1 Tsp. Fresh Lemon Juice
1 Tsp. Paprika
2 Cups Wide Noodles
¼ Cup Almonds, slivered
1 - 4 Oz. Can Sliced Mushrooms,
    drained

Mix the soup and sour cream. Add ¼ cup of this mixture to the beef, parsley, salt, pepper, crumbs, and egg; mix well. Shape into 16 small meatballs. Cook in 1 tablespoon of butter until well browned. Remove meatballs. Cook onion and garlic in fat remaining in skillet until lightly browned. Drain off any remaining fat. Add meatballs, remaining soup mixture, bay leaf, lemon juice, and paprika. Bring to a boil; cover and simmer for 20 minutes. Uncover and cook for 10 minutes longer. Cook and drain noodles. Saute' almonds and mushrooms slowly in 2 tablespoons of butter until almonds are golden brown. Stir frequently. Mix with noodles and arrange on a hot platter as a border. Put meatballs in center with sauce. Makes 4 servings.

SHREDDED BEEF AND VEGETABLES

1 Lb. Boneless Sirloin or Round Steak
3 Tbs. Vegetable Oil
2 Cloves Garlic, chopped
½ Small Head Cauliflower, broken into
    flowerettes
1 Green Pepper, seeded and cut into
    strips
3 Carrots, thinly sliced
1 - 1 Lb. Can Bean Sprouts, drained
4 Water Chestnuts, thinly sliced
    (optional)
½ Tsp. Ground Ginger
1/3 Cup Soy Sauce
1 Cup Water
1 Tbs. Cornstarch
2 Cups Hot Cooked Rice

Cut meat in very thin strips across the grain. Saute' in hot oil in a large skillet for 3 min. over high heat, turning to brown. Remove from skillet and keep warm. Add garlic, cauliflower, pepper and carrots to skillet & cook, stirring constantly, until vegetables are tender crisp, about 3 minutes. Add bean sprouts, water chestnuts, ginger, soy sauce and water. Cook, covered, 5 minutes longer and add meat. Blend cornstarch with 2 tbs. water in a cup; add to skillet. Cook for 1 minute, or until thickened and bubbly. Serve over rice. Makes 4 servings.

KIDNEY BEANS AND BEEF

1½ Lbs. Beef Round Steak,
   cut into 1″ cubes
2 Tbs. Olive Oil or Vegetable Oil
3 Onions, peeled and coarsely chopped
2 Large Garlic Cloves, minced
1 Tsp. Salt
¼ Tsp. Pepper
1 Cup Canned Beef Broth
1 - 8 Oz. Can Tomato Sauce
1 - 16 Oz. Can Tomatoes, undrained
2 - 16 Oz. Cans Red Kidney Beans,
   drained and rinsed
1 - 5½ Oz. Can Pitted Ripe Olives,
   drained

Brown meat in oil in a large skillet. Remove beef with slotted spoon and put into an electric cooker. Add onion and garlic to fat in skillet and cook until lightly browned. Add to cooker and sprinkle with salt and pepper. Add broth and stir well. Cover and cook on low for 8 to 10 hours. Stir in tomato sauce, tomatoes and kidney beans. Cover & cook on low for 1 hr. Before serving, stir in ripe olives. Ladle into bowls to serve; makes 8 servings.

BAKED SIRLOIN STEAK

4 to 5 Lb. Sirloin Steak, about
   2½″ thick
Salt and Pepper
¼ Cup Butter
2 Tbs. All-purpose Flour
½ Tsp. Hot Pepper Sauce
4 Onions, sliced thin
2 Carrots, shredded
1 Cup Ketchup, or tomato sauce
½ Cup Water

Heat a large iron skillet to sizzling hot. Sear steak quickly until brown on both sides. Remove steak to platter and season with salt and pepper. Add remaining ingredients to skillet; mix well. Cook for 5 minutes and pour off into small bowl.

Return steak to skillet; top with sauce. Bake in preheated very hot oven (450° F.) for 20 to 30 minutes. Makes 6 servings.

BEEF ROLL with HERB STUFFING

1 Flank Steak (1½ to 2 lbs.)
3 Medium Onions, chopped (1½ cups)
4 Tbs. Butter or Margarine
2 Cups Packaged Bread Stuffing (half
   of an 8 oz. package)
¼ Cup Chopped Parsley
2 Tbs. Grated Parmesan Cheese
½ Tsp. Garlic Salt
½ Cup Water
¼ Cup Unsifted All-purpose Flour
¼ Cup Vegetable Oil
2 Envelopes Spaghetti Sauce Mix
4 Cups Tomato Juice
1 - 2 Lb. Can Italian Tomatoes
2 - 4 Oz. Cans Mushroom Stems
   and Pieces

Have the butcher split the flank steak, butterfly fashion. You can also do this yourself, using a sharp long-blade knife. Work very slowly, cutting with a sawing motion, as evenly as possible. Saute' ¼ cup onion in butter or margarine just until soft in a medium saucepan. Stir in bread stuffing, parsley, Parmesan cheese, garlic salt, and water; toss with a fork until moist & well mixed.

Lay steak flat on counter top; spread the stuffing over steak to within 1″ of edges. Starting at one end, roll up, jelly-roll style, and fasten with 2 or 3 wooden picks. Fold up ends of roll to hold in stuffing; fasten with more wooden picks. Rub roll well with flour; brown in vegetable oil in heavy kettle or Dutch oven. Stir in remaining 1¼ cups onion, and saute' just until soft. Stir in spaghetti sauce mix, tomato juice, tomatoes and mushrooms (with the liquid); cover and simmer for 1½ hours, or until meat is tender. Remove roll to carving board; take out wooden picks. Carve meat in ½-inch thick slices. Serve sauce with meat roll. There will be sauce remaining, which can be used for spaghetti or manicotti dinner. Makes 6 servings.

STEAK ROLLUPS
(Bavarian Style)

1 Slice Round Steak, 1" thick
  (about 2 lbs.)
6 Sweet Italian Sausages or
  6 Smoked Link Sausages
2 Tbs. Vegetable Oil
1 Medium Onion, chopped (½ cup)
1 - 1 Lb. 11 Oz. Can Sauerkraut
1 - 1 Lb. 4 Oz. Can Tomatoes
1 Tbs. Caraway Seeds
1 Tbs. Brown Sugar
1 Tsp. Salt

Cut steak into 6 even-size pieces; pound
very thin with a wooden mallet or rolling
pin. Roll each piece around a sausage &
fasten with one or two wooden picks.
Brown pieces of steak slowly in vegetable
oil in a large frying pan. Remove from
pan and add onion; saute' just until soft.
Drain liquid from sauerkraut into frying
pan. Stir in tomatoes, caraway seeds,
brown sugar and salt. Return meat to
pan. Cover and simmer for 1 hour. Now
spoon sauerkraut in a layer on top of the
meat. Cover again and simmer for 30
minutes longer, or until meat is tender.
Spoon sauerkraut into a heated serving
dish; arrange meat rolls, spoke fashion,
on top. Spoon sauce from pan over the
top. Makes 6 servings.

SWEET AND SOUR MEAT BALLS
(From Shanghai)

3 Large Green Peppers, seeded
4 Pineapple Slices
1 Lb. Ground Beef
Soy Sauce
Salt and Pepper
Seasoned Salt
1 Tbs. Flour
2 Tbs. Butter
1 Cup Chicken Broth
½ Cup Juice from Pineapple
¼ Cup Vinegar
2 Tbs. Cornstarch
1 Tbs. Sugar

Wash the peppers and cut each into 6 pieces.
Cook in boiling water, to cover, for 3 min.
Drain. Cut each slice of pineapple into
6 pieces. Drain. Combine the meat, 2

tsp. soy sauce, ¾ tsp. salt, 1 tsp. seasoned
salt, ¼ tsp. pepper and blend well. Shape
the mixture into 16 small balls and roll
them in the flour. Heat the butter and
brown meatballs on all sides over medium
heat; cover and simmer for 5 minutes. Remove to a hot dish and keep warm. Add
to the butter ½ cup chicken broth, the
green peppers and pineapple pieces; cover
and simmer for 8 minutes. Meanwhile,
combine the remaining broth, pineapple
juice, vinegar, cornstarch, sugar, 2 tsp.
soy sauce and ½ tsp. salt. Add to green
pepper mixture and stir constantly until
the sauce is thickened and clear. Pour
the pepper mixture over the meat balls
and serve hot, with boiled rice. Makes 4
servings.

CURRIED BEEF
(From the Mideast)

1 Lb. Beef Stew Meat, cut into
  pieces
½ Tbs. Ground Coriander
½ Tsp. Ground Cumin
½ Tsp. Ground Mustard
½ Tsp. Cayenne Pepper
1 Tsp. Ground Turmeric
¼ Tsp. Ground Black Pepper
¼ Tsp. Ginger
Wine Vinegar
1 Large Onion, sliced thin
2 Garlic Cloves, sliced thin
2 Fresh or Pickled Green Chilies,
  finely chopped
4 Tbs. Shortening or Cooking Oil
Salt to taste
Lemon Juice to taste

Combine the spices and mix with enough
of the wine vinegar to make a paste. Saute'
onion, garlic and chopped chilies in shortening or oil for 3 or 4 minutes. Add the
spice paste and cook for 3 or 4 minutes
longer. Add the meat; cover pan and let
meat simmer in its own juice for 1 to 1½
hours. Add just enough water from time
to time to keep meat from sticking to pan.
The juices will form a thick, rich gravy.
Add salt and lemon juice to taste. Makes
4 servings.

NOODLE, BEEF AND CHEESE CASSEROLE

2 Tbs. Vegetable Oil
1 Onion, chopped
2 Lbs. Ground Beef
4 - 10¼ Oz. Cans Meatless Mushroom
   Sauce (for spaghetti)
1 Tsp. Salt
1 Lb. Fine Noodles, cooked and drained
1 Lb. Sharp Cheddar Cheese, grated or
   shredded
Seasoning Salt

Heat oil; add onion and cook until golden.
Add meat and cook until meat loses its
red color, stirring occasionally. Add the
mushroom sauce and salt; heat. Arrange
half of the noodles in a casserole; top
with half of sauce and half of cheese;
sprinkle with seasoning salt. Make another
layer of noodles; add sauce and top with
cheese. Bake in preheated 325°F. oven
for 1 hour. The top should be nicely
browned. Makes 8 to 10 generous
servings.

PEPPERY BROILED STEAK

1 Round Steak, cut 1" thick
   (about 2 lbs.)
Unseasoned Meat Tenderizer
1¼ Cups Wine Vinegar or Cider Vinegar
½ Cup Olive Oil or Vegetable Oil
1 Tbs. Mixed Italian Herbs
2 Cloves Garlic, minced
1 Bay Leaf
1 Tbs. Seasoned Pepper

Moisten steak and sprinkle with meat tenderizer, following directions on label. Put
steak into a shallow glass or plastic dish.
Mix the wine vinegar, or cider vinegar,
olive oil or vegetable oil, herbs, garlic and
bay leaf in a 2-cup measure; pour over the
meat. Cover and chill about 2 hours, turning meat several times so it will season
evenly. When ready to broil, remove the
steak from marinade (save marinade to
strain, heat and use as a dip or sauce for
steak). Place steak on broiler rack and
sprinkle top evenly with half of the seasoned pepper. Broil, about 6 inches from
the heat, for 10 to 12 minutes. Turn and
sprinkle with remaining seasoned pepper.
Broil 8 to 10 minutes longer for rare, or
until steak is done as you like it. Remove
to cutting board and slice diagonally into
¼-inch to ½-inch slices. Makes 6 servings.

FRIKADELLER
(Danish Meatballs)

1 Large Onion
1 Tbs. Butter
¾ Cup Soft Bread Crumbs
¾ Cup Milk
¾ Lb. Very Finely-ground Beef
   or Veal, ground 2 to 3 times
¾ Lb. Very Finely-ground Pork,
   ground 2 to 3 times
2 Eggs, beaten
1½ Tsp. Salt
¼ Tsp. Ground Allspice
Pepper
1 Cup Warm Milk
2 Tbs. Butter
2 Tbs. Oil
¼ Cup All-purpose Flour
1½ Cups Meat Stock or Consomme'

Chop the onion and cook in the butter
until soft. Soak the bread crumbs in the
milk and combine with onion, meats,
eggs and seasonings. Mix well. Gradually
beat in the warm milk (this will be easier
if you use an electric mixer). Add as
much of the milk as the mixture will
take. Chill, then form into meatballs
(about 12). Flatten the meatballs slightly.
Heat together the butter and oil; brown
meatballs. Drain off fat; sprinkle meatballs slightly with flour and add stock to
the pan. Simmer for 5 to 10 minutes before serving. Milk may be used instead
of stock, or 1 cup of dairy sour cream
may be added toward the end of the
cooking. Makes 6 servings.

SPICY SWISS STEAK

1½ Tsp. Salt
½ Tsp. Ground Allspice
¼ Tsp. Pepper
2 Lbs. Beef Round Steak, about 1"
  thick
1/3 Cup All-purpose Flour
3 Tbs. Shortening or Salad Oil
1 Medium Onion, minced
3 Cups Peeled Chopped Tomatoes,
  fresh or canned

Rub salt, allspice, and pepper well into
steak. Dredge meat with flour. Pound in
flour with edge of a plate. Heat shortening in heavy casserole. Brown meat quickly
in hot fat on both sides. Add onion and
tomatoes. Cover and bake in preheated
oven (350°F.) for about 1½ hours, or until meat is tender. Check occasionally to
be sure there is enough liquid in the
casserole, adding a little hot water, bouillon
or more tomato to prevent sticking. Makes
about 4 servings.

PEPPER POT ORIENTAL

1 Lb. Ground Beef
½ Cup Thinly-sliced Green Onions
1 Clove Garlic, minced
1½ Tsp. Sugar
¼ Cup Soy Sauce
2 Lbs. Fresh Haddock Fillets,
  cut into 2" pieces
1 Large Onion, chopped (1 cup)
6 Large Mushrooms, trimmed and
  sliced
4 Medium Carrots, pared and cut into
  2"-long sticks
½ Cup Sliced Celery
1½ Tsp. Salt
1 Tsp. Pepper
¼ Tsp. Ground Ginger
¾ Cup Water
1 Egg
1 Tbs. Butter or Margarine

Mix ground beef with green onions, garlic,
sugar and 2 tablespoons of the soy sauce
until well blended in a bowl. Reserve the
remaining 2 tablespoons of soy sauce for
use later. Spread half of the meat mixture
evenly in a 12-cup baking dish; top with
half each of the haddock, chopped onion,
mushrooms, carrots and celery. Mix salt,
pepper and ginger in a cup; sprinkle half
over layers in dish. Repeat with remaining ground-beef mixture; haddock, vegetables and seasoning mixture. Combine
remaining 2 tablespoons of soy sauce &
water in a cup; pour over layers. Cover
tightly and bake in 350°F. oven for one
hour, or until haddock flakes easily and
all vegetables are tender. Just before
serving, beat egg slightly in a cup; cook
in butter or margarine, turning once, just
until firm. Cut in thin strips and mound
in a petal design in center of baking dish.
Mixture is souplike, so serve in soup
plates or shallow bowls. Makes 6 servings.

SPANISH MEATBALLS

1 Lb. Ground Beef
¼ Cup White Cornmeal
1 Egg
1 Clove Garlic, minced
1 Small Onion, minced
½ Tsp. Crumbled, Dried Oregano
1¼ Tsp. Salt
½ Tsp. Pepper
Chili-Tomato Sauce (see recipe
  below)

Mix beef, cornmeal, egg, garlic, onion, &
seasonings. Shape into tiny balls about
½" in diameter. Drop into boiling sauce;
cover and simmer for 5 minutes. Makes
4 servings.

Chili-Tomato Sauce:
1 Tbs. Shortening
1 Small Onion, chopped
1 Garlic Clove, minced
2 to 3 Tbs. Chili Powder
3 Cups Tomato Juice
Salt to taste

Melt shortening in large saucepan. Add
onion and garlic and cook slowly until
lightly browned. Add the chili powder,
tomato juice and salt to taste. Cook
for 10 minutes before adding meatballs.
Makes about 3 cups.

TANTALIZING POT ROAST

1 Chuck Beef Roast (about 4 lbs.)
2 Tbs. Lemon Juice
6 Slices Bacon, diced
1 Medium Onion, chopped (½ cup)
1 Garlic Clove, minced
1½ Cups Orange Juice
1 Cup Diced, Peeled Ripe Tomato
   (1 large)
1 Tbs. Sugar
3 Tsp. Salt
1 Tsp. Leaf Thyme, crumbled
½ Tsp. Ground Nutmeg
¼ Tsp. Pepper
1 Bay Leaf
3 Tbs. Cornstarch
¼ Cup Water

Brush beef with lemon juice; let stand for
about 5 minutes. Saute' bacon with onion
and garlic in Dutch oven or electric skillet
until bacon is crisp; remove and set aside.
Brown beef in bacon drippings in same pan
over medium heat; stir in bacon mixture,
orange juice, tomato and seasonings. Cover
and simmer for 3 hours, or until meat is
very tender. Remove to heated platter;
keep hot while making gravy. Pour the
liquid into a 4-cup measure; let stand for
about 1 minute, or until fat rises to top.
Skim off fat and remove bay leaf. Add
water, if needed, to make three cups of
liquid. Return to pan and heat to boiling.
Blend cornstarch with water in a cup; stir
into the hot liquid. Cook, stirring constantly, until gravy thickens and boils for
3 minutes. Carve meat into thin slices
and serve with gravy. Makes 6 servings.

TERIYAKI FLANK STEAK

¾ Cup Cooking Oil
¼ Cup Soy Sauce
¼ Cup Honey
2 Tbs. Cider Vinegar
2 Tbs. Finely Chopped Green Onions
1 Large Garlic Clove, minced or mashed
1½ Tsp. Ground Ginger
1 Flank Steak, about 2 pounds (not
   scored)

Combine soy sauce, oil, honey, vinegar,
onion, garlic and ginger. Pour over the
steak and allow to marinate for 4 hours
or more; turn occasionally.

This steak may be oven-broiled or it may
be broiled over hot coals in your barbecue
(about 5 minutes each side for medium
rare). Baste occasionally with marinade.
Carve into thin slices, cutting on the
diagonal from top to bottom of steak (as
for London Broil). Makes 4 servings.

BEEF BROILED IN SAUCE

1 Lb. Beef Rump
2 Tbs. Sugar
¼ Cup Soy Sauce
2 Tbs. Minced Onion
1½ Tsp. Minced Garlic
1 Tsp. Minced Gingerroot
2 Tsp. Ground Toasted Sesame Seed
½ Tsp. Pepper
1 Tbs. Sesame-seed Oil
Minced Pine Nuts

Cut the meat into 1/8" slices. This is easier
to do if meat is first frozen until hard. Mix
meat slices with the sugar and let stand for
a minute or two. Grill lightly until surface
of meat is just seared and then pound. Dip
the meat into sauce made of soy sauce,
onion, garlic, gingerroot, sesame seed, pepper, and sesame-seed oil.

Grill lightly once more, turning the meat to
brown it on both sides. Pound and dip
again into the same sauce and grill once
more. Cut into 1" squares and sprinkle
lightly with minced pine nuts. Makes 4 to
6 servings.

CHILI--RIO GRANDE STYLE

4 Lbs. Beef Chuck, cut into
   2" cubes
1/3 Cup All-purpose Flour
1 Tsp. Ground Cumin
3 Tbs. Chili Powder
1 Tbs. Curry Powder
1½ Tsp. Salt
Freshly-ground Black Pepper,
   to taste
1 Tsp. Oregano
2 Tbs. Vegetable Oil
2 Tbs. Butter
1 Cup Chopped Onions
4 Cloves Garlic, crushed
2 Cups Beef Stock, or 2 Beef
   Bouillon Cubes combined
   with 2 cups hot water
1 Cup Dry Red Wine

Combine flour, cumin, chili powder, curry powder, salt, pepper and oregano. Dredge the meat in this mixture and set aside. Put oil and butter in a large, heavy skillet; add the onions and garlic and saute' for several minutes, until soft. Remove the garlic and onions to an ovenproof casserole. Using the same pan, saute' the meat cubes, a few at a time, until they are browned on all sides. Add to the casserole. Add the beef stock to the skillet and heat and stir, loosening the browned bits from the bottom of the pan. Pour this into the casserole, together with the red wine. Cover tightly and bake in a 300°F. oven for 2½ to 3 hours, until the meat is tender. Adjust the seasonings to your taste and serve immediately. Makes 8 to 10 servings.

HUNGARIAN GOULASH

¼ Cup Salad Oil
3 Lbs. Boneless Beef Chuck,
   cut into 1" cubes
1 Lb. Onions, peeled and
   sliced (about 3 cups)
1 Tbs. Paprika
1½ Tsp. Salt
1/8 Tsp. Pepper
1 - 10½ Oz. Can Condensed Beef
   Broth, undiluted
3 Tbs. Flour
1 Cup Dairy Sour Cream

In Dutch oven, heat oil over high heat. Add the beef cubes, in a single layer at a time, & cook over medium heat until cubes are well browned on all sides. As they brown, remove to a bowl. This will take about 15 to 20 minutes in all. Add onion to drippings; saute' until tender and golden brown--about 10 minutes. Return meat to Dutch oven. Add paprika, salt and pepper, stirring until well blended with meat. Stir in ¾ cup of the beef broth. Bring to boiling; reduce heat and simmer, covered, for 2 hours, or until beef cubes are fork-tender.

In small bowl, combine the flour and remaining beef broth, stirring until smooth. Gradually add to beef mixture, stirring constantly. Simmer, uncovered and stirring occasionally, 15 minutes longer. Just before serving, place sour cream in small bowl. Slowly add ½ cup hot gravy. Slowly add to beef mixture, stirring until well blended. Heat, but do not boil. Serve the goulash with noodles. Makes 6 servings.

MEAT LOAF

1 Lb. Ground Pork
1 Lb. Ground Veal
1 Lb. Ground Beef
2 Eggs
1/3 Cup Chopped Onion
2 Tsp. Salt
¼ Tsp. Dry Mustard
1/8 Tsp. Seasoned Salt (optional)
1/8 Tsp. Celery Salt
1/8 Tsp. Paprika
¼ Tsp. Black Pepper

Grind meat only once in a food chopper (use coarse blade). Combine meats thoroughly in large bowl.

Beat the eggs well and add onion and other seasonings. Mix well. Add this to the meat and stir or knead until blended. Pack into an oiled glass bread loaf pan (10x5¼x3½") and unmold onto a flat baking pan.

Bake at 350° for 1 hour. Let stand for 15 minutes before slicing.

PEPPERONI-STUFFED BEEF ROAST

1 Eye of Round Beef Roast, about 4 lbs.
1 - 5 Oz. Pkg. Whole Pepperoni
1 - 10½ Oz. Can Condensed Beef Bouillon
¼ Cup Cider Vinegar
Several Drops Liquid Red Pepper Seasoning
4 Tbs. All-purpose Flour
½ Cup Water
1 Tbs. Brown Sugar

Stand the roast on end and cut a small hole through the center with a sharp thin-bladed knife; stuff hole with pepperoni, twisting and pushing it in as you work (do not remove strings from roast). Brown the roast in a large frying pan or Dutch oven; drain off all fat. Stir in bouillon, vinegar and red pepper seasoning. Cover and simmer, turning meat several times, for 3 hours, or until tender. Remove to a serving platter and keep warm while making gravy. Heat liquid in pan to boiling. Smooth flour & water to a paste in a cup; stir into boiling liquid with brown sugar. Cook, stirring constantly, until gravy thickens and boils for 1 minute. Carve part of roast into ¼" thick slices. Makes 6 servings for each of two meals.

BEEF, LAMB and PORK STEW

½ Lb. Beef for Stew
½ Lb. Lamb for Stew
½ Lb. Pork Cubes
2 Tbs. Butter or Margarine
3 Onions, peeled and chopped
4 Green Peppers, seeded and cut into pieces
1 Garlic Clove, crushed
1 Tbs. Paprika
1 Tsp. Salt
1 Tsp. Cumin Seed, crushed
1 Cup Water
3 Medium Tomatoes, peeled and diced
1 Cup Dairy Sour Cream

Cut the meat into 1" to 1½" cubes. Brown meat on all sides in butter in a skillet. Add onion, green pepper, garlic and paprika; stir. Cook for 3 to 4 minutes. Turn contents of skillet into an electric cooker. Sprinkle with salt and cumin. Add water to skillet; heat and stir to loosen browned particles. Pour into cooker; stir. Cover and cook on low for 8 to 10 hours. Add tomato and sour cream to stew; mix. Cover and cook on high for 30 minutes. Serve hot with fluffy hot rice. Makes 6 to 8 servings.

BEEF RAGOUT

2/3 Cup Flour
1 Tbs. Salt
1/8 Tsp. Pepper
3 Lbs. Beef Chuck, cut into 1½" cubes
1/3 Cup Salad Oil
1 Cup Chopped Onion
1 Cup Chopped Celery
½ Cup Chopped Green Pepper
2 Cloves Garlic, crushed
2 - 10½ Oz. Size Condensed Beef Consomme', undiluted
1 - 1 Lb. Can Tomatoes, undrained
1 - 6 Oz. Can Tomato Paste
2 Tbs. Chopped Parsley
2 Tsp. Paprika
2 Tsp. Worcestershire Sauce
12 New Potatoes, scrubbed (about 1 lb.)

On waxed paper, combine flour, salt and pepper. Use to coat beef cubes. Reserve remaining flour mixture. In 3 tablespoons of hot oil in Dutch oven, brown beef cubes, a third at a time. Remove as they are browned. Add more oil as needed. Add onion, celery, green pepper, and garlic to drippings in Dutch oven; saute' until tender--about 5 minutes. Remove from heat. Stir in reserved flour mixture, stirring until well blended. Gradually stir in consomme'. Add tomatoes, tomato paste, parsley, paprika, Worcestershire, and the browned beef. Bring to boiling, stirring occasionally. Reduce heat and simmer, covered, for 1¾ hours. Add potatoes and cook, covered, 45 minutes longer, or until the potatoes and meat are tender. Sprinkle with more chopped parsley before serving. Makes 6 to 8 servings.

CHINESE FLANK STEAK

1 Flank Steak (about 1½ lbs.)
2 Tbs. Soy Sauce
1 Tsp. Worcestershire Sauce
Dash of Liquid Red Pepper Seasoning
3 Tbs. Vegetable Oil
1 Medium Onion, peeled and sliced
½ Green Pepper, seeded and cut
  into strips
1 Small Garlic Clove, minced
1 - 4 Oz. Can Sliced Mushrooms
2 Tbs. Cornstarch
1½ Cups Beef Broth or Consomme'

Slice steak very thin diagonally; place in
a bowl. Sprinkle with soy sauce and
Worcestershire sauce and red pepper seasoning; toss to mix well. Heat oil until hot in
a large frying pan; add seasoned meat. Cook
quickly, stirring constantly, until meat loses
its pink color; remove from frying pan with
a slotted spoon. Stir onion, green pepper
and garlic into drippings in pan; saute' until soft. Stir in mushrooms and liquid.
Blend cornstarch into beef broth until it
forms a smooth liquid; stir into vegetables.
Cook, stirring constantly, until sauce thickens and boils 3 minutes. Return meat to
pan and heat slowly just until hot. Makes
4 servings.

PASTELLS
(From West India)

2 Tbs. Butter
1 Lb. Ground Beef
1 Cup Finely-chopped Onion
½ Cup Finely-chopped Celery
1 Green Pepper, chopped
3 Tbs. Oatmeal
1 Tsp. Salt
1 Tsp. Prepared Mustard
1 Tsp. Summer Savory
2 Cups Hot Mashed Potatoes
1 Recipe Pastry

Boil and mash the potatoes. Make the
pastry and chill. Melt butter in a large
frying pan and cook the onions and the
ground beef until onions are limp. Add
chopped celery and green pepper. Add

oatmeal, salt, mustard and summer savory
to the meat mixture; blend and cook until meat is done (about 20 minutes). Stir
the hot mashed potatoes into the meat
mixture.

Roll out pastry on a lightly-floured board &
cut as many 6" circles as you will need individual servings. Preheat oven to 425°F.
Cut a few small vents on one half of each
circle. Place 2 or 3 large spoonfuls of meat
mixture on the other half of the circle. Lift
the vent side of the pastry over the meat
mixture to form a covering. Pinch and flute
edges together. Bake pastells on a cookie
sheet at 425°F. for 25 minutes. Rice may
be substituted for the potato and curry may
be substituted for the mustard if desired.

STUFFED MEAT LOAF

1 Lb. Ground Beef
1 Egg
2 Slices Crumbled Bread, without
  crusts (soaked in ¼ cup milk)
3 Tbs. Grated Romano Cheese
Dash of Marjoram
1 Tbs. Minced Fresh Parsley,
  or 1 Tsp. Dry Parsley
1 Small Onion, chopped
Salt and Pepper to taste

Stuffing:
2 Strips Prosciutto
5 Thin Strips Provolone (3" long
  and ¼" wide)
1 Hard-cooked Egg, sliced lengthwise

Topping:
1 - 8 Oz. Can Tomato Sauce

In a large bowl, combine beef, egg, bread,
cheese, marjoram, parsley, onion, salt and
pepper. Mix thoroughly. Divide in half.
In a shallow 7x11" baking pan, greased
with olive oil, mold half of the meat into
an oval shape. Flatten slightly. Arrange
the prosciutto, provolone and egg on meat.
Place remaining meat on top and mold,
pressing edges down. Bake in a preheated
375°F. oven for 25 minutes, or until brown.
Top with tomato sauce and bake 5 minutes
more or until well heated. Makes 4 servings.

BEEF SLICES

1 Lb. Beef Rump, sliced into
   thin slices
1 Tbs. Butter or Coconut Oil
1 Large Onion, thinly-sliced
1 Large Tomato, peeled and chopped
2 Inches of Stick Cinnamon
2 Whole Cloves

Marinade:
1 Large Onion, finely chopped
3 Garlic Cloves, finely chopped
10 Peppercorns, crushed
3 Tbs. Dark Soy Sauce
3 Tbs. Brown Sugar
Grated Nutmeg

Pound the beef slices with a meat mallet
until they are very thin. To prepare the
marinade, mash the onion and garlic to a
fine paste; combine this with the pepper,
soy sauce, brown sugar and nutmeg (just
a pinch). Marinate the meat in this sauce
for 30 minutes to 1 hour.

Heat the butter or oil in a large skillet or
wok, add the sliced onion and fry it until
soft. Add the beef slices and marinade &
stir-fry for 1 minute. Add the tomato and
a little water. Stir and allow to cook, uncovered, until the meat is tender, the tomato
soft and there is not too much gravy--about
5 minutes. Makes 3 to 4 servings.

CHINESE PEPPER STEAK

1 Envelope Instant Beef Broth
   (or 1 Tsp. Granulated Beef
   Bouillon)
¼ Cup Boiling Water
2 Lbs. Ground Beef
1 Tbs. Vegetable Oil
1 Large Green Pepper, halved,
   seeded and sliced
¾ Cup Thinly-sliced Celery
¼ Cup Sliced Green Onions
1 - 1 Lb. Can Tomatoes
2 Tbs. Cornstarch
2 Tbs. Soy Sauce
Hot Cooked Rice

Dissolve the beef broth in boiling water
in a cup; stir lightly into ground beef
in a large bowl. Shape into 6 patties
about 1" thick. Brown the patties in
vegetable oil, turning once, in a large
frying pan. Remove with a slotted
spoon and place in a shallow pan. Stir
green pepper, celery, and green onions
into drippings in pan; saute' until soft.
Stir in tomatoes; place beef patties in
sauce. Cover and simmer for 20 min.
Place patties on a heated deep serving
platter. Blend cornstarch with soy
sauce and a little water to a paste in
a cup. Stir into mixture in pan. Cook,
stirring constantly, until sauce thickens
and boils for 3 minutes. Pour over the
beef patties. Serve over rice. Makes 6
servings.

GOURMET GOULASH

1 Lb. Ground Beef
1 Cup Chopped Onion
1 Garlic Clove, crushed
1 Tsp. Salt
3 Cups (4 Oz.) Medium Noodles
1 Can Tomato Juice (2½ cups)
1½ Tsp. Worcestershire Sauce
1½ Tsp. Celery Salt
1 Tsp. Salt
Dash of Pepper
1 Can Condensed Beef Broth
½ Cup Water
1/3 Cup Chopped Green Pepper
1 Cup Dairy Sour Cream
1 - 3 Oz. Can (2/3 Cup) Broiled,
   Sliced Mushrooms, drained

Place beef, onion, garlic and 1 tsp. salt in
an electric skillet. Heat to about 350°F.
Cook and stir until beef is browned. Add
noodles. Combine tomato juice, Worcestershire sauce, celery salt, salt, pepper, beef
broth and water. Pour over noodles.
Cover and simmer at 220°F. for 20 minutes, stirring occasionally. Add green pepper. Cover and cook 10 minutes, or until
noodles are tender. Stir in mushrooms &
cream; heat but do not boil. Makes 5 or
6 servings.

FRENCH COUNTRY-STYLE PORK CHOPS

4 Medium Carrots
2 Small White Turnips
2 Celery Stalks
4 Leeks, white part only, or
    8 Green Onions, white part only
4 Small White Onions, chopped
1 - 1 Lb. 13 Oz. Can Tomatoes
    (3½ cups)
1/8 Tsp. Ground Marjoram
1 Bay Leaf
¼ Cup Chopped Parsley
¾ Tsp. Salt
½ Tsp. Pepper
1/3 Cup Consomme'
1½ to 2 Lbs. Blade Pork Chops,
    trimmed of excess fat

Cut carrots, turnips, celery, and leeks into 1½'' long julienne strips. Combine with next 7 ingredients in large heavy kettle. Add consomme'; bring to a boil. Simmer, covered, for 5 minutes. Put pork chops on top of vegetables. Cover and simmer for about 1 hour, or until thoroughly done. When ready to serve, place vegetables in center of serving dish and surround with pork chops. Makes 4 servings.

PORK CHOP CASSEROLE

6 Pork Chops
1 Onion, sliced thin
2 Tbs. Butter or Margarine
8 Cloves
½ Tsp. Salt
1 Tsp. Crushed Coriander Seeds
1 Medium Pineapple
1 Cup Sugar
½ Cup Fresh Lemon Juice
½ Tsp. Ground Ginger
1 Cup Uncooked Rice
½ Tsp. Ground Cinnamon

Brown chops on both sides; remove from skillet. Cook onion in butter with cloves, salt and coriander. Add the chops and 1½ cups of water and simmer for 20 minutes. Remove chops; strain gravy, adding water if necessary, to make 1 cup liquid. Cut peeled pineapple into ½'' slices. Boil the sugar, lemon juice and ginger for 5 min.

Add pineapple and cook until just tender, adding water if necessary to keep it from sticking. Cook and drain rice. Cut half of pineapple into pieces and add to the rice. Put rice in casserole, arrange chops over it, and top with pineapple slices. Sprinkle with cinnamon and pour gravy over all. Cover and bake in preheated 300°F. oven for 35 to 40 minutes. Makes 6 servings.

GLAZED HAM LOAF

½ Cup Milk
1 Egg
1 Tbs. Catsup
1 Tbs. Prepared Mustard
1/8 Tsp. Pepper
1 Cup Soft White Bread Crumbs
1 Lb. Ground Ham
½ Lb. Ground Veal
2 Tbs. Finely-chopped Onion
1 Tbs. Chopped Parsley

Fruit Glaze:

1 - 8¾ Oz. Can Fruits for Salad
¼ Cup Light Brown Sugar, firmly
    packed
2 Tbs. Cider Vinegar

Preheat oven to 350°F. In a large bowl, combine milk, egg, catsup, mustard, and pepper; beat until well blended. Stir in crumbs. Let mixture stand for several minutes. Add ham, veal, onion and parsley and mix well. In shallow baking pan, shape meat into loaf about 8'' long and 4'' wide. Bake ham loaf, uncovered, for 30 minutes.

In the meantime, drain syrup from fruit into a small saucepan. Add brown sugar and vinegar. Bring to boiling, stirring constantly. Add fruit. Reduce heat and simmer for 5 minutes. Remove saucepan from heat.

Remove ham loaf from oven. Pour the glaze over the loaf, arranging the fruit attractively on top. Then bake ham loaf for 30 minutes longer. With wide spatula, remove ham loaf to a warm platter. Spoon glaze from pan over top of loaf. Serve with mustard. Makes 6 servings.

SWEET-AND-SOUR SPARERIBS

3 Lbs. Pork Spareribs
1¼ Cups Vinegar
¾ Cup Cornstarch
2½ Tbs. Honey
1¼ Tbs. Soy Sauce
Oil, for frying
5/8 Cup Syrup from Canned
   Pineapple
2½ Tbs. Brown Sugar
½ Tsp. Salt
4 Pineapple Rings
1 Onion
1 Red Pepper

Cut the spareribs into serving-size pieces, chopping through the bone if necessary. Fill a large saucepan half full of water & add 4 tablespoons of the vinegar to it; bring to a boil. Add the spareribs and simmer for 20 minutes; drain. Place the cornstarch, honey and soy sauce in a bowl and mix well. Coat the spareribs with this mixture. Heat about 1 inch of oil in a large frying pan and fry the spareribs until golden. Drain well on absorbent kitchen paper.

Put the pineapple syrup into a large saucepan with 5/8 cup of water, brown sugar, salt and the remaining vinegar. Bring to a boil; add spareribs. Cover and simmer for 30 minutes, turning occasionally. Add the pineapple and vegetables to the pan 5 min. before cooking time is finished. Serve hot. Makes 4 to 6 servings.

MIDWEST HAM STEAK

1 Fully-cooked Ham Steak, cut
   1" thick (about 1 lb.)
1 Small Onion, chopped (¼ cup)
2 Tbs. Butter or Margarine
3 Flat Cornmeal Cakes
1 - 12 Oz. Can Mexican-style Corn,
   drained
1 Egg, slightly beaten
1 Tsp. Dry Mustard
Dash of Pepper
2 Envelopes Mushroom Gravy Mix
Water
¼ Cup Dry Sherry

Trim any excess fat from the ham steak; score fat edge and place steak in a shallow baking pan. Saute' onion in butter or margarine until soft in a large frying pan; remove from heat. Crumble corn cakes into frying pan; add corn, egg, mustard and pepper; toss lightly to mix. Spoon on top of ham; cover pan tightly with foil. Bake in 350°F. oven for 40 minutes. While ham bakes, prepare mushroom gravy mix with water, following directions on the label. Stir in sherry. Lift ham, with stuffing, onto a heated serving platter. Carve into ½" thick slices, cutting through stuffing. Serve gravy separately to spoon over top. Makes 4 servings.

ORIENTAL PORK AND SHRIMP

2 Eggs, beaten
½ Lb. Ground Pork
1 - 7 Oz. Pkg. Frozen, Cleaned
   and Shelled Shrimp, thawed
   (about 1 cup)
1 - 5 Oz. Can Water Chestnuts,
   drained and chopped
2 Tbs. Chopped Green Onion
1 Tsp. Soy Sauce
½ Tsp. Sugar
½ Cup Fine, Dry Bread Crumbs
Fat, for frying
Sweet-Sour Sauce (recipe below)

After the shrimp are thawed, chop very fine. Combine first 7 ingredients and ¼ tsp. salt; mix well. Shape into 36 balls. Roll in bread crumbs. Fry in deep, hot fat (360°F.) until brown, about 1½ to 2 minutes.

Sweet-Sour Sauce:
¾ Cup Water
¼ Cup Sugar
2 Tbs. Vinegar
1 Tbs. Soy Sauce
¼ Tsp. Salt
1 Tbs. Cornstarch
1 Tbs. Cold Water

In a saucepan, combine the water, sugar, vinegar, soy sauce and salt. Heat to boiling. Blend together the cornstarch and cold water. Slowly stir into boiling mixture. Cook and stir until bubbly. Makes 6 servings.

HAM AND OYSTER GUMBO

1 Roasting Chicken (3½ to 5 lbs.),
  cut into pieces
2 Tbs. Cooking Oil
¼ Cup Butter
1 Lb. Ham, cut into 1" cubes
3 Tbs. All-purpose Flour
1 Small Onion, minced
2 Medium Tomatoes, chopped
1½ Quarts Boiling Water
1 Bay Leaf
3 Parsley Sprigs
1 Tsp. Ground Thyme
Salt and Pepper
Dash of Hot Red Pepper Sauce
2 Dozen Oysters, shucked
1 Tbs. File' Powder

Trim fat off chicken pieces. Heat oil and
half of butter together in a large, deep skillet. Saute' ham until golden. Remove ham
to Dutch oven or deep saucepan and set
aside. Fry chicken pieces until browned
but not cooked through. Remove chicken
to Dutch oven. Stir flour into pan juices
and cook until lightly browned. Add onion and cook until soft, stirring constantly.
Add tomato and boiling water; blend thoroughly. Pour sauce on ham and chicken
in Dutch oven. Add bay leaf, parsley,
thyme, salt and pepper to taste, and hot
pepper sauce. Cook, covered, over moderate heat for about 30 minutes, or until
chicken is tender. Stir occasionally. Add
oysters and remaining butter. Cook over
low heat, stirring occasionally, for 5 minutes longer. Remove from heat and stir
in file' powder, blending thoroughly.
Serve with cooked rice. Makes 6 to 8
servings.

PINEAPPLE HAM LOAF

1 No. 2 Can Pineapple Slices
½ Cup Brown Sugar
1½ Lbs. Smoked Ground Ham
1 Lb. Ground Fresh Pork
¾ Cup Crushed Bite-size
  Shredded Corn Biscuits
½ Cup Chopped Onion
1 Tsp. Dry Mustard
2 Eggs, beaten
1 Cup Milk

Drain the pineapple. Reserve 2 tbs. of the
pineapple syrup. Add brown sugar to the
syrup and heat, stirring, until sugar dissolves.
Pour into a 9½x5x3" loaf pan. Combine remaining ingredients thoroughly. Lightly
pack over the brown-sugar mixture. Refrigerate overnight. Bake at 350°F. for 1 hour
45 minutes to 2 hours, or until done. Remove from oven and let stand 10 minutes.
In the meantime, brush pineapple slices with
melted butter and broil, 3 inches from heat,
for about 5 minutes. Pour off excess liquid
from the loaf and invert the loaf on a serving plate. Arrange pineapple slices around
the loaf. Cherries may be set in the center
of the pineapple slices. Makes 8 to 10
servings.

PORK CHOPS with
TANGY SAUCE

6 Rib Pork Chops, ¾" thick
2 Tbs. Salad Oil
1 Tsp. Salt
½ Cup Maple-blended Syrup
½ Cup Hickory-flavor Ketchup
2 Tbs. Lemon Juice
2 Tsp. Worcestershire Sauce
1 Unpeeled Large Tart Apple,
  cored and cut into 6 rings
1 Tbs. Cornstarch
1/3 Cup Water

Brown the pork chops in salad oil; season
with salt. Drain off the oil. Combine
syrup, ketchup, lemon juice and Worcestershire sauce. Reserve ½ cup of mixture;
pour remaining mixture over chops. Simmer, covered, over low heat for 25 minutes. Place an apple slice on each chop;
top with remaining ½ cup sauce mixture.
Cover and simmer 25 minutes longer. Remove chops to a hot platter. Blend cornstarch with water and stir into sauce in
skillet. Cook, stirring constantly, until
the sauce comes to a boil and thickens.
Serve over the pork chops. Makes 6
servings.

JAMAICAN PORK

1 - 5 Lb. Fresh Pork Shoulder
2 Tsp. Salt
½ Tsp. Pepper
2 Tbs. Vegetable Oil
3 Large Onions, chopped (3 cups)
2 Cups Water
¼ Cup Cider Vinegar
2 Tbs. Honey
½ Cup Sliced, Pitted Ripe Olives
½ Cup Seedless Raisins
2 Tbs. Capers
1/3 Cup Flour

Trim skin and any excess fat from the pork. Sprinkle salt and pepper over meat. Brown slowly in vegetable oil in a heavy skillet or Dutch oven. Remove and set aside. Pour all drippings from the kettle, then measure out 2 tablespoonfuls and return to kettle. Stir onions into drippings; saute' until soft. Stir in water, vinegar, honey, olives, raisins and capers; heat to boiling. Place pork in sauce. Cover and simmer, turning several times, for 2½ hours, or until pork is tender. Remove to a heated serving platter; keep warm. Let liquid in kettle stand until fat rises to top, then skim off. Reheat liquid to boiling.

Blend flour with about 3 tablespoons of water in a cup; stir into boiling liquid. Cook, stirring constantly, until sauce thickens and boils 1 minute. Carve pork into ¼-inch thick slices; serve sauce separately to spoon over meat. Makes 6 servings.

HAM BALLS WITH SOUR-CREAM SAUCE

2 Lbs. Ground Cooked Ham
½ Cup Minced Onion
½ Tsp. Pepper
2 Eggs, slightly beaten
Sour-Cream Sauce (see recipe
    below)

Mix all ingredients, except sauce, and shape into balls. Allow about ¼ cup of mixture for each ball. Put into a baking pan (13x9x2"). Bake in preheated hot oven (400°F.) for 35 to 40 minutes. Serve with sour-cream sauce. Makes 12 servings.

Sour-Cream Sauce:

1/3 Cup Butter or Margarine
1/3 Cup All-purpose Flour
1-1/3 Cups Water
2-2/3 Cups Dairy Sour Cream
¾ Tsp. Marjoram
¾ Tsp. Dillseed
Salt and Pepper to taste

Melt butter and blend in flour. Add the water, sour cream, marjoram, and dillseed. Cook, stirring constantly, until thickened. Cook for 10 minutes longer. Add salt and pepper to taste. Sauce can be kept warm over hot water. Makes 4 cups of sauce.

DUTCH PORK HOT POT

2 Lbs. Boneless Pork Shoulder,
    cut into 1" cubes
¼ Cup Unsifted All-purpose Flour
3 Tsp. Salt
1 Tsp. Leaf Thyme, crumbled
1 Tsp. Coriander Seeds, crushed
¼ Tsp. Pepper
1 - 1 Lb. Can Red Kidney Beans
Boiling Water
4 Medium Potatoes, pared and cut
    into ¼" slices
4 Medium Onions, sliced and separated
    into rings
8 Carrots, pared and cut into 4" lengths
2 Tbs. Butter or Margarine

Trim all fat from the pork. Shake cubes, a few at a time, with flour in a paper bag to coat well. Mix salt, thyme, coriander and pepper in a cup. Drain liquid from kidney beans into a 2-cup measure; add boiling water to make 1½ cups. Layer the vegetables and meat in a 12-cup deep baking dish as follows: half each of potatoes, onions, pork, kidney beans and carrots, sprinkling each layer lightly with seasoning mixture. Repeat with remaining vegetables, pork and seasoning mixture. Pour liquid over; dot with butter or margarine. Cover and bake in a 350°F. oven for 3 hours, or until the pork is tender. Makes 6 to 8 servings.

HOME-MADE PORK SAUSAGE

4 Lbs. Ground Fresh, Lean Pork
3 Medium Pods Dry Hot Red
  Pepper, crushed fine
1½ Tsp. Black Pepper
1 Tbs. Salt
2 Tsp. Sage

Choose very fresh lean pork loin or pork shoulder. Put meat and red pepper through food chopper, using medium knife. Add rest of seasonings and mix thoroughly. Pack firmly into clean bowls or loaf pans. Cover tightly and keep refrigerated until ready to fry. Measure out sausage meat by half cupfuls and shape into patties about 3" in diameter. If shaped in loaf pan, cut cold sausage meat into ½" slices. No shaping is required. Brown on both sides in a hot skillet, then reduce heat, cover and cook slowly until thoroughly done, about 20 minutes. When cut in half, thoroughly cooked patties are never pink in the center but a grayish white. One pound makes 4 to 5 servings.

HAM-STUFFED GREEN PEPPERS

6 Large Green Peppers
1 - 1 Lb. Canned Ham, drained
1 Medium Onion, peeled and
  quartered
2 Medium Potatoes, cooked, peeled
  and diced
1 Egg, beaten
1 Tsp. Leaf Marjoram, crumbled
2 Tbs. Butter or Margarine

Cut a thin slice from stem end of each pepper; scoop out seeds. Parboil pepper cups in boiling water in a kettle for 5 minutes, or until almost tender; drain well. Cut ham into chunks; put ham and onion through a food chopper, using a coarse blade. Combine with potatoes, egg and marjoram in a medium bowl; toss lightly to mix. Spoon into pepper cups; dot with butter or margarine. Stand peppers in a shallow baking dish and bake in 350°F. oven for 30 minutes, or until peppers are tender and filling is hot. Top with mustard sauce (recipe below). Makes 6 servings.

Mustard Sauce: Melt 2 tablespoons butter or margarine in small saucepan; stir in 2 tablespoons of all-purpose flour, 2 teaspoons dry mustard, and ½ teaspoon of salt; cook, stirring constantly, until bubbly. Stir in 1½ cups milk and a few drops liquid red pepper seasoning. Continue to cook and stir until sauce thickens and boils 1 minute. Makes about 1½ cups.

PORK--TAHITIAN STYLE

1 - 6 Lb. Fresh Ham, butt half
1 - 6 Oz. Can Pineapple Juice
¼ Cup Lime Juice
½ Cup Brown Sugar, firmly packed
½ Tsp. Whole Cloves
2 - 3" Pieces Stick Cinnamon
Lime Slices, halved

Trim skin and any excess fat from pork. Place roast on a rack in a shallow baking pan. Insert meat thermometer into roast so bulb reaches thickest part without touching bone. Roast in slow oven (325° F.) for 3½ hours, or until thermometer registers 180°F. While pork roasts, combine pineapple and lime juices, brown sugar, cloves and cinnamon in a small saucepan; heat to boiling. Simmer for 5 minutes. Brush part over roast. Continue roasting, brushing every 10 minutes with remaining pineapple mixture, for 30 minutes, or until thermometer registers 185°F. and pork is tender and richly glazed. Remove to a heated serving platter. Make two cuts lengthwise across the top of roast; tuck halved lime slices into cuts. Brush with any remaining pineapple mixture. Garnish platter with parsley. Carve roast into ¼" slices. Makes 6 servings.

PORK CHOP SUEY

3 Lbs. Lean Boneless Pork Shoulder,
    cut into 1-inch cubes
2 Large Onions, chopped (about
    2 cups)
1 Tbs. Brown Sugar
2 Tsp. Ground Ginger
½ Tsp. Salt
¼ Tsp. Pepper
4 Envelopes Instant Chicken Broth,
    or 4 Chicken-Bouillon Cubes
1 - 6 Oz. Can Sliced Mushrooms
4½ Cups Water
4 Cups Thinly-sliced Celery
3 Tbs. Cornstarch
2 Tbs. Soy Sauce
1 - 1 Lb. Can Bean Sprouts, drained

Brown the pork cubes, a few at a time, in
a large frying pan. Remove from pan. Add
onions and saute' just until soft. Return
pork to the pan. Stir in brown sugar, ginger,
salt, pepper, chicken broth, mushrooms and
liquid, and 4 cups of water. Cover and simmer for 40 minutes, or until pork is tender.
Stir in celery; cover and simmer for 10 min.
Blend cornstarch, soy sauce and remaining
½ cup water in a cup; stir into meat mixture
and cook, stirring constantly, until it thickens and boils. Boil for 3 minutes. Stir in
the drained bean sprouts; heat again just until bubbly-hot. Serve over your choice of
rice or Chinese fried noodles. Makes 12
servings.

PORK CHOPS WITH CRANBERRY-MUSHROOM STUFFING

6 Cups Cubed White Bread
6 Loin Pork Chops, cut 1" thick
1 Large Onion, chopped (1 cup)
1 Cup Thinly-sliced Celery
6 Tbs. Butter or Margarine
1 Chicken Bouillon Cube
1 Cup Water
½ Cup Cranberry-Orange Relish
1 - 6 Oz. Can Chopped Mushrooms,
    drained
½ Tsp. Salt
½ Tsp. Leaf Thyme, crumbled
½ Tsp. Leaf Sage, crumbled
¼ Tsp. Pepper

Place bread cubes in a shallow pan and toast
in a moderate oven (350°F.) for 20 minutes,
or until golden brown. Trim all fat from the
pork chops. Saute' a few of the trimmings
in a large frying pan; remove and discard.
Place chops in drippings and saute' slowly,
turning once, until richly browned. Remove
from pan and keep warm. Saute' onion and
celery in butter or margarine in same pan until soft. Stir in bouillon cube (crush with
a spoon), water, cranberry-orange relish,
mushrooms, salt, thyme, sage and pepper.
Heat to boiling and pour over bread cubes
and toss until evenly moist. Spoon into a
lightly-greased baking pan, 13x9x2". Arrange the browned chops in a single layer
on top. Cover and bake in 350°F. oven
for 1 hour and 30 minutes, or until chops
are tender. Remove chops from the pan.
Spoon dressing onto a heated serving platter and arrange chops on top of dressing.
Garnish as desired. Makes 6 servings.

SWEET-SOUR HAM ROLLS

¾ Lb. Ground Cooked Pork
½ Lb. Ground Cooked Ham
1 Cup Cracker or Bread Crumbs
1 Egg
¾ Cup Milk
½ Tsp. Salt
½ Cup Brown Sugar, packed
½ Tsp. Dry Mustard
¼ Cup Vinegar
¼ Cup Hot Water
2 Tbs. Seedless Raisins or
    Currants

Mix meats together with crumbs, well-
beaten egg, milk and salt. Shape into
4 servings-size rolls. Place in a greased,
shallow 1-quart baking dish. Mix remaining ingredients in glass or enamel saucepan.
Heat, stirring until sugar dissolves. Spoon
about half of the sauce over the rolls.
Bake for 50 minutes in 325°F. oven.
Baste frequently with sauce. Serve hot
with any remaining sauce. Makes 4
servings.

PORK with ORANGE GLAZE

1 - 4 Lb. Loin of Pork
1 Small Onion, grated
1 Tbs. Butter or Margarine
2 Tbs. Brown Sugar
1½ Tsp. Cornstarch
½ Tsp. Ground Ginger
1 Cup Orange Juice
1 Tbs. Bottled Steak Sauce

Place pork, fat side up, on a rack in a roasting pan. If using a meat thermometer, insert bulb into center of meat without touching bone. Roast in 325°F. oven for 1 hour. While pork roasts, saute' the onion in butter or margarine until soft (use a small saucepan). Stir in remaining ingredients and cook, stirring constantly, until thick. Brush part over meat. Continue roasting, brushing meat every 15 minutes, for 1 hour longer. Roast should be richly glazed and the thermometer should register 170°F. Carve meat into chops. Makes 4 servings.

HAM-CORN BREAD RING with CREAMED PEAS

¾ Cup Yellow Cornmeal
1 Cup All-purpose Flour
¼ Cup Sugar
2 Tsp. Baking Powder
½ Tsp. Baking Soda
¾ Tsp. Salt
1 Cup Dairy Sour Cream
¼ Cup Milk
1 Egg, beaten
2 Tbs. Margarine, melted
1 Cup Ground, Cooked Ham
Creamed Cooked Peas

Mix all ingredients, except peas, just to blend. Pour into a well-greased six-cup ring mold, patting mixture down and leveling off top. Bake in hot oven (425° F.), preheated, for about 20 minutes. Let stand for 2 or 3 minutes. Turn out on hot serving plate. Fill center with peas. Makes 6 servings. Other creamed vegetables such as onions, asparagus, broccoli, or mixed vegetables may be substituted for the creamed peas.

PORK PLATTER-- KOREAN STYLE

1½ Lbs. Lean, Boneless Pork
      Shoulder, cut into 1" cubes
2 Tbs. Flour
4 Tbs. Vegetable Oil
3 Tsp. Curry Powder
1 Tbs. Sugar
1/3 Cup Soy Sauce
¾ Cup Water
2 Large Onions, peeled, sliced
      and separated into rings
2 Cups Sliced Celery
1 - 9 Oz. Pkg. Frozen, Cut Green
      Beans
2 Medium Yellow Squash, trimmed,
      halved lengthwise and sliced
1 Tsp. Celery Salt

Shake the pork cubes with flour in a paper bag to coat evenly. Brown in 2 tablespoons of the vegetable oil in a large frying pan; remove and set aside. Stir curry powder into drippings in frying pan; cook 3 minutes. Stir in sugar, soy sauce and ½ cup of water; cook, stirring constantly and scraping bottom of pan, until bubbly; stir in pork and cover. Simmer 1 hr. and 15 min., or until pork is tender.

While meat cooks, saute' onion rings in remaining 2 tablespoons of vegetable oil for 3 minutes, in a second large frying pan. Push onion rings to one side. Stir in celery and cook for 3 minutes. Stir in green beans and squash. Sprinkle with celery salt and toss to mix. Add remaining ¼ cup of water; cover and steam for 10 minutes, or until the vegetables are tender but crisp; drain. Spoon vegetables onto a heated platter; spoon pork on top. Makes 6 servings.

POLYNESIAN PORK PLATTER

2 Cups Uncooked Regular Rice
½ Cup Thinly-sliced Celery
1 - 3 Lb. Canned Pork Picnic
   Shoulder
¼ Cup Unsifted All-purpose Flour
1 Tsp. Ground Ginger
5 Tbs. Butter or Margarine
1 - 1 Lb. 4 Oz. Can Pineapple Chunks,
   in juice
¼ Cup Cornstarch
½ Cup Water
¼ Cup Light Brown Sugar, firmly
   packed
¼ Cup Cider Vinegar
¼ Cup Light Molasses
1 - 15 Oz. Can Sliced Small Tomatoes
1 - 1 Lb. Can Italian Green Beans

Combine the rice and celery and cook, following directions on rice label; keep warm. Scrape gelatin coating from pork into a small bowl. Cut pork into 1" cubes, discarding any fat. Shake pork in a mixture of flour and ginger in a plastic bag to coat evenly. Saute' pieces in 4 tablespoons of the butter or margarine until crusty-brown in a large frying pan. Remove with a slotted spoon; keep warm. Drain juice from pineapple into frying pan. Smooth cornstarch and water to a paste in a cup; stir into frying pan, then stir in the brown sugar, vinegar, molasses and gelatin from pork. Cook, stirring constantly, until mixture thickens and boils 3 minutes; add pineapple and pork. Heat until bubbly.

Heat tomatoes and beans in their liquids to boiling in separate small saucepans. When ready to serve, spoon rice mixture into an oval or ring on a large serving platter; pile pork mixture in center. Drain liquids from tomatoes and beans and spoon part of each vegetable at ends of meat. Season vegetables with remaining 1 tablespoon of butter or margarine and sprinkle lightly with salt and pepper. Garnish with green-pepper rings, if you wish. Makes 8 servings.

MAPLE-BARBECUED SPARERIBS

1½ Cups Maple Syrup
2 Tbs. Chili Sauce
2 Tbs. Cider Vinegar
1½ Tbs. Finely-chopped Onion
1 Tbs. Worcestershire Sauce
1 Tsp. Salt
½ Tsp. Dry Mustard
1/8 Tsp. Pepper
3 Lbs. Spareribs, cut into
   serving-size pieces

Preheat oven to 350°F. In a medium bowl, combine maple syrup with rest of ingredients, except spareribs. Mix well. Wipe spareribs with damp paper towels. Brush on both sides with maple basting sauce. Place ribs, in single layer, on rack in shallow, open roasting pan. Roast 1½ hours, or until tender, brushing frequently with sauce and turning occasionally to glaze evenly. Makes 4 servings.

BAKED STUFFED HAM STEAKS

1 Cup Mashed Cooked Sweet Potatoes
3 Cups Toasted Bread Cubes
1/3 Cup Finely Chopped Celery
¼ Cup Finely Chopped Onion
4 Sausage Links
¾ Tsp. Salt
¾ Tsp. Poultry Seasoning
1½ Tbs. Butter or Margarine,
   melted
2 Fully-cooked Ham Steaks, center
   cut, ½" thick each

Combine sweet potatoes, bread cubes, celery and onion. Cut sausage links into ½" pieces, brown and add to the mixture, discarding the fat. Blend in salt, poultry seasoning and butter. Slash fat around the ham steaks to prevent curling and place 1 steak in a greased baking dish. Spread with the stuffing. Top with remaining steak. Cover and bake in preheated oven (325°F.) for 30 minutes. Remove cover and bake for 30 minutes longer. Makes 6 servings.

SOUTHERN HAM BAKE

2 Medium Sweet Potatoes, pared and
  sliced thin
3 Medium Pears, pared, quartered,
  cored and sliced
3 Cups Diced Cooked Ham (about
  1 lb.)
3 Tbs. Brown Sugar
½ Tsp. Salt
¼ Tsp. Pepper
¼ Tsp. Curry Powder
1/3 Cup Apple Cider
1 Cup Pancake Mix
½ Tsp. Dry Mustard
1 Cup Milk
2 Tbs. Melted Butter or Margarine

Layer half of sweet potatoes, pears and
ham in an 8-cup baking dish. Mix the
brown sugar, salt, pepper and curry powder in a cup. Sprinkle half on top of
layers in baking dish. Repeat with remaining sweet potatoes, pears, ham and
seasonings. Pour apple cider over and
cover. Bake in moderate oven (375°F.)
for 40 minutes, or until sweet potatoes
are tender. While ham mixture bakes,
combine pancake mix, mustard, milk &
melted butter or margarine in a medium
bowl, blending well to make a thin batter. Pour over hot ham mixture. Bake,
uncovered, 20 minutes longer, or until
pancake topping is puffed and golden.
Makes 6 servings.

CHERRY PORK CHOPS

4 Pork Chops
Salt and Pepper to taste
1 - 1 Lb. 1 Oz. Can Pitted Light
  Sweet Cherries
¼ Cup Slivered Almonds
6 Whole Cloves
1 Tbs. Cider Vinegar

Brown the pork chops on both sides.
Season with salt and pepper. Combine
the cherries and syrup from can with
almonds, cloves and vinegar. A little
red food coloring may be added if
desired. Pour over chops and simmer,
covered, for 30 minutes. Makes 4
servings.

RANCH-STYLE RIBS

3 to 4 Lbs. Loin Back Ribs,
  or Spareribs, cut into strips
  3" wide
1 Cup Catsup
1 Tbs. Worcestershire Sauce
2 or 3 Dashes Hot Pepper Sauce
1 Cup Water
¼ Cup Vinegar
1 Tbs. Sugar
1 Tsp. Salt
1 Tsp. Celery Seed

Season ribs with salt and pepper; place in
a shallow roasting pan, meaty side up.
Roast in a very hot oven, 450°F., for 30
minutes. Reduce temperature to 350°F.
and continue to bake for 30 minutes more.
Spoon off excess fat. Combine remaining
ingredients; bring to a boil and pour over
the ribs. Continue baking at 350°F. for
about 45 minutes, or until ribs are tender.
Baste with sauce every 15 minutes. If
sauce becomes too thick, add more water.
Makes 4 servings.

FILIPINO-STYLE
PORK FRICASSEE

1 Fresh Ham (about 8 lbs.)
½ Cup Soy Sauce
Juice of 1 Lemon
2 Tsp. Poultry Seasoning
1½ Tsp. Salt
½ Tsp. Pepper
1 Tsp. Ground Ginger
2 Medium Onions, chopped
2 Cups Water
6 Tbs. Cornstarch

Have meat sliced into 1" slices. Remove
bones, trim off fat and cut slices into
pieces about 1x1½". Combine remaining
ingredients, except water and cornstarch.
Pour over meat and let stand for at least
30 minutes. Put in a large kettle; add
water and bring to a boil. Cover and simmer for 1½ hours, or until tender. Skim
fat from broth. Thicken with cornstarch
mixed with a little cold water. Simmer
for about 5 minutes. Makes 12 servings.

HAM LOAF WITH PLUM SAUCE

1 Lb. Ground Smoked Ham
1 Lb. Ground Lean Pork
4 Cups Cornflakes
2 Eggs
1 Cup Milk
½ Tsp. Salt
3 Tbs. Chopped Green Pepper
½ Cup Brown Sugar
1 Tsp. Whole Cloves

Combine meats with eggs, milk, salt and green pepper and mix well. Crush corn flakes into coarse crumbs with rolling pin (measure cornflakes before they are crushed). Add the crushed cornflakes to the meat mixture and mix thoroughly.

Pat the brown sugar into the bottom of a lightly-greased loaf pan (9½ x5½x2¾"). Sprinkle with cloves. Add the meat mixture, packing down carefully. Bake in a moderate oven (350°F.) for 1 to 1½ hours or until loaf is thoroughly cooked through to the center. Turn out on a platter to serve. Remove the cloves if desired.

Plum Sauce:

1 No. 2½ Can Blue Plums (drain
    juice and reserve)
One-inch piece of Stick Cinnamon
2 Tbs. Cornstarch
¼ Tsp. Salt
3 Tbs. Water
1/16 Tsp. Allspice (if desired)
2 Tbs. Lemon Juice
Blue Plums, stoned and cut in half

Heat the plum juice to boiling with the cinnamon. Mix cornstarch and salt with cold water and add to boiling juice, stirring constantly until mixture boils again and is thick. Add remaining ingredients and simmer sauce slowly for 10 minutes. Serve hot over ham loaf.

SPARERIBS WITH PINEAPPLE STUFFING

1 Rack Spareribs (about 3 lbs.)
¼ Cup Chopped Celery
2 Tbs. Chopped Onion
2 Tbs. Butter or Margarine
1 - 13¼ Oz. Can Pineapple Tidbits,
    drained (reserve syrup)
½ Tsp. Cloves
2 Cups Packaged Seasoned Stuffing

Tie spareribs in a circle; place bone tips up on a rack in an open shallow roasting pan. Do not add water and do not cover; roast in 325°F. oven for 2 hours. Cook celery and onion in butter until tender, stirring occasionally. Mix with pineapple, cloves, stuffing and enough reserved pineapple syrup to moisten. Spoon dressing into the circle of ribs. Bake, uncovered, about 30 minutes longer, or until meat is tender. Makes 4 servings.

BARBECUED SPARERIBS

5 Lbs. Lean Pork Spareribs
½ Cup Chopped Onion
1/3 Cup Red Wine
Salt and Pepper to taste
1½ Cups Ketchup
Juice of 1½ Lemons (or 3 tbs.)
½ Cup Dark Brown Sugar,
    firmly packed
¼ Tsp. Hot Pepper Sauce
1 Tsp. Worcestershire
1 Tsp. Mustard Seeds

Put spareribs into a shallow dish. Cover with a mixture of onion, wine, salt and pepper. Marinate for 1 hour, turning occasionally. Combine remaining ingredients. Cook, stirring often, for 5 minutes, or until thickened. String ribs, accordion style, on skewer of grill and secure tightly with clamps. Brush well with the marinade. Have coals ready in rear of barbecue kettle. Attach skewer and turn on motor. Put a drip pan under the ribs. Cook for 1½ hours, or until tender, basting with the sauce during the last hour. Makes 4 servings.

INDONESIAN SKEWERED PORK

1 Cup Salted Peanuts
2 Tbs. Ground Coriander
2 Garlic Cloves
1 Tsp. Crushed Red Pepper
1 Cup Sliced Onion
¼ Cup Fresh Lemon Juice
2 Tbs. Brown Sugar
¼ Cup Soy Sauce
½ Tsp. Pepper
½ Cup Butter or Margarine
½ Cup Bouillon or Water
2 Lbs. Lean Pork, cut into 1" cubes

Combine all ingredients except last 3 in container of electric blender. Whirl to a fine puree. Transfer puree to a saucepan and bring to boil. Stir in butter; add bouillon & remove from heat. Cool and pour over the pork. Marinate for at least 3 hours. Thread pork on skewers and broil slowly over charcoal or under broiler for 25 to 30 minutes, turning frequently to brown and cook on all sides. If any marinade remains after cooking, heat and pour over meat. Makes 4 to 6 servings.

SPICY GLAZED PORK CHOPS WITH APRICOTS

1 - 1 Lb. 14 Oz. Can Whole Apricots
1 Tbs. Bottled Steak Sauce
1 Tsp. Salt
6 Rib or Loin Pork Chops, ½" thick
1 Tsp. Whole Cloves

Drain syrup from apricots into medium-size saucepan; stir in steak sauce and salt. Heat to boiling and cook, uncovered, for 15 min., or until syrup thickens slightly. Brush the chops on both sides with half of syrup and arrange in single layer in shallow baking pan. Do not cover. Bake in hot oven (400° F.) for 45 minutes, then turn. Stud apricots with cloves and arrange around chops; brush with remaining syrup and bake 30 minutes longer, or until chops are tender and richly glazed. Makes 6 servings.

CHOPSTICK PORK

3 Cups Cubed Roast Pork
4 Tbs. Soy Sauce
6 Medium Carrots, peeled and sliced
   ½" thick
2 Medium Green Peppers, halved, seeded
   and cut into 1" pieces
1 - 1 Lb. Can Sliced Cling Peaches
3 Tbs. Vegetable Oil
1 Large Onion, chopped (1 cup)
1 - 14 Oz. Can Chicken Broth
¼ Cup Cider Vinegar
3 Tbs. Cornstarch
3 Tbs. Water
3 Medium Bananas
1 - 3 Oz. Can Chinese Fried Noodles

Combine pork and soy sauce in a medium bowl; toss lightly to mix and let stand while cooking vegetables. Cook carrots in boiling salted water for 15 minutes, or just until tender-crisp. Drain. Parboil green peppers in boiling salted water in a small saucepan for 5 minutes; drain. Set both carrots and peppers aside.

Drain syrup from peaches into a 1-cup measure. Set peaches aside. Drain pork, saving soy sauce in a cup. Brown pork in salad oil in a large frying pan; remove and set aside. Stir onion into drippings in pan; saute' just until soft. Stir in ½ cup of the peach syrup, chicken broth, vinegar & reserved soy sauce. Smooth cornstarch and water to a paste in a cup; stir into onion mixture. Cook, stirring constantly, until mixture thickens and boils 3 minutes. Remove from heat. Peel bananas; halve lengthwise and cut into 2" pieces. Arrange with cooked carrots, green peppers, and peach slices in separate mounds in a shallow 8-cup baking dish. Pile browned pork in center. Pour hot onion sauce evenly over top. Sprinkle noodles between mounds; top with a ring of water-chestnut slices if you wish. Bake, uncovered, in 350°F. oven for 30 minutes, or until bubbly-hot in center. Makes 6 servings.

PORK TENDERLOIN WITH PEARS

2 Cups Chicken Stock, or 2 Chicken Bouillon Cubes dissolved in 2 cups of hot water
3 Large Ripe Pears (still firm)
2¼ Lbs. Pork Tenderloin, cut into 18 fillets (2 oz. each)
5 to 6 Tablespoons Butter
Salt and Pepper to taste
2 Tbs. Minced Shallots
6 Oz. Mild Blue Cheese

Pour chicken stock into a pan wide enough to accommodate the pears. Bring to a gentle boil. Peel pears, slice in half lengthwise and remove cores. Poach pear halves in the simmering stock for 2 to 3 minutes, covered, just until tender. Remove the pears and set them aside. Boil chicken stock rapidly until reduced to 1 cup. Set aside.

Pound fillets to flatten slightly. Melt 2 to 3 tablespoons of butter in a large frying pan over medium heat. Saute' fillets, 6 to 8 at a time, 2 minutes on each side, until lightly browned. When browned, place fillets in a large, shallow baking dish. Add more butter, as needed, to finish sauteeing the pork. Season the fillets with salt and pepper to taste. When all of the meat is browned, prepare a thin sauce by sauteeing shallots over medium heat in the same frying pan, adding additional butter if necessary. Cook the shallots for 2 to 3 minutes, until soft. Pour into the pan the reserved chicken stock and simmer sauce for a minute or two, scraping the pan as you stir. Keep sauce warm. Fill the poached pears with equal portions of blue cheese, then place pears on top of the sauteed pork fillets. Bake at 350°F. for 15 to 20 minutes, or until cheese melts and meat is cooked through. When meat is done, pour the sauce over it. Serve immediately. Makes 6 servings.

HAM PATTIES WITH CARROTS AND APPLES

4 Large Carrots, peeled and sliced crosswise (2 cups)
4 Cooking Apples, peeled and thickly sliced (4 cups)
¼ Cup Brown Sugar
1 Tbs. Butter or Margarine
1 Beaten Egg
¼ Cup Milk
½ Cup Soft Bread Crumbs
2 Cups Ground Fully-cooked Ham
Shortening

Simmer carrots in salted water for 10 min. and then drain. In a 2-quart casserole, layer the carrots, then apples, then brown sugar. Dot with butter. Combine egg, milk and bread crumbs. Add ground ham and mix well. Shape into 8 patties. Brown in hot shortening. Lay ham patties on top of apple-carrot mixture. Bake, covered, at 350° F. for 45 minutes. Makes 4 servings.

NEAPOLITAN PORK CHOPS AND SPAGHETTI

1 - 28 Oz. Can Italian Tomatoes
1 - 6 Oz. Can Tomato Paste
2 Garlic Cloves, minced
2 Tsp. Salt
¼ Tsp. Pepper
½ Tsp. Oregano
½ Tsp. Sweet Basil
¼ Tsp. Sage
1 Bay Leaf
2 Cups Water
4 Lean Pork Chops, about 1½ lbs.
8 Oz. Fine Spaghetti

Put first 10 ingredients into a large saucepan. Bring to a boil and simmer, uncovered, for 1 hour, stirring occasionally. Trim meat from chops, leaving it in large pieces. Brown on all sides in skillet. Add meat and drippings to sauce and simmer for 1 hour longer. Cook and drain spaghetti. Put on hot platter and cover with pork and sauce. Makes 4 servings.

PEKING CHICKEN with WALNUTS

1 Whole Chicken Breast, skinned, boned and diced
1 Tsp. Salt
1 Tbs. Cornstarch
1 Egg White
1 Cup Walnuts, blanched in boiling water for 3 minutes, drained and skinned
2 Tbs. Vegetable Oil, plus enough additional for deep frying
1 Green Pepper, halved, seeded, deribbed and diced
1 Sweet Red Pepper, halved, seeded, deribbed and diced
2 Tbs. Bean Paste (purchased in Oriental food store)
2 Tbs. Sugar
1 Tbs. Dry White Wine
Chicken Stock

Mix the chicken with the salt, cornstarch and egg white, tossing well. Put the walnuts into a strainer and deep fry them in enough oil heated to 300°F. to cover them by 1 inch. Dip them up and down in the oil to get them as brown as you like, but be careful because they burn easily. Drain them well and set aside. Reserve the oil.

Saute' the peppers in 1 tablespoon of fresh oil for 1 minute; drain them. Add another tablespoon of oil to the pan and saute' the bean paste for 3 minutes, stirring constantly. Add the sugar.

Deep fry the chicken pieces in the reserved oil heated to 375°F. for 1 minute. Drain the pieces and put them into the bean paste. Add the wine. If the sauce is too thick for your taste, thin it with up to ¼ cup of chicken stock. Toss furiously. Add the peppers and walnuts, and allow to heat through, stirring constantly. Makes 6 servings.

BARBECUED CHICKEN

1 - 3 Lb. Broiler-Fryer Chicken
1 Cup Gingerale
½ Cup Orange Juice
½ Cup Finely-chopped Onion
¼ Cup Corn Syrup
½ Tsp. Salt
½ Tsp. Ginger
¼ Tsp. Pepper

Combine the gingerale and remaining ingredients (except chicken) in a plastic bag. Add the chicken and allow to marinate for about 2 hours. Drain the chicken, reserving the liquid. Put chicken on a barbecue spit and cook, rotating spit, over medium hot coals for 1½ hours, or until chicken is tender. Baste occasionally with the remaining liquid. Makes 3 to 4 servings.

CHEESY CHICKEN ON A BUN

1 Tbs. Butter
1 Tbs. Flour
1 Tsp. Dry Mustard
½ Tsp. Salt
1/8 Tsp. Paprika
1¼ Cups Milk
1 Cup Grated Sharp American Cheese (¼ Lb.)
1 Egg, beaten
½ Lb. Thinly-sliced, Cold Cooked Chicken
Parsley

Melt butter in top of double boiler over boiling water. Blend in flour and seasonings and gradually add milk, stirring constantly. Continue to cook over boiling water until mixture is smooth and thickened. Stir to keep smooth. Add cheese, cover and let stand over hot (not boiling) water until cheese is melted and well blended. Stir occasionally. Slowly add part of the hot mixture to egg; stir to mix well and return to double boiler. Cook for 2 minutes longer, stirring. Remove from heat but keep over hot water. Split and toast buns; arrange chicken slices on top. Pour cheese sauce over all. Garnish with dash of paprika and a sprig of parsley and serve immediately. Makes 4 servings.

TURKEY WITH MEAT STUFFING

1 - 10 Lb. Turkey
Butter
3 Tbs. Olive Oil

Stuffing:
¾ Lb. Ground Beef
½ Lb. Ground Pork
1 Small Onion, minced
2 Slices Chopped Prosciutto
  or Ham
1 Sprig Fresh Parsley, chopped
4 Tbs. Grated Parmesan Cheese
½ Tsp. Basil
1 Cup Cooked Rice
8 Chopped Mushrooms
8 Roasted Chestnuts, chopped
Meat from 4 Walnuts, chopped
2 Eggs
Salt and Pepper to taste
5 Strips Salt Pork

Clean, wash and dry turkey. Rub inside
with butter. Heat olive oil in a large skillet over medium heat and cook beef, pork
and onion until light brown. Place in a
large bowl. Add prosciutto, parsley, cheese,
basil, rice, mushrooms, chestnuts, walnuts,
eggs, salt and pepper. Mix well and stuff
turkey. Sew or skewer together. Rub outside with butter. Arrange salt pork strips
over turkey. Place turkey in a 10x14x2"
roasting pan. Cook in a preheated oven
at 325°F. for 4½ hours, or until tender.
Baste frequently. Remove from oven and
let stand for 20 minutes for easier carving.
Serves 10 to 12.

CHICKEN-FILLED TORTILLAS

12 Tortillas
2 Tbs. Cooking Oil
1 Green Onion, minced
1 - 8¼ Oz. Can Tomatoes,
  drained and chopped
2 Cups Chopped Cooked Chicken
Salt
1 - 8 Oz. Can Tomato Sauce
1 Hot Dried Red Pepper
Dash of Oregano

Fry tortillas in 1 tablespoon of the oil until
crisp. Cook onion in remaining oil for 2

minutes. Add tomatoes and cook for 5 min.
Add chicken, heat and add salt to taste.
Spread on tortillas and fold over. Top with
remaining ingredients, heated together.
Makes 12.

VEGETABLE-STUFFED PHEASANT
(Baked in Dough Blanket)

1 Pheasant (2 lbs.)

Vegetable Stuffing:
¾ Cup Finely-chopped Onion
3 Tbs. Butter or Margarine
¾ Cup Coarsely-grated Carrot
¾ Cup Finely-diced Celery
2 Tbs. Chopped Parsley
¾ Tsp. Salt
1/8 Tsp. Pepper

Dough Blanket:
1½ Cups All-purpose Flour
1 Tsp. Salt
2 Tbs. Shortening
½ Cup Water

Rinse pheasant inside and out with several
changes of warm water. Remove pin feath-
ers and singe pheasant if necessary. Be
sure cavity is well drained. Remove neck
and cook with giblets for gravy.

Fill salted cavity with vegetable stuffing,
made as follows: Lightly saute' onion in
heated butter. Add the remaining vegetables and seasonings and toss to mix well.
Fill the cavity and close opening with
skewers and string.

To make dough blanket, sift together the
flour and salt; cut in fat with pastry blender
or two knives until particles are the size of
rice grains. Add water gradually, stirring to
make a dough soft enough to roll. Roll out
on a lightly-floured board from 1/8 to ¼"
thick and into a 15x10" rectangle. Wrap
dough around pheasant, completely covering it. Moisten edges and pinch together
to seal. Place pheasant, breast side up, on
a trivet in a shallow roasting pan and roast
uncovered in a 350°F. oven for 1½ to 2½
hours. Prepare giblet gravy from drippings.
Break away crusty golden brown blanket
in pieces and serve with the pheasant and
giblet gravy. Makes 4 servings.

JAMBALAYA

1 Broiler-Fryer (about 2½ Lbs.)
2 Cups Water
3 Tsp. Salt
¼ Tsp. Pepper
1 Bay Leaf
2 Large Onions, chopped (about
  2 cups)
1 Large Garlic Clove, crushed
¼ Cup Butter or Margarine
1 Lb. Cooked Ham, cubed
1 - 1 Lb. 12 Oz. Can Tomatoes
1 Large Green Pepper, halved,
  seeded and chopped
½ Tsp. Leaf Thyme, crumbled
¼ Tsp. Cayenne
1 Cup Uncooked Regular Rice

Place the chicken in a large kettle or Dutch oven. Add water, salt, pepper and bay leaf. Bring to boiling; reduce heat, cover & simmer for 45 minutes, or until chicken is tender. Remove chicken from broth and set aside. When cool enough to handle, remove meat from bones and cut into cubes; reserve. Pour broth into a 2-cup measure; remove bay leaf. Add water, if necessary, to make 2 cups; reserve. Saute' onions & garlic in butter or margarine until soft in same kettle; add ham, tomatoes, green pepper, thyme, cayenne and reserved chicken and broth. Heat to boiling; stir in rice. Reduce heat; cover and simmer, following directions on box of rice for cooking. Serve in large bowls. Sprinkle generously with chopped parsley and serve with French bread, if you wish. Makes 8 servings.

FARMER-STYLE BRAISED CHICKEN

1 - 3 to 4 Lb. Chicken, seasoned
  inside with salt and pepper
  and trussed
6 Tbs. Butter
1 Medium Onion, finely sliced
4 Young Carrots, thinly sliced
1 Small Celery Heart, finely sliced
3 or 4 Thin Slices Prosciutto
1/3 Cup Shelled Fresh Peas
½ Cup Sliced Fresh Green Beans
½ Cup Chicken or Veal Stock

Melt 4 tablespoons of butter in a small saute' pan. Add the onion and cook gently for 4 to 5 minutes (do not brown). Add the carrots and celery. Steam them gently over very low heat for 15 minutes. Shake the pan to toss the vegetables, rather than risk breaking them by turning them with a spoon. They should be softened but not at all brown. The onion should be a golden color and the butter should remain clear. Set the pan aside.

Melt the remaining butter in a heatproof casserole over low heat. Add the chicken and brown it lightly. Remove the chicken and line the casserole with the prosciutto. Replace the chicken, breast up, and surround it with all the cooked and raw vegetables mixed together. Add the stock and cover the casserole. Place the casserole in the oven and cook for 45 to 50 min. Make sure that you use moderate heat, since the vegetables will burn if the liquid reduces. Bake until done. Makes 4 servings.

DUCK AND SWEET-POTATO CASSEROLE

2 Large Ducks, quartered
Salt and Pepper
8 Partially-cooked Sweet
  Potatoes, halved
½ Cup Chicken Bouillon
1½ Cups Fresh Orange Juice
Grated Rind of 1 Orange
1 - 8 Oz. Can Mandarin Oranges,
  juice reserved
1 Tbs. Cornstarch
Curacao

Sprinkle duck with salt and pepper and bake in a shallow pan in preheated hot oven (400° F.) for 1 hour. Drain off fat. Put duck in a large casserole and add sweet potatoes. Combine bouillon, orange juice and rind, & juice drained from mandarin oranges. Bring to a boil and thicken with cornstarch mixed with a little cold water. Cook until clear; add a little Curacao. Pour over duck and potatoes. Cover and bake for about 45 minutes, or until tender. Baste several times with sauce in pan. At serving time, top with mandarin oranges. Makes 8 servings.

ISLANDER CHICKEN

1 - 3 Lb. Broiler-Fryer Chicken,
   cut into serving pieces
1/3 Cup Olive Oil
¾ Cup Diced Raw Ham
1 Cup Sliced Onions
2 Cloves Garlic, minced
3 Medium Tomatoes, peeled
   and chopped
2½ Cups Water
2½ Cups Uncooked Rice
¾ Cup Chopped Green Pepper
1 Small Bay Leaf
2½ Tsp. Salt
½ Tsp. Cumin Seed
1/8 Tsp. Saffron

Heat the olive oil in a Dutch oven; add the
chicken, ham, onions and garlic and brown
the chicken on all sides. Add the tomatoes
and simmer, covered, for about 20 minutes.
Add the remaining ingredients and bring to
a boil. Lower the heat; cover and simmer
slowly until the rice is tender (about twenty
minutes). Add more liquid if necessary.
Remove the chicken. Heap the rice mixture
in the center of a large platter and surround
it with the chicken pieces. Makes 6 servings.

CHICKEN BREASTS
BAKED IN WINE

1 Cup Red Wine
¼ Cup Soy Sauce
¼ Cup Salad Oil
2 Tbs. Water
1 Clove Garlic, peeled and sliced
1 Tsp. Powdered Ginger
¼ Tsp. Oregano
1 Tbs. Brown Sugar
3 Chicken Breasts, split in halves
3 or 4 Cups Cooked Wild Rice

Combine all sauce ingredients and mix well.
Place chicken in large casserole. Pour mixture over all and cover dish. Bake about
1½ hours at 375°F., or until chicken is tender and done. Uncover for last 15 minutes
of baking, unless pan juices have cooked
down to almost nothing. Serve at once,
surrounded by mounds of hot cooked wild
rice. Makes 6 servings.

CHICKEN AND RICE STUFFED
CANTALOUPE (From Israel)

3 Large, Ripe Cantaloupes, about
   3 lbs. each
2 Cups Long-grain White Rice
3 Tbs. Olive Oil
2 Cups Chicken Stock
2 Cups Water
2 Tsp. Salt
1 Cup Chopped Onion
2 Large, Whole Chicken Breasts
   (about 2 lbs. of chicken)
¼ Cup Brandy
¼ Lb. Mushrooms, cleaned and
   coarsely chopped
1 Cup Black Olives, coarsely chopped
Boston or Red Leaf Lettuce, for garnish
1 Cup Roasted, Unsalted Pistachio
   Nuts, coarsely chopped, for garnish

Skin and bone the chicken breasts and dice
meat into ½" pieces. Halve the cantaloupes,
using a decorative zigzag cut. Remove seeds.
Scoop out balls of fruit with a small melon
baller, leaving a sturdy shell for stuffing.
Set aside melon shells and fruit. Saute' rice
in 1 tbs. olive oil over medium-high heat until golden brown. Pour in chicken stock,
water, and salt and bring to a boil. Cover
pan, reduce heat, and simmer 20 to 25 minutes, until rice has absorbed all liquid and
is tender. Fluff with a fork and set aside.

In a large heavy frying pan, saute' onions in
remaining 2 tablespoons of oil for 2 or 3
minutes over medium heat, until onions are
tender and translucent. Add diced chicken
meat and saute' 3 or 4 minutes longer, until
chicken turns white and is cooked through.
Pour in the brandy and flambe'. When the
flames die out, add the chopped mushrooms
and olives. Continue cooking 1 to 2 minutes
more. Stir the boiled rice and melon balls
into the chicken mixture and heat until all
components are hot. Taste and adjust the
seasoning if desired.

To serve, line 6 small dinner plates with
leaf lettuce. Place a melon shell on each
lettuce bed and fill loosely, mounding
high, with hot rice mixture. There should
be enough filling left over for second servings for those with hearty appetites. Sprinkle chopped pistachios over the mixture &
serve while filling is still hot. 6 servings.

FINGER DRUMSTICKS

3 Lbs. Small Chicken Wings
   (about 15)
½ Cup Sugar
3 Tbs. Cornstarch
1 Tsp. Salt
½ Tsp. Ground Ginger
¼ Tsp. Pepper
¾ Cup Water
1/3 Cup Lemon Juice
¼ Cup Soy Sauce

Singe chicken wings, if needed. Cut off
tips and discard. Divide each wing in half
by cutting through joint with a sharp knife.
Place in a single layer on rack in broiler pan.
Bake in hot oven (400°F.) for 30 minutes,
turning once.

Mix sugar, cornstarch, salt, ginger and pepper in a small saucepan; stir in water, lemon
juice and soy sauce. Cook, stirring constantly, until mixture thickens and boils
for 3 minutes. Brush part over chicken
wings. Continue baking, turning and brushing several times with remaining lemon mixture, for 40 minutes, or until richly glazed.
When ready to serve, place in a chafing dish
or keep-hot server. Frame with a ring of
thin lemon slices, if you wish. Serve hot.

ROAST DUCKLING
(Hawaiian Style)

2 - 5 Lb. Ducklings, ready to cook
2 Tsp. Salt
2 Tbs. Lemon Juice
9 Slices White Bread, toasted and
   cubed
1 Cup Sliced Green Onions
2 Clove Garlic, sliced
½ Tsp. Ground Ginger
2 - 4 Oz. Cans Chopped Mushrooms,
   drained
1 - 1 Lb. 14 Oz. Can Sliced Pineapple
¾ Cup Butter or Margarine, melted
¼ Cup Soy Sauce
¼ Cup Honey
Mint

Wash ducklings inside and out with cold
water; dry well. Sprinkle salt and lemon
juice into cavities. Smooth neck skin over

back, then twist wing tips until they rest
flat against sides. Combine bread cubes,
green onions, garlic, ginger and mushrooms
in a large bowl. Drain syrup from pineapple into a small bowl and set aside for the
sauce. Dice 4 slices of the pineapple and
add to bread mixture. Drizzle ½ cup of
the melted butter or margarine over top;
toss lightly to mix. Spoon dressing into
cavities in ducklings, packing in lightly.
Lace openings together with poultry pins
or skewers and string. Place ducklings on
a rack in a shallow roasting pan. Do not
add any water or cover pan. Roast in
325°F. oven for 1½ hours, then pour all
drippings from pan. Combine remaining
¼ cup melted butter or margarine with
soy sauce and honey in a small saucepan;
heat, stirring constantly, to boiling. Brush
part of mixture over the ducklings. Continue roasting, brushing with remaining
soy mixture every 15 minutes, for 1 hour,
or until a drumstick moves easily and the
ducklings are richly golden. Remove the
ducklings to a heated large serving platter.
Garnish with remaining pineapple slices,
cut in half, and mint. Carve ducklings
into quarters or cut with kitchen scissors.
Serve with Mandarin Sauce. Makes 8
servings.

Mandarin Sauce:
2 Tbs. Cornstarch
½ Tsp. Ground Ginger
2 Envelopes Instant Chicken Broth
   or 2 Tsp. Granulated Chicken
   Bouillon
1 - 11 Oz. Can Mandarin Orange
   Segments

Mix the cornstarch with the ginger and instant chicken bouillon in a small saucepan.
Drain the syrup from mandarin orange segments into a 2-cup measure. Add pineapple syrup and water, if needed, to make 2
cups. Stir into cornstarch mixture. Cook,
stirring constantly, until sauce thickens &
boils for 3 minutes. Remove from heat
and fold in orange segments. Serve warm.
Makes about 2½ cups sauce.

CHICKEN ROYALE

3 Chicken Breasts (about 12 oz.
   each), halved
4 Cups Water
Few Celery Tops
2½ Tsp. Salt
½ Lb. Meat-loaf Mixture (ground
   beef and pork)
6 Tbs. Flour
Dash of Pepper
1 Egg
2 Tsp. Grated Onion
¼ Cup Milk
3 Medium Carrots, pared and sliced
1 Cup Frozen Peas
4 Tbs. Butter or Margarine
1 Tbs. Lemon Juice
Liquid Red Pepper Seasoning
   (a few drops)
1 - 5 Oz. Can Shrimp, drained,
   rinsed and deveined
2 Tbs. Chopped Parsley

Combine chicken breasts, water, celery tops and 2 tsp. of salt in a large saucepan; cover and simmer for 30 minutes, or until chicken is tender. Remove from broth and cool until easy to handle. Pull off skin and take meat from bones in one piece; set aside. Set broth aside also.

Combine meat-loaf mixture, 2 tbs. flour, remaining ½ tsp. salt, pepper, egg, onion, and milk in a medium bowl; mix with a fork until well-blended. Shape into 18 small balls. Set remaining flour aside for making sauce.

Reheat chicken broth to boiling; add meat balls. Cover and poach for 10 minutes, or until cooked through; lift out with a slotted spoon and place in a bowl. Cook carrots, covered, in part of the same chicken broth for 20 minutes, or until tender. Cook the peas in remaining broth, following directions on label. Drain liquid from peas & carrots and strain into a 4-cup measure. Add more water, if needed, to make 4 cups. Keep carrots and peas hot.

Melt butter or margarine in a large saucepan; blend in 4 tbs. flour. Cook, stirring constantly, just until bubbly. Stir in the 4 cups chicken broth; continue cooking & stirring until sauce thickens and boils for

1 minute. Stir in lemon juice and liquid red pepper seasoning.

Cut each half chicken breast into three pieces; add to sauce with meat balls, carrots, and peas. Heat slowly just to boiling; spoon into a chafing dish or a heated serving dish. Arrange shrimp on top; sprinkle with parsley. Makes 6 servings.

INDIAN-STYLE CHICKEN

1/3 Cup Butter
8 Small Chicken Breasts, skinned,
   boned and quartered
1 Cup Chopped Onion
1 Clove Garlic, chopped
2 Tsp. Salt
1 Tbs. Powdered Ginger
¼ Tsp. Chili Powder
½ Cup Drained, Canned Tomatoes
1 Cup Clear Chicken Broth or
   Yogurt
½ Cup Ground Cashew Nuts
½ Cup Flaked Coconut
2 Tbs. Cornstarch
1 Cup Heavy Cream

In a deep skillet, or a 3½-quart Dutch oven, melt half of the butter. Brown the chicken, about eight pieces at a time, adding the remaining butter as necessary. Remove the chicken. Add onion and garlic to the pan and cook for 5 minutes. Return the chicken to the pan. Add the salt, ginger, chili powder, tomatoes and broth. Mix lightly; cover and cook for 15 minutes. Add the nuts and coconut; cover and cook over low heat until the chicken is tender, about 10 minutes longer.

Slowly add the cream to the cornstarch and blend well; stir into the cooking liquid. Stir constantly until the sauce returns to a boil. Simmer over low heat for 5 minutes. If desired, this may be cooled and refrigerated at this point. Near serving time, bring to room temperature and then reheat over very low heat. Serve with noodles. Makes 10 or more servings.

TURKEY STEW

Butter or Margarine
1 Large Onion, sliced
2 Medium Zucchini, sliced (about
    3 cups)
½ Cup Sliced Celery
4 Cups Cooked Turkey, in
    large chunks (about 1½" cubes)
½ Lb. Small Fresh Mushrooms
1 - 1 Lb. Can Whole Carrots,
    drained
2/3 Cup Dry White Wine
2/3 Cup Canned Condensed Chicken
    Broth
1 - 10½ Oz. Can Condensed Cream
    of Celery Soup
1 - 10½ Oz. Can Condensed Cream
    of Chicken Soup
¼ Tsp. Dried Thyme Leaves
¼ Tsp. Dried Marjoram Leaves
Chopped Parsley

In 4 tablespoons of hot butter in a large,
heavy skillet, saute' onion, zucchini and
celery until almost tender and lightly
browned--about 10 to 15 minutes. Combine with turkey in a 3-quart casserole.
In the same skillet, brown mushrooms,
adding more butter if needed. Add to
turkey mixture in casserole. Add carrots.
Stir wine into drippings in skillet, then
stir in undiluted chicken broth, celery
soup, chicken soup, thyme and marjoram.
Bring to boiling, stirring to loosen browned
bits in pan. Pour wine mixture over the
turkey and vegetables in casserole. Mix
lightly with a fork. Bake, covered, for
1 hour, or until bubbling in center.
Sprinkle with chopped parsley. Makes
6 servings.

ROCK CORNISH HENS
(with Pineapple-Walnut Stuffing)

4 Rock Cornish Hens
Pineapple Walnut Stuffing
    (recipe below)
¼ Cup Lemon Juice
½ Cup Honey
¼ Cup Grenadine Syrup
½ Cup Soft Butter or Margarine

Thaw the hens, if frozen. Stuff them; combine lemon juice, honey and grenadine syrup.
Set aside ½ cup for basting; blend remainder
with butter and spread over the surface of
the birds. Roast at 350°F. for about 1 hr.,
or until done, brushing occasionally with
honey mixture. Makes 4 servings.

Pineapple-Walnut Stuffing:
½ Cup Water
¼ Cup Butter or Margarine
½ Pkg. Bread Stuffing Mix
1 Egg, slightly beaten
½ Cup Crushed Pineapple
¼ Cup Finely-chopped Walnuts

Heat water; add butter and heat until
melted. Stir in remaining ingredients.
Makes enough stuffing for 4 hens.

CHICKEN WITH TOASTED ALMONDS

3 - 2 Lb. Broiler Fryers
5 Tbs. Salad Oil
2 Tbs. Soy Sauce
2 Tsp. Salt
1½ Tsp. Sugar
Dash of Pepper
¼ Cup Cornstarch
1 - 13¾ Oz. Can Clear Chicken Broth
1 - 5 Oz. Can Water Chestnuts, drained
    and chopped
½ Cup Peas, drained (use either thawed,
    frozen peas or canned peas)
1 Cup Thinly-sliced Celery
1 - 4 Oz. Can Whole Mushrooms, drained
½ Cup Toasted Slivered Almonds

Have the butcher bone and skin the broiler
fryers. To make them easier to slice, store
in freezing compartment until partially
frozen. Slice into long, thin slivers; let thaw
completely at room temperature. Heat oil
in large skillet. Add chicken slivers, soy
sauce, salt, sugar and pepper. Cook, stirring,
a few minutes, or just until chicken is no
longer pink.

In small bowl, make a smooth paste of cornstarch and 1/3 cup water. Stir into chicken
mixture, with chicken broth, water chestnuts,
peas, celery, and mushrooms. Cook, stirring,
until slightly thickened and translucent.
Sprinkle top with almonds. Makes 6 servings.

MAIN DISHES (POULTRY) 48

CHICKEN MORNAY

6 Tbs. Butter or Margarine
6 Tbs. All-purpose Flour
3 Cups Milk
6 Stuffed Olives, sliced
½ Cup Diced Pimiento
¼ Cup Sherry
3 Cups Diced Cooked Chicken
Salt and Pepper
8 Oz. Wide Noodles, cooked and
    drained
1 Cup Grated Parmesan or Hard Gruyere
    Cheese

Melt butter and blend in flour. Gradually add the milk and cook, stirring constantly, until smooth and thickened. Add olives, pimiento, sherry and chicken. Season with salt and pepper to taste. Line a shallow baking dish (2-quart) with noodles. Cover with the chicken mixture. Sprinkle with cheese. Bake in hot oven (400°F.), preheated, for 15 to 20 minutes. Makes 6 servings.

INDONESIAN BAKED CHICKEN

¼ Cup Dark Brown Sugar, firmly
    packed
1 Tbs. Boiling Water
3 Tbs. Indonesian Sweet Soy Sauce
3 Tbs. Paprika
2 Tbs. Mashed Garlic (about
    7 cloves)
2 Tbs. Fresh Lime Juice
1 Tsp. Salt
1 - 3 Lb. Chicken, cut into serving-
    sized pieces

Place brown sugar in a small bowl. Stir in boiling water, then add the remaining marinade ingredients. Mix well. Brush chicken pieces with this sauce. Refrigerate, if possible, for several hours, allowing the flavors in the sauce time to permeate the chicken. Bake prepared chicken in a preheated 350°F. oven for about 1 hour, or until chicken is tender. The sauce is also good on broiled or barbecued chicken. Makes 4 servings.

CHICKEN CASSEROLE

1 - 4 to 5 Lb. Stewing Chicken
1 Large Onion, quartered
1½ Tsp. Salt
½ Cup Butter or Margarine
½ Cup Flour
2 - 4 Oz. Cans Mushrooms, drained
1 Cup Evaporated Milk
1 Tsp. Salt
1/8 Tsp. Pepper
½ Tsp. Ground Turmeric
½ Tsp. Oregano Leaves
1 Cup Rice, uncooked
2½ Cups Boiling Water
1½ Tsp. Salt
1 Tbs. Butter
½ Cup Chopped Green Onions
½ Cup Shredded Mild Cheese

Cook the chicken until tender in water to cover, with onion and 1½ tsp. salt added. Cool chicken (reserve broth); remove skin and cut chicken meat into small pieces with kitchen scissors.

Melt butter or margarine in saucepan; stir in flour. Add 4 cups liquid (juice drained from the mushrooms and the rest chicken broth) and evaporated milk. Cook and stir until sauce is thick and smooth. Add 1 tsp. salt, pepper, turmeric and oregano. Combine the rice with boiling water, 1½ tsp. salt, and 1 tbs. butter. Cover and bake in 400°F. oven for 30 minutes, or until tender. Spread rice on bottom of a large casserole or baking dish. Top with chicken, then with green onions, sauce and mushrooms. Sprinkle the cheese over the top. Bake in 350°F. oven for 30 minutes. Makes 10 to 12 servings.

SPANISH-STYLE CHICKEN WITH RICE

1 Frying Chicken, cut up
  (about 2½ lbs.)
Salt
3 Tbs. Olive Oil
1 Large Onion, chopped
1 Garlic Clove, minced
1 Medium Green Pepper, chopped
1 - 1 Lb. 3 Oz. Can Tomatoes
  (about 2-1/3 cups)
1/3 Cup Sherry
¼ Tsp. Pepper
Pinch of Ground Saffron
½ Tsp. Paprika
2 Whole Cloves
1 Bay Leaf, crumbled
1 Cup Water
1¼ Cups Uncooked Long-grain Rice
1 Cup Cooked Peas
1 Pimiento, cut up

Season the chicken with salt and brown in oil. Add onion, garlic and green pepper & brown for about 5 minutes longer. Add remaining ingredients, except rice, peas and pimiento; simmer, covered, for 15 minutes. Add rice, bring to a boil, stirring constantly. Cover and simmer for about 30 minutes. Garnish with peas and pimiento. Makes 4 to 6 servings.

CHICKEN SUPPER CASSEROLE

1 Cup Flour
2 Tsp. Baking Powder
½ Tsp. Salt
2 Eggs, slightly beaten
½ Cup Milk
1 Cup Shredded Cheddar Cheese
1 Tsp. Worcestershire Sauce
¾ Cup Chopped Onion
½ Cup Chopped Celery
1 Green Onion Top, chopped
¼ Cup Chicken Broth or Water
1 - 10½ Oz. Can Cream of Chicken
  Soup
1 Cup Milk
½ Cup Mushrooms, cooked
3 Cups Cubed, Cooked Chicken
Salt and Pepper to taste
3 Slices Bacon, fried crisp

Combine first 6 ingredients in mixing bowl and blend. Simmer onions, celery, chicken broth in pan for 20 minutes. Combine in a 2-quart casserole the soup, milk, chicken, mushrooms, bacon, salt, pepper and cooked vegetables. Stir in Worcestershire sauce and mix well. Drop the biscuits by tablespoonful into casserole. Bake in 350°F. oven for 45 minutes, until golden brown. Sprinkle with cheese. Return to oven until the cheese melts.

COQ AU VIN

1 - 4 Lb. Stewing Chicken, cut
  into serving-size pieces
1/3 Cup Unsifted All-purpose Flour
1½ Tsp. Salt
3 Tbs. Butter or Margarine
½ Cup Diced Cooked Ham
12 Small White Onions, peeled
1 - 12 Oz. Can Mixed Vegetable
  Juice (1½ cups)
1½ Cups Apple Cider
1 - 4 Oz. Can Mushroom Caps
1 Clove Garlic, minced
6 Peppercorns
6 Whole Cloves
1 Bay Leaf

Wash chicken pieces; pat dry. Shake with flour and salt in a paper bag; coat well. Brown chicken pieces, a few at a time, in butter or margarine in a large frying pan. Place in a 12-cup baking dish; sprinkle with ham and top with onions. Stir vegetable juices, cider, mushrooms and liquid, and garlic into drippings in pan; heat to boiling, scraping brown bits from bottom of pan. Pour over chicken. Tie seasonings in a cheesecloth bag; add to baking dish. Cover and bake in 350°F. oven for 2 hrs. 15 min., or until chicken is very tender. Uncover; remove bag of spices and let the chicken stand for 5 to 10 minutes, or until fat rises to top. Skim off fat. Garnish with parsley if you wish. Makes 4 servings.

GRANOLA-RICE STUFFING

1 Small Orange
1½ Cups Cooked Rice
1 Cup Granola Cereal
1 Small Apple, peeled, cored and
   chopped (about 2/3 cup)
¾ Tsp. Salt
¼ Tsp. Ground Cinnamon
1/3 Cup Chopped Celery
¼ Cup Chopped Onion
2 Tbs. Butter or Margarine

Peel and section the orange over a medium-size bowl so that the juice is not lost. Chop the orange sections (should have about 1/3 cup) and add to the juice in the bowl. Add the cooked rice, granola cereal, chopped apple, salt, and cinnamon. Set aside.

In a small saucepan, cook the celery and onion in butter or margarine until tender but not brown. Add to the rice mixture, tossing lightly until well mixed. Will stuff six 1 to 1½ pound Cornish game hens or two 2½ to 3 pound broiler-fryer chickens. If desired, the stuffing may be baked, covered, in a 1-quart casserole at 375°F. for 25 to 30 minutes. Makes about 3½ cups of stuffing.

ROCK CORNISH GAME HENS INDIENNE

6 Frozen Rock Cornish Game Hens
   (about 1 lb. each), thawed
¼ Tsp. Pepper
¼ Tsp. Leaf Thyme, crumbled
½ Cup Butter or Margarine, melted
4 Slices Bacon, diced
1 Medium Onion, chopped
1 Tbs. Flour
1 Tbs. Sugar
2 Tsp. Curry Powder
2 Tsp. Instant Chicken Bouillon
1 Cup Apricot Nectar
1 Tbs. Lemon Juice
Parsley Rice (see recipe below)
Buttered Carrots

Remove giblets from body cavities of hens and save to simmer for soup. Rinse hens inside and out; pat dry with paper toweling.

Mix 1 teaspoon salt with pepper and thyme in a cup; sprinkle ¼ teaspoonful inside each hen. Tie legs together. Place hens, breast side up, in a jelly roll pan. Brush with part of the melted butter or margarine. Roast in a moderate oven (375°F.), brushing once or twice with remaining melted butter or margarine and drippings in pan. Roast for 1 hour. Cut away strings with scissors; spoon all drippings from pan.

While hens roast, saute' bacon until almost crisp in a medium-size saucepan. Remove from pan with a slotted spoon and drain on paper towels. Stir onion into drippings and saute' until soft. Blend in flour, sugar, curry powder, chicken bouillon and ½ tsp. salt. Cook, stirring constantly, until bubbly. Stir in apricot nectar and lemon juice. Heat, stirring constantly, to boiling; simmer 5 minutes, or until mixture thickens slightly. Spoon about half of mixture over hens. Roast 10 minutes. Spoon remaining curry mixture over top to make a thick coating. Continue roasting for 10 minutes, or until hens are tender and richly glazed.

Spread Parsley Rice on a large deep serving platter; arrange hens on top. Spoon buttered carrots at each end.

Parsley Rice:

1 Cup Uncooked Rice
2 Tbs. Butter or Margarine
2 Tsp. Instant Chicken Bouillon
2¼ Cups Boiling Water
¼ Cup Chopped Parsley

Combine rice, butter or margarine, chicken bouillon and boiling water in a 6-cup baking dish. Cover and bake along with hens in a moderate oven (375°F.) for 1 hour, or until rice is tender and liquid is absorbed. Fluff rice with a fork & stir in chopped parsley. Makes 6 servings.

MACUTO CHICKEN

2 Large Chicken Breasts, halved,
   skinned and boned
¼ Tsp. Salt
1/8 Tsp. Pepper
2 Ripe, but firm, Bananas
1 Tsp. Angostura Bitters
3 or 4 Oz. Cooked Ham, thinly
   sliced
½ Cup All-purpose Flour
3 Eggs, lightly beaten
1 Cup Freshly-grated Coconut
Sufficient Oil for deep frying
Sweet and Sour Sauce (recipe
   below)

Lay each chicken breast half between waxed paper and flatten out with a mallot until approximately ¼" thick. Season chicken with a portion of the salt and pepper. Peel the bananas and cut in half, or into pieces that are approximately the length of the chicken breasts. Sprinkle bitters on sliced ham and wrap around bananas. Place ham-wrapped bananas on each breast. Roll tightly to enclose filling completely. Secure with toothpicks. At this point, the chicken rolls may be wrapped tightly in foil and refrigerated up to 24 hours. When ready to use, dredge the breasts in flour, dip into beaten eggs, then roll in coconut. Deep-fry each chicken roll 5 to 7 minutes at 375°F., until golden brown and cooked through. Drain, remove toothpicks, and serve with Sweet and Sour Sauce.

Sauce:
1 Cup Orange Juice
2 Tbs. Vinegar
1 Tbs. Dark Brown Sugar
1 Tbs. Cornstarch
1 Tbs. Dark Rum
1 Tsp. Angostura Bitters

In a small saucepan, whisk together the juice, vinegar, sugar and cornstarch. Place pan over heat and bring to a slow boil; simmer for 1 minute. Take off heat and add rum and bitters. Serve warm. Makes 4 servings.

JAMAICAN-STYLE CHICKEN

1 - 4 Lb. Roasting Chicken
2 Tbs. Butter or Margarine
1½ Cups Chicken Broth
¾ Cup Sliced Celery
1 Medium Onion, chopped
½ Tsp. Garlic Salt
2 Dried Red Peppers, crushed
1 Tbs. Vinegar
¼ Tsp. Ground Allspice
½ Cup Sliced Green Olives
1 Medium Green Pepper, sliced
2 Tbs. Cornstarch
Salt and Pepper

Brown chicken on all sides in butter in a heavy kettle. Put chicken on a rack in a kettle. Add the next 7 ingredients, cover and simmer for 1½ hours, or until chicken is tender. Add olives and green pepper; cook for 10 minutes more. Remove the chicken to a hot platter and thicken the liquid in the kettle with cornstarch blended with a little cold water. Season to taste with salt and pepper; pour over chicken. Makes 4 servings.

HONEY-PECAN CHICKEN

2 - 3 Lb. Frying Chickens, cut
   into serving pieces
4 Cups Buttermilk
1 Cup All-purpose Flour
¾ Tsp. Salt
¼ Tsp. Pepper
Oil, for deep frying

Place chicken pieces in a large bowl and cover with buttermilk. Let chicken soak at least 1 hour, refrigerated. When ready to cook, drain chicken, then coat thoroughly with flour that has been seasoned with salt and pepper. Fry the chicken in hot oil until crisp golden brown and cooked through.

Honey-Pecan Sauce:
1 Cup Butter
½ Cup Honey
½ Cup Chopped Pecans

Bring ingredients to a gentle boil in a small saucepan. Arrange hot chicken on serving dishes; drizzle honey-pecan sauce over it & serve immediately. Makes 6 to 8 servings.

EGG ROLLS with CHICKEN STUFFING

Pancakes:
4 Eggs
1½ Cups Water
1½ Cups Sifted All-purpose Flour
1 Tsp. Salt
Peanut Oil or Vegetable Oil,
   for cooking

Filling:
1 Large Onion, diced (1 cup)
1 Cup Thinly-sliced Celery
1 Tsp. Vegetable Oil
1 Tbs. Soy Sauce
2 Cups Diced, Cooked Chicken

Prepare filling first and let stand while making pancakes. Combine onion, celery and vegetable oil in a small saucepan; cover and cook over low heat for 10 min., or until soft. Stir in soy sauce. Pour over chicken in a medium bowl; toss to mix well.

To make pancakes, beat eggs with water until foamy (use medium bowl). Beat in flour and salt just until smooth. Batter will be thin. Heat an 8″ frying pan slowly; test temperature by sprinkling in a few drops of water. When drops bounce about, temperature is right. Add about 1 teaspoon of peanut oil or vegetable oil, tilting pan to cover bottom completely. Pour ¼ cup of batter into pan; cook 1 to 2 minutes, or until top appears dry and underside is golden. Lift out onto paper towels to cool (only one side is baked). Repeat with remaining batter, adding a little oil before each baking. Make 12 pancakes. Cool each separately on paper towels.

When ready to fill, spoon ¼ cup chicken mixture slightly off center on baked side of each pancake. Fold short end up over filling, then fold both sides toward center and roll up, jelly-roll fashion, to cover filling completely. Fasten with one or two wooden picks. Place in a shallow dish; cover and chill overnight. When ready to cook, heat peanut oil or vegetable oil (1½-inch depth) to 400°F. in an electric skillet or deep heavy frying pan. Drop in chilled rolls, 2 or 3 at a time, and fry, turning once. Fry 5 to 8 minutes, or until golden.

Drain on paper towels. Keep rolls hot in warm oven until all are cooked. Remove picks. Serve rolls plain or with a bottled sweet-sour sauce, if you prefer. Makes 6 servings of 2 rolls each.

FRUIT-NUT STUFFING

1 Box Triscuit wafers, crumbled
½ Lb. Prunes, cooked and pitted
1 Cup Juice from Prunes
2 Onions, peeled and diced
2 Green Peppers, diced
1 Cup Diced Celery
½ Cup Finely-cut Parsley
1 - 3 Oz. Can Chopped Mushrooms
3 Tbs. Butter or Margarine
1 - 6 Oz. Can Chopped Salted Almonds
½ Tsp. Thyme or Savory
1 Tsp. Pepper
2 Tsp. Salt

Make the dressing the day before needed. Soak crumbled wafers in juice from cooked prunes. Saute' onions, green peppers, celery, parsley and mushrooms in butter or margarine until soft but not too brown. Stir in almonds. Blend herb, pepper & salt into mixture. Cut up prunes and mix in. Stir soaked wafer crumbs and juice into prune mixture. Store in covered bowl overnight in refrigerator. When bird is ready for cooking, stuff this flavorful mixture loosely in neck and cavity. Roast at once. Makes enough for large capon or roasting chicken, or small (6 to 8 lb.) turkey. Double recipe for large turkey.

TURKEY CASSEROLE with OYSTERS AND HAM

½ Cup Butter or Margarine
¼ Cup Flour
2 Cups Milk
½ Tsp. Salt
1/8 Tsp. Pepper
¼ Tsp. Dry Mustard
2 Cups Diced, Cooked Turkey
1 Cup Ground, Cooked Ham
1 Pint Oysters, preheated in juice
3 Cups Mashed Potatoes
Paprika

Melt butter; stir in the flour and blend together. Add milk, salt, pepper and mustard. Cook over low heat, stirring constantly, until smooth and thickened. Add the turkey, ham and oysters. Pour into greased 1½-quart casserole. Arrange the mashed potatoes around the edge of the casserole; sprinkle with paprika. Bake in 350°F. oven for 30 minutes. Makes 6 to 8 servings.

SCOTCH COCK-A-LEEKIE

1 - 5 Lb. Stewing Chicken, cut up
3 Onions, quartered
¼ Cup Chopped Parsley
2 Celery Stalks, slivered
¼ Cup Chopped Celery Leaves
½ Tsp. Poultry Seasoning
Salt and Pepper
1 Bay Leaf
2½ Quarts Cold Water
2 Tbs. Barley
12 Leeks, with tops, cleaned and sliced
3 Potatoes, peeled and diced
Chopped Parsley

Place all ingredients except barley, leeks, potatoes and parsley in kettle; bring to a boil and simmer for 2 hours, or until the chicken is tender. Remove the chicken and slice thin; set aside. Strain the broth. Add the barley, leeks, and potatoes to the broth and continue to simmer for 30 min. Place the sliced chicken in a soup tureen; pour soup over the chicken and garnish with chopped parsley.

With French bread and a salad, this makes a one-dish meal. Makes about 3 quarts.

CHICKEN HAWAIIAN

1 Pkg. Frozen Chicken Breasts
1 Pkg. Frozen Chicken Legs or Thighs
¼ Cup Soy Sauce
¼ Cup Dry White Wine
Juice of 1 Lime
1 Clove Garlic, mashed or minced
1 Tsp. Curry Powder
1 Tsp. Minced Gingerroot
¼ Tsp. Dried Thyme
¼ Tsp. Dried Oregano
¼ Tsp. Freshly Ground Pepper
2 Medium-size Onions, thinly sliced
¼ Cup Butter (4 tbs.)
2 Cups Uncooked Rice
8 Slices of Pineapple
1 Tbs. Butter
½ Cup Toasted Slivered Almonds
16 Dates, sliced
1 Pimiento, cut into small pieces
¼ Cup Dry White Wine

Thaw chicken breasts and legs; cut each chicken breast into two pieces. Mix together the soy sauce, wine, lime juice, garlic, curry, gingerroot, thyme, oregano and pepper (no salt). Pour over chicken and marinate for several hours, turning chicken occasionally. Fry the onions in 2 tablespoons of the butter until light yellow and remove from pan.

Add the other 2 tablespoons of butter to pan and then fry the chicken pieces (which have been drained and dusted with flour) until brown on all sides. Pour in the marinade, cover and steam until tender. This should take about 45 minutes. Uncover the pan for the last 15 minutes.

While the chicken is steaming, cook rice by whichever method you prefer. Saute' the pineapple slices in the tablespoon of butter until lightly browned. To serve, mix the almonds, dates and pimiento with the rice and heap on a large chop plate. Arrange chicken and fried pineapple rings around the rice. Add the other ¼ cup of wine to the drippings in the pan and stir. Serve gravy separately. Makes 8 servings.

TURKEY TETRAZZINI

2/3 Cup Butter or Margarine
½ Cup All-purpose Flour
1 Cup Hot Milk
1 Cup Hot Chicken Bouillon
½ Tsp. Salt
½ Tsp. Pepper
1/8 Tsp. Ground Nutmeg
¼ Cup Dry Sherry
¾ Cup Heavy Cream
1 Lb. Thin Spaghetti
½ Lb. Mushrooms, sliced, or
   2 - 4 Oz. Cans Mushrooms, drained
2 to 3 Cups Diced, Cooked Turkey
½ Cup Grated Parmesan or Romano
   Cheese

Heat ½ cup butter and stir in flour. Combine milk and bouillon and stir into flour mixture. Cook, stirring, until sauce is smooth and thickened. Blend in salt, pepper, nutmeg and sherry. Stir in cream and remove mixture from heat. Cook and drain spaghetti. Saute' mushrooms in 2 tablespoons butter for 5 minutes. Mix half of sauce with spaghetti and mushrooms. Place in buttered shallow baking dish. Make well in center of spaghetti mixture. Mix remaining sauce with turkey and place in well. Sprinkle with Parmesan cheese. Bake in preheated hot oven (400°F.) for 20 min. Makes 6 to 8 servings.

TARRAGON-SEASONED CHICKEN BREASTS

3 Whole Chicken Breasts,
   boned and halved
Salt and Freshly-ground Pepper
   to taste
¼ Cup Flour
¼ Cup Butter
1 Tbs. Chopped Shallots or Onion
¼ Cup Dry White Bordeaux Wine
1 Tsp. Freshly-chopped Tarragon
   or ½ Tsp. Dried Tarragon
¼ Cup Chicken Broth
¼ Cup Heavy Cream

Skin the chicken breasts. Sprinkle with salt and pepper and dredge with the flour. Reserve the remaining flour. In a large skillet, heat 3 tbs. of butter; add the chicken and brown on both sides. Transfer to a heated platter. Add the shallots to the skillet and saute' briefly. Add the wine. Cook the liquid over high heat until it is nearly evaporated, while scraping loose all the brown particles in the pan. Add the reserved flour and stir to make a thick paste. Sprinkle with the tarragon and stir in the chicken broth. Return the chicken to the skillet; cover and cook until tender, about 25 min. Transfer the chicken to a heated platter & keep hot. Add the remaining butter and the cream to the skillet; heat, stirring, and pour the sauce over the chicken. Makes 6 servings.

CHICKEN SALTIMBOCCA

3 Whole, Large Chicken Breasts,
   skinned, boned and halved
   lengthwise
6 Thin Slices Boiled Ham
6 Slices Process Swiss Cheese
1 Medium Tomato, peeled, seeded
   and chopped
Dried Sage, crushed
1/3 Cup Fine Dry Bread Crumbs
2 Tbs. Grated Parmesan Cheese
2 Tbs. Snipped Parsley
¼ Cup Butter or Margarine, melted

Place chicken, boned side up, between two pieces of waxed paper or plastic wrap. Beginning at the center and working out to the edges, pound each piece of chicken lightly with a meat mallet until the piece measures 5½x5½''. Remove the paper or plastic wrap. Place a ham slice and a slice of cheese on each cutlet, cutting to fit within ¼'' of edges. Top with some of the chopped tomato and sprinkle lightly with sage. Fold in sides; roll up jelly-roll fashion, pressing to seal well. Combine the bread crumbs, Parmesan cheese and parsley. Dip the chicken rolls into butter, then roll in the crumb mixture. Bake in a shallow baking pan at 350°F. for 40 to 45 minutes. Remove rolls to a warm platter. Blend the juices remaining in the pan until they are smooth. Serve over the chicken. Makes 6 servings.

CHICKEN TAMALES

1 - 4 to 5 Lb. Stewing
  Chicken, cut up
1 Large Onion, chopped
1 Garlic Clove, minced or
  crushed
2 Tbs. Salad Oil
Paprika
Salt
Ground Red Pepper
Chili Powder
Cumin Powder
10 Cups Chicken Broth
  (heated)
2 Cups Cornmeal
1½ Tsp. Salt
Corn Shucks
Salad Oil, for greasing
  the corn shucks

Place chicken in a large kettle; cover with
hot water. Simmer until tender and meat
falls from bones, about 3 hours. Remove
from broth; take meat off bones. Grind
the meat, using a coarse blade.

Cook the liver, heart and gizzard separately;
grind and mix with the chicken. Cook onion and garlic in oil until soft and clear.
Add chicken and seasonings.

Bring chicken broth to a boil; prepare the
cornmeal mush, using broth, cornmeal &
salt. Trim and brush shucks for wrapping
tamales. Rinse with cold water. Place in
a pan and cover with boiling water. Let
stand until soft and pliable. Drain on paper towels. Grease with the oil. On each
shuck, spread a layer of mush, then a layer
of chicken mixture. Roll as for jelly roll.
Secure each end of shuck with string cut
from corn "silk".

Place tamales on rack in a large kettle,
over enough water in bottom of kettle
to prevent burning. Cover kettle and
steam tamales about 3 hours over low
heat. Makes 6 to 8 servings.

GERMAN-STYLE CHICKEN

1 - 2½ to 3 Lb. Broiler-Fryer
  Chicken, cut up
2 Tbs. Cooking Oil or Shortening
1 Cup Water
2 Tbs. Brown Sugar
2 Tbs. Vinegar
1½ Tsp. Salt
¼ Tsp. Pepper
1 Medium Head Cabbage, cut into
  eight wedges
½ Tsp. Caraway Seed

In a 12-inch skillet, brown chicken pieces
in hot oil over medium heat for about 15
minutes. Combine water, brown sugar,
vinegar, salt and pepper and pour over the
chicken. Cover and simmer for 20 minutes.
Add cabbage wedges and caraway seed;
cover and cook until chicken and cabbage
are tender, about 15 minutes longer. Arrange chicken and cabbage on serving platter; spoon pan juices over and serve. Makes
4 servings.

ROAST GOOSE WITH POTATO STUFFING

5 Lbs. Potatoes
¼ Cup Butter
1½ Cups Milk
2 Tsp. Salt
¼ Tsp. Pepper
½ Tsp. Poultry Seasoning
1 Egg, beaten
¼ Cup Finely-chopped Parsley, lightly
  packed
1 - 12 Lb. Goose
1 Tbs. Salt

Peel, boil and mash potatoes. Add the next
seven ingredients and beat until light and
fluffy. Prepare goose for roasting. Rub the
tablespoon of salt on inside. Fill goose with
stuffing; skewer and lace together. Place
breast-side up on rack in an open roasting
pan and bake, uncovered, in moderately slow
oven (325°F.) for 4½ to 5 hours, or until
tender. Do not prick skin to release excess
fat during baking. Boil giblets in a small
amount of salted water until tender. Chop
and add giblets to drippings along with their
cooking liquid for gravy. Makes 10 to 12
servings.

STUFFED CHICKEN
(From Portugal)

1 - 4 Lb. Roasting Chicken
2 Tbs. Butter
Salt and Pepper to taste
½ Tsp. Oregano
2 Tbs. Olive Oil

Stuffing:
½ Lb. Ground Beef, cooked
4 Slices Milk-soaked Bread
    (without crusts)
1 Egg
2 Tbs. Grated Romano Cheese
1 Tbs. Fresh Minced Parsley, or
    1 Tsp. Dry Parsley
1 Small Onion, minced
Salt and Pepper to taste
Pinch of Poultry Seasoning

Wash the chicken and dry. Rub inside with
1 tbs. butter. Combine stuffing ingredients.
Stuff the chicken. Sew or skewer together
to prevent stuffing from falling out. Rub
outside of chicken with 1 tbs. butter. Sprinkle with salt, pepper and oregano. Grease
the bottom of a 9x13x2" roasting pan with
olive oil. Place chicken in pan and roast in
a preheated 350°F. oven for 1 hour 15 minutes, or until tender. Baste occasionally.
Makes 6 servings.

CHICKEN WITH SWEET
AND SOUR SAUCE

2 Large Chicken Breasts, halved,
    skinned and boned
¼ Tsp. Salt
1/8 Tsp. Pepper
2 Ripe, but firm, Bananas
1 Tsp. Angostura Bitters
3 to 4 Oz. Cooked Ham, thinly
    sliced
½ Cup All-purpose Flour
3 Eggs, beaten slightly
1 Cup Flaked Coconut
Oil, for deep frying
Sweet and Sour Sauce (see
    recipe below)

Lay each chicken breast half between wax
paper and flatten out with a mallot until
approximately ¼" thick. Season chicken
with a portion of the salt and pepper. Peel
bananas and cut in half or into pieces that
are approximately the length of the chicken
breasts. Sprinkle bitters on sliced ham and
wrap around bananas. Place ham-wrapped
bananas on each breast. Roll tightly to
enclose filling completely. Secure with
toothpicks. Dredge breasts in flour, dip
into beaten eggs, then roll in coconut.
Deep fry each chicken roll 5 to 7 minutes
at 375°F., until golden brown and cooked
through. Drain, remove toothpicks and
serve with sweet and sour sauce. Serves 4.

Sauce:
1 Cup Orange Juice
2 Tbs. Vinegar
1 Tbs. Dark Brown Sugar
1 Tbs. Cornstarch
1 Tbs. Dark Rum
1 Tsp. Angostura Bitters

Whisk together the orange juice, vinegar,
sugar and cornstarch in a small saucepan.
Place pan over heat and bring to a slow
boil; simmer for 1 minute. Remove from
heat and pour in rum and bitters. Serve
warm.

ROAST CHICKEN
(Indian Style)

1 Roasting Chicken (3½ to 4 pounds)
½ Cup Raw Rice
1 Can (10½ oz.) Condensed Mushroom
    Soup
½ Tsp. Curry Powder
6 Ripe Olives, chopped
2 Tbs. Chopped Onion
2 Tbs. Butter or Margarine, melted

Wash and dry chicken. Cook and drain the
rice. Mix rice, ½ cup soup, ¼ tsp. curry
powder, olives and onion. Stuff chicken
with the mixture and roll up. Put in baking
pan and brush with butter. Cover lightly
with foil and roast in preheated slow oven
(325°F.) for 2½ to 3 hours, removing foil
about 45 minutes before end of roasting
time to allow for browning. Serve chicken
and stuffing with sauce made from remaining soup, heated, and ¼ teaspoon curry
powder. Makes 5 to 6 servings.

CHICKEN MEXICALI

2 Broiler-Fryers, cut up (about
   3 lbs. each)
2 Tbs. Butter or Margarine
2 Tbs. Olive Oil or Vegetable Oil
1 Large Onion, chopped (1 cup)
1 Large Sweet Green Pepper,
   quartered, seeded and chopped
1 Large Sweet Red Pepper, quartered,
   seeded and chopped
3 Tsp. Chili Powder
¼ Cup Sifted All-purpose Flour
1 - 2 Lb. Can Italian Tomatoes
3 Tsp. Salt
1 Tsp. Sugar
¼ Tsp. Pepper

Wash chicken pieces and pat dry. Brown,
a few pieces at a time, in butter or margarine and olive oil or vegetable oil in a
large frying pan; remove all pieces from the
pan and set aside while making the sauce.

Stir onion and green and red peppers into
pan drippings; saute' until soft. Stir in
chili powder and cook for 1 minute. Sprinkle flour over top, then blend in. Stir in
tomatoes, salt, sugar and pepper. Cook,
stirring constantly, until sauce thickens &
boils 1 minute. Layer browned chicken,
topping each with part of the sauce, in a
12-cup baking dish. Cover and bake in a
350°F. oven for 1 hour. Uncover and bake
bake 30 minutes longer, or until chicken
is tender and sauce is slightly thickened.
Makes 8 servings.

CHICKEN PARMIGIANA

3 Chicken Breasts (about 12 oz.
   each), split, skinned & boned
2 Eggs, lightly beaten
1 Tsp. Salt
1/8 Tsp. Pepper
¾ Cup Fine, Dry Bread Crumbs
½ Cup Vegetable Oil
2 Cups Tomato Sauce
¼ Tsp. Basil
1/8 Tsp. Garlic Powder
1 Tbs. Butter or Margarine
½ Cup Grated Parmesan Cheese
8 Oz. Mozzarella Cheese,
   sliced and cut into triangles

Place the chicken breasts on a cutting
board and pound lightly with side of a
heavy knife or cleaver until meat is
about ¼" thick. Combine eggs, salt &
pepper. Dip chicken into egg mixture,
then into crumbs. Heat oil until very
hot in a large frying pan. Quickly brown
the chicken on both sides; remove to a
shallow baking dish. Pour excess oil
from frying pan. Stir tomato sauce,
basil, and garlic powder into frying pan.
Heat to boiling; simmer 10 minutes, or
until thickened. Stir in butter or margarine. Pour over chicken; sprinkle
with cheese. Cover and bake in moderate oven (350°F.) for 30 minutes.
Uncover. Place mozzarella over the
chicken. Bake 10 minutes longer, or
until cheese melts.

CHICKEN WITH APPLES

1 - 2½ to 3 Lb. Broiler-Fryer
   Chicken, cut up
¼ Cup Butter or Margarine
1 Tsp. Salt
¼ Tsp. Pepper
1 Cup Apple Cider or Apple Juice
1 Tsp. Lemon Juice
4 Tart Cooking Apples, peeled
   and sliced (3 cups)
1 Tbs. Cornstarch
1 Tbs. Brown Sugar
¼ Tsp. Ground Cinnamon

In a skillet, brown the chicken slowly in
butter for about 10 minutes; turn often.
Remove from heat and drain off fat. Sprinkle chicken with salt and pepper. Add the
cider and lemon juice. Cover and simmer
for about 25 minutes. Add the apples and
simmer until just tender, about 5 to 10
minutes longer. Remove chicken and apples to platter and keep warm. Skim fat
from the juices in the pan. Measure the
juices and add water, if needed, to make
1 cup of liquid. In a saucepan, blend the
cornstarch, brown sugar and cinnamon.
Stir in the 1 cup of juices. Cook and stir
until thickened and bubbly. Season to
taste with salt and pepper. Spoon some
of the sauce over the chicken and apples.
Pass the remaining sauce. Makes 4 servings.

MORAVIAN CHICKEN

3½ to 4 Lb. Roasting Chicken,
   Pullet or Young Fowl
1 Tbs. Salt
1 Quart Boiling Water
3 Celery Leaves
1 Medium Carrot
1 Medium Onion, cut in half
1 Small Piece Bay Leaf
1 Red Pepper Pod
1 Lb. Whole Green Beans
4 Oz. Medium Noodles (2 cups)

Cut the singed, cleaned chicken into serving
portions. Place in a 4-quart kettle that has
a tight-fitting cover. Add salt, then cover
with water. Add celery leaves, carrot, onion
bay leaf and pepper. Cover and simmer for
2 hours, or until almost tender, removing
bay leaf after ½ hour. Add beans and cook
20 minutes, then add noodles. Continue
cooking about 10 minutes longer. Makes
4 to 6 servings.

CHICKEN GUMBO

1 - 3½ Lb. Frying Chicken, cut up
2 Cups Water
2 Medium Onions, sliced
Tops from 2 Celery Stalks
2 Bay Leaves
1 Tsp. Monosodium Glutamate
2 Tsp. Salt
2 Tbs. Butter or Margarine
1 Medium Green Pepper, chopped
2 - 1 Lb. Cans Tomatoes (4 cups)
3 Parsley Sprigs, chopped
½ Tsp. Hot Pepper Sauce
1/3 Cup Uncooked Rice
½ Lb. Fresh Okra, sliced
1 Tsp. File' Powder

Wash chicken pieces and put in kettle.
Add water, 1 onion, celery, bay leaves,
monosodium glutamate, and 1 teaspoon
of salt. Bring to boil; cover and simmer
for 40 minutes. Remove from heat;
strain broth and return to kettle. Remove
meat from bones in large pieces. Cut into
bite-size pieces; return to broth. Melt
butter. Add remaining onion and green
pepper, and cook for about 5 minutes.
Add to chicken with 1 teaspoon salt,
tomatoes, parsley and hot pepper sauce.
Simmer for 20 minutes. Add rice and
okra; simmer for another 20 minutes.
Remove from heat and stir in file' powder. Makes 4 servings.

CHICKEN PAPRIKA

2½ to 3½ Lbs. Chicken, cut into
   serving pieces
1 Tsp. Salt
½ Tsp. Pepper
¼ Cup Flour
4 Tbs. Butter or Margarine
2 Medium Onions, peeled and chopped
Paprika
¼ Cup Water
1 - 3 Oz. Can Sliced Mushrooms
1 Cup Commercial Sour Cream

If frozen chicken is used, thaw according to
directions on package. Combine the salt &
pepper with 3 tablespoons of flour in paper
bag. Shake chicken in bag until pieces are
well coated with flour mixture. Melt butter
or margarine in heavy skillet. Cook chicken
over medium heat until browned on all
sides. Add onions, 1 teaspoon paprika, water, mushrooms and their liquid. Cover and
cook over low heat for about 30 minutes,
or until chicken is tender and done. Remove chicken to hot platter.

Stir remaining 1 tablespoon of flour into
mixture in skillet until smooth. Add sour
cream. Stir over low heat 1 or 2 minutes,
until hot and bubbly. Pour over chicken.
Sprinkle lightly with paprika. Serve hot.
Makes 4 to 6 servings.

TURKEY DRUMSTICKS
(with Tangerine Risotto)

4 Frozen Turkey Drumsticks
  (about 1 lb. each), thawed
2 Tbs. Vegetable Oil
1 Large Onion, chopped
1 Tsp. Salt
¼ Tsp. Pepper
1 - 14 Oz. Can Chicken Broth
½ Cup Ginger Marmalade (from
  a 12-ounce jar)
1/3 Cup Light Molasses
1/3 Cup Cider Vinegar
1/3 Cup Prepared Mustard
1 Tsp. Ground Ginger
Tangerine Risotto (see recipe
  below)

Brown the drumsticks slowly in vegetable
oil in a large frying pan; remove from pan.
Stir onion into drippings and saute' until
soft. Stir in salt, pepper, and chicken
broth. Heat to a boil. Place drumsticks
in sauce; cover and simmer, turning several
times, for 1½ hours, or until tender. Remove drumsticks from pan and place on a
rack in a shallow baking pan.

Blend marmalade, molasses, vinegar, mustard, and ginger in a small saucepan; heat
slowly to boiling. Brush part of this mixture over the drumsticks. Bake in moderate oven (375°F.) for 40 minutes, or until
richly glazed (turn and brush several times
with remaining molasses mixture). Spoon
Tangerine Risotto onto a heated large
serving platter; arrange turkey drumsticks
on top. Garnish platter with parsley and
small cubes of jellied cranberry sauce, if
desired.

Tangerine Risotto:

1 Cup Uncooked Regular Rice
4 Tbs. Butter or Margarine
1 Medium-size Seedless Orange
1 Large Onion, chopped
1/3 Cup Thawed Frozen Concentrated
  Tangerine Juice
1 - 5 Oz. Can Water Chestnuts,
  drained and sliced
1 Tsp. Sugar
½ Tsp. Salt

Cook rice in a large saucepan, following
directions on the label. Stir in 2 tbs. of
the butter or margarine; keep rice warm.
While rice cooks, pare orange; section over
a small bowl to catch the juice; cut each
section in half. Saute' onion in remaining
2 tbs. of butter or margarine until soft in
a medium-size frying pan; stir in orange
sections and juice, concentrated tangerine
juice, water chestnuts, sugar and salt. Heat
slowly to boiling. Pour over rice mixture
and toss lightly to mix. Makes 4 servings.

POACHED CHICKEN
AND VEGETABLES

1 - 4 Lb. Stewing Checken
6 to 9 Cups Chicken Stock
2 Tbs. Fresh Lemon Juice
2 Carrots, peeled and julienned
  into 1½" pieces
2 Celery Stalks, julienned into
  1½" pieces
3 Green Onions, trimmed and
  julienned into 1½" pieces
¼ Lb. Fresh Mushrooms, cleaned
  and quartered
¼ Cup Chopped Onion
1 Large Garlic Clove, minced
2 Bay Leaves
2 Whole Cloves
¼ Tsp. Ground Cardamom
¼ Tsp. Oregano
¼ Tsp. Pepper
4 Large Tomatoes, quartered
  and seeded
1 Tsp. Chopped Fresh Mint Leaves
  or ½ Tsp. Dried Mint
¼ Tsp. Rosemary
Chopped Parsley, for garnish

Place trussed chicken in a large pot. Pour
in enough stock to cover the bird. Bring
to a boil, then lower heat to simmer. Add
remaining ingredients, except tomatoes,
mint and rosemary. Poach, partially covered,
for 35 minutes. After 35 minutes, add the
tomatoes, mint and rosemary. Simmer the
dish 25 minutes longer, or until juices in
the bird run clear when pierced with a knife.
To serve, place chicken on a large platter, un-
tie, and surround it with the vegetables.
Spoon over it 1 cup cooking stock, then
garnish with chopped parsley, if desired.
Strain and degrease additional cooking stock
for a natural gravy. Makes 4 servings.

CHICKEN (Deep-Fried)

1 Chicken (broiler-fryer), 2 Lbs.
Oil for deep frying
1 Slice Fresh Gingerroot
1 Green Onion, cut into 1-inch pieces

Marinade:

1 Tbs. Sherry
1 Tbs. Cornstarch
5 Tsp. Soy Sauce

Place chicken in a saucepan and add enough water to cover. Bring to a boil, turn down heat, and simmer for about 1 hour. Remove chicken from broth. Bone the chicken, cutting meat into shreds about 2 inches long. Allow meat to cool.

Coat the chicken with the marinade and allow it to stand for a few minutes. Heat a deep frying pan and add enough oil for deep frying. Add gingerroot and green onion. Fry the pieces of chicken in hot oil for about 1 minute, or until they become brown and crisp. Serve immediately. Makes 2 servings.

LEMON CHICKEN

¼ Cup All-purpose Flour
1 - 2½ to 3 Lb. Broiler-Fryer
   Chicken, cut up
2 Tbs. Cooking Oil
1 - 6 Oz. Can Frozen Lemonade
   Concentrate, thawed
½ Cup Water
3 Tbs. Brown Sugar
3 Tbs. Catsup
1 Tbs. Vinegar
1 Tbs. Cornstarch
Hot Cooked Rice

In a plastic bag, combine flour and 1 tsp. salt. Add chicken pieces, a few at a time, and shake well to coat. In skillet brown chicken in hot oil for 15 minutes. Spoon off fat. Blend lemonade concentrate, ½ cup water, brown sugar, catsup and vinegar. Pour over chicken. Bring to boiling; cover and simmer until tender, 45 to 50 minutes. Remove chicken to platter; keep warm. Skim fat from pan juices. Measure juices

and add water, if needed, to make 1¼ cups of liquid. Return to pan. Blend 1 tablespoon of cold water into cornstarch; stir into pan juices. Cook and stir until thickened and bubbly. Pass sauce with chicken; serve over rice. Makes 4 servings.

CHICKEN with CURRANT-RICE STUFFING

1 - 2½ to 3 Lb. Chicken
1 Chicken Liver
Vegetable Oil or Butter
½ Cup Slivered Blanched Almonds
¾ Cup Uncooked Long-grain Rice
½ Cup Dry White Wine
1¼ Cups Water
Salt
1 Tsp. Ground Cinnamon
Sugar
½ Cup Dried Currants

Wash and dry the chicken; set aside. Heat 3 tablespoons of oil or butter in a medium saucepan & saute' the almonds and chicken liver in it. When they are lightly browned, remove them from the pan with a slotted spoon. Chop the liver and set it aside with the nuts. Add the rice to the fat in the pan and saute' over medium heat, stirring constantly. Pour in the wine and water; add the salt, cinnamon and a pinch of sugar. Cover and cook for 12 minutes, or until the rice is almost tender. Stir in the almonds, liver and currants and remove the pan from the heat. Spoon the stuffing into the cavity of the chicken & close tightly with skewers. Truss the chicken and brush the surface lightly with melted butter or oil. Set the bird on a rack in a roasting pan, breast side up, and roast it in a preheated moderate oven (350°F.) for 1¼ hours, or until tender. Turn the bird with two wooden spoons every 20 minutes and baste it frequently with the pan drippings. When the bird is finished cooking, remove the stuffing from the cavity and transfer it to the center of a warmed platter. Carve the chicken and arrange the pieces around the stuffing. Serve warm. Makes 5 to 6 servings.

CHICKEN CROQUETTES

2 Tbs. Butter
¼ Cup All-purpose Flour
¾ Tsp. Salt
1/8 Tsp. Pepper
1 Cup Milk
1 Tsp. Minced Parsley
1 Tsp. Minced Onion
2 Cups Ground, Cooked Chicken
½ Tsp. Fresh Lemon Juice
Salt and Pepper, to taste
Pinch of Ground Sage
Fine, Dry Bread Crumbs
1 Egg
1 Tbs. Water
Fat, for deep frying

Melt the butter; add flour, salt and pepper and mix well. Gradually add milk & cook until thick, stirring constantly. Combine the next 7 ingredients with the white sauce. Chill. Shape into 8 croquettes; roll in the crumbs, dip into slightly-beaten egg mixed with water, and then roll again in crumbs. Fry in deep fat (375°F. on frying thermometer) for about 5 minutes, or until golden. Makes 4 servings.

CHICKEN FRICASSEE with CORNMEAL DUMPLINGS

1 Large Stewing Chicken
    (about 6 lbs.), cut up
All-purpose Flour
Salt and Pepper to taste
¼ Cup Fat or Oil
Celery Tops
1 Onion, peeled
1 Bay Leaf
4½ Cups Water
2 Chicken Bouillon Cubes
Cornmeal Dumpling Batter
    (see recipe below)

Wash chicken pieces. Drain and pat dry. Dredge pieces with flour mixed with salt and pepper. Brown the chicken on all sides in hot fat or oil. Add celery tops, onion, bay leaf, 4 cups water, and bouillon cubes. Bring to a boil, lower heat, cover and simmer for 1½ hours, or until chicken is tender. Blend 6 tablespoons flour with remaining water. Stir mixture gradually into hot liquid. Cook until thickened, stirring constantly. Season to taste with salt and pepper. Make the dumpling batter and drop by teaspoonfuls into gently boiling fricassee. Cover and simmer for 12 minutes, or until the dumplings are done when tested with a toothpick. Makes 4 servings.

Dumpling Batter:
1 Egg, beaten
¼ Cup Milk
1 Tbs. Cooking Oil
½ Cup Yellow Cornmeal
¼ Tsp. Poultry Seasoning
½ Cup All-purpose Flour
1 Tsp. Baking Powder
½ Tsp. Salt

Mix egg with milk, oil, cornmeal, and poultry seasoning. Sift in remaining ingredients. Blend well. Makes 12 to 16 small dumplings.

CHICKEN KEBABS

4 Whole Chicken Breasts, skinned and
    boned
½ Tsp. Ground Ginger
¼ Tsp. Dried Chili Peppers
1/8 Tsp. Powdered Mustard
1/8 Tsp. Ground Cardamom or
    finely crushed cardamom seed
1/8 Tsp. Turmeric
1 Tsp. Curry Powder
1 Tbs. Yogurt or Buttermilk
2 Tsp. Fresh Lemon Juice
1 Tsp. Salt
Small Onions, cut in ¼-inch slices
Lemon Quarters, sprinkled with paprika
Parsley

Flatten skinned and boned chicken with hands and cut into 2" pieces. Mix remaining ingredients, except for last 3, to a thick paste. Add chicken pieces and stir to coat well. Let stand for 1 hour at room temperature. Thread on skewers, alternating several pieces with a slice of onion. Repeat until 4 skewers are filled. Set across a shallow pan and broil slowly for 15 minutes, or until done, turning once during cooking. Serve at once garnished with lemon quarters and parsley. Makes 4 servings.

COUNTRY-CAPTAIN CHICKEN

½ Cup Chopped Onion
½ Cup Chopped Green Pepper
1 Clove Garlic, minced
2 Tbs. Butter or Margarine
1 - 28 Oz. Can Tomatoes,
    cut up
¼ Cup Dried Currants
¼ Cup Snipped Parsley
2 to 3 Tsp. Curry Powder
1 Tsp. Ground Mace
1 Tsp. Salt
1/8 Tsp. Pepper

Melt butter or margarine in a large sauce-pan. Add onion, green pepper and garlic and cook until tender but not brown. Stir in the undrained tomatoes, currants, parsley, curry, mace, 1 tsp. salt, and 1/8 tsp. pepper. Cook, uncovered, for 15 minutes.

1/3 Cup All-purpose Flour
1 Tsp. Salt
¼ Tsp. Pepper
¼ Tsp. Paprika
2 - 2½ to 3 Lb. Broiler-Fryer
    Chickens, cut into serving pieces
2 Tbs. Cooking Oil
2 Tbs. Cold Water
1 Tbs. Cornstarch

While sauce is cooking, combine flour, 1 tsp. salt, ¼ tsp. pepper and the paprika in a paper or plastic bag. Add the chicken pieces, 2 or 3 at a time; shake to coat the chicken evenly. Lightly brown the chicken pieces on all sides in hot oil for about 15 minutes. Arrange chicken in a 13x9x2" baking dish; top with sauce. Cover and bake at 325°F. until chicken is tender, about 1 hour. Remove chicken to a warm platter; keep warm. Skim excess fat from the sauce; transfer remaining sauce to a medium saucepan. Blend cold water into the cornstarch; stir into the sauce. Cook and stir until sauce is thickened and bubbly. Serve chicken and sauce over rice. Makes 8 to 10 servings.

SESAME CHICKEN

2 Frying Chickens (2½ Lbs. each),
    quartered
½ Cup Sesame Seeds
1/3 Cup Cooking Oil
¼ Cup Minced Onion
2 Tsp. Salt
½ Tsp. Ground Cardamom
½ Tsp. Ground Ginger
1 Garlic Clove, minced
Dash of Ground Cloves
Dash of Ground Chili Powder
Pan Gravy

Wash and dry chicken pieces. Put in a shallow broilerproof baking dish, skin side down. Mix next 9 ingredients and brush some on chicken. Bake in 350°F. oven for 30 minutes, basting frequently with remaining sesame mixture. Turn skin-side up and bake for about 30 min. longer. Put under broiler and brown lightly. Serve with Pan Gravy. Makes 4 servings.

Pan Gravy: Remove chicken from baking pan. Blend 1 tablespoon cornstarch and 1 cup water. Stir into drippings. Cook, stirring, until thickened.

HAWAIIAN PINEAPPLE AND CHICKEN

½ Cup Sliced Water Chestnuts
½ Cup Sliced Bamboo Shoots
½ Cup Sliced Celery
¼ Cup Sliced Chinese Cabbage
2 Tbs. Cooking Oil
2 Cups Diced Cooked Chicken
1 Tbs. Brown Sugar
1 Tbs. Vinegar
3 Tbs. Soy Sauce
2 Cups Chicken Bouillon
1 Cup Drained Pineapple Cubes
3 Tbs. Cornstarch
3 Tbs. Cold Water
¼ Cup Chopped Green Onion
Chow-mein Noodles

Cook vegetables in oil for 5 minutes, stirring. Add next 7 ingredients and bring to a boil. Stir in cornstarch blended with water. Cook, stirring constantly until thickened. Sprinkle with onion and serve on noodles. Makes 4 servings.

CHICKEN KIEV

12 Tbs. Butter or Margarine
6 Chicken Breasts (about 12 oz. each)
4 Tbs. Finely-chopped Parsley
½ Tsp. Sugar
2 Eggs
1 Cup Fine, Dry Bread Crumbs
1 Tsp. Salt
1/8 Tsp. Pepper
Shortening or Vegetable Oil,
    for frying

Cut butter or margarine into 12 even-length sticks; chill in freezer while fixing chicken (butter should be very cold). Pull skin from chicken breasts; halve breasts and cut meat in one piece from the bones. Place each half, boned-side up, between wax paper and pound very thin with a mallet or rolling pin to form a "cutlet." (Be careful not to pound holes in the meat.)

Place 1 piece of very cold butter or margarine, 1 tsp. parsley, and a dash of sugar on end of each cutlet; fold sides over to seal in butter, then roll up. Hold in place with wooden picks. Beat eggs slightly in a pie plate; mix bread crumbs, salt and pepper in a second pie plate. Dip stuffed rolls in egg, then in crumb mixture to coat well. Chill at least an hour. You can prepare this ahead to this point. When ready to fry, melt enough shortening or pour in enough vegetable oil to make a 2" depth in an electric deep-fat fryer or large saucepan. Heat oil to 350°F. Fry rolls, 3 or 4 at a time and turning often, for 7 minutes, or until tender and crisply golden. Lift out with a slotted spoon; drain well. Keep hot until all rolls are cooked.

SHAKER CHICKEN PUDDING

2 to 3 Cups Cooked Chicken Meat,
    diced
1 Apple, diced
1 Onion, chopped (½ cup)
1 Celery Stalk, chopped (½ cup)
6 Tbs. Butter
½ Cup Apple Cider
½ Tsp. Salt
¼ Tsp. Pepper
Grated Nutmeg
1 Cup Bread Crumbs

Sauce:
2 Tbs. Flour
1 Cup Heavy Cream

Prepare the chicken, preferably from a freshly-poached chicken. Gently saute' the apple, onion and celery in 4 tablespoons of butter until they are soft. Add the cider, salt, pepper and a pinch of nutmeg. Simmer, covered, for 30 minutes, or until the vegetables are very soft. Uncover the pot and continue to cook this mixture until it is thickened.

To make the sauce, cook the flour and 2 tablespoons of butter in a saucepan for a few minutes, stirring until the mixture just begins to change color. Add the cream and cook, stirring, until the sauce thickens. Mix into this sauce the cooked vegetable hash and the chicken. Pour the mixture into a buttered baking dish, and sprinkle with bread crumbs and the remaining 2 tablespoons of butter, melted. Bake in an oven, preheated to 350°F., for 20 minutes, or until browned. Makes 4 to 6 servings.

BARBECUED CHICKEN
(Texas Style)

1½ Cups Butter
¾ Cup Sugar
2 Garlic Cloves, crushed
1 Tsp. Paprika
½ Cup Tarragon Vinegar
3 Cups Ketchup
2 Tbs. Worcestershire Sauce
1½ Tsp. Prepared Mustard
1½ Tsp. Salt
½ Tsp. Pepper
2 Tsp. Chili Powder
6 Broiler-Fryer Chickens (2½ lbs.
    each), cut into halves
Salt and Pepper to taste

Combine all ingredients except last 4. Simmer for 20 minutes until thick, stirring occasionally. Makes 3 cups of sauce. Rub chickens with salt and pepper. Place, skin side up, on grill after coals are ready. Cook, basting with the sauce and turning often, for about 1 hour, or until the meat is tender & no pink can be seen. Makes 12 servings.

COSTA BRAVA PAELLA

1 - 2 Lb. Broiler-Fryer, cut
   into serving-size pieces
1 Large Onion, chopped (1 cup)
1 Garlic Clove, minced
1 Cup Uncooked Regular Rice
6 Small Slices Salami, diced
2 Tsp. Salt
1 Tsp. Sugar
¼ Tsp. Pepper
1/8 Tsp. Crushed Saffron
1 - 1 Lb. Can Tomatoes
1½ Cups Water
1 Envelope Instant Chicken Broth
   or 1 Chicken Bouillon Cube
1 Lb. Fresh Shrimp, shelled and
   deveined or 1 - 12 Oz. Pkg. Frozen
   Shrimp, shelled and deveined
1 - 4 Oz. Can Pimiento, drained
   and cut into large pieces

Remove skin from chicken. Place chicken, meaty side down, in a single layer on rack of broiler pan. Broil, 4 inches from the heat, for 10 minutes; turn and broil for 10 minutes longer, or until lightly browned. Set aside. Pour the drippings from the broiler pan into a medium frying pan and stir in the onion and garlic. Saute' until soft. Spoon mixture into a 12-cup baking dish with rice, salami, salt, sugar, pepper and saffron. Combine tomatoes with water and instant chicken broth or bouillon cube in same frying pan; heat to boiling, crushing bouillon cube with a spoon. Stir into rice mixture with shrimp. Arrange chicken and pimientos on top; cover and bake in 350°F. oven for 1 hour, or until liquid is absorbed and chicken is tender. Makes 6 servings.

CHICKEN IN WALNUT SAUCE

3 Lbs. Chicken Pieces (breasts,
   thighs, drumsticks)
1 Small Onion, peeled and
   quartered
1 Carrot, peeled and coarsely
   chopped
4 Tsp. Salt
6½ Cups Water
3 Slices Day-old White Bread
3¾ Cups Walnuts (14 oz.),
   finely ground
1 Small Onion, peeled and finely
   chopped
4 Tsp. Paprika

Place chicken, quartered onion, chopped carrot, and 2 teaspoons of salt in a large pot. Pour in 6 cups of water and bring to a boil over high heat. Reduce heat to low, partially cover, and simmer chicken 45 minutes or longer, until tender. Take pan off of heat and allow chicken to cool down, uncovered, in the pan.

When cool, take chicken pieces and vegetables out of the broth. Set chicken aside & discard vegetables. Put broth back on the fire and boil, uncovered, over high heat for 30 minutes, until liquid is reduced to approximately 3 cups. Skin and bone the cooked chicken. Shred or cut meat into thin pieces 1" long. Set aside.

To prepare the sauce, begin by soaking the bread briefly in ½ cup water until soft. When soft, put the bread into a food processor or blender. Add most of the ground walnuts, saving a small amount for garnish. Also add the finely-chopped onion, 3 teaspoons of paprika, and remaining 2 teaspoons of salt. Puree until the mixture forms a thick paste. Depending on the size of your processor or blender, this may have to be done in batches. Place walnut paste in a large bowl; slowly pour in 2 or more cups of the reduced chicken stock and beat until the sauce has the consistency of thin mayonnaise. Pour half of the walnut sauce over the shredded chicken and mix thoroughly. Select a shallow serving dish on which to mound the masked chicken. Pour as much remaining walnut sauce as desired over the chicken. Sprinkle with 1 tsp. paprika and the reserved walnuts. Serve at room temperature. Makes 8 servings.

CHICKEN WITH TOMATO SAUCE

1 - 4 Lb. Stewing Chicken, cut up
¼ Cup Flour
¼ Cup Olive Oil or Vegetable Oil
2 Garlic Cloves, minced
½ Cup Chopped Onion
½ Lb. Cooked Ham, cut in
   julienne strips
1 - 16 Oz. Can Tomatoes, undrained
1 - 8 Oz. Can Tomato Sauce
2 Chicken Bouillon Cubes, crushed
½ Tsp. Crushed Basil
3 Drops Hot Pepper Sauce
1 Tsp. Grated Lemon Peel
½ Cup Walnuts, chopped
½ Cup Pimiento-stuffed Olives
Hot, cooked Rice

Rinse chicken and pat dry with paper towels. Coat chicken with flour. Heat olive oil with garlic in a large heavy skillet; add chicken & brown pieces on all sides. Put the browned chicken into an electric cooker. Add onion, ham, tomatoes and a mixture of the tomato sauce, crushed bouillon cubes, basil, hot pepper sauce and lemon peel; stir well. Cover and cook on low for 8 to 10 hours. Add walnuts and olives to contents of cooker. Serve chicken in sauce over hot, cooked rice in a heated serving dish. Garnish with additional stuffed olives, if desired. Makes 6 servings.

CHICKEN/RICE TETRAZZINI

1 Quart Water
2 Tsp. Salt
1 - 4 to 5 Lb. Stewing Chicken,
   cut into pieces
1¾ Cups Chicken Broth
1 - 4 Oz. Can Sliced Mushrooms
2 Tbs. Flour
½ Tsp. Garlic Salt
1/8 Tsp. Pepper
½ Cup Light Cream
1 Cup Grated Cheddar Cheese
4 Cups Cooked Rice
1 Tbs. Chopped Parsley
4 Strips Bacon, cooked crisp and
   crumbled
¼ Cup Cracker Crumbs
¼ Tsp. Poultry Seasoning

Heat water in saucepan; add salt & chicken. Cover and simmer for 2½ to 3 hours, or until the thigh meat is tender. Take meat from bones and cut it into chunks. Heat chicken broth with juice from mushrooms. Blend flour, garlic salt, pepper and cream together and stir into broth; cook, stirring constantly until thickened. Remove from heat; stir in cheese.

Combine rice, chicken, mushrooms and parsley in another bowl. Alternate layers of the chicken mixture and sauce in a buttered 3-quart casserole. Combine bacon, crumbs and seasoning; sprinkle over casserole. Bake in a very hot oven (450°F) for 30 minutes. Makes 10 servings.

CHICKEN IN BURGUNDY WINE

5 Tbs. Butter or Margarine
3 Slices of Bacon, cut into very
   thin pieces (matchstick size)
1 Medium Onion, thinly sliced
1 Broiler-Fryer Chicken, cut into
   pieces (2½ to 3 lbs.)
1 Tbs. All-purpose Flour
2 Tbs. Brandy
2 Cups Burgundy or other dry red
   wine
1 Bay Leaf
2 Tbs. Chopped Parsley
¼ Tsp. Crumbled Dried Thyme
1 Tsp. Salt
½ Tsp. Pepper
1/8 Tsp. Ground Nutmeg
1 Cup Chopped Fresh Mushrooms,
   sauteed in butter

Melt ¼ cup butter over medium heat, stirring occasionally. Cook bacon and onion in it until soft and transparent. Remove bacon and onion with slotted spoon and reserve. Brown chicken on all sides in remaining fat. Sprinkle with flour. Add brandy, Burgundy, bay leaf, parsley, thyme, salt, pepper & nutmeg. Cook, covered, in preheated 350°F. oven for 30 minutes, or until tender. Stir in reserved bacon and onion mixture, and the mushrooms. Return to oven and cook, covered, for another 5 to 10 minutes. Remove; stir remaining butter into the sauce. Serve with noodles or mashed potatoes. Makes 4 servings.

GREEK MARINATED FRIED CHICKEN

1 - 2½ Lb. Chicken, cut into
    serving pieces
Salt and Pepper
¾ Cup Flour
Olive or Peanut Oil
Small Tomatoes or Tomato Wedges
Watercress and Parsley Sprigs

Marinade:
¼ Cup Olive Oil
¼ Cup White Wine Vinegar
¼ Cup Fresh Lemon Juice
½ Cup Dry White Wine
2 Garlic Cloves, chopped
1 Small Onion, sliced
1 Bay Leaf, crushed
1 Tsp. Dried Thyme, Marjoram
    or Oregano
2 Peppercorns, crushed
2 or 3 Juniper Berries
4 Coriander Seeds, cracked

Combine all the marinade ingredients in a
bowl. Place the chicken in the marinade,
coating the pieces on all sides. Cover and
refrigerate for at least 2 hours, or overnight if desired. Drain the chicken, then
season lightly with salt and pepper. Put
the flour in a paper bag; add the chicken
pieces and shake lightly until they are
coated with flour.

Pour oil in a heavy skillet to a depth of
½" and heat almost to the smoking point.
Slip the chicken into the hot oil and fry
to a light brown on all sides. Using tongs,
remove the chicken to a roasting pan, discarding the oil remaining in the skillet.

Bake in a preheated 350°F. oven for 30
minutes, or until tender, pouring off the
oil as it collects in the pan. The chicken
should now be crisp and a rich chestnut
color. Arrange the chicken on a platter,
alternating tomatoes, watercress and
parsley around the edge. Makes 4 to 5
servings.

CHICKEN MARENGO

6 Slices Bacon, cut into 1" pieces
2 - 2 Lb. Broiler-Fryers, cut up
½ Cup Sifted All-purpose Flour
2 Tsp. Salt
¼ Tsp. Pepper
2 Medium Onions, chopped (1 cup)
1 Clove Garlic, minced
1 - 4 Oz. Can Whole Mushrooms
2 - 1 Lb. Cans Tomatoes
¼ Cup Chopped Parsley
Liquid Red Pepper Seasoning (a
    few drops)

Fry the bacon until almost crisp in a large
frying pan. Lift out with a slotted spoon;
drain on paper towels and set aside for
later. Leave bacon drippings in the pan.

Wash and dry the chicken pieces well. Snip
off the small rib bones with a kitchen scissors, if you wish. Shake the chicken pieces
in a mixture of flour, salt and pepper in a
paper bag to coat well. Reserve any leftover
flour mixture. Brown the chicken, a few
pieces at a time, in the bacon drippings; put
chicken pieces in a 12-cup shallow baking
dish. Saute' onion and garlic until soft in
same frying pan; stir in reserved flour mixture. Drain liquid from mushrooms; save
the mushrooms for later. Stir mushroom
liquid, tomatoes, parsley and a few drops
of liquid red pepper seasoning into the frying pan; heat to boiling, stirring constantly.
Spoon mixture over chicken in baking dish;
cover. Bake in 350°F. oven for 1 hr. and
20 min., or until chicken is tender. Sprinkle with reserved bacon pieces and mushrooms. Bake, uncovered, 10 minutes longer,
or until the bacon is crisp. Sprinkle with
croutons just before serving. Makes 8
servings.

TURKEY AND BROCCOLI WITH ALMONDS

4 Oz. Medium Noodles (about
   2 cups)
1 - 10 Oz. Pkg. Frozen Broccoli,
   cooked
2 Tbs. Butter or Margarine
2 Tbs. All-purpose Flour
1 Cup Evaporated Milk (undiluted)
1 Cup Turkey or Chicken Broth
1 Cup Diced Cheddar Cheese
½ Tsp. Monosodium Glutamate
1 Tsp. Worcestershire
¼ Tsp. Pepper
2 Cups Diced Cooked Turkey
Salt
¼ Cup Toasted Slivered Blanched
   Almonds

Cook and drain noodles; put in shallow baking dish. Cut broccoli into 1" pieces and reserve blossoms. Arrange stems on noodles. Make a sauce with butter, flour and liquids. Add cheese, monosodium glutamate, Worcestershire, and pepper; stir until cheese is melted. Add turkey and salt to taste. Pour over ingredients in dish. Arrange the broccoli blossoms on top and sprinkle with almonds. Bake in 350°F. oven for about 30 minutes. Makes 4 servings.

CHICKEN--CALIFORNIA STYLE

1 - 4 to 5 Lb. Chicken, cut
   into serving pieces
½ Cup Olive Oil or Vegetable Oil
½ Cup Cornmeal (plus extra for
   thickening sauce)
Salt
1 Cup Finely-chopped Onion
3 Garlic Cloves, finely chopped
½ Tsp. Grated Nutmeg
1 Tsp. Cumin Seeds
1 Tsp. Ground Coriander
1 Cup Water
1 Cup Dry Red Wine
4 Tbs. Chili Powder
1 Cup Blanched Almonds
1 Cup Green Olives
Chopped Fresh Coriander Leaves
1 Tsp. Sesame Seeds

Heat the oil in a deep braising pan or heavy iron or cast-aluminum skillet. Roll the chicken in the cornmeal and brown quickly on both sides. Salt the chicken while it is browning. When nicely colored, add the onion, garlic, nutmeg, cumin and ground coriander. Turn the chicken so that the flavors of the seasonings blend. Add the water & wine, and bring to a boil. Reduce the heat, cover and simmer until the chicken is just tender--about 45 minutes to 1 hour. Do not let it overcook. Add the chili powder, turn the chicken pieces and simmer a few minutes more. Transfer the chicken to a warmed platter. Add the almonds and the olives to the sauce. Continue to stir until the sauce thickens slightly. Correct the seasoning and pour the sauce over the chicken. Sprinkle with chopped coriander leaves, if available, and the sesame seeds. Serve with rice or cornmeal. Makes 4 to 6 servings.

CHICKEN CACCIATORE

2 - 2 Lb. Broiler Fryers, cut up
3 Tbs. Olive Oil or Salad Oil
2 Tbs. Butter or Margarine
1 - 15 Oz. Can Tomato Sauce
1 - 1 Lb. 12 Oz. Can Whole Tomatoes,
   undrained
¾ Cup Dry Red Wine
1 Tsp. Dried Basil Leaves
1 Tsp. Dried Oregano Leaves
¼ Tsp. Minced Garlic
2 Tbs. Chopped Parsley
¾ Tsp. Salt
¼ Tsp. Pepper
3 Tbs. Flour
1 - 6 Oz. Can Whole Mushrooms,
   drained

Wash chicken and pat dry with paper towels. Heat oil and butter in a 6-quart Dutch oven. Add chicken, a few pieces at a time, and brown well on all sides. Remove pieces as they are browned. Return chicken to Dutch oven; add tomato sauce, tomatoes, wine, basil, oregano, garlic, parsley, salt and pepper. Simmer, covered 45 to 50 minutes, or until chicken is tender. Combine flour with 3 tablespoons water; stir into sauce. Add mushrooms; cook for 10 minutes longer, or until sauce is thickened. Makes 6 servings.

ORIENTAL CHICKEN AND VEGETABLES

4 Chicken Breasts, about 9 oz. each
1 Tsp. Salt
1 - 10 Oz. Pkg. Frozen French-style
   Green Beans
1 Cup Diced Celery
1 - 1 Lb. Can Bean Sprouts, drained
¾ Cup Water
3 Tbs. Cider Vinegar
¼ Tsp. Pepper
2 Tbs. Cornstarch
3 Tbs. Soy Sauce
2 Medium Tomatoes, each cut into
   6 wedges
3 Cups Hot Cooked Rice

Strip skin from chicken. Cut meat from bones and then cut into ¼" wide strips. Sprinkle salt in a large frying pan. Add the chicken and saute', stirring often, for 10 minutes. Push to one side. Place the frozen beans in frying pan; cook, breaking beans apart as they thaw, 5 minutes. Stir in celery, bean sprouts, ¾ cup water, vinegar and pepper. Heat to boiling. Cover and simmer for 5 minutes.

Blend cornstarch with 2 tablespoons water until smooth; stir in soy sauce and stir into mixture in frying pan. Cook, stirring constantly, until mixture thickens and boils for 3 minutes. Lay tomato wedges on top; cover again and steam 5 minutes, or just until tomatoes are heated through.

Spoon a ring of rice around edge of each of 6 heated serving plates; spoon chicken mixture into centers, placing tomato wedges on top. Makes 6 servings.

BARBECUE FRIED CHICKEN

1 - 2½ to 3 Lb. Broiler-Fryer
   Chicken, cut up
¼ Cup All-purpose Flour
1 Tsp. Salt
2 Tbs. Cooking Oil
1 Cup Catsup
½ Cup Chopped Onion
½ Cup Water
1 Small Clove Garlic, minced
1 Tsp. Salt
¼ Tsp. Pepper
3 Tbs. Lemon Juice

Coat the chicken pieces with a mixture of flour and 1 tsp. salt. In a large skillet, brown the chicken pieces in hot oil over medium heat for about 15 minutes, turning to brown evenly. While chicken pieces are browning, combine catsup, onion, water, garlic, 1 tsp. salt and ¼ tsp. pepper in a saucepan and bring to a boil. Simmer, uncovered, for 20 minutes. Remove from heat; blend in the lemon juice. Pour the catsup mixture over the chicken. Cover and cook over low heat until tender, approximately 35 to 40 minutes, turning occasionally. Makes 4 servings.

FRENCH-STYLE CHICKEN

1 - 4 Lb. Roasting Chicken, ready
   for cooking
Salt and Pepper
3 Tbs. Butter
½ Lb. Sliced Ham, cut into strips
1/8 Tsp. Thyme
1 Bay Leaf
2 Cloves
1/8 Tsp. Mace
2 Sprigs Parsley
1 Shallot, sliced

Cut chicken into serving pieces and remove bones carefully. Season chicken lightly with salt and pepper. Melt butter in a deep skillet or saucepan. Stir in remaining ingredients. Mix. Cook 1 or 2 minutes over low heat. Place chicken pieces in mixture, turning chicken to coat well. Cover pan and cook slowly about 1 hour, or until chicken is tender. Stir frequently. Uncover the pan for the last few minutes of cooking. Place chicken on warmed serving dish. In French restaurants the following sauce is usually poured over this chicken.

3 Tbs. Tarragon Vinegar
1 Tsp. Sugar
¼ Cup Chopped Mushrooms
1 Recipe White Sauce, seasoned
   to taste with onion
2 Egg Yolks

Mix vinegar, sugar and mushrooms into hot cream sauce over hot, not boiling, water. Stir slowly until blended. Beat egg yolks slightly. Stir into sauce. Pour hot sauce over chicken and serve at once. Makes 6 servings of chicken.

CALYPSO CHICKEN

1 - 3 to 4 Lb. Chicken, cut
   into serving pieces
1/3 Cup Olive Oil or Vegetable
   Oil
2 Cups Raw, Unprocessed Rice
1 Medium Onion, finely-chopped
1 Green Pepper, halved, seeded,
   deribbed and finely chopped
1 Garlic Clove, finely chopped
1 Small Fresh Green Chili, stemmed,
   seeded and finely chopped
½ Lb. Fresh Mushrooms, sliced
½ Tsp. Ground Saffron
1 Strip Lime Peel, about 2" long
1 Tbs. Strained Fresh Lime Juice
¼ Tsp. Angostura Bitters
1 Qt. Chicken Stock
Salt and Pepper
3 Tbs. Light Rum

Heat 3 tablespoons of oil in a skillet and saute' the chicken pieces until brown all over. Remove chicken to a heavy, flame-proof casserole. Add the rice, onion, garlic, green pepper and hot green chili to the oil remaining in the skillet; saute', stirring constantly, until the oil is absorbed. Be careful that the rice does not burn. Add rice mixture to the chicken in the casserole. Add remaining 2 tbs. of oil to the skillet and saute' the mushrooms over fairly high heat for 5 minutes. Add them to the casserole with the saffron, lime peel, lime juice, bitters and chicken stock. Add salt and pepper to taste. Bring to a boil; cover and simmer gently until the rice and chicken are tender and the liquid is absorbed--about 30 minutes. Add the rum and cook, uncovered, for 5 minutes longer. Makes 6 servings.

LEMON BBQ CHICKEN DRUMETTES

2 Tbs. Cooking Oil
2 Lbs. Chicken Wing Drumettes
1½ (8 oz.) Cans Tomato Sauce
¼ Cup Fresh Lemon Juice
¼ Cup Packed Brown Sugar
½ Tsp. Ground Cloves
½ Tsp. Ground Allspice
½ Tbs. Prepared Mustard
Dash Salt & Pepper
8 Lemon Slices

Brown drumettes in skillet, in 2 tbs. cooking oil. Lower heat to simmer for 15 minutes. Remove drumettes from skillet and place into rows in a casserole dish, cover with sauce. Bake at 350 degrees for 30 minutes.

Sauce: In saucepan, mix tomato sauce, brown sugar, lemon juice, spices and mustard. Stir until smooth. Cook over medium heat until bubbly. Pour over drumettes and bake for 30 minutes. Garnish with fresh cut lemon slices.

CHICKEN CURRY

1 - 4 Lb. Stewing Chicken,
   cut up
3 Cups Hot Water
2½ Tsp. Salt
3 Peppercorns
1 Onion, studded with 4 cloves
1 Small Carrot
2 Tbs. Butter
2/3 Cup Minced Onion
3 Tbs. Curry Powder
1 Cup Canned Coconut Milk
1/8 Tsp. Freshly-ground Black
   Pepper
3 Tbs. Chopped Preserved or
   Crystallized Ginger
¼ Tsp. Ground Cloves
1 Tsp. Chopped Fresh Mint, or
   ½ Tsp. Crushed Dried Mint
¼ Cup Lime Juice
½ Cup Heavy Cream

Place the chicken in a deep kettle or Dutch oven with the water, two teaspoons of salt, the peppercorns, onion and carrot. Cover and simmer for 1 hour. Remove the chicken from the broth and cool. Reserve the broth. Cut the chicken into small pieces, removing the skin and bones. Melt the butter in a large skillet. Add the onion and saute' until tender, but not brown. Stir in the curry powder. Gradually stir in the coconut milk and 1 cup of the strained chicken broth. Add the pepper, remaining salt, ginger, cloves and mint. Cover and cook over low heat for 30 minutes. Add the chicken pieces and continue cooking until the chicken is tender, about 30 minutes longer. Just before serving, stir in the lime juice and then the cream. Serve on hot rice with chutney and other condiments. Makes 6 servings.

SCALLOP AND MACARONI BAKE

1 Lb. Fresh or Frozen Sea Scallops
1 Tsp. Shrimp Spice
1 Slice Lemon
2 Cups Water
1 - 8 Oz. Pkg. Elbow Macaroni
3 Tbs. Butter or Margarine
1 Cup Coarse, Soft Bread Crumbs
   (2 slices)
2 Tbs. All-purpose Flour
1 Tsp. Dry Mustard
½ Tsp. Salt
2½ Cups Milk
¼ Cup Chili Sauce
1 - 4 Oz. Pkg. Shredded Cheddar
   Cheese
3 Small Tomatoes

Wash the fresh scallops under running cold water, or partly thaw frozen scallops. Cut into small pieces. Combine shrimp spice, lemon and water in a medium saucepan; heat to boiling. Add scallops. Cover and then remove pan from heat; let stand 5 minutes, then drain. Cook the macaroni in a kettle, following directions on the label. Drain and return to kettle.

While the macaroni is cooking, melt butter or margarine in a medium saucepan; toss 1 tablespoonful with the bread crumbs in a small bowl and set aside for topping. Stir flour, mustard and salt into the remaining butter in saucepan. Cook, stirring constantly, just until bubbly. Stir in milk; continue cooking and stirring until sauce thickens slightly and boils for 1 minute. Remove from heat and stir in chili sauce.

Pour sauce over the macaroni, then stir in the scallops. Spoon into a buttered 8-cup baking dish and sprinkle with cheese. Cut stem ends from tomatoes; halve tomatoes crosswise and sprinkle lightly with sugar, salt and pepper, if you wish. Place on top of macaroni mixture; sprinkle buttered crumbs around edge. Bake in 350°F. oven for 30 minutes, or until browned and bubbly. Makes 6 servings.

CRISPY BROILED SALMON STEAKS

½ Cup Butter or Margarine, melted
1 Tsp. Salt
1/8 Tsp. Paprika
6 Salmon Steaks, ¾" thick (6 to
   8 oz. each)
1 Cup Crushed Saltines
1 Cup Crushed Potato Chips
6 Lemon Wedges
6 Parsley Sprigs

Combine butter, salt and paprika. Wipe steaks with damp cloth. Dip each into butter mixture, then roll in combined saltines and potato chips. Arrange the steaks on lightly-greased broiler rack in broiler pan. Broil, 6 inches from heat, for 5 minutes. Turn and broil 5 to 8 minutes, or until fish flakes easily with a fork. Serve each steak with a lemon wedge and parsley sprig. Makes 6 servings.

FRIED PRAWNS
(Indonesian)

1½ Lbs. Large Prawns
Salt and Pepper
3 Eggs
Oil for Deep Frying
1 Tbs. Butter
1 Tbs. Flour
2 Tbs. Tomato Sauce
1 Tsp. Vinegar
1 Tsp. Soy Sauce
1 Tsp. Sugar
2 Large Onions, sliced and fried
   until brown
3 Potatoes, sliced thin and fried
   with the onions

Shell and wash the prawns, then rub them with salt and pepper. Dip the prawns into the lightly-beaten eggs, then fry them in hot oil until cooked.

To prepare the sauce, heat the butter in a pan and fry the flour brown. Put in the tomato sauce, vinegar, soy sauce, sugar, onions and a little water; add salt to taste. Last, put in the prawns and cook for a few minutes, till done. Serve with the potato chips.

BROILED STUFFED LOBSTER TAILS

8 Frozen Lobster Tails, about
   ½ lb. each
1/3 Cup Butter or Margarine
2 Tsp. Instant Green Onion
1/3 Cup Flour
1 Tsp. Salt
1/8 Tsp. Pepper
Few Grains Turmeric (if desired)
1½ Cups Milk
½ Cup Light Cream or Half-and-Half
1 Lb. Shrimp, cooked and peeled
1 - 7 Oz. Can Minced Clams
¾ Cup Soft, Buttered Crumbs

Cook the lobster tails in water according
to the directions on the package. Cool;
remove meat, leaving trimmed shells intact.
Cut lobster meat into bite-size pieces. Melt
butter; add instant green onion and cook 5
minutes over low heat. Blend in flour, salt,
pepper and turmeric. Combine milk and
cream; add all at once. Cook and stir over
medium heat until smooth and thick. Dice
shrimp, reserving 8 for garnish; combine with
lobster meat. Drain the clams and add the
diced shrimp, lobster and clams to sauce.
Refill shells. Sprinkle with buttered crumbs
and broil, with surface of food about 4"
below heat, until golden brown. Garnish
tops with whole shrimp and broil a few
seconds longer. Makes 8 servings.

STUFFED SHRIMP TEMPURA

1 Lb. Large Fresh Shrimp, in shells
1 - 8 Oz. Jar Mixed Candied Fruits
1 Cup Sifted All-purpose Flour
1 Tsp. Baking Powder
¼ Tsp. Salt
¾ Cup Milk
Vegetable Shortening or Oil
Flour (for coating)

Wash shrimp in colander under running cold
water. Peel off shells, but leave tails on.
Make a shallow cut down the back of each
shrimp with a sharp-pointed knife; lift out
the black line or sand vein, then make the
same cut deeper for a pocket for stuffing.

Dry shrimp well on paper towels. Chop
candied fruits very fine (should be paste-
like). Stuff about 1 teaspoonful into pocket
in each shrimp. Set aside any remaining
fruit. Combine the 1 cup sifted flour, baking powder and salt in a medium bowl;
beat in milk until smooth (batter will be
medium thick).

Melt enough vegetable shortening or pour
in vegetable oil to make a 2-inch depth in
an electric skillet or large heavy saucepan;
heat to 380°F. While shortening heats,
dip stuffed shrimp very carefully into some
additional flour in a pie plate to coat generously, then, holding each by the tail, dip
into batter, letting excess drip back into
the bowl. Fry, a few at a time, in hot fat,
turning once, 3 to 4 minutes, or until a
golden brown. Lift out with a slotted
spoon and drain on paper toweling. Serve
hot with mustard fruits (see recipe below)
and lemon wedges. Makes 6 servings.

Mustard Fruits:
2 Tbs. Butter or Margarine
2 Tbs. All-purpose Flour
½ Tsp. Sugar
¼ Tsp. Salt
¼ Tsp. Ground Ginger
1¼ Cups Milk
1 Tbs. Lemon Juice
1 Tbs. Chili Sauce
1 Tsp. Prepared Mustard

Melt butter or margarine over low heat in a
small saucepan; blend in flour, sugar, salt &
ginger. Cook, stirring constantly, just until
bubbly. Stir in milk and continue to cook
and stir until sauce thickens and boils for
1 minute. Remove from heat. Stir in the
reserved chopped candied fruits (from the
stuffing), the lemon juice, chili sauce, and
prepared mustard. Serve warm. Makes
about 1½ cups.

PHILIPPINE-STYLE SHRIMP

3 Lbs. Large, Fresh Shrimp, in
   shells
2¼ Cups Sifted All-purpose Flour
1 Tsp. Baking Powder
½ Tsp. Salt
2 Eggs
¼ Cup Lemon Juice
1¼ Cups Water
3 - 3½ Oz. Cans Flaked Coconut
Vegetable Oil or Shortening, for frying

Wash shrimp in cold water; peel off shells,
but leave tails on. Make a cut along underside of each with a sharp-tipped knife, cutting not quite through. Lift out the black
line, or sand vein. Press shrimp open until
they lie flat.

Sift flour, baking powder and salt into a
medium bowl. Beat eggs with lemon juice
and water until blended; pour over flour
mixture and beat until smooth. Holding
each shrimp by the tail, dip into batter,
letting any excess drip back into the bowl.
Sprinkle with coconut to coat well; pat in
firmly. Place on wax-paper-covered wire
racks and chill for at least 1 hour.

Melt enough vegetable oil or shortening in
a deep-fat fryer or heavy large saucepan to
fill two-thirds full. Heat to 350°F. Fry
shrimp, a few at a time, turning once, for
2 minutes, or until golden. Lift out with
a slotted spoon and drain on paper towels.
Makes 8 servings.

SOLE WITH ORANGE SAUCE

¾ Lb. Sole Fillets (or cod, flounder,
   or turbot)
2 Oranges
1 Lemon
¼ Cup Heavy Cream
3 Large Egg Yolks
½ Cup Dry White Wine
Salt and Pepper
Cayenne Pepper
8 Tbs. Butter
Flour, seasoned with salt and
   pepper
Chopped Fresh Parsley

Sprinkle the fish with the juice of half a
lemon and leave in a cool place while the
sauce is being made. Beat together in a
large heatproof bowl the cream, egg yolks,
wine and the juice of 1 orange and the
other half of the lemon. Cut the second
orange into wedges and set aside for garnish.

Set the bowl over a pan of simmering water,
or transfer the sauce to a heavy pan set directly over the heat if you are used to cooking egg-thickened sauces. Stir until the sauce
reaches the consistency of heavy cream or is
a little thicker. Season with salt, black pepper and cayenne pepper. Beat in 4 tablespoons of the butter. Reduce the heat so
that the sauce keeps warm without cooking
more.

Dip the sole fillets in the flour, and fry to
a golden brown in the remaining butter.
Arrange the sole on a platter with the
orange wedges tucked in between them,
and a little parsley scattered on top. Serve
the sauce separately in a warmed bowl.
Makes 6 servings.

TUNA SOUFFLE

¼ Cup Butter
1/3 Cup Flour
1¼ Cups Milk
4 Eggs, separated
1 Tsp. Chopped Onion
¼ Tsp. Salt
Dash of Pepper
2 Tbs. Chopped Parsley
7 Oz. Tin Tuna

Melt the butter and blend in flour until
smooth. Gradually add the milk and cook
over low heat until sauce boils and thickens,
stirring constantly to keep smooth. Thoroughly beat egg yolks. Add white sauce
gradually, stirring to keep smooth. Add the
onion, salt, pepper, parsley and flaked tuna.
Cool slightly. Beat egg whites until stiff;
fold carefully into first mixture. Turn into
an ungreased 6-cup mold or casserole. Bake
in a moderately slow oven (325°F.) about
one hour, or until puffy and high and delicately browned on top. Serve immediately.
Makes 5 servings.

FILLET OF SOLE with CRAB STUFFING

1 - 7 Oz. Can Crabmeat
6 Fresh Fillets of Sole (about
   2 lbs.), or 2 - 1 Lb. Pkgs.
   Frozen Fillet of Sole, partially
   thawed
3 Bay Leaves
2 Tsp. Salt
1 Cup Water
2 Tbs. Lemon Juice
6 Medium Carrots, peeled and
   cut into sticks
2 Cups Frozen Peas
3 Tbs. Flour
1 Egg
1 Lemon, cut into thin slices

Drain liquid from crabmeat into a cup & set aside for making sauce. Break crabmeat into large chunks, removing any bony tissue. Cut fresh or frozen fillets in half lengthwise. Set aside a few pieces of crabmeat for garnish. Place remaining crabmeat on thick end of each fillet, dividing evenly, and roll up, jelly-roll fashion. Fasten with wooden picks. Stand rolls in a medium-size frying pan. Add bay leaves, salt, water and 1 tablespoon of lemon juice. Cover and heat to boiling; simmer 15 minutes, or until fish flakes easily.

While fish is cooking, cook carrot stick, covered, in boiling salted water in a medium saucepan for 20 minutes, or until tender. Drain and keep hot. Cook peas, following directions on the label; drain & keep hot.

Remove fish fillets from liquid with a slotted spoon; keep fillets hot while making sauce. Pour liquid into a 2-cup measure; discard bay leaves. Add water, if necessary, to make 1½ cups liquid. Combine with ¼ cup of the reserved crab liquid in a small saucepan. Stir in flour, and cook, stirring constantly, until sauce thickens and boils for 1 minute. Beat egg with remaining 1 tablespoon of lemon juice in a small bowl; slowly stir in about 1 cup of the hot sauce, then stir back into remaining liquid in saucepan. Remove from heat. Place fish rolls on heated serving plates; spoon carrots and peas around them. Spoon hot sauce over all. Garnish with reserved pieces of crabmeat and a lemon slice. Makes 6 servings.

BAKED FISH with CRUSTY TOPPING

1 Lb. Fish Fillets
3 Tbs. Flour
½ Tsp. Salt
1/8 Tsp. Paprika
1/8 Tsp. Celery Salt
½ Tbs. Finely-cut Parsley
1 Cup Milk
4 Tbs. Butter or Margarine,
   melted
1 Cup Cracker Crumbs, or dry
   bread crumbs

Preheat oven to 375°F. Butter a 1½-quart shallow baking dish. Place fish in buttered baking dish. Sprinkle with flour, seasonings, and parsley. Combine milk, butter or margarine, and crumbs and spread over the fish. Bake 25 minutes, or until top is browned. Serve in baking dish or on a warmed platter. Makes 4 servings.

AVOCADO SHRIMP BOATS

2 Large Ripe Avocados
Lemon Juice
2 Medium Tomatoes
1 Tsp. Sugar
½ Tsp. Salt
Pepper
1/8 Tsp. Ground Turmeric
1 Tsp. Chopped Parsley
2 Green Onions, minced
Sprig of Fresh Mint, chopped fine
½ Tbs. Cider Vinegar
½ Tbs. Water
Dash of Cayenne
2 Tbs. French Dressing
1 Cup Cooked Shrimp
Watercress

Cut avocados in half and remove the seed. Scoop out pulp and dice. Rub the shells with lemon juice and set aside. Peel and chop the tomatoes. Mix all remaining ingredients except shrimp and watercress. Pour over tomatoes and avocado pieces. Mix carefully; fold in shrimp and pile mixture in avocado shells. Top with sprigs of watercress. Chill. Makes 4 servings.

POACHED HALIBUT STEAKS
with CURRY SAUCE

1½ to 2 Lbs. Halibut Steaks
Boiling Water
1 Slice of Onion
Parsley
Celery Tops
Salt
Peppercorns

Cut the halibut steaks into individual pieces. Cover with boiling water; season with slice of onion, some parsley, a few celery tops, salt and a few peppercorns. Simmer gently for 10 to 15 minutes, or until fish is tender. Remove fish to a hot platter and reserve the stock. Serve with curry sauce. Makes 3 to 4 servings.

Curry Sauce:

3 Tbs. Butter or Margarine
½ Onion, grated
1½ Tbs. Flour
2 to 4 Tsp. Curry Powder
½ Tsp. Salt
1¼ Cups Fish Stock (add water
     if necessary to make 1¼ cups)
¼ Cup Cream or Undiluted Evaporated
     Milk

Cook onion in butter for 1 to 2 minutes. Blend in flour and seasonings. Add fish stock gradually; cook until thickened, stirring constantly. Add cream before serving. Makes about 1½ cups of sauce.

MACKEREL COOKED IN
PORT WINE

8 Whole Mackerel (or cod, mullet, or
     whiting)
3 Tbs. Butter
1 Carrot, sliced
1 Large Onion, coarsely chopped
1 Bouquet Garni
Salt and Pepper
1 Cup Port Wine
1½ Cups Water
5 Leeks, white parts only, sliced
     crosswise (or use green onions)
1 Tbs. Flour

Clean the fish, remove heads and tails and set aside. Cut each fish into 3 crosswise pieces. Melt 1 tablespoon of the butter in a large saucepan and saute' the fish heads and tails for 5 minutes. Add the carrot, onion, bouquet garni, salt and pepper, port wine, and water. Cover and cook over medium heat for 15 minutes. Strain the stock; return stock to the cleaned pan and leave to simmer over low heat.

In another pan, saute' leeks or onions in 1 tablespoon of butter for 2 or 3 minutes. Add the leeks and pieces of mackerel to the simmering stock and let them simmer very gently, covered, for 10 minutes. With a slotted spoon, remove the fish and leeks to a warmed serving dish. Blend the remaining flour and butter together and stir this into the stock. Cook for a minute or two until lightly thickened. Pour the sauce over the fish and serve immediately. Makes 8 servings.

SHRIMP AND HAM WITH RICE

3 Cups Uncooked Rice
6 Cups Water
3 Tsp. Salt
1 Cup Butter
½ Tsp. Very-finely-minced
     Dry Red Chili Peppers
¾ Cup Finely-chopped Salted Peanuts
½ Cup Finely-chopped Onion
1½ Cups Cubed, Cooked Ham or
     1 Can (12 oz.) Luncheon Meat,
     cut into ½" cubes
1 Lb. Medium Prawns (20 to
     25), cooked, shelled and cleaned
Salt to taste

Cook the rice in boiling, salted water until tender but not mushy. Melt the butter in a small saucepan and stir in chili peppers (they should be almost powdery). Add peanuts and onions and cook slowly for 5 minutes. Pour over the rice and add the cubed meat and prawns. Toss together carefully with 2 forks. Taste for seasoning. Set aside to season and blend flavors. Place over low heat just before serving time; toss occasionally to prevent scorching. Makes 8 servings.

BAKED STUFFED SHRIMP

15 Frozen Deveined Large Shrimp
½ Cup Butter or Margarine, melted
1 Cup Fine, Dry Bread Crumbs
¼ Cup Grated Parmesan Cheese
½ Tsp. Salt
½ Tsp. Pepper
2 Tbs. Lemon Juice
2 Tbs. Dry Sherry

Place the frozen shrimp in an 8x8x2"
baking pan; brush each lightly with part
of melted butter or margarine. Heat in
slow oven (325°F.) while preparing the
crumb topping. Blend remaining butter
or margarine with bread crumbs, cheese,
salt, pepper, lemon juice and sherry in a
small bowl; spoon evenly over shrimp.
Bake for 25 minutes, or until topping is
golden. Makes 3 servings.

CREOLE JAMBALAYA

2 Tbs. Butter
1 Lb. Raw Smoked Ham, coarsely diced
2 Large Onions, chopped
2 Garlic Cloves, minced
1 Medium Green Pepper, cut up
2 - 1 Lb. 3 Oz. Cans Tomatoes,
    about 4-2/3 cups
3 Cups Meat Broth, or 2 Chicken
    Bouillon Cubes and 3 cups water
1 Bay Leaf, crushed
½ Tsp. Dried Thyme
½ Tsp. Chili Powder
¼ Tsp. Pepper
2 Cups Long-grain Rice
1 Lb. Fresh Shrimp, cooked, shelled
    and cleaned (or 1 - 12 Oz. Pkg.
    Frozen Shrimp, shelled, cleaned
    and cooked

Melt the butter in a top-of-the-stove casserole or a Dutch oven. Add ham, onion
and garlic. Cook until lightly browned.
Add remaining ingredients, except rice &
shrimp, and bring to a boil. Gradually
stir in rice. Cover and simmer for 30 min.,
or until rice is tender and liquid is absorbed. Add shrimp and more seasoning
if desired. Makes 6 servings.

MARDI GRAS SEAFOOD BAKE

1 Large Onion, chopped (1 cup)
1 Garlic Clove, minced
¼ Cup Olive Oil or Vegetable Oil
1½ Cups Uncooked Regular Rice
6 Strands Saffron, crushed
1 Vegetable Bouillon Cube
1½ Tsp. Salt
1 - 1 Lb. Can Tomatoes
1 - 8 Oz. Bottle Clam Juice
1 Cup Water
1 - 1 Lb. Pkg. Frozen Haddock or
    Flounder Fillets, thawed
1 - 11 Oz. Can Minced Clams
1 - 10 Oz. Pkg. Frozen Lobster Tails
3 Tbs. Butter or Margarine, melted
1 - 10 Oz. Pkg. Frozen Peas

Saute' onion and garlic in olive oil or vegetable oil until soft (use large frying pan); remove from pan. Stir rice and saffron into
drippings in pan; saute' stirring constantly,
until rice is golden. Return onion mixture
to pan, then stir in vegetable bouillon cube,
salt, tomatoes, clam juice and water. Heat
to boiling; remove from heat.

Set aside 3 of the fish fillets for use later.
Cut remaining fish fillets into bite-size
pieces; stir into rice mixture with clams &
liquid. Spoon into a deep 12-cup baking
dish; cover. Bake in 350°F. oven for 30
minutes.

While casserole is baking, cook lobster tails
in boiling, salted water, following directions
on package. Drain and cool until easy to
handle. With scissors, cut through the thick
membrane on underside of shell and remove.
Take out lobster meat by peeling hard shell
back with fingers of one hand and pulling
meat toward you with the other; split each
piece of meat in half. Roll up saved fish
fillets. Arrange lobster meat and rolled fillets on top of rice mixture in baking dish.
Brush with part of the melted butter or
margarine; cover and bake 30 minutes longer
or until rice and fish are tender. Cook the
peas, following directions on package; season with remaining melted butter or margarine. Spoon around edge of dish. Garnish fish rolls with pimiento, if desired.
Makes 6 servings.

DEVILED TUNA CASSEROLE

2 Tbs. Butter or Margarine
2 Tbs. All-purpose Flour
1 Tsp. Dry Mustard
½ Tsp. Salt
1½ Cups Milk
¼ Tsp. Liquid Red Pepper Seasoning
1 Tbs. Lemon Juice
1 - 7 Oz. Can Tuna, drained
   and flaked
¾ Cup Coarsely Crumbled Soda
   Crackers (9 crackers)
4 Hard-cooked Eggs, shelled
Parsley

Melt butter or margarine in medium saucepan; remove from heat and blend in flour,
mustard and salt. Slowly stir in the milk.
Cook, stirring constantly, until sauce thickens and boils for 1 minute. Stir in liquid
red pepper seasoning, lemon juice, tuna &
½ cup cracker crumbs (save remaining
crumbs and 1 egg for topping and garnish).
Chop remaining 3 eggs coarsely; stir into
tuna mixture and pour into a buttered
shallow 4-cup baking dish or 9" pie plate.
Sprinkle reserved cracker crumbs over top.
Bake in 350°F. oven for 20 minutes, or
until crumbs are golden. Quarter saved
egg lengthwise and arrange on casserole
to form a petal design. Center with a
sprig of parsley. Makes 4 servings.

SOLE AU GRATIN

4 Sole Fillets, ½ lb. each
12 Tbs. Butter
4 Tbs. Chopped Fresh Parsley
4 Scallions, white parts only,
   chopped
2 Cups Chopped Fresh Mushrooms
Salt and White Pepper
4 Tbs. Toasted Bread Crumbs
½ Cup Dry White Wine

Butter a large gratin dish and sprinkle the
base with half of the parsley, scallions and
mushrooms. Season with salt and white
pepper. Lay the fish on top. Cover with
the rest of the chopped ingredients and top
with the bread crumbs. Add the wine; melt
the remaining butter and sprinkle it over

the top. Bake in a preheated 425°F. oven
for 15 minutes, or until the fish is cooked
and the top is crisp and golden. At the end
of the cooking, the dish may be broiled
quickly if necessary to brown the top.
Makes 4 servings.

FINNISH FISH AND
POTATO SOUP

2 Lbs. Halibut Steaks or
   Turbot Fillets
6 Cups Regular Strength Chicken
   Broth
1 Lb. New Potatoes, peeled and cut
   into ½" cubes
1 Large Onion, finely chopped
1 Tsp. Dill Weed
1 Medium White or Red Onion
   (mild flavor), chopped
6 Tbs. Melted Butter
Salt and Pepper
Dill Weed

Place the fish in a saucepan and add broth.
Cover and bring to a boil over medium heat;
then reduce heat and simmer 2 to 4 minutes,
or until fish breaks easily when moved with
a fork. Set aside for at least 20 minutes (or
you can chill the fish in the broth to inten-
sify the fish flavor). Lift fish out of broth
with a slotted spoon. Remove and discard
any skin and bones; cut fish into bite-size
chunks. Return saucepan with broth to high
heat. Add potatoes, the chopped onion, and
1 teaspoon of dill weed. Boil, covered, for
about 10 minutes, or until potatoes are tender enough to mash. Add fish and heat thoroughly. Ladle soup into bowls; sprinkle each
serving with chopped, uncooked onion, salt
and pepper to taste, melted butter, and an
additional sprinkling of dill weed. Makes
5 to 6 servings.

FINNAN HADDIE

2 Lbs. Finnan Haddie
2 Cups Water
2 Cups Milk
1 Green Pepper, cut fine
8 Onions, peeled and chopped
½ Cup Butter or Margarine
½ Cup Flour
2½ Cups Light Cream
2 Cups Poaching Liquid
White Pepper
½ Cup Buttered Crumbs

Soak finnan haddie in combined water and milk for about 2 hrs. Simmer fish gently in same liquid 15 minutes. Drain fish and save the liquid. Preheat oven to 400°F. Saute' green pepper and onions in butter or margarine in a 2-quart saucepan until onion is transparent. Stir flour in slowly until smooth. Add cream, stirring constantly. Add 2 cups of poaching liquid. Cook, still stirring, until sauce is smooth and thick. Add flaked fish and a quick grind of pepper. Pour mixture into 2½-quart baking dish. Cover with crumbs & bake 20 minutes, or until top is browned. Serve hot. Makes 6 servings. Serve on thin toast slices.

JELLIED FISH WITH LEMON
(Egyptian-style)

2½ Lbs. Fish Steaks (bass, cod
    or halibut)
5 Tbs. Olive Oil
2 Garlic Cloves, chopped
1 Quart Water
¾ Cup Fresh Lemon Juice
2 Tsp. Salt
Pepper
1 Tsp. Curry Powder (optional)
5 Tbs. Chopped Fresh Parsley

Heat the oil in a large pan and fry the garlic in it. Add the water, lemon juice, seasonings and parsley. Add the steaks. Simmer slowly for 30 minutes. Transfer the fish and the liquid to a deep serving dish. Serve the fish cold in its jelly. Makes 6 to 8 servings.

ARMENIAN ROCKFISH

1 Medium Onion, sliced
½ Clove Garlic, mashed or minced
1½ Tbs. Olive Oil
1 Cup Water
1 - 1 Lb. 4 Oz. Can Solid Pack
    Tomatoes
1 Tsp. Salt
½ Tsp. Pepper
1 Cup Crabmeat, fresh or canned
1½ Lbs. Rockfish Fillets

In a heavy kettle, saute' onion and garlic in olive oil until golden brown, then add water, tomatoes, salt and pepper, and simmer for 20 minutes. Drop in crabmeat & continue cooking for 10 minutes. Cut fillets in thin strips, then drop into tomato mixture and simmer very slowly for 20 minutes. To avoid breaking up fish, do not stir the mixture, but shake pan occasionally. Serve immediately. Makes 6 servings.

INDIAN BROILED SHRIMP

1 Lb. Raw Shrimp, shelled and
    deveined
1 Cup Boiling Water
1 Tsp. Salt
1 Tsp. Ground Coriander
½ Small Onion, minced
8 Peppercorns
¼ Cup Cooking Oil
1 Tsp. Salt
½ Tsp. Ground Cuminseed
1 Tsp. Ground Turmeric
1 Tbs. Fresh Lemon Juice or
    Lime Juice
1 Large Lemon or Lime, cut
    into wedges

Combine shrimp, boiling water, salt, coriander, onion and peppercorns in saucepan. Bring to a boil. Cook for 2 to 3 minutes, or until shrimp just begin to turn pink. Remove from water; reserve. Heat oil in skillet. Remove from heat. Stir in salt, cuminseed, turmeric and lemon juice.

Add shrimp and toss to coat with mixture. Place shrimp in shallow baking pan. Broil under medium heat for about 5 min., or until shrimp are pink and slightly browned on the edges. Serve with lemon or lime wedges. Makes 4 to 6 servings.

SALMON LOAF

½ Cup Buttered Crumbs
1 - 1 Lb. Can Salmon
Dash of Pepper
1 Tbs. Chopped Parsley
2 Eggs, beaten
1 Tsp. Lemon Juice
½ Tsp. Sage
1 Tbs. Melted Butter
½ Cup Milk
½ Tsp. Salt
2 Tsp. Chopped Onion

Combine ingredients in order given. Pack firmly into a buttered loaf pan and bake in a 350°F. oven for 30 to 40 minutes.

CRAB FU YUNG

1 Cup Crabmeat
1 Cup Bean Sprouts
½ Cup Shredded Onion
½ Cup Finely-sliced Celery
3 Tbs. Cooking Oil
6 Eggs
1 Tbs. Soy Sauce
1 Tbs. Cornstarch
1 Tsp. Salt
Dash of Pepper
Sauce (see recipe below)

If using canned bean sprouts, rinse and drain first. Put crabmeat and bean sprouts into a large bowl. To cut onion into shreds, cut it into halves from top to bottom. Put on cutting board, cut side down, and finely slice with the grain of the onion, or from top to bottom. Saute' onion and celery in oil until limp (about 5 min.). Add to crabmeat.

Beat the eggs, add soy sauce, cornstarch, salt and pepper. Pour over crabmeat and vegetables and mix thoroughly. Put 1 tbs. of mixture on greased griddle or skillet and brown. Turn and brown on other side. Keep hot until all are cooked. Pour sauce over top. Makes 4 servings.

Sauce:

Cook until thick ½ cup water, 2 teaspoons sherry, 1 tablespoon soy sauce, and 2 teaspoons cornstarch.

SCALLOPS WITH RICE
(From the Mideast)

1 Large Onion, finely chopped
¼ Cup Butter
2 Lbs. Scallops
1 Cup Uncooked Rice
2 Tbs. Olive Oil
Water
1½ Tsp. Salt
Parsley

Saute' onion in butter until golden. Wash scallops and add. Simmer for 15 minutes, turning occasionally. Brown rice in olive oil until golden. Put into a 2-quart casserole. Drain the juice from the scallops and add water to make 2½ cups. Add salt and pour over rice. Bake, covered, in a hot oven (400°F.), preheated, for 20 minutes. Stir in scallops and onion and bake for 10 minutes longer. Sprinkle with chopped parsley. Makes 6 to 8 servings.

PORTUGUESE STUFFED SOLE

1 Large Sole
½ Cup Chopped Cooked Bacon or Ham
1 Onion, diced
1 Tbs. Olive Oil
1 Tbs. Melted Butter
Salt and Pepper to taste
2 Egg Yolks, beaten
Bread Crumbs
2 Tbs. Port
1 Tbs. Fresh Lemon Juice
Mashed Potatoes
Parsley

Skin sole and remove backbone. Fill space with bacon. Put diced onion and fish in a flat casserole which has been spread with olive oil. Pour melted butter over fish. Season with salt and pepper. Cover fish with beaten egg yolks, then sprinkle with bread crumbs. Add wine and lemon juice. Bake in moderate oven (375°F.), preheated, for about 30 minutes. Border with mashed potatoes or potato chips. Bake for about 5 minutes longer. Garnish with parsley. Makes 3 or 4 servings.

Note: As a variation, chopped shrimp, clams, or scallops can be used for the filling.

CHINESE VEAL

1 Lb. Veal Shoulder
1 Tbs. Butter or Margarine
2 Cups Shredded Green Cabbage
1 Cup Diced Green Pepper
2 Cups Diced Celery
2 Chicken Bouillon Cubes
2 Cups Hot Water
2 Tbs. Cornstarch
2 Tbs. Soy Sauce
1½ Tbs. Dark Molasses
1 Tbs. Bead Molasses
1 Tsp. Vinegar
1 Tsp. Salt
½ Cup Water
2 Large Tomatoes, cubed
3 to 4 Cups Cooked Rice
   (or Chinese noodles)
¼ Cup Blanched Almonds

Wipe meat with a damp cloth. Cut into 1" cubes and saute' in hot butter in a ten-inch heavy skillet for 10 minutes. Add cabbage, green pepper, celery, and the bouillon cubes dissolved in the hot water. Simmer slowly uncovered for 15 minutes. Make a thin paste of the cornstarch and the next 6 ingredients and add it to meat mixture. Stir gently until mixture boils and thickens. Add tomatoes and stir carefully to mix them through the meat and vegetables without breaking them up. Continue to cook for 1 minute longer. Serve at once on hot rice or noodles and garnish with the almonds. Makes 4 servings.

LAMB SHOULDER CHOPS
(Creole Style)

2½ Lbs. Lamb Chops
1½ Tbs. Fat
2 Tsp. Salt
1/3 Cup Sliced Onion
1½ Cups Tomato Juice
2 Medium Carrots, sliced
1 Tsp. Chopped Parsley

Wipe the chops clean with a damp cloth and brown them slowly on both sides in the fat. Add remaining ingredients; cover closely and simmer until tender (about 1½ hours). Makes 5 or 6 servings.

RUMAKI
(Chicken Livers)

16 Chicken Livers
1 Cup Soy Sauce
½ Cup Cream Sherry
16 Slices Bacon, halved crosswise

Wash chicken livers; dry well on paper towels. Cut each liver in half, removing any stringy portion. Turn livers into a large bowl. Combine soy sauce and sherry; mix well. Pour over chicken livers; toss lightly to mix well. Wrap each halved chicken liver with half a bacon slice; secure with wooden pick. Arrange on broiler rack in broiler pan. Brush each side with soy mixture. Broil, 3 inches from heat, for 2 or 3 minutes on each side, turning once or twice, until bacon is crisp and livers are cooked through. Makes 32.

PERUVIAN LAMB STEW

1 - 2 Lb. Lamb Shoulder
Boiling Broth
Juice of 1 Lemon
2 Tbs. Minced Onion
1 Clove Garlic, crushed
1/8 Tsp. Ground Allspice
½ Tsp. Pepper
3 Tbs. Fat
¾ Tsp. Salt
4 Cups Cooked, Seasoned Lima
   Beans (fresh, frozen or canned)

Trim bones and skin from meat; cut meat into 2" pieces. Prepare broth from bones and trimmings. Place meat in a heavy pan with lemon juice, onion, garlic, allspice & pepper; let stand in this marinade for about 2 hours. Remove meat, reserving marinade mixture. Drain meat; brown well in hot fat in a heavy skillet. Place meat in a stew pot; add marinade, then boiling broth to cover ¾ of the meat. Cover pot and bake in a 275°F. oven until tender, adding salt at the end of the first hour. When meat is done, remove it from the broth. Skim off all fat. Add limas; simmer on top of stove for about 15 minutes. If gravy is not thick enough, blend 1 tbs. fat with 1 tbs. flour; stir into gravy. Makes 6 to 8 servings.

LIVER LYONNAISE

1 Lb. Sliced Liver
3 Tbs. Flour
1 Tsp. Salt
1/8 Tsp. Pepper
3 Tbs. Fat
3½ Cups Cubed Potatoes
1 Cup Thinly-sliced Onions
1 Can Condensed Cream of Celery
   Soup
½ Cup Milk
1 Tsp. Salt
1/8 Tsp. Pepper

Cut liver into 1½" cubes. Blend flour, 1 tsp. salt and 1/8 tsp. pepper together. Roll the liver pieces in the flour mixture. Brown on all sides in hot fat in a heavy skillet; remove liver from the pan. Fry potatoes and onions in remaining fat until lightly browned and the potatoes are tender. Alternate liver and potato-onion mixture in a 1½-quart baking dish. Combine soup, milk, 1 tsp. salt and 1/8 tsp. pepper and pour over the contents of the baking dish. Cover and bake in a moderate oven, 375°F., for 40 minutes, or until done. Makes 6 servings.

LEG OF LAMB, CREOLE

½ Cup Chili Sauce
2 Tbs. Cider Vinegar
½ Cup Dry Red Wine
2 Tbs. Olive Oil
1 Cup Beef Bouillon
1 Tbs. Sugar
1 Tsp. Salt
½ Tsp. Pepper
1 Bay Leaf
2 Onions, minced
2 Garlic Cloves, minced
8 Lb. Leg of Lamb

Mix all ingredients, except lamb. Pour the sauce over the meat. Let stand in refrigerator for at least 6 hours, basting meat occationally with the sauce. Put lamb on a rack in roasting pan. Add sauce and roast, uncovered, in preheated 325°F. oven for about 4 hours, basting occasionally with the sauce. Add boiling water if liquid evaporates. Remove lamb to a hot platter and thicken gravy. Makes 8 to 10 servings.

CONTINENTAL VEAL PIE

1½ Lbs. Veal Shoulder, cut into
   1" cubes
3 Tbs. All-purpose Flour
3 Tbs. Olive Oil or Vegetable Oil
2 Italian Hot Sausages, sliced ½" thick
12 Small White Onions, peeled
1 Envelope Spaghetti Sauce Mix, with
   tomato (2¼ oz. size)
3 Cups Water
12 Small Carrots, pared and cut in
   sticks
6 Medium Zucchini, trimmed and cut
   into sticks
¼ Lb. Fresh Mushrooms, sliced (or
   1 - 4 Oz. Can Sliced Mushrooms)
1 Pkg. Pie Crust Mix
1 Egg
1 Tbs. Milk
Liquid Red Pepper Seasoning
   (a few drops)

Put flour into a paper bag. Shake veal, a few pieces at a time, in flour to coat evenly. Brown quickly in olive oil or vegetable oil in large heavy kettle or Dutch oven; push to one side. Brown sausages in same kettle; push to one side. Add onions and brown lightly. Combine spaghetti sauce mix and water in 4-cup measure (mix has tomato right in it, so all you need to add is the water). Stir into kettle; cover and simmer for 1½ hours, or until veal is tender.

Cook carrots and zucchini sticks together in boiling salted water in large saucepan for 15 minutes, or just until tender; drain well. Mound veal mixture, cooked vegetables, and mushrooms in an 8-cup baking dish. Prepare pie crust mix, following label directions, or make pastry from your own favorite one-crust recipe. Roll out on lightly floured pastry cloth or board to a circle 3" larger than baking dish. Cut a 4" cross in center. Fold points of cross back so gravy won't darken pastry. Lay circle over rolling pin and transfer to baking dish. Trim overhang to 1"; fold under flush with rim and flute. Bake at 425°F. for 30 minutes. Makes 6 servings.

CURRIED LAMB

1½ Lbs. Lean Lamb, cut into
   1" cubes
2 Tbs. Shortening
1 Tbs. Curry Powder
1 Medium Onion, minced
1 Garlic Clove, minced
1 Apple, peeled and chopped
1½ Cups Beef Bouillon
¼ Cup Cream

Saute' the lamb in shortening until well-
browned on all sides; add curry powder,
onion and garlic. Cook until onion is soft.
Add apple and bouillon. Simmer, covered,
for 1½ hours, or until meat is tender. Stir
in cream and heat through. Makes 6
servings.

ROMAN VEAL SCALLOPINI

8 Tbs. Butter or Margarine
¾ Lb. Mushrooms, sliced
1 Small Onion, finely chopped
1 Clove Garlic, peeled
3 Cups Coarsely-chopped Peeled
   Fresh Tomatoes (about 2 lbs.)
2/3 Cup Dry White Wine
Salt
¼ Tsp. Dried Tarragon Leaves, crushed
12 Thin Veal Scallops (1½ lbs.)
1/8 Tsp. Pepper
Grated Parmesan Cheese

In 5 tablespoons of hot butter, in skillet,
saute' mushrooms until golden-brown--
about 5 minutes. Add onion and garlic,
and cook about 5 minutes, or until onion
is golden. Add tomatoes, wine, ¾ teaspoon salt, and the tarragon, stirring until well blended. Reduce heat; simmer,
covered and stirring occasionally, 30 min.

Meanwhile, wipe veal with damp paper
towels. Sprinkle with ½ teaspoon salt
and the pepper. Heat 3 tablespoons butter in another skillet. Add veal, a few
pieces at a time, and cook until lightly
browned on both sides--about 5 minutes.
Remove, and keep warm. Return veal to
skillet. Remove garlic from sauce. Pour
sauce over veal; simmer, covered, for 5
minutes. Sprinkle with Parmesan cheese.
Makes 6 servings.

LAMB DAUBE

1 Cup Dry Red Wine
2/3 Cup Olive Oil
1 Tbs. Salt
1 Tsp. Pepper
1 Tsp. Dried Oregano
1 Tsp. Dried Rosemary
1 Bay Leaf
2 Cloves
1 Carrot, cut up
4 Garlic Cloves
1 Shoulder of Lamb (4 to 5 lbs.),
   boned and rolled
2 Onions, stuck with 2 cloves
1 Tsp. Dried Tarragon
1 Green Pepper, finely sliced
3 Tbs. Tomato Paste
24 Black Olives, pitted

Place first 9 ingredients for marinade in
a pot and bring to a boil. Lower heat &
simmer for 5 minutes. Remove from heat
and cool. Cut garlic into slivers. Make
tiny slits in the flesh of the meat and
insert garlic slivers. Soak lamb in marinade for 12 to 24 hours. When ready to
cook, put meat in braising pan or heavy
Dutch oven and add onions, tarragon,
and green pepper. Strain marinade and
pour over meat. Cover pot and cook in
preheated moderate oven (350°F.) for
1 hour. Reduce heat to slow oven
(300°F.), and add tomato paste and
olives. Add additional seasoning if desired. Cook for 45 to 60 minutes, or
until lamb is tender. Remove meat.
Strain sauce, chill and skim off fat.
Reheat lamb, covered, in sauce. Slice
meat; serve sauce separately. Makes 8
servings.

HARVEST VEGETABLE CASSEROLE

¼ Cup Salad Oil
4 Large Onions, sliced & separated into rings
3 Large Green Peppers, cut into 1" strips
1 Cup Barley
2 Envelopes Beef-flavored Bouillon
4 Large Carrots, cut into chunks
4 Large Tomatoes, peeled and quartered
3 Medium Zucchini, cut into chunks
1½ Lbs. Green Beans, each cut in half
1 - 10 Oz. Pkg. Frozen Peas
1 Small Head Cauliflower, separated into flowerets
¼ Cup Lemon Juice
3 Cloves Garlic, crushed
2 Tbs. Salt
2 Tsp. Paprika
½ Tsp. Pepper
½ Cup Parsley, chopped
Water

In a 12" skillet, over medium heat, in hot oil, cook onions, green peppers until browned, about 10 minutes, stirring often.

In each of two 13"x9" baking dishes, or two 3½ qt. casseroles, combine 1 cup water, ½ cup barley and 1 envelope of bouillon. Top each with half the carrots, tomatoes, zucchini, green beans, peas, cauliflower, then onion mixture.

In a cup combine lemon juice, garlic. Pour half into each casserole. Sprinkle vegetables with salt, paprika and pepper. Cover casseroles. Bake one casserole in a 400 degree oven only 1 hr.; freeze and serve later. Bake second casserole 1½ hrs. or until barley is tender; stir in ¼ cup parsley and serve. Each casserole makes 12 servings.

To freeze and serve up to 1 month later; Stir remaining parsley into casserole to freeze. Cool at room temperature until easy to handle. Cover; freeze. To serve, thaw overnight in refrigerator. Bake, covered, in a 350 degree oven for 1½ hrs. or until hot.

BAKED STUFFED EGGPLANT

1 - 2 Lb. Eggplant
2 Cups Chopped, Cooked Meat
1 Cup Fresh or Canned Tomatoes
2 Tbs. Chopped Onion
1 Egg
1 Tsp. Sugar
1 Cup Cooked Rice
2 Tbs. Butter
1 Tsp. Salt
Paprika to taste
Black Pepper to taste
½ Cup Buttered Crumbs

Cut eggplant in halves lengthwise and scoop out pulp, leaving shells about ¼" thick. Put shells into cold water. Combine chopped eggplant pulp with meat, tomato, onion, egg, sugar, rice, butter and seasonings. Heat until boiling. Drain shells and fill with hot mixture. Sprinkle bread crumbs over top and bake 1 hour in a moderate oven (350°F.). Serve on heated platter, cutting through eggplant, stuffing and all, for each serving. Makes 5 servings.

HARVARD GREEN OR WAX BEANS

3 to 4 Cups Water
¾ Tsp. Salt
1½ Lbs. Green or Wax Beans
3 to 4 Tbs. Sugar
3 Tsp. Cornstarch
3 Tbs. Cider Vinegar
Pimiento

Heat water to boiling; add salt and beans which have been washed, trimmed and cut into 1" lengths. Cook, uncovered, in rapidly-boiling water until tender--20 to 30 minutes. Drain, saving the cooking water. Mix the sugar and cornstarch. Measure ¾ cup of cooking water, add to cornstarch mixture and cook, stirring constantly until sauce boils and becomes clear. Add vinegar; pour over beans and let stand in warm place for about 20 minutes to blend flavors. Add a few strips of pimiento and reheat before serving. Makes 5 servings.

SWEET-POTATO BALLS

2½ Cups Mashed Canned or Cooked
   Sweet Potatoes (1 - 1 Lb. 2 Oz.
   Can or about 2 Lbs. fresh)
½ Tsp. Salt
Dash of Pepper
2 Tbs. Butter or Margarine, melted
1/3 Cup Honey
1 Tbs. Butter or Margarine
1 Cup Chopped Pecans.

Combine mashed sweet potatoes, salt, pepper, and 2 tbs. butter; chill for easier handling. Shape into 8 balls. Heat honey and 1 tbs. butter in a small, heavy skillet over high heat. When syrup is hot, remove from heat and add potato balls, one at a time. Spoon glaze over, coating completely. Roll in chopped nuts. Place balls so they do not touch each other in a greased shallow baking dish or pan. Bake in 350°F. oven for 20 to 25 minutes. Makes 4 servings.

SOUTHERN FRIED CABBAGE

1 Small Head Green Cabbage,
   cored and shredded
3 to 4 Tbs. Bacon Fat
2 Tsp. Red Pepper Flakes
Salt to taste

Heat the bacon fat in a skillet; toss in the cabbage and stir until it is glistening. Lower the heat and add the pepper flakes; season with salt to taste and continue cooking and turning the cabbage until it is tender-crisp. This will bake about 10 minutes. Makes 4 servings.

POTATO KUGEL

3 to 4 Medium Potatoes, peeled,
   grated and drained (about 3
   cups)
3 Eggs
1/3 Cup Potato Flour
½ Tsp. Baking Powder
1½ Tsp. Salt
1/8 Tsp. Pepper
3 Tbs. Grated Onion
4 Tbs. Butter, melted

In a large bowl, beat the eggs until they are thick. Stir in the potatoes, potato flour, baking powder, salt, pepper, onion and melted butter. Turn the mixture into a greased 1½-quart baking dish and bake in a preheated 350°F. oven for about 1 hour, or until browned. Serve the kugel hot. Serves 6 to 8.

ARTICHOKES WITH LAMB STUFFING

4 Whole Fresh Artichokes
1 Lb. Ground Lamb
¾ Cup Chopped Onion
2 Tbs. Salad Oil
½ Cup Fine Dry Bread Crumbs
¼ Cup Snipped Parsley
2 Eggs, beaten
¼ Tsp. Ground Nutmeg
¼ Tsp. Pepper
Sauterne Sauce (recipe below)

Wash the artichokes; cut off stem close to base. Cook in boiling salted water for 25 to 30 minutes, or till stalk can be pierced easily and leaf pulled out readily. Drain upside down. Cut off top third of leaves with kitchen shears; remove center leaves and chokes.

Brown lamb and onion in hot oil; drain. Add crumbs and next 4 ingredients, and ½ teaspoon of salt; mix well. Spread the artichoke leaves slightly; fill centers with meat mixture. Place in a 9x9x2" baking dish. Pour hot water around artichokes, to depth of 1". Bake, uncovered, at 375° F. for 35 minutes.

Sauterne Sauce:
¼ Cup Sauterne
1 Tbs. Instant Minced Onion
¾ Cup Mayonnaise
2 Tbs. Snipped Parsley
1 Tbs. Lemon Juice

Combine sauterne with instant minced onion and let stand for 10 minutes. Add mayonnaise, snipped parsley, and lemon juice and mix well. Cook and stir until hot; do not boil. Makes 4 servings.

GREEN BEANS with CHEESE TOPPING

1 - 9 Oz. Pkg. Frozen Green Beans
 (French cut)
1 Small Onion, peeled and chopped
3 Tbs. Butter or Margarine
¼ Cup Flour
2 Cups Milk
2 Tsp. Salt
1/8 Tsp. Pepper
¼ Tsp. Thyme
¼ Tsp. Savory
½ Tsp. Accent
1 Tbs. Finely-cut Parsley
6 Hard-cooked Eggs
½ Cup Grated Swiss or Processed
 Cheese
¼ Cup Bread Crumbs

Cook frozen beans as directed on package. Drain and set aside. Cook onion in 2 tbs. of butter or margarine until golden. Stir in flour until smooth. Add milk gradually, stirring. Cook, stirring constantly, until bubbly. Season with salt, pepper, herbs, Accent and parsley. Remove from heat. Cut eggs in slices. Mix with green beans in 1½-quart baking dish. Pour parsley sauce over mixture. Sprinkle with cheese and crumbs. Dot with remaining 1 tbs. butter or margarine. Bake 30 minutes in preheated 350°F. oven (until brown). Makes 4 servings.

TOMATO-CELERY STEW

½ Cup Chopped Onion
¼ Cup Chopped Green Pepper
1 Small Garlic Clove, minced
3 Tbs. Butter or Margarine
¾ Lb. Celery, cut diagonally in
 1" pieces
2 - 16 Oz. Cans Tomatoes, undrained
1 Tsp. Sugar
¼ Tsp. Crushed Thyme
1/8 Tsp. Pepper
1 Vegetable Bouillon Cube
2 Tbs. Minced Parsley
½ Cup Uncooked Rice
1 Lb. Canned Ham, cut into
 short strips

Cook onion, green pepper and garlic in butter in a large skillet until onion is soft, about 2 minutes; stir occasionally. Put this mixture into an electric cooker. Add celery, tomatoes, sugar, thyme, pepper, bouillon cube, parsley and rice. Cover and cook on low for 4 to 6 hours. Add ham and heat thoroughly. Sprinkle shredded Parmesan cheese over top before serving. Makes 6 servings.

HAM AND BROCCOLI CASSEROLE

1 Cup Uncooked Regular Rice
2 - 10 Oz. Pkgs. Frozen Broccoli
 Spears
6 Tbs. Butter or Margarine
2 Cups Fresh Bread Crumbs
 (4 slices)
2 Large Onions, chopped fine
 (2 cups)
3 Tbs. All-purpose Flour
1 Tsp. Salt
¼ Tsp. Pepper
3 Cups Milk
4 Cups Cubed Cooked Ham
 (1½ lbs.)
1 - 8 Oz. Pkg. Sliced Process
 American Cheese

Cook the rice, following directions on the label. Spoon into a greased refrigerator-to-oven baking dish, 13x9x2". Cook the broccoli, following directions on the package; drain well. Place in a single layer over the rice in baking dish. Melt butter or margarine in a large frying pan; measure out 2 tablespoons of butter and sprinkle over bread crumbs in a small bowl; set aside. Stir onions into remaining butter in frying pan; saute' until soft. Stir in flour, salt and pepper; cook, stirring constantly, until bubbly. Stir in milk and continue cooking and stirring until sauce thickens and boils 1 minute. Stir in ham; heat again just until bubbly; pour over layers in baking dish. Place cheese slices over sauce; sprinkle buttered bread crumbs over all. Cover and chill in refrigerator. About 45 minutes before serving time, uncover baking dish and place in 350°F. oven; bake 45 minutes, or until bubbly and crumb topping is golden. Makes 8 servings.

CRUNCHY WALNUT CARROTS

5 Cups Carrot Sticks (use young
    carrots and cut sticks 3" long)
1½ Cups Water
½ Tsp. Salt
½ Cup Melted Butter or Margarine
2 Tsp. Honey
½ Tsp. Salt
¼ Tsp. Coarse Pepper
2 Tbs. Lemon Juice
¼ Tsp. Grated Lemon Peel
½ Cup Coarsely-broken Walnuts

Cook carrots in water with ½ teaspoon of
salt added, just until tender. Drain well.
While carrots are cooking, heat remaining
ingredients, except the walnuts. Pour this
topping over the hot carrots. Toss in the
walnuts. Makes 8 servings.

WYOMING BASQUE POTATOES

1 Medium-size Onion, chopped
    (about ½ cup)
1 Small Garlic Clove, crushed
2 Tbs. Olive Oil
¾ Cup Chopped Parsley
¼ Cup Chopped Pimiento
1 Tsp. Salt
1/8 Tsp. Pepper
1 Envelope Instant Chicken Broth
    or 1 Tsp. Granulated Chicken
    Bouillon
1 Cup Water
6 Medium Potatoes (about 3 lbs.)

Saute' onion and garlic in olive oil until
soft. Use a medium skillet. Stir in parsley,
pimiento, salt, pepper, chicken broth and
water. Remove from heat.

Pare potatoes and slice thin (you should
have about 6 cups). Layer potato slices
in the broth in the skillet; heat to boiling.
Reduce heat, cover and simmer for about
20 minutes, or until tender. Remove the
potatoes with a slotted spoon to a heated
serving dish. Spoon remaining cooking
liquid over potatoes. Makes 8 servings.

EGGPLANT SUPREME

¼ Cup Butter or Margarine
3 Medium Onions, sliced
1 Small Eggplant (1 Lb.), peeled
    and sliced
2 Eggs
1 Tbs. Cold Water
½ Cup Fine Dry Bread Crumbs

Sauce:

1 Tsp. Paprika
1 Tsp. Curry Powder
1 Tsp. Mustard
½ Tsp. Horseradish
½ Tsp. Celery Seed
½ Tsp. Salt
½ Cup French Dressing

Melt 2 tablespoons of butter in a skillet.
Add the onions and saute' until soft (3
to 5 minutes). Remove onions. Add
the rest of the butter, and the eggplant
which has been dipped in one beaten
egg diluted with the water and then in
bread crumbs. Brown delicately on both
sides. Add onions again and the thoroughly blended ingredients of the sauce,
combined with the other beaten egg.
Cover and simmer slowly for 20 minutes.
Arrange slices on a hot platter. Makes
5 servings.

CABBAGE-FILLED PEPPERS

6 Sweet Red Peppers
½ Head Cabbage, finely cut
1½ Tsp. Salt
1 Tbs. Yellow Mustard Seed
2 Cups Cider Vinegar

Remove stems and cut off tops of the peppers. Remove seeds without breaking the
shell. Add salt and mustard seed to the cabbage, mixing thoroughly. Spoon mixture
into peppers, pressing it in tightly. Place
tops on pepper shells and fasten down with
wooden picks. Place upright in a stone jar
and cover with cold vinegar. Cover jar and
store in a cool place (several months if desired). Makes 6 servings.

SPINACH SOUP with DUMPLINGS

Soup:
6 Cups Chicken Stock
1/3 Cup Chinese Mushrooms
½ Chicken Breast
½ Egg White, slightly beaten
1 Lb. Fresh Spinach
1/3 Cup Water Chestnuts
¼ Tsp. White Pepper,
   freshly ground
Salt to taste

Dumplings:
½ Lb. Shrimp
¼ Cup Ham, minced
1 Scallion, chopped (use both
   white and green parts)
1 Egg, slightly beaten
2 Tbs. Water Chestnut Powder
   (obtain from oriental food store)
½ Tsp. Salt
1 Tsp. Sugar
2 Tsp. Soy Sauce

Shell, devein, wash, drain, dry and mince the shrimp. Mince the ham; chop scallion. Blend together thoroughly the egg, water chestnut powder, salt, sugar and soy sauce. Combine with minced ham, shrimp and chopped scallion. Bring chicken stock to a boil; turn flame to low and drop dumpling mixture, one full teaspoon at a time, into the simmering chicken stock. The dumplings will float when they are done, but continue to let them simmer for 1 minute more to avoid any taste of the water chestnut powder. Remove the dumplings from the soup with a slotted spoon and set aside.

Rinse the mushrooms; cover with warm water and soak for 30 to 60 minutes, or until soft. Stem and dice. Add mushroom stock to chicken stock. Bone the chicken breast and freeze partially; cut chicken breast into 1x1x¼" slices. Mix chicken slices with egg white. Wash spinach and cut into 1½" pieces. Peel water chestnuts and slice each one in 3 or 4 pieces.

Bring chicken stock to a boil over high heat in a saucepan. Add mushroom pieces and boil for 2 minutes. Add the spinach and stir with a wooden spoon.

When stock returns to a boil, add chicken pieces and mix well in a figure-eight motion to prevent chicken pieces from sticking together. When stock returns to a boil, add water chestnuts, dumplings and pepper. Add salt, if necessary. When soup returns to a boil again, turn off the flame. Pour into a soup tureen and serve immediately. Makes 6 servings.

VEGETABLE GOULASH

1 - 15 Oz. Can Kidney Beans,
   undrained
1½ Cups Fresh Corn Kernels
   (about 3 ears)
1 Cup Chopped Celery
1 Cup Chopped Onion
½ Cup Chopped Green Pepper
1 - 8 Oz. Can Tomato Sauce
1 Tsp. Brown Sugar
½ to ¾ Tsp. Chili Powder
1/8 Tsp. Pepper

Combine all ingredients in electric cooker. Cover and cook on high for 4 hours, or until vegetables are tender.

CELERY GRATIN WITH ALMONDS

3 Tbs. Butter or Margarine
3 Cups Thinly-sliced Raw Celery
1 Cup Shredded Blanched Almonds
3 Tbs. Flour
2 Cups Hot Milk
Salt and Pepper to taste
¼ Cup Grated Sharp Cheddar or
   Parmesan Cheese

Melt butter in heavy skillet. Add celery and almonds. Saute', covered, over low heat for 10 to 15 minutes, or until celery is tender. Blend in flour. Stir in hot milk gradually. Cook, stirring constantly, until sauce is smooth and thickened. Season with salt and pepper. Turn into greased 1-quart baking dish. Sprinkle with grated cheese. Bake in preheated hot oven (400° F.) until bubbly, or glaze briefly under hot broiler. Makes 4 to 6 servings.

INDIAN-STYLE MIXED VEGETABLES

¼ Cup Butter
1 Medium Onion, sliced
¼ Tsp. Ground Turmeric
½ Tsp. Summer Savory
1 Large Potato, peeled and cubed
1½ Cups Water
1 Small Head Cabbage, shredded
1 Small Cauliflower, cut into
    small pieces
1 Cup Fresh or Frozen Peas
2 Fresh Tomatoes, peeled and cut
    into wedges
1 Bunch Spinach, washed and stems
    removed
Salt to taste

Melt the butter in a 5-quart kettle; add the onion, turmeric and savory. Saute' onion until it is limp--about 5 minutes. Add the potato and water. Cover and cook about 5 minutes. Add the cabbage and cauliflower and simmer for about 5 minutes. Add peas, tomatoes and spinach; cook about 3 to 5 minutes longer. Add salt to taste and stir gently. Transfer to serving bowl and keep warm on buffet table. Makes 12 servings.

POTLUCK CASSEROLE

2 - 10 Oz. Pkgs. Frozen Asparagus
1 Cup Chopped Onion
¼ Cup Butter or Margarine
6 Tbs. Flour
3 Cups Milk
2 Tsp. Salt
¼ Tsp. Pepper
4 Hard-cooked Eggs, sliced
½ Cup Shredded Cheddar Cheese
½ Cup Dry Bread Crumbs

Cook asparagus just until barely tender, according to directions on package. Drain well. In a large skillet, cook onion in butter until tender but not brown. Stir in the flour. Add milk and cook, stirring constantly, until thickened. Mix in salt, pepper, eggs and asparagus. Turn into a 2-quart casserole. Top with cheese and crumbs. Bake in a moderate oven, 350°F., for about 30 minutes, until hot and bubbly. Makes 8 servings.

CABBAGE PATCH STEW

½ Lb. Ground Beef
2 Tbs. Fat
2 Medium Onions, sliced thin
1 Cup Shredded Cabbage
½ Cup Diced Celery
1 - 1 Lb. Can Red Kidney Beans
1 Cup Cooked Tomatoes
Salt and Pepper to taste
1 Tsp. Chili Powder
Hot Mashed Potatoes

Brown the ground beef in hot fat over medium heat; add onions, cabbage and celery. Cook until yellow. Add water to cover, about 2 cups. Simmer for 15 minutes. Add beans, tomatoes and seasonings; cook for 15 to 25 minutes longer. Serve in bowls topped with spoonfuls of mashed potato. Makes 6 servings.

CHINESE PEAS AND BEAN SPROUTS

2 Lbs. Chinese Peas (edible pod)
1 Lb. Fresh Bean Sprouts
1 Large Onion
½ Green Pepper
2 Stalks Celery
1 Slice Raw Ham, cut ¼" thick
2 Tbs. Soy Sauce
1 Tbs. Cornstarch
1 Cup Water
½ Tsp. Salt

Remove tips and strings from peas. If pods are large, cut them in half. Mix peas and bean sprouts. Cut onion, green pepper, and celery into small pieces (don't chop). Cut ham, including fat, into thin strips. Put ham into large kettle and fry a few minutes to bring out fat. Add onion, green pepper, and celery and cook until they are wilted slightly. Add the mixed peas and bean sprouts; cover and cook for 10 minutes, or until wilted. Mix together the soy sauce, cornstarch, water and salt. Pour this over the vegetables and cook a few minutes longer, stirring occasionally.
Serves 8 to 10 as a vegetable, 6 as a main dish.

POTATO KNISHES

2½ Cups Sifted All-purpose Flour
1 Tsp. Baking Powder
½ Tsp. Salt
2 Eggs
½ Cup Cooking Oil
2 Tbs. Water
Potato Filling (see recipe below)

Sift flour with baking powder and salt. Make a well in the center and add eggs, oil and water. Mix with the hands and then knead on lightly-floured board until smooth. Roll out dough on a lightly floured board as thin as possible. Cut into 3" rounds. Place 1 tablespoon of potato filling on each round. Moisten edges of dough and pull together to enclose filling completely and to form a ball. Place, pinched-side down, on an oiled cookie sheet. Bake in preheated 350°F. oven for 35 minutes, or until brown. Makes about 2 dozen.

Potato Filling:

1 Cup Chopped Onion
1/3 Cup Chicken Fat
2 Cups Mashed Potatoes
1 Egg, well beaten
1 Tsp. Salt
1/8 Tsp. White Pepper

Saute' onions in fat until golden brown. Beat in remaining ingredients.

The knishes can also be filled with pot cheese, ground meat or chicken, or with cooked and seasoned buckwheat groats.

MEXICAN HOMINY

1 Medium Onion, minced
1 Medium Green Pepper, chopped
¼ Cup Butter or Bacon Fat
1 - 1 Lb. 13 Oz. Can Hominy,
   drained (about 3½ cups)
1 Tsp. Chili Powder
½ Tsp. Salt
1/8 Tsp. Pepper

Cook onion and green pepper in the butter in top pan of chafing dish, over direct heat, for about 10 minutes. Add remaining ingredients; heat and serve. Makes 4 servings.

BAKED SQUASH
(Bavarian Style)

2 Small Butternut or Acorn Squashes
2 Tbs. Bacon Drippings or Butter
1 Tbs. Brown Sugar
½ Tsp. Salt
¼ Tsp. Dry Mustard
1/8 Tsp. Pepper
1 Cup Soft Bread Crumbs (2 slices)
1 Cup Drained Sauerkraut

Cut squash in half lengthwise; remove seeds. Cook, covered, in a small amount of boiling salted water in a large saucepan for 15 to 20 minutes, or until tender. Drain.

Scoop pulp from shells into a large bowl, leaving a thin rim to hold shells in shape. Mash pulp with bacon drippings or butter, sugar, salt, mustard and pepper; stir in the crumbs and sauerkraut. Pile lightly into shells; place in a baking pan. Bake in 400° F. oven for 20 minutes, or until heated through. Makes 4 servings.

EGGPLANT SCALLOP

1 Large Onion, chopped
   (about 1 cup)
1 Tsp. Curry Powder
2 Tbs. Vegetable Oil
2 Tbs. Sugar
2 Tsp. Mixed Italian Herbs
2 Tsp. Salt
1 Envelope Instant Beef Bouillon,
   or 1 Beef Bouillon Cube
1 Tbs. Cider Vinegar
1 Tsp. Worcestershire Sauce
¼ Cup Water
½ Cup Pitted Sliced Ripe Olives
1 Large Eggplant, diced (about
   8 cups)
4 Large Ripe Tomatoes, diced
2 Cups Sliced Celery

Saute' onion with curry powder in salad oil just until onion is soft. Use large frying pan. Remove from heat. Stir in seasonings, then remaining ingredients; cover. Heat to boiling, then simmer, stirring once or twice, for 15 minutes. Uncover and simmer for 10 minutes longer, or until eggplant and celery are tender. Makes 6 servings.

HAWAIIAN SWEET POTATOES

6 Sweet Potatoes
Boiling Water
1 - 8½ Oz. Can Crushed Pineapple
½ Cup Butter or Margarine, melted
1/3 Cup Granulated Sugar
1 Tsp. Cinnamon
½ Cup Chopped Pecans
1/3 Cup Light Brown Sugar,
   firmly packed
¼ Cup Butter or Margarine, melted

Scrub potatoes; cut each in half and cook in boiling water, to cover, for 20 minutes, or just until tender; drain. When cool enough to handle, scoop potato out of shells, being careful to keep shells intact. Preheat oven to 375°F. Drain pineapple, reserving syrup. In a large bowl, combine sweet potato, pineapple, ½ cup butter, granulated sugar and cinnamon. Beat until well blended and creamy. Fold in pecans. Dip potato shells in reserved pineapple syrup. Arrange in shallow baking dish. Fill with potato mixture. Sprinkle with brown sugar and drizzle with melted butter. Bake 15 minutes, or until bubbling hot. Makes 6 servings.

VEGETABLE PIE
(From Malta)

1 Large Onion, peeled and sliced
2 Tbs. Olive Oil
2 Tsp. Tomato Puree
1 Lb. Shelled Peas (about 2 cups)
2 Lbs. Lima Beans
2 Lbs. Spinach, chopped
3 Carrots, sliced thin
4 Artichoke Hearts, quartered
   (optional)
½ Cup Water
10 Anchovy Fillets (soak in cold
   water 10 minutes, pat dry and
   chop fine)
Pitted Olives, chopped
Salt and Pepper to taste
Pastry for 1 - 10" Deep-dish Pie
   (double crust)

In a large skillet, fry onion in olive oil until translucent but not brown. Add tomato puree and continue cooking over moderate heat for a few minutes. Add all of the other vegetables, together with ½ cup water. Cover and cook for 10 minutes, or until the vegetables are tender. Add more water if necessary to keep vegetables from sticking. Remove the pan from the heat and stir in the anchovies and olives. Season to taste with salt and pepper. Pour mixture into a pastry-lined 10" deep-dish pie plate. Cover with a pastry top and cut two or three slits in top. Bake in preheated 400°F. oven for 25 minutes, then lower heat to 350°F. and bake for an additional 30 to 45 minutes. Makes 4 servings.

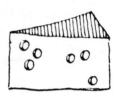

SWISS CHARD with CHEESE

2 Lbs. Swiss Chard
2 Tbs. Butter or Margarine
2 Tbs. Flour
1 Tsp. Salt
½ Cup Milk
½ Lb. Diced Process Cheese
½ Cup Bread Crumbs
2 Tbs. Melted Butter

Cut the stalks from washed chard leaves into 1" pieces. Place in bottom of a large kettle; cover with boiling salted water. Cover and cook for 5 minutes. Add the torn leaves and continue cooking until tender, about 5 minutes. Drain thoroughly in a colander, pressing out the liquid. You should have about 5 cups of chard.

While the chard is cooking, melt the butter; blend in flour and salt. Add milk and cook, stirring constantly, until mixture comes to a boil. Add cheese, stirring until cheese is melted and blended. Place chard in greased 2-quart casserole. Stir in the sauce. Toss the crumbs with melted butter; sprinkle over the casserole. Bake in a 350°F. oven until bubbly, about 25 minutes. Makes 6 servings.

ARTICHOKES WITH LEMON SAUCE

¼ Cup Salad Oil or Olive Oil
6 Lemon Slices
2 Bay Leaves
1 Clove Garlic, split
1 Tsp. Salt
1/8 Tsp. Pepper
4 Large Artichokes (about 3 lbs.)

Lemon Sauce:

¼ Cup Melted Butter
2 Tbs. Olive Oil
2 Tbs. Lemon Juice

In large kettle, combine 3 quarts of water with ¼ cup olive oil, lemon slices, bay leaves, garlic, salt and pepper; bring to a boil. Meanwhile, trim stalk from base of artichokes; cut a 1" slice from tops.

Remove discolored leaves; snip off spike ends. Wash the artichokes in cold water; drain. Add to boiling mixture. Reduce heat; simmer, covered, for 40 to 45 min., or until artichoke bases feel soft. Drain artichokes well. Meanwhile, make the lemon sauce. In a small bowl, mix the butter, 2 tablespoons of olive oil, and the lemon juice until well combined.

To serve: Place artichoke and small cup of sauce on individual plates. To eat, pull out leaves, one at a time, and dip in sauce. Discard prickly choke. Makes 4 servings.

NEW POTATOES WITH MUSHROOMS

1½ Lbs. Small New Potatoes, peeled
3 Tbs. Butter
1 Scallion, finely chopped (include some of green top)
1½ Cups Finely-chopped Fresh Mushrooms
2 Tbs. Flour
1½ Cups Chicken Stock or Chicken Bouillon
1 Bay Leaf
2 Tsp. Finely-chopped Fresh Parsley or Mint

Boil the potatoes in salted water until they are tender--about 15 minutes. Drain and set aside. Melt butter in a heavy saucepan. Saute' the scallion for 2 to 3 minutes, then stir in mushrooms and saute' for 3 to 4 minutes. Add flour and stir until smooth. Gradually add the stock, stirring all the time until smooth. Add the bay leaf and bring mixture to a boil. Reduce heat and simmer, uncovered, for 8 minutes. Add cooked potatoes to the sauce and heat through over low heat, stirring occasionally. Adjust the seasonings. Sprinkle with parsley or mint and serve. Makes 4 servings.

CAULIFLOWER WITH YOGURT SAUCE

1 Large Head Cauliflower
1 Tbs. Vegetable Oil
8 to 10 Whole Cloves
¼ Tsp. Crushed Cardamom Seeds, or ¼ Tsp. Ground Cardamom
1½ Tsp. Ground Ginger
1 Tsp. Anise Seed
1 Tsp. Chili Powder, more or less, according to taste
1 Tsp. Salt
1 Cup Plain Yogurt, lightly beaten
Chopped Fresh Coriander or Parsley, for garnish

Cut off tough end of the cauliflower stem and snap off any green leaves. Steam or boil the cauliflower until tender but still slightly crisp. Remove; drain if necessary and place cauliflower in a buttered baking dish. Heat the oil in a small, heavy pan. Add all the spices and saute' briefly, 30 seconds or so. Stir in the beaten yogurt and simmer the sauce for 1 to 2 minutes. Pour the yogurt sauce over the warm cauliflower. Place dish in preheated 350°F. oven and bake 12 to 15 minutes, until the sauce is golden brown on top. Serve hot, garnished with chopped coriander or parsley. Remove the whole cloves before serving. Makes 6 to 8 servings.

VEGETARIAN PILAF

1 - 8 Oz. Container Ricotta Cheese
Oil, for deep frying
1 Tbs. Turmeric
1 Cup Hot Water
¼ Cup Butter
¼ Cup Vegetable Oil
½ Cup Blanched, Slivered Almonds
½ Onion, thinly sliced
1½ Tbs. Minced Garlic
3 Tbs. Minced Fresh Gingerroot
5 Cardamom Pods, pounded lightly
1 Stick Cinnamon
3 Whole Cloves
10 Peppercorns
1 Cup Small Cauliflower Flowerettes
1 Cup Green Peas
2 Cups Long-grain White Rice
2 Tsp. Salt
4 Cups Boiling Water
½ Cup Dark Raisins
½ Cup Sweet Red Cherries, pitted
  and quartered

Enclose the ricotta cheese in cheesecloth
and form a rectangle. Place the cheese between 2 small cheese or bread boards and
put a light weight on top. Let it sit for
about 1 hour to condense the cheese and
squeeze excess moisture from it. Cut the
cheese into ½" cubes.

Heat oil to 375°F. Fry cubes of cheese in
small batches until they are golden brown.
This should take 45 to 60 seconds per
batch. Drain the cheese and discard the
oil. Mix the turmeric with 1 cup hot water;
place the fried cheese into the turmeric mixture and set aside.

Place butter and oil in a large skillet over
medium-high heat. Fry almonds until they
are golden, 2 to 3 minutes; remove with a
slotted spoon and set aside. Add onion,
garlic, ginger, cardamom, cinnamon, cloves,
and peppercorns to the pan. Saute' until
onions are golden, about 5 minutes. Add
cauliflower and peas; fry 2 minutes longer.
In the same pan, put the rice. Add 2 tsp.
salt and 4 cups boiling water. Cover and
bring to a boil; lower heat and simmer 20
to 25 minutes, until all liquid is absorbed.
Remove from the heat; discard the whole
spices, then stir in the cubed cheese, half
the fried almonds and ¼ cup of the raisins.

Place on a serving platter; sprinkle with the
remaining almonds and raisins and the sweet
cherries. Makes 10 to 12 servings.

CORN AND TOMATO CASSEROLE

8 to 12 Ears Fresh Corn
¼ Cup Butter (or bacon drippings)
2 Cups Water
4 Slices Crisp Bacon, crumbled
1 Tsp. Salt (or to taste)
2 Large Tomatoes, peeled and sliced

Cut corn from cob. There should be 4 to
5 cups of cut corn. Melt the butter or
drippings in a skillet; add the corn and
saute' quickly for about five minutes.
Add water, bacon and salt and arrange in
a buttered casserole in alternate layers with
the sliced tomato on top. Bake (uncovered)
in a moderate oven (350°F.) for about 30
minutes. Serve hot. Makes 5 to 6 servings.

ZUCCHINI, ARMENIAN STYLE

2 Lbs. Zucchini, washed and
  trimmed
1 Cup Ground Lamb Shoulder,
  or 1 Lb. Lamb Patties
½ Cup Raw Rice
1 Small Onion, chopped fine
1 Tbs. Chopped Parsley
½ Cup Stewed Tomatoes
Salt, to taste
Freshly Ground Black Pepper,
  to taste

Peel the zucchini and cut into 3" pieces.
Scoop out the centers. Soak the zucchini
in cold salted water for about ½ hour. Mix
the lamb with the rice, onion, parsley, tomatoes, salt and pepper. Drain the zucchini
and fill the hollows with the lamb mixture.
Arrange in a saucepan and add water to the
depth of 1". The water should not reach
more than halfway up the sides of the
zucchini. Cover pan tightly and simmer
over low heat until the rice is tender,
about 1 hour. Check from time to time
to see whether more water is needed.
Makes 6 servings.

BRUSSELS SPROUTS WITH CHESTNUT SAUCE

1 Lb. Brussels Sprouts
1 Tsp. Salt
½ Lb. Chestnuts, roasted and
   peeled
1/3 Cup Butter or Margarine

Cut off stem end of Brussels sprouts. Soak in cold water 15 minutes; drain. Place in a medium saucepan with 3 cups of water and the salt; bring to boiling. Lower heat, and simmer, uncovered, 10 minutes, or until tender. Drain.

Quarter chestnuts; saute' in hot butter in saucepan for 5 minutes. Toss with drained Brussels sprouts. Makes 6 servings.

Note: To roast chestnuts, first make a slit in each shell with a sharp knife. Bake at 500°F for 15 minutes. Remove shells and skin.

CHICKEN CORN CHOWDER

1 Whole Small Chicken Breast,
   halved lengthwise (about 8 oz.)
½ Cup Water
¼ Cup Chopped Onion
¼ Cup Chopped Celery
1 - 10¾ Oz. Can Condensed Cream
   of Chicken Soup
1 - 8¾ Oz. Can Whole Kernel Corn
½ Cup Milk
½ Cup Shredded Sharp American
   Cheese (about 2 oz.)
2 Tbs. Chopped Pimiento

In a medium saucepan, combine chicken, water, onion and celery. Bring to a boil; reduce heat, cover and simmer until tender, about 15 to 20 minutes. Remove chicken; cool slightly. Discard skin and bones and cut up the meat. Return chicken to broth; stir in soup, undrained corn, milk, cheese and pimiento. Cook, uncovered, until heated through, about 10 minutes, stirring occasionally. Makes 4 or 5 servings.

SQUASH MEDLEY

4 Medium Summer Squash,
   fresh and unpeeled (about
   4 cups)
½ Green Pepper, chopped
2 Ripe Tomatoes, peeled and
   chopped
6 Slices Bacon, fried and
   crumbled
1½ Cups Shredded Process Cheese
1/3 Cup Chopped Onion
½ Tsp. Salt
½ Cup Fine Bread Crumbs
2 Tbs. Butter

Parboil squash. If you use frozen squash, do not parboil. To make filling, combine remaining ingredients, except for crumbs and butter. Mix well. Slice the parboiled squash thinly. Place in baking dish, alternating squash and filling. Top with bread crumbs and dabs of butter. Bake in a 375°F. oven for 35 minutes. Makes 6 to 8 servings.

Note: If using zucchini, parboil for 3 minutes; if using yellow crooknecks or small white pattypans, parboil for 5 minutes; and if using white scallops, parboil for 15 to 20 minutes.

SWEDISH RUTABAGAS

2 Medium Rutabagas, peeled,
   quartered and sliced ¼" thick
2 Tbs. Brown Sugar
½ Tsp. Ground Ginger
½ Tsp. Salt
1/8 Tsp. Pepper
2 Tbs. Butter

Cook rutabagas in boiling, salted water; drain. Combine brown sugar, ginger, salt and pepper; mix thoroughly. Add sugar mixture, along with butter, to the rutabagas. Stir gently over low heat until the sugar melts, 2 to 3 minutes. Makes 6 servings.

HONEY-GLAZED ONIONS

12 Small Boiling Onions (use
    onions no larger than 1½"
    in diameter)
4 Tbs. Butter
2 Tbs. Honey
½ Tsp. Salt

Drop the onions into boiling water to
cover and cook briskly, uncovered, for
about 1 minute. Drain onions. With
a small, sharp knife, trim the stem ends,
remove white, parchment-like skins and
cut tops from onions. Arrange onions
in a baking dish in single layer. In a
small skillet, melt the butter over moderate heat. Add the honey and salt, &
stir until mixture is hot and fluid. Pour
honey mixture over onions, turning them
with a spoon to coat them evenly. Bake
onions in preheated 400°F. oven for about
45 minutes, basting occasionally with the
cooking liquid, until they are golden brown
and tender. Serve at once. Makes 4
servings.

GREEN BEAN SOUP

1½ Lb. Ham Bone, with meat
15 Whole Allspice
8 to 10 Sprigs Parsley
4 Sprigs Summer Savory (or
    1 Tsp. Dried Savory Leaves)
1 Small Onion, minced
1½ Cups Peeled, Diced Potatoes
2 Cups Cut Green Beans
½ Cup Light Cream
1 Tbs. Butter or Margarine
2 Tsp. Salt

Place ham bone in a soup kettle with water
to cover. Tie allspice, parsley and savory
in a small cheesecloth bag or put in a tea
ball. Add to the kettle and simmer for 2
hours, adding more water if needed. Add
onion, potatoes and beans; cook until the
vegetables are tender, 20 to 30 minutes.
Remove the spice ball. Just before serving,
blend in cream, butter and salt. Makes 8
to 10 servings.

NUTTY BAKED SQUASH

2 Acorn Squash, 1 lb. each
2/3 Cup Graham Cracker Crumbs
1/3 Cup Coarsely Chopped Pecans
1/3 Cup Soft Butter or Margarine
3 Tbs. Brown Sugar
¼ Tsp. Salt
¼ Tsp. Nutmeg

Heat oven to 400°F. Cut each squash in
half; remove seeds and fibers. Stir together
remaining ingredients and spoon one-fourth
of crumb mixture into each squash half.
Arrange squash halves in ungreased baking
dish, 11x7x1½". Pour water into baking
dish to depth of ¼". Cover and bake for
35 to 40 minutes, or until squash is tender.
Makes 4 servings.

CARROT SOUFFLE'
(Grecian Style)

1½ Lbs. Carrots
1 Cup Soft, Stale Bread Crumbs
1 Cup Milk
Melted Butter or Margarine
3 Egg Yolks
1 Tsp. Salt
4 Egg Whites

Wash carrots, scrape and cut into pieces.
Cover with lightly salted boiling water &
cook for 20 min., or until tender. Drain.
Whirl in blender. Combine crumbs and
milk; beat in 3 tablespoons of melted butter. Beat egg yolks and beat into crumb
mixture. Add salt. Combine with carrots.
Beat egg whites until stiff but not dry.
Fold egg whites into carrot mixture.
Grease a 2-quart baking dish; pour in the
carrot mixture. Set in shallow pan of hot
water. Bake in preheated 350°F. oven
for 30 to 45 minutes, until risen, set and
lightly browned. Serve at once with ½
cup melted butter poured over the top.
Makes 6 servings.

SCALLOPED CORN

1 - 20 Oz. Can Cream Style Corn
1 Small Onion, finely chopped
2 Slices Bread, finely diced
Bacon Strips
Grated Cheese
¾ Cup Milk
1 Egg
¼ Tsp. Salt
Freshly-ground Black Pepper

Preheat oven to 350°F. Grease a casserole dish. Prepare bread crumbs, grated cheese and chopped onion. Place milk, egg, salt & pepper in bowl. Beat well. Add onion and corn to beaten mixture. Blend in crumbs. Turn into a greased casserole. Top with bacon strips cut in pieces. Sprinkle with grated cheese. Bake 25 minutes at 350°F. If desired, braise bacon strips under broiler just before serving.

FRESH VEGETABLE SOUP

1 Lb. Lean Shin or Chuck Beef,
    cut into 1" cubes
1 Beef Knucklebone, cracked
6 Cups Water
2 - 1 Lb. Cans Tomatoes
3 Carrots, sliced
1 Onion, sliced
1 Clove Garlic, minced
2 Bay Leaves
1 Tbs. Sugar
2 Tsp. Salt
2 Cups Chopped Cabbage
1 Cup Sliced Zucchini
1 Cup Cut-up Green Beans
1 Cup Broken Macaroni
¼ Cup Chopped Parsley
Grated Parmesan Cheese

Simmer beef and bone with water, tomatoes, carrots, leek or onion, garlic, bay leaves, sugar and salt in kettle for about 3 hours; remove bone. Cool soup slightly and skim off fat. Add cabbage, zucchini, green beans and macaroni; cook 45 minutes longer, or until beans are tender. Sprinkle with parsley; serve with grated cheese. Makes about 12 cups.

OKRA, CORN AND TOMATO MEDLEY

½ Lb. Okra, cut into ¼" slices
    (about 2 cups)
4 Ears Corn, scraped (about 2
    cups of kernels)
3 Large Tomatoes, peeled and
    diced
4 Slices Bacon
1 Onion, finely chopped
1 Small Green Pepper, chopped
1 Tsp. Sugar
Salt and Pepper
Tabasco

In a large skillet, fry the bacon until it is crisp. Remove the bacon; drain and crumble it. Set the bacon aside. Discard all but 4 tablespoons of the bacon fat from the pan. Stir the okra and onion into the bacon fat, add the corn & cook over medium heat for 10 minutes. Stir constantly. Add the tomatoes, green pepper and sugar and season with salt, pepper and a dash of Tabasco. Cover & simmer for about 25 minutes, or until all the vegetables are tender; stir occasionally. Correct the seasoning; pour mixture into a serving dish and sprinkle with the crumbled bacon. Makes 6 servings.

CHINESE-STYLE ASPARAGUS

2 Lbs. Fresh Asparagus
¾ Cup Chicken Stock
1 Tbs. Cornstarch
1 Tbs. Cold Water
2 Tbs. Soy Sauce
1 Clove Garlic, minced or mashed
Salt and Pepper to taste
2 Tbs. Olive Oil or Salad Oil

Wash the asparagus well and snap off lower stalks. Cut diagonally into very thin slices. Heat chicken stock to boiling and stir in a mixture of the cornstarch, water, and soy sauce; stirring constantly, cook until thickened. Add garlic and salt and pepper to taste. Saute' sliced asparagus in hot oil for 2 minutes. Pour over sauce and stirring constantly, cook 1 minute longer. Serve at once. Serves 6.

BEETS IN ORANGE SAUCE

3 Tbs. Sugar
2 Tbs. Cornstarch
¼ Tsp. Salt
½ Cup Orange Juice
¼ Cup Lemon Juice
1/8 Tsp. Orange Rind
1/8 Tsp. Lemon Rind
3 Cups Coarsely-shredded, Cooked
   Fresh Beets, or canned

Blend the first three ingredients together in the top of a double boiler. Add the orange and lemon juice and cook over boiling water until thick and transparent, stirring constantly. Add the orange and lemon rinds and the beets. Mix lightly. Cook over boiling water until thoroughly heated through. Serve at once. Makes 4 servings.

HUNGARIAN POTATOES

2 Chicken Bouillon Cubes
2 Cups Boiling Water
2 Tbs. All-purpose Flour
1 Tsp. Salt
1 Tsp. Paprika
¼ Tsp. Pepper
1 Large Onion, chopped (1 cup)
4 Cups Thinly-sliced Pared Raw
   Potatoes (about 6 medium)
2 Medium Tomatoes, cut into
   wedges
2 Tbs. Butter or Margarine

Dissolve bouillon cubes in boiling water in a 2-cup measure. Combine flour, salt, paprika and pepper in a cup. Spread onion over bottom of a buttered 8-cup baking dish. Layer half the potatoes, flour mixture and tomatoes; repeat, ending with tomatoes. Dot with butter or margarine. Slowly pour the bouillon over; cover with lid or foil. Bake in 325°F. oven for 30 minutes; uncover and bake, pressing potatoes down several times with spoon to keep moist, for 2 hours more, or until tender. Let stand about 10 minutes, to let potatoes absorb some of the liquid. Makes 6 servings.

PEAS--ITALIAN STYLE

1 Lb. Shelled Peas
1 Slice Bacon or Ham, cut up
   into small pieces
1 Clove Garlic
2 Tbs. Olive Oil
Salt and Pepper to taste
Water

Put all of the ingredients into a small saucepan and cook slowly until the peas are tender. Remove the garlic before serving.

CABBAGE AND POTATO CASSEROLE

2 Lbs. Potatoes
Boiling Water
3 Tsp. Salt
4 Cups Coarsely-shredded
   Green Cabbage
1½ Cups Sliced Scallions
1/3 Cup Milk
½ Cup Butter or Margarine
¼ Tsp. Pepper

Peel potatoes and cut each into quarters. In ½" boiling water, with 1 tsp. salt, in a medium saucepan, cook potato, covered, for 15 to 20 minutes, or until fork tender and completely cooked. Drain. Return pan to low heat, shaking to dry potatoes.

While potatoes are cooking, cook the cabbage in a medium saucepan with ½" water and ½ teaspoon of salt. Pan should be covered and cabbage cooked for 8 to 10 minutes, or just until tender. Drain well.

Heat scallions with milk and ½ teaspoon of salt. Bring to boiling; reduce heat and simmer for 10 minutes.

In saucepan, with electric mixer at medium speed, beat potato with 4 tablespoons of butter, 1 teaspoon salt, and the pepper. Beat in scallions and hot milk, beating until potato is very light and fluffy. Stir in cabbage, combining well. Heat over low heat for 5 minutes. Turn mixture into a heated serving dish. Make a depression in the center and fill with remaining butter. Makes 8 servings.

NEAPOLITAN POTATO PIE

2 Lbs. Potatoes
8 Oz. Grated Mozzarella Cheese
2 Slices Minced Prosciutto
    or Ham
6 Large Eggs
4 Tbs. Grated Romano Cheese
2 Tsp. Chopped Fresh Parsley
Salt and Pepper to taste
Bread Crumbs

Scrub potatoes thoroughly. Boil potatoes with skins in salted, boiling water for 20 minutes, or until tender. Peel and put the potatoes through a ricer or mash until smooth. Place in a large bowl. Add the mozzarella, prosciutto, eggs, cheese, parsley, salt and pepper and mix well. Grease an 8x8x2" baking dish. Sprinkle the bottom lightly with bread crumbs. Place the potato mixture in dish. Bake in a preheated 375°F. oven until golden brown. Serves 8.

BAKED POTATOES
with SWISS CHEESE

4 Medium Potatoes
¼ Cup Melted Butter
½ Cup Consomme'
½ Tsp. Salt
½ Tsp. Pepper
½ Cup Grated Swiss-type Cheese
¼ Cup Sweet Butter

Peel potatoes and slice into ½" rounds. Cook over low heat in melted butter until potatoes are just tender, adding some of the consomme' as necessary. Put the potatoes and remaining consomme' into a buttered 1-quart baking dish; sprinkle with salt and pepper. Cover with grated cheese and dot with butter. Bake in preheated 400°F. oven for 10 minutes. Makes 3 or 4 servings.

TOMATO SOUP
from FIJI

¾ Cup Rice
1/3 Cup Chopped Onion
2 Tbs. Drippings
2 Cups Cut-up Tomatoes
2 to 3 Slices Red Pepper
½ Tsp. Salt
1 Tbs. Chopped Parsley
1 Tsp. Sugar
1/8 Tsp. Paprika

Wash the rice; add to 3 cups boiling water and boil for 30 minutes. Cook the onion in a pan with the drippings until tender but not brown; add the tomatoes and pepper and simmer for 10 minutes. Rub the mixture through a strainer into the boiling rice and water. Add salt, pepper and sugar and sprinkle with parsley and paprika on top of the soup when serving.

GREEN BEANS with
PEARS AND BACON

1 Lb. Green Beans, trimmed and
    broken into pieces
6 Firm Ripe Pears, peeled,
    cored and sliced
½ Cup Water
1 Thin Sliver Lemon Peel
1 Tsp. Salt
6 Slices Bacon
¼ Cup Sugar
2 Tbs. Vinegar
1 Tsp. Fresh Lemon Juice

Place pear slices in a saucepan with the water and lemon peel; bring to a boil. Lower the heat and simmer, uncovered, for 5 minutes. Stir in green beans and salt and continue cooking. Fry the bacon in a skillet. When crisp, remove the bacon to a paper towel and drain. Pour off all but 2 tablespoons of the fat in the skillet. Add sugar, vinegar and lemon juice to the fat in skillet and simmer for 3 minutes. Pour sauce over pears and beans and cook until tender. Crumble the bacon and sprinkle it on top of beans and pears just before serving. Makes 6 servings.

PIQUANT PINEAPPLE AND BEETS

½ Cup Crushed Pineapple
2 Tbs. Vinegar
2 Tbs. Sugar
2 Tbs. Cornstarch
1 - 1 Lb. Can Sliced or Diced Beets,
   drained (about 2 cups)
2 Tbs. Butter or Margarine
Salt and Pepper to taste

Bring pineapple and vinegar to boil. Combine sugar and cornstarch and stir into mixture. Cook, stirring constantly, until smooth and thickened. Add beets and butter. Heat well and season to taste. Serve hot as a relish. Makes 4 servings.

ONION PIE
(German Main Dish)

1½ Cups Sifted Flour
¾ Tsp. Salt
1½ Tsp. Caraway Seeds
½ Cup Shortening
2 to 3 Tbs. Water
3 Cups Peeled Onions, thinly sliced
3 Tbs. Melted Butter or Margarine
½ Cup Milk
1½ Cups Dairy Sour Cream
1 Tsp. Salt
2 Eggs, well beaten
3 Tbs. Flour
Bacon Slices, cooked crisp

To make the pastry, combine the flour, salt and caraway seeds. Add shortening; cut into flour until mixture resembles coarse cornmeal. Stir water in lightly with a fork; stir until mixture adheres and follows fork around the bowl. Turn onto a floured board; roll to 1/8" thickness. Fit into a 10" pie pan and flute the edges. Bake in a 425°F. oven for 10 minutes, or until lightly browned.

While pie crust is baking, prepare the filling. Saute' onions in butter until lightly browned. Spoon into pastry shell. Add milk, 1¼ cups sour cream, and salt to the eggs. Blend 3 tablespoons of flour with the remaining ¼ cup sour cream; combine with the egg mixture and pour over the onions. Bake in slow oven, 325°F., for

30 minutes, or until firm in the center. Garnish with crisp bacon. Makes 8 servings.

PORK CABBAGE ROLLS

1 Large Head Cabbage
2½ Cups Ground or Finely-
   chopped Cooked Pork Roast
½ Cup Fine Bread Crumbs
1/3 Cups Finely-chopped Onion
1 Egg, slightly beaten
1 Tbs. Chopped Parsley
1 Tsp. Caraway Seeds
1½ Tsp. Salt
¼ Tsp. Freshly-ground Pepper
1 - 8 Oz. Can Tomato Sauce
½ Cup Water
1 Tsp. Cornstarch
½ Tsp. Sugar
1 Tbs. Lemon Juice

Discard the wilted outer leaves of the cabbage and remove core. Carefully remove 10 to 12 whole, large leaves. Steam leaves for 3 minutes in small amount of boiling, salted water, covered. Drain and cool.

Mix pork, bread crumbs, onion, egg, parsley, caraway seeds, salt and pepper. Put a heaping tablespoonful of pork mixture near the stem end of each cabbage leaf. Fold in the two sides, then roll leaf. Put cabbage rolls close together in a large skillet. Mix tomato sauce, water, cornstarch, sugar and lemon juice; pour over rolls. Cover tightly and simmer for 30 minutes, or until leaves are tender. Makes 10 to 12 rolls.

ONION RINGS

6 Large Onions
½ Cup Flour
Salt and Pepper
½ Tsp. Paprika

Peel and slice onions. Separate into rings. Cover with milk and let stand 30 minutes. Drain well. Combine flour, salt and pepper, and paprika and shake over onion rings. Fry in hot shortening; drain. Sprinkle with salt.

BARLEY BEAN SOUP

2 Slices Beef Shank, sawed into
   pieces 1½" thick
2 Small Ham Knuckles
½ Cup Dried Navy Beans
¼ Cup Pearl Barley
2 Sliced Celery Tops
1 Onion, chopped
8 Cups Cold Water

Place beef shank, ham knuckles, navy
beans, barley, celery tops, and onion in
a large kettle. Pour over cold water;
cover and simmer for 3 hours. Remove
meat, and when cool enough to handle,
slice from the bone and cut into small
pieces. Return meat to soup, season
with salt and pepper and heat. Serve
with a sprinkling of chopped parsley.
Makes 8 servings.

MANICOTTI

1 - 12 Oz. Pkg. Manicotti Noodles
2 Cups Cream-style Cottage Cheese
1 - 8 Oz. Pkg. Cream Cheese
1 - 9 Oz. Pkg. Frozen, Chopped
   Spinach, thawed and drained
¼ Lb. Liverwurst, diced
2 Eggs
1 Tsp. Salt
1/8 Tsp. Pepper
6 Cups Meat-seasoned Tomato Sauce
   (use your favorite recipe)
1 - 8 Oz. Pkg. Sliced Mozzarella or
   Pizza Cheese, cut into triangles

Cook the manicotti noodles, a few at a time,
in a large amount of boiling salted water, following directions on box. Lift out carefully
with slotted spoon so as not to break; place
in a pan of cold water until ready to fill.

Mix the cottage cheese, cream cheese, spinach, liverwurst, eggs, salt and pepper until
well blended in a medium bowl. Heat the
tomato sauce in a medium saucepan and
keep hot. Lift manicotti noodles, 1 at a
time, from the water; drain. Fill with the
cheese mixture, using a long-handled teaspoon (or fill a plastic bag with the cheese
mixture; fold to make a cone-shape and snip

an opening in one corner, squeezing filling
into noodles). Arrange filled noodles in
rows in a single layer in a 16-cup shallow
baking pan. Spoon hot tomato sauce over
and around the noodles. Cover and bake
in a 350°F. oven for 30 minutes; uncover
and arrange cheese triangles, overlapping, on
noodles. Bake 10 minutes longer, or until
cheese is melted and bubbly. Makes 8
servings.

ITALIAN MINESTRONE

½ Lb. Dry White Beans, soaked
   in water overnight
3 Quarts Salted Water
1 Tsp. Olive Oil
1/8 Lb. Salt Pork, cut into small
   pieces
1 Clove Garlic, chopped fine
1 Small Onion, chopped
1 Leek, diced and washed
1 Tsp. Chopped Parsley
1 Tsp. Chopped Basil
1 Tbs. Tomato Paste
3 Tomatoes, peeled, seeded
   and chopped
3 Stalks Celery, chopped
2 Carrots, sliced
2 Potatoes, diced
1 Small Turnip, peeled and diced
¼ Small Cabbage, shredded
2 Zucchini, diced
1½ Quarts Water
Salt to taste
½ Tsp. Freshly-ground Black Pepper
1 Cup Elbow Macaroni
6 Tbs. Grated Parmesan Cheese

Drain the beans and boil them in the salted
water about 1 hour, or until tender. Place
the olive oil in a large kettle and add the
salt pork, garlic, onion, leek, parsley and
basil. Brown lightly. Add the tomato paste
thinned with a little water and cook 5 min.
Add the tomatoes, celery, carrots, potatoes,
turnip, cabbage, zucchini, water, salt & pepper and cook slowly 45 minutes to 1 hour.
Add the beans. Add the elbow macaroni &
cook 10 minutes, or until tender. Adjust
the seasonings and pour soup into heated
bowls. Serve immediately, sprinkled with
grated Parmesan cheese. Makes 6 servings.

SEAFOOD LASAGNA

½ Lb. Lasagna Noodles
1 Tbs. Olive Oil or Vegetable Oil
2 - 10 Oz. Cans Frozen Condensed
    Cream of Shrimp Soup
2 - 7 Oz. Cans King Crabmeat
2 Cups Cream-style Cottage Cheese
1 - 8 Oz. Pkg. Cream Cheese,
    softened
1 Large Onion, chopped (1 cup)
1 Egg
2 Tsp. Leaf Basil, crumbled
1 Tsp. Salt
¼ Tsp. Pepper
4 Medium-size Ripe Tomatoes, peeled
    and sliced
2 Tsp. Sugar
1 Cup Grated Cheddar Cheese
    (¼ lb.)

Slide lasagna noodles into a large kettle of
boiling salted water (a few at a time so they
do not break). Add olive oil or vegetable
oil to keep noodles from sticking. Cook,
stirring often and gently with a wooden
spoon, for about 15 minutes, or just until
noodles are tender. Drain and cover with
cold water.

While the lasagna noodles are cooking,
thaw the soup slowly, stirring often, in a
large heavy saucepan or double boiler.
Drain and flake the crabmeat, carefully
removing any bony tissue. Stir the crabmeat into soup; heat until bubbly.

Blend cottage cheese and cream cheese with
onion, egg, basil, salt and pepper in a large
bowl. Line the bottom of a lightly-oiled
13x9x2" baking dish with a single layer of
noodles. Top with half of cheese mixture,
another single layer of noodles, then all
of crab sauce. Cover with remaining noodles,
then remaining cheese mixture. Arrange the
tomato slices in a single layer on top; sprinkle with sugar. (If desired, you can prepare
casserole to this point then refrigerate and
keep until ready to use later in the day.
Remove it from the refrigerator 30 minutes before baking and let stand at room
temperature.) Bake in 350°F. oven for 15
minutes. Sprinkle with grated cheese, then
bake 45 minutes longer, or until crusty
brown. Let stand about 15 minutes to set,
then cut into 8 servings; lift out with wide
spatula. Makes 8 servings.

BAKED BEANS

1 Lb. Dried Beans
½ Tbs. Dry Mustard
1/3 Cup Brown Sugar
¼ Cup Molasses
1 Tsp. Salt
1/8 Tsp. Pepper
¼ Lb. Diced Salt Pork

Soak the beans overnight in water to cover.
Bring beans to a boil in a large kettle and
simmer gently for 1½ hours; drain and put
into pressure cooker. Add remaining ingredients. Add one medium sliced onion, if
desired. Pressure cook at 15 lbs. pressure
for 40 to 45 minutes. Reduce pressure
gradually; turn beans into a baking dish and
brown in 375°F. oven for about 30 minutes.
If you do not wish to use a pressure cooker,
bake the beans in a slow oven, 300°F., for
6 to 8 hours, covered. Add boiling water,
as necessary, to keep beans moist. Uncover
during the last hour of baking to brown the
beans on top if desired.

SPANISH CHICK-PEA SOUP

1¾ Cups Chick-peas, washed
    and drained
4 Cups Water
1 Clove Garlic, minced
2 Onions, chopped
1 Green Pepper, chopped
1 Tbs. Cooking Oil
4 Cups Ham Broth
1 Large Potato, diced
1/3 Cup Diced Ham
½ Lb. Chorizos (Spanish Sausage)
    (or frankfurters)
Salt and Cayenne

Soak peas overnight in water; do not drain.
Cook garlic, onions, and green pepper in oil
in heavy kettle for about 5 minutes; do not
brown. Add soaked undrained chick-peas
and ham broth; simmer for about 1½ hrs.,
until chick-peas are just tender. Add potato,
ham and sliced chorizos; cook for about 30
minutes, until potato is tender. Season to
taste with salt and cayenne. Makes about
2 quarts or 8 to 10 servings.

ITALIAN RICE AND PEAS

½ Cup Chopped Onion
3 Tbs. Butter or Margarine
1½ Cups Shelled Peas
½ Cup Chopped, Cooked Ham
   (optional)
1 Cup Uncooked Rice
3 to 5 Cups Chicken or Beef
   Bouillon
2 Tbs. Grated Parmesan Cheese

Cook onion in 2 tablespoons butter until
golden. Add peas, cook for 1 minute,
then add ham (if used) and rice. Cook,
stirring, over low heat until the rice becomes golden. Add 3 cups of bouillon.
Cover, turn heat low, or put in preheated
oven (350°F.) and cook until the rice is
tender, adding more bouillon if necessary.
Stir lightly occasionally with a fork to
prevent sticking. This will take about
18 to 30 minutes. The liquid should be
absorbed, the rice tender but not mushy.
Stir in 1 tablespoon butter and the cheese
and serve at once, garnished with a little
pimiento if desired. Makes 4 to 6 servings.

Note: Frozen peas may be used; add
when rice is half cooked.

LIMA BEAN CHOWDER

1 Cup Dried Lima Beans
3 Cups Cold Water
½ Tsp. Salt
4 Slices Bacon
¼ Cup Onion, finely chopped
2 Cups Diced Raw Potatoes
1 Cup Diced Carrot
1 Cup Water
¾ Tsp. Salt
2 Cups Milk
2 Tbs. Finely-chopped Parsley

Wash the lima beans thoroughly and put
into a soup kettle. Add water and salt;
heat to boiling, reduce heat and simmer
for 45 minutes. Reserve ½ cup of the
whole limas. Puree the remainder along
with the liquid left from cooking. Pan
fry the bacon until done. Remove the
bacon and add the onion to the fat; saute'
until soft. Add potatoes, carrots, 1 cup of

water and ¾ teaspoon of salt. Simmer for
15 minutes, or until vegetables are tender.
Add milk, the pureed and the whole beans.
Heat to boiling. Serve immediately.
Crumble the bacon and sprinkle it and the
parsley over chowder. Makes 4 generous
servings.

RICE IN VINEGAR DRESSING
(Sushi)

Vinegar Dressing:
¼ Cup Rice Vinegar (or 3 tbs.
   mild white vinegar)
3½ Tbs. Sugar
2½ Tsp. Salt
1½ Tbs. Sweet Sake (or 1 tbs.
   pale dry sherry)

2 Cups Unconverted White Rice
1 - 2" Square Kombu (dried
   kelp), cut from package of
   Kombu and washed under
   cold running water

Dressing: Combine the vinegar, sugar, salt
and sweet sake or dry sherry in a 1½-quart
stainless steel saucepan. Bring to a boil,
uncovered; cool to room temperature. Combine 2½ cups cold water with the rice in a
2-quart stainless steel saucepan and let the
rice soak for 30 minutes. Add the square
of dried kelp and bring to a boil over high
heat. Cover the pan, reduce the heat to
moderate, and cook for about 10 minutes,
or until the rice has absorbed all of the water. Reduce the heat to its lowest point &
simmer another 5 minutes. Let the rice rest
off the heat for an additional 5 minutes before removing the cover and discarding the
kelp. Transfer the hot rice to a large non-
metallic platter or tray (wood, enamel,
ceramic, glass or plastic). Immediately pour
on the vinegar dressing and mix thoroughly
with a fork. The rice is ready to use when
it has cooled to room temperature. It may
be covered and left at room temperature for
as long as 5 hours before serving. Makes
about 6 cups.

NOODLES CANTONESE

½ Lb. Lean Pork
1 Tbs. Fat or Oil
Salt and Pepper
½ Cup Water
2 Cups Cooked Noodles
  (4 oz. pkg.)
1 Cup Sliced Celery
1 Cup Thinly-sliced Fresh or
  Frozen French Green Beans
1½ Tbs. Grated Onion
2 Tbs. Soy Sauce

Cut pork into very thin slivers; brown in hot fat. Add seasoning and water; cook 20 minutes. While meat is cooking, cook noodles in 2 quarts of boiling salted water (2 tsp. salt). Combine all ingredients; cook for 5 minutes. Makes 4 servings.

SPLIT PEA SOUP
(Indian Style)

1 Ham Hock (about 1 lb.), cracked
Water
1½ Cups Green or Yellow
  Split Peas
1 Small Onion, chopped
1 Tsp. Ground Coriander
1 Tsp. Ground Cumin
¼ Tsp. Ground Turmeric
1 Tsp. Lemon Juice
4 Tsp. Sugar
Salt and Pepper to taste
2 Tbs. Chopped Fresh Coriander
  or Parsley
Chopped Salted Peanuts

Place ham hock in a Dutch oven; cover with water. Cover and bring to a boil; simmer 10 minutes. Drain. Rinse and pick over split peas; add to the ham hock with 1½ quarts of water and the onion. Cover and simmer for about 1½ hours, or until peas mash easily. Remove ham hock; discard bone & fat. Cut meat into small pieces and return to pan. Add ground coriander, cumin, turmeric, lemon juice, sugar, salt and pepper to taste. Simmer 10 minutes longer. Serve with fresh coriander and chopped peanuts. Makes about 6 servings.

CHINESE PORK-FRIED RICE

1 Lb. Pork
1 Garlic Clove, minced
1 Onion, chopped
1 Cup Uncooked Rice
Salt and Pepper
1 - 3 Oz. Can Sliced Mushrooms,
  undrained
1¾ Cups Water
1 Egg
Soy Sauce

Cut pork into thin strips. Brown in skillet with garlic and onion. Add rice and cook until lightly browned, stirring frequently. Add 1 tsp. salt, ¼ tsp. pepper, the mushrooms and the water. Bring to a boil; cover and simmer for 25 minutes, or until rice is tender. Beat egg with salt and pepper to taste. Put into hot greased 8″ skillet. Fry until firm, turning once; cut into strips. Put rice mixture in serving bowl; arrange egg strips on top. Serve at once with soy sauce. Makes 4 servings.

BAKED BEANS
(Michigan Style)

1 Lb. Dried Great Northern Beans
6 Cups Water
2 Tsp. Salt
½ Tsp. Dry Mustard
1 Large Onion, minced
1/3 Cup Firmly-packed Dark Brown Sugar
1/3 Cup Dark Molasses
½ Cup Chili Sauce
2-1/3 Cups Tomatoes (one 1 lb. 3 oz. can)
8 Slices Bacon

Cover beans with water and bring to a boil; boil for 2 minutes. Cover pan and let stand for 1 hour. Simmer until beans are almost tender, about 1½ hours. Drain the liquid and save. Add remaining ingredients to the beans, except for bacon. Pour beans into a shallow baking pan. Top with bacon slices, cut into halves. Bake in preheated 300°F. oven for 2 hours, adding more bean liquid if necessary. Makes 6 servings.

BAKED PASTA WITH MEAT AND WHITE SAUCE

1 Lb. Mezzani (pasta), or Ziti
7 Oz. Ground Beef
¼ Lb. Sliced Italian Sweet Sausage
4 Tbs. Butter, divided
1 Tbs. Chopped Parsley
2 Eggs
Salt and Pepper to taste
2 Tbs. Flour
2 Cups Milk
Fine Dry Bread Crumbs
2 Tbs. Grated Parmesan Cheese

In a medium skillet, brown ground beef in 1 tbs. of butter. Place in a bowl. Add the parsley, eggs, salt and pepper and mix well. For the white sauce, melt 2 tbs. of butter in a small saucepan over low heat. Add the flour and blend until smooth. Add milk gradually and stir constantly until sauce is thickened. If it becomes too thick, add a small amount of milk.

Fry the sausage slices for about 2 minutes over low heat in a large skillet. Set aside. Cook mezzani in 6 quarts of boiling water, salted, for 10 to 12 minutes or until al dente. Drain and season with remaining tablespoon of butter and the cheese; mix well.

In a buttered 3-quart casserole, place a layer of mezzani. Distribute half each of beef & sausage on top. Add another layer of mezzani and the remainder of the meats. Cover with white sauce. Sprinkle top with fine dry bread crumbs and dot with butter. Bake in a preheated 350°F. oven until golden brown. Makes 4 servings.

ORANGE RICE

3 Tbs. Butter
2/3 Cup Sliced Celery
2 Tbs. Chopped Onion
1½ Cups Water
2 Tbs. Grated Orange Peel
1 Cup Orange Juice
1¼ Tsp. Salt
1 Cup Uncooked Rice

Melt butter in a heavy saucepan with a cover; add celery and onion and cook, stirring occasionally, until tender and light brown. Stir in water, orange peel and juice, and salt; then bring to a boil. Add rice, cover and steam over low heat for 20 to 25 minutes, or until rice is tender. Makes 6 servings. This goes well with ham or poultry.

INDONESIAN FRIED RICE

4 Cups Water
2 Envelopes Instant Chicken Broth
   or 2 Chicken Bouillon Cubes
1 Tsp. Cumin Seeds or ½ tsp.
   curry powder
2 Cups Uncooked Regular Rice
1 Large Onion, chopped (1 cup)
1 Garlic Clove, minced
6 Tbs. Peanut Oil or Vegetable Oil
1 Tsp. Salt
½ Tsp. Chili Powder
¼ Tsp. Ground Mace
½ Cup Toasted Slivered Almonds
1 Lb. Fresh Shrimp, cooked and
   deveined (or 1 - 5 oz. can shrimp,
   deveined, drained and rinsed)

Heat water with chicken broth or bouillon cubes and cumin seeds (or curry powder) in large saucepan; stir in rice. Cover and cook 15 to 20 minutes, or just until rice is tender and liquid is absorbed. Spoon into a large bowl; cool, then chill, for the rice should be very dry, with each grain separate, before frying. Saute' onion and garlic in 2 tablespoons of peanut oil or vegetable oil just until soft in large frying pan; remove and set aside. Turn rice out onto paper toweling; fluff with a fork to separate grains. Saute' lightly, half at a time, in same pan, adding 2 tablespoons of oil for each. Return all rice to pan; stir in onion mixture, seasonings and almonds. Save one or two whole shrimp for garnish; cut up remaining shrimp and stir into rice mixture. Cover and heat slowly for 5 minutes, or until heated through. Spoon rice mixture onto a large, heated serving platter or tray and garnish with saved whole shrimp. Makes 8 servings.

FINNISH MACARONI

1½ Cups Small Elbow Macaroni
2 Quarts Hot Milk
1½ Tsp. Salt
1 Tsp. Sugar
1 Tbs. Butter
2 Egg Yolks
½ Cup Light Cream
White Pepper

Cook macaroni in hot milk in top part of double boiler over boiling water until soft, about 30 minutes. Stir in salt, sugar, and butter. Beat together egg yolks and cream. Add to macaroni. Season with pepper. Makes 4 to 6 servings.

LASAGNA ROLL-UPS

1 - 2½ Lb. Broiler-Fryer
1½ Cups Water
1 Small Onion, peeled and
   sliced
1 Tsp. Salt
¼ Tsp. Pepper
1 Envelope Spaghetti Sauce Mix
1 - 1 Lb. 12 Oz. Can Tomato
   Puree
Dash of Sugar
2 Tbs. Butter or Margarine
1 - 10 Oz. Pkg. Frozen, Chopped
   Spinach, thawed
¼ Tsp. Ground Nutmeg
1 Lb. Lasagna Noodles
1 - 6 Oz. Pkg. Sliced Mozzarella
   Cheese

Cook the chicken with water, onion, salt and pepper for about 40 minutes, or until tender. Use a large saucepan. While the chicken is cooking, combine spaghetti sauce mix, tomato puree, sugar and butter or margarine in a medium saucepan. Heat to boiling; reduce heat. Cover and simmer for 30 minutes. Remove chicken from broth; cool. Reserve the broth. Remove skin and bones from chicken; cut meat into small pieces.

Combine ½ cup of the reserved broth with half of the chicken and half of the spinach in an electric blender container.

Process until smooth, about 1 minute. Place mixture in a bowl, scraping sides of blender container with a rubber spatula. Repeat with remaining chicken, spinach and ½ cup broth. Add to the mixture in the bowl; add nutmeg and blend well.

Cook lasagna noodles in a kettle, following directions on the label. Drain and put into a large bowl of cold water. To make roll-ups, remove lasagna noodles, one at a time, from cold water and pat dry with paper toweling. Spread a scant ¼ cup chicken mixture on noodle and roll up, jelly-roll fashion. Repeat with remaining noodles. Pour 2 cups of the tomato sauce into the bottom of a shallow 12-cup baking dish. Arrange roll-ups on sauce, making two layers if necessary. Spoon remaining sauce over roll-ups. Bake in 375°F. oven for 20 minutes. Cut mozzarella cheese into lengthwise strips and arrange on roll-ups. Bake 10 minutes longer, or until cheese is melted and sauce is bubbly-hot. Makes 6 to 8 servings.

CHEESE AND RICE BALLS

2 Cups Cooked Rice
½ Cup Grated Parmesan Cheese
1 Egg, well beaten
1 Tbs. Melted Butter
2 Tsp. Prepared Mustard (optional)
1 Tsp. Salt
Dash of Pepper
½" Cubes of Cheese (your favorite)
Bread Crumbs
Fat, for deep frying

Mix rice and grated cheese. Add the eggs, butter and seasonings. Blend well. Cover each cube of cheese with rice mixture & form into balls. Be sure that there are no open places in the rice balls so that cheese won't seep out and separate from the rice. Dip into bread crumbs. Fry in deep hot fat (365°F.) for 5 to 8 minutes, or until slightly brown on all sides. Makes 12 to 16 balls, depending on size. These are a fine way to use leftover rice. May be used as snacks.

RANCH-HOUSE BEANS

4 Cups Dried Pinto Beans, washed and
    drained
8 Cups Water
½ Lb. Salt Pork
2 to 4 Tbs. Chili Powder (depending
    on taste)
¼ to ½ Tsp. Hot Pepper Sauce
    (depending on taste)
Salt to taste

Bring beans and water to a boil. Remove
from heat, cover and let stand for 1 hour.
Add the salt pork and simmer, covered,
for 1½ to 2 hours, or until beans are tender
and water is almost absorbed.

While the beans are cooking, remove the
scum from the top and stir occasionally.
Remove salt pork and stir in enough chili
powder, hot pepper sauce, and salt to give
the beans a spicy flavor. The beans may
be prepared ahead of time and reheated.
Makes 10 to 12 servings.

SPAGHETTI WITH CABBAGE

¾ Lb. Spaghetti, broken
    into 3" pieces
1 Head Cabbage (about 2 lbs.)
¼ Cup Olive Oil
1 Small Onion, chopped
Salt and Pepper to taste
¼ to ½ Cup Grated Romano or
    Parmesan Cheese

Wash cabbage. Remove core and cut the
cabbage into bite-size pieces. In a large
saucepan, cook onion in hot olive oil over
low heat until slightly yellow. Add the
cabbage, salt and pepper. Stir. Cover and
steam for 30 minutes or until tender, stirring occasionally. If necessary, add a small
amount of hot water.

Cook spaghetti in 5 quarts of rapidly boiling, salted water for 15 minutes, or until
tender. Do not drain completely; leave
spaghetti slightly moist. Turn onto platter.
Add cabbage mixture. Toss well. Serve
with grated Romano or Parmesan cheese.
Serves 4 to 6.

RIGATONI with CHICKEN

1 - 3 Lb. Chicken, cut into
    serving pieces
2 Tbs. Butter
2 Tbs. Olive Oil
½ Cup Dry White Wine
2 Garlic Cloves, chopped
Ground Sage and Dried Rosemary
1 Tsp. Salt
Freshly-ground Black Pepper
2 Cups Chicken Stock
3 Anchovy Fillets, soaked in
    cold water for 10 minutes
    and patted dry
½ Tbs. Wine Vinegar
6 Plum Tomatoes, peeled and
    diced
½ Lb. Rigatoni (or any other large
    macaroni product)
Parmesan Cheese, grated

Heat the butter and oil in a deep saucepan.
Saute' the chicken pieces in it, browning
them evenly. Pour in the wine and continue
cooking, uncovered, until the wine evaporates. Add the garlic, a pinch each of sage
and rosemary, the salt, a liberal amount of
pepper and the chicken stock. Cover the
pan and simmer for 1 hour, or until chicken
is fork-tender. Transfer the chicken to a
warm platter in a low oven. Chop the anchovies, then mash them into a paste in the
vinegar. Stir this into the sauce; add the tomatoes. Simmer over low heat, uncovered,
stirring often, for 20 minutes, or until the
sauce is smooth and thick. Meanwhile, cook
the rigatoni al dente, drain it and place it in
a large, hot bowl. Pour in two thirds of the
sauce; toss well. Serve immediately in hot
soup bowls. Serve the chicken separately,
topped with the remaining sauce. Pass the
grated Parmesan cheese. Makes 4 servings.

KIDNEY BEAN CASSEROLE

¼ Cup Chopped Onion
½ Cup Chopped Green Pepper
2 Tbs. Butter or Margarine
1 - 1 Lb. 4 Oz. Can Kidney
    Beans, drained (about 2½ cups)
2 Tbs. Ketchup
1 Tsp. Worcestershire Sauce
½ Tsp. Salt
1/8 Tsp. Pepper
½ Lb. Process Cheese, diced

Saute' the onion and green pepper in butter until soft. Add beans, ketchup, Worcestershire sauce and seasonings. Alternate layers of bean mixture and cheese in a greased 1-quart casserole. Bake in a 350°F. oven for about 20 minutes. Makes 4 servings.

SPAGHETTI with LEMON MEAT SAUCE

2 Lbs. Ground Beef
¾ Cup Finely-chopped Onion
½ Cup Chopped Green Pepper
2 Cloves Garlic, crushed
¼ Cup Brown Sugar, firmly packed
1 Tsp. Salt
¼ Tsp. Pepper
1 Tsp. Thyme
½ Tsp. Basil
2 - 8 Oz. Cans Tomato Sauce
2 - 6 Oz. Cans Tomato Paste
1 - 6 Oz. Can Sliced, Broiled
    Mushrooms, undrained
1 Tbs. Grated Lemon Peel
¼ Cup Lemon Juice
Hot Cooked Spaghetti

Put meat, onion, green pepper and garlic into a heated saucepan. Cook until meat loses its pink color. Remove mixture from the saucepan with a slotted spoon and put into an electric cooker. Add brown sugar, seasonings, tomato sauce and tomato paste; mix well. Cover and cook on low for 10 to 12 hours. Stir in mushrooms, lemon peel and lemon juice; heat thoroughly. Spoon over hot spaghetti and sprinkle with grated Parmesan cheese, if desired. Makes 10 to 12 servings.

NEAPOLITAN LASAGNE

Sauce:
2 Tbs. Finely-chopped Onion
½ Tsp. Minced Garlic
1/3 Cup Salad Oil
1 - 2 Lb. 3 Oz. Can Plum
    Tomatoes, sieved
2 Beef Bouillon Cubes
1 Cup Water
1 - 6 Oz. Can Tomato Paste
½ Bay Leaf
2 Whole Cloves
½ Tsp. Basil Leaves
½ Tsp. Oregano Leaves
½ Tsp. Salt
¼ Tsp. Pepper
¼ Tsp. Sugar

Filling:
1 Lb. Creamed Cottage Cheese
1 - 10 Oz. Pkg. Frozen Spinach,
    cooked, drained and chopped
2 Eggs, slightly beaten
½ Cup Grated Parmesan Cheese
¼ Tsp. Salt
¼ Tsp. Ground Nutmeg
1/8 Tsp. Pepper
1 - 1 Lb. Pkg. Lasagne Noodles,
    cooked and drained
¼ Lb. Mozzarella Cheese,
    shredded
Grated Parmesan Cheese

Saute' onion and garlic in oil; stir in remaining sauce ingredients. Bring to a boil; simmer 1 hour, stirring occasionally. Remove bay leaf and cloves.

Blend together the cottage cheese, spinach, eggs, ½ cup Parmesan cheese, salt, nutmeg and pepper; set aside. Spread 1 cup of the sauce in a 13x9x2" baking dish. Lay a third of the noodles in a single layer on top. Spread with sauce; spoon on half of spinach mixture; sprinkle with a third of mozzarella cheese. Repeat layers, topping with sauce. Add remaining noodles; cover with remaining sauce. Sprinkle with mozzarella and Parmesan cheeses. Cover loosely with foil and bake in 350°F. oven for 40 min. Makes 12 servings.

LIMA BEAN-HAM SOUP

1 Lb. Dried Lima Beans
10 Cups Cold Water
1 Ham Bone, with scraps
1 Onion, peeled and sliced
2 Celery Stalks, sliced
8 Whole Black Peppercorns
2 Carrots, peeled and cut in chunks
¼ Tsp. Powdered Mustard
1 Bay Leaf
1 Leek, sliced (optional)
3 Tbs. Butter or Margarine
2 Tbs. All-purpose Flour
1½ Cups Milk

Pick over and wash beans. Put in large kettle and add the water. Bring to a boil and boil for 2 minutes. Cover and let stand for 1 hour. Add the next 8 ingredients; bring to a boil then cover & simmer for about 1½ hours. Remove ham bone and force the bean mixture through a sieve or food mill. You may whirl this bean mixture in the blender until smooth, if preferred. Melt butter and blend in the flour. Add milk and cook, stirring, until thickened. Add to bean mixture with any ham scraps removed from bone. Heat. Makes 6 to 8 servings, or approximately 2½ quarts.

SPAGHETTI WITH FOUR CHEESES
(Mexico City - Style)

½ Cup Butter
2/3 Cup Shredded Mozzarella Cheese
2/3 Cup Grated Gouda or Edam Cheese
2/3 Cup Grated Swiss Cheese
2/3 Cup Grated Parmesan Cheese
1 Lb. Spaghetti
Salt and Pepper

Melt butter in the top part of double boiler. Have cheeses ready. Cook spaghetti to your taste in boiling, salted water. Drain well & turn into a chafing dish or electric skillet turned to low. Add mozzarella and gouda and toss well. Add half of butter and the Swiss cheese. Give it a thorough mixing & add freshly-ground pepper. Finally, add remaining butter and the Parmesan cheese. Toss again and serve very hot. Makes 4 servings.

JAMAICAN SPLIT-PEA SOUP

2 Cups Split Peas
2 Onions, coarsely chopped
6 Cups Water
3 Cups Chicken Bouillon or Consomme'
   (or Beef Bouillon or Consomme')
Salt and Pepper to taste
4 Strips of Bacon, cooked and
   crumbled
Croutons

Boil split peas and onions in water for 30 minutes. Simmer for 1½ hours. Whirl this puree in a blender for a few seconds. Return to pot and add bouillon. Season to taste. Garnish with crumbled bacon & croutons. Makes about 6 servings.

BRETON BAKED BEANS

1 Cup Dried Pinto Beans
1 Cup Dried Navy or Pea Beans
1 Cup Dried Baby Lima Beans
6 Cups Cold Water
1 Large Onion, chopped (about
   1 cup)
2 Bay Leaves
2 Tsp. Leaf Thyme, crumbled
¼ Tsp. Pepper
4 Smoked Pork Hocks (about 2
   pounds)
1 - 1 Lb. 13 Oz. Can Tomatoes
1 - 12 or 16 Oz. Can Whole-Kernel
   Corn
2 Cups Sliced Celery
1 Tbs. Sugar

Pick over the beans, then rinse in cold water. Combine with 6 cups cold water in kettle or Dutch oven; cover and bring to a boil. Cook for 2 minutes; remove from heat and let stand for 1 hour. Stir in onion, bay leaves, thyme and pepper; add pork hocks, poking them down into the beans. Cover and simmer for 1 hour. Remove pork hocks; let stand until cool enough to handle. Remove the skin, then cut meat from bones and dice. Stir meat, tomatoes, corn and liquid, celery and sugar into beans; spoon into a 16-cup baking dish. Bake, uncovered, in a 350°F. oven for 2 hours, or until meat and beans are tender. Remove bay leaves before serving. Makes 8 to 10 servings.

BISCUIT SANDWICHES
(A Square Meal)

1 Recipe Baking Powder Biscuits
   (use your favorite)
1 Lb. Ground Beef
1 Tsp. Salt
3 Tbs. Butter or Bacon Drippings
¼ Lb. Mushrooms, cleaned
¼ Cup Flour
1½ Cups Milk
¾ Tsp. Salt
¾ Cup Grated Sharp Cheese
2 Cups Cooked Green Beans

Turn biscuit dough onto a floured board and roll to ¼" thickness in a 12½x5" rectangle. Cut into ten 2½" squares. Transfer to a slightly greased baking sheet and bake in a hot oven (425°F.) for 8 to 10 minutes.

In the meantime, combine the meat with the salt and shape in 5 thin patties. Pan fry in a hot, slightly greased skillet until done. Melt butter in top of double boiler. Add sliced mushrooms; cover and saute' just long enough for the mushrooms to be covered with their own juices--2 or 3 minutes. Blend in the flour; add the milk. Stir constantly over direct heat until the sauce boils and thickens. Add ¾ teaspoon of salt and cheese; stir until cheese is melted. Add the green beans and keep hot over boiling water. To serve, place a meat patty between 2 biscuits and pour the hot sauce over all. Serve immediately. Makes 5 servings.

EGGS TETRAZZINI

¼ Cup Finely Chopped Onion
¼ Cup Finely Chopped Celery
2 Tbs. Almonds, blanched and slivered
2 Tbs. Chopped Green Pepper
2 Tbs. Butter
1 Cup Cold Water
2½ Oz. Pkg. Dry Mushroom Soup Mix
1 Cup Milk
4 Hard-cooked Eggs, diced
2 Cups Hot Cooked Spaghetti
Chopped Parsley

Saute' onion, celery, almonds and green pepper in the butter for 5 minutes. Meanwhile, gradually add the water to the soup mix in a saucepan. Stir until well blended and smooth; add milk and heat to boiling over medium heat, stirring constantly. Simmer for 5 minutes, stirring occasionally.

Add sauteed ingredients and the eggs. Heat thoroughly and pour over hot drained spaghetti. Garnish with parsley and serve immediately. Makes 4 servings.

BORDELAISE SAUCE

¼ Cup Butter or Margarine
2 Shallots, finely chopped
2 Garlic Cloves, finely chopped
2 Slices Onion
2 Slices Carrot
2 Sprigs Parsley
10 Whole Black Peppercorns
2 Whole Cloves
2 Bay Leaves
3 Tbs. Flour
½ Tsp. Meat-extract Paste (do
   not use liquid meat extract)
1 - 10½ Oz. Can Condensed Beef
   Broth, undiluted
1 Cup Burgundy
¼ Tsp. Salt
1/8 Tsp. Pepper
2 Tbs. Finely-chopped Parsley

Heat butter in a medium skillet. Saute' shallots, garlic, onion, carrot, parsley, peppercorns, cloves and bay leaves until onion is golden--about 3 minutes. Remove from heat; stir in flour until smooth. Cook, stirring, over very low heat, until flour is lightly browned-- about 5 minutes. Remove from heat & add meat-extract paste. Stir in beef broth and ¾ cup Burgundy. Bring just to a boil, over medium heat, stirring constantly. Reduce heat and simmer, uncovered, for 10 minutes, stirring occasionally. Strain the sauce, discarding vegetables and spices. Return sauce to skillet. Add salt, pepper, parsley and remaining ¼ cup of Burgundy. Reheat gently but do not boil. Taste; add more meat extract if desired. Serve with filet of beef, steak, or hamburger. Makes about 2 cups.

MEXICAN PUCHERO

¼ Lb. Salt Pork, diced
3 Cups Cubed Boneless Beef
1 Clove Garlic
1 Medium Onion, minced
1 Cup Chopped Cabbage
1 Tsp. Crumbled Oregano
½ Tsp. Ground Coriander
½ Tsp. Ground Cuminseed
2½ Cups Canned Tomatoes
2 Tbs. Chopped Parsley
¾ Cup Soaked Garbanzos or
    Chick-peas
1/3 Cup Rice
1 Cup Fresh-cut Whole Kernel Corn
Salt and Pepper to taste

Brown the salt pork. Add remaining ingredients, except for corn and salt and pepper. Cover and simmer, stirring occasionally, for 1½ hours, or until meat is tender. Add corn and salt and pepper to taste. Cook for a few minutes longer to reheat. Drain broth and serve separately with the meat and vegetables. Makes 4 to 6 servings.

SKILLET RAGOUT

1 Lb. Sausage Meat
1 Lb. Ground Veal
2 Eggs
1 Cup Soft Bread Crumbs
    (2 slices of bread)
¼ Cup Chopped Parsley
½ Tsp. Salt
1 Large Onion, chopped (1 cup)
1 Medium Head of Cabbage (about
    3 lbs.)
1 Cup Sliced Carrots
1 Cup Mixed Vegetable Juices
1 Tsp. Salt
½ Tsp. Basil
¼ Tsp. Pepper
1 - 10 Oz. Pkg. Frozen Lima Beans
1 - 10 Oz. Pkg. Frozen Peas

Mix sausage, veal, eggs, bread crumbs, parsley and ½ tsp. salt in medium bowl. Shape lightly into 48 small balls. Brown slowly, turning several times, in a large frying pan (or use an electric frying pan). Remove the meatballs and set aside. Drain all fat from pan, then return 3 tablespoonfuls to pan; stir in onion and saute' just until soft. Cut cabbage in half; slice one half into 8 wedges, then shred other half finely to make about 6 cups. Stir shredded cabbage into onion in pan and cook for 2 minutes, or just until wilted. Stir in carrots, mixed vegetable juices, 1 teaspoon of salt, basil & pepper. Arrange cabbage wedges on top. Cover & heat to boiling, then simmer for 15 minutes. Separate frozen limas and peas; stir into vegetables in frying pan. Top with meatballs; cover and cook 15 minutes longer, or until limas are tender and meatballs are heated through. Serve right from skillet, or spoon into heated serving bowl and arrange the cabbage wedges around the edge. Makes 8 servings.

CHEESE-EGG SCRAMBLE

4 English Muffins or Crumpets,
    split and toasted
4 Tbs. Liver Spread or Deviled
    Ham (from a 4½-oz. can)
6 Eggs
1/3 Cup Milk
½ Tsp. Salt
Dash of Pepper
2 Tbs. Butter or Margarine
4 Slices Process American Cheese,
    cut in half

Spread each muffin half with liver spread or deviled ham; place on a cookie sheet. Set aside. Beat eggs with milk, salt and pepper until foamy (use a medium-size bowl). Melt butter or margarine over low heat in a medium frying pan, tipping pan to coat side. Pour in egg mixture. Cook very slowly, stirring gently from bottom and side of pan just until eggs start to set and are creamy-soft. Remove from heat. Spoon onto prepared muffin halves, dividing evenly. Crisscross top of each with 2 half slices of cheese. Broil 2 to 3 minutes, or just until cheese melts and is bubbly. Makes 4 servings.

POLYNESIAN FRANKS

1 Large Onion, chopped (about
   1 cup)
3 Tbs. Vegetable Oil
2 Tbs. Cornstarch
1 Tbs. Curry Powder
¼ Tsp. Ground Allspice
1 Tsp. Salt
1 - 1 Lb. 5 Oz. Can Crushed
   Pineapple
2 Tbs. Cider Vinegar
12 Frankfurters, cut diagonally
   into 1" lengths

In a large frying pan, saute' onion in vegetable oil until soft. Mix cornstarch, curry powder, allspice and salt in a cup; stir into onions and cook, stirring constantly, just until bubbly. Stir in pineapple & syrup and vinegar; cook over low heat, stirring constantly, until sauce mixture thickens & boils for 3 minutes. Place frankfurters into sauce; heat to boiling. Cover and simmer for 15 minutes, or until heated through. Serve as is or over hamburger buns. Makes 8 servings.

SAUCE ALLEMANDE

2 Tbs. Butter
2 Tbs. Flour
2 Cups Hot Fish, Veal, Chicken,
   or Clear Vegetable Stock
Salt and Pepper
¾ Cup Strong Chicken Stock, heated
2 Egg Yolks, slightly beaten
2 Tbs. Heavy Cream
1 Tbs. Fresh Lemon Juice
1 Tbs. Butter, softened

Melt 2 tablespoons of butter in top part of double boiler. Stir in flour and blend thoroughly. Gradually stir in hot stock. Cook, covered, over simmering, not boiling water for 30 to 45 min., stirring occasionally. Season with salt and pepper to taste. Strain through a fine sieve into a saucepan. Stir additional hot chicken stock into sauce. Blend thoroughly.

Over medium heat, let sauce cook down to two thirds of its original volume, stirring constantly. Remove from heat. Beat egg yolks with cream. Gradually stir hot sauce into egg-yolk mixture. Return sauce to saucepan. Reheat over low heat, but do not boil. Just before serving stir in lemon juice and butter. Stir over low heat until butter is melted. Makes about 1-2/3 cups sauce. One-fourth cup of thinly-sliced sauteed mushrooms may be added to sauce if desired.

QUICHE LORRAINE

½ Pkg. Piecrust Mix
6 Slices Bacon
1 Medium Onion, chopped (½ cup)
8 Oz. Swiss Cheese, shredded
   (2 cups)
4 Eggs
2 Cups Milk
1 Tsp. Salt
¼ Tsp. Ground Nutmeg
1/8 Tsp. Pepper

Prepare piecrust mix, following directions on label (or make your own single-crust pastry recipe). Roll out to a 12" round on a lightly-floured pastry board. Fit into a 9" pie plate or fluted quiche dish. Trim overhang to ½"; turn under, flush with rim and flute to make a stand-up edge. Prick shell well all over with a fork (if using a quiche dish, level pastry so that it is even with rim). Bake in a 425°F. oven for 5 minutes; remove to wire rack and cool slightly. Increase oven temperature to 450°F.

Fry bacon in small skillet until crisp; drain all but 1 tablespoon of fat. Crumble bacon. Saute' onion in bacon fat until soft. Sprinkle cheese evenly in a layer in partly-baked pastry shell; add bacon and onion. Beat eggs slightly in a medium bowl; slowly beat in milk, salt, nutmeg & pepper. Pour mixture into pastry shell. Bake in hot oven (450°F.) for 15 min., then lower the temperature to 350°F. and bake for an additional 15 minutes, or until center is almost set but still soft. Do not overbake as the custard will set as it cools. Let stand for 15 minutes before serving. Cut into wedges. Makes 6 servings.

POLISH-STYLE HAMBURGERS

1 Onion, peeled
1 Carrot, peeled
1 Stalk Celery
1 Medium Potato, peeled
Few Parsley Sprigs
¾ Lb. Beef Chuck, ground
2 Slices of Bread, crumbled
1 Egg
1½ Tsp. Seasoned Salt
¼ Tsp. Seasoned Pepper
2 Tbs. Butter or Margarine
1 Cup Dairy Sour Cream
2/3 Cup Canned French-fried
    Onion Rings

Force first 5 ingredients through medium blade of food chopper. Add to next 5 ingredients and mix lightly but thoroughly. Shape into 8 patties and brown on both sides in butter. Remove from skillet and blend sour cream into drippings. Put the patties back into skillet. Cover and simmer for about 20 minutes. Top with onion rings. Makes 4 servings.

ORIENTAL OMELET

4 Eggs, separated
Dash of White Pepper
¼ Tsp. Salt
¼ Tsp. Cream of Tartar
Butter
¼ Cup Soy Sauce
¼ Cup Brown Sugar, packed
2 Tbs. Vinegar
2 Tbs. Cornstarch
½ Tsp. Dry Mustard
½ Cup Green Pea Pods, thawed
    and drained
¼ Cup Water Chestnuts, cut in
    strips
¼ Cup Green Pepper Strips
¼ Cup Red Pepper Strips
1¼ Cups Shredded Cheddar Cheese

Beat egg yolks and pepper in a small mixing bowl until thick and lemon colored. Beat egg whites, ¼ cup water, salt and cream of tartar in a small mixing bowl until stiff but not dry. Fold beaten yolks into beaten egg whites. Melt 2 teaspoons of butter in a 10-inch skillet with heatproof handle until just hot enough to sizzle a drop of water. Turn egg mixture into skillet. Cook over low heat until puffy and browned on bottom; about 5 minutes. Transfer to preheated 325°F. oven. Bake for 12 to 15 minutes, or until knife inserted near center comes out clean.

Heat 1 cup water, soy sauce, brown sugar, vinegar, cornstarch and dry mustard in a 1-quart saucepan. Cook over medium heat, stirring constantly, until thickened. Cook 2 minutes longer. Remove from heat and stir in 2 tablespoons of butter until melted. Add pea pods, water chestnuts and pepper strips. Keep warm. Remove omelet to a heated platter. Score omelet down the center with a sharp knife. Spread 1 cup of cheese on bottom half of omelet. Fold in half. Top with remaining cheese. Spoon ½ cup sauce over omelet. Serve remaining sauce separately. Makes 4 servings.

SWISSED ELK OR VENISON ROUND STEAK

2 Round Steaks, cut about ¾" thick
    (about 1½ lbs.)
¼ Cup Flour
2 Tsp. Salt
1/16 Tsp. Pepper
¼ Cup Butter or Margarine
1 Cup Water
1 Medium Onion, chopped
1 Cup Diced Celery
½ Cup Sour Cream

Wipe steaks clean with a damp cloth. Combine flour, salt and pepper and pound well into the steak, using the back of a heavy butcher knife blade or the edge of a sturdy saucer. Brown both sides of steak and any remaining seasoned flour slowly in the heated butter. Add ¼ cup of water. Cover and simmer slowly, adding the rest of the water as needed. When the meat is almost tender (1 to 2 hours), add the onion and celery and cook until thoroughly tender. Stir in the sour cream and cook for 2 minutes longer. Serve at once. From 1½ to 2½ hours of cooking will be required, the time depending upon the age of the animal. Makes 5 servings.

ITALIAN-STYLE STUFFED MUSHROOMS

16 Large Fresh Mushrooms
6 Oz. Sweet Italian Sausage
1 Garlic Clove, minced
3 Tbs. Olive Oil
2 Tbs. Minced Parsley
¼ Cup Grated Parmesan Cheese
¼ Cup Water

Wash mushrooms. Remove stems and chop fine. Remove casing from sausage and put the meat into a skillet with the chopped mushrooms, garlic, and 1 tablespoon of oil. Cook, breaking up meat with fork, until lightly browned. Add 1 tablespoon of oil, the parsley and cheese. Fill mushroom cavities with the mixture, rounding tops, and put in shallow baking pan. Put remaining oil & the water in bottom of pan. Bake in preheated 350°F. oven for approximately 20 minutes. Makes 4 servings.

EUROPEAN CASSEROLE

1 Small Onion, minced
2 Tbs. Butter or Margarine
1 - 3 Oz. Can Chopped Mushrooms, drained
3 Cups Diced Cooked Meat (such as ham, chicken, beef or veal)
1 Cup Diced, Cooked Potato
1 Dill Pickle, diced
½ Cup Chopped Olives
Salt and Pepper
1½ Cups Dairy Sour Cream
2 Hard-cooked Eggs, chopped
2 Tomatoes, peeled and sliced
½ Cup Grated Cheddar Cheese

Cook the onion in butter for 2 or 3 min. Add mushrooms and cook for 2 minutes longer. Add to the meats, potato, pickle and olives; mix well. Season with sale and pepper. Stir in the sour cream. Put into a shallow 2-quart baking dish and sprinkle with eggs. Put tomato slices around the edge, and sprinkle cheese over the top. Bake in a moderate oven, pre-heated (350°F). Bake for 25 to 30 min. Makes 6 to 8 servings.

UKRAINIAN BORSCH

1 Lb. Beef Chuck, in one piece
8 Cups Beef Bouillon
Salt and Pepper to taste
1 Bay Leaf
2 Tbs. Butter
1 Onion, chopped
2 Carrots, sliced
3 Medium Raw Beets, shredded
½ Medium Cabbage, shredded
1 Tbs. Minced Parsley
1 - 8 Oz. Can Tomato Sauce
1 Tbs. Vinegar
2 Medium Potatoes, cubed
Dairy Sour Cream

Place beef and cold beef bouillon into a deep kettle. Add salt and pepper & bay leaf. Bring to a boil; skim and simmer, covered, for about 30 minutes. In another pan, melt butter and saute' the onion, carrots, beets, cabbage and parsley for 3 minutes. Add tomato sauce and vinegar and simmer over low heat for 10 minutes. Add to soup, along with potatoes. Simmer, covered, for about 1 hour, or until meat is tender. Skim when needed. Correct seasonings. Remove beef to platter; slice and serve separately. Serve with sour cream. Makes 6 to 8 servings.

RANCHERS' EGGS
(Huevos Rancheros)

1 Garlic Clove, minced
2 Large Onions, chopped
3 Tbs. Butter
1 or 2 Dried Hot Peppers
1 Pimiento, chopped
3½ Cups Tomatoes (1 - 1 Lb. 12 Oz. Can)
Salt to taste
8 Eggs

Cook the garlic and onion in 2 table-spoons of butter until lightly browned. Add crumbled hot pepper, chopped pimiento and tomatoes. Simmer for 45 minutes, or until thickened. Add salt to taste. Fry eggs in remaining but-ter. Serve with the sauce. Makes four servings.

GERMAN KÖNIGSBERGER KLOPS

1 - 2 Oz. Can Anchovy Fillets
5 Slices Dry Bread
1 Cup Milk
1½ Cups Chopped Onion
2 Tbs. Butter or Margarine
2 Eggs, beaten
1½ Tsp. Salt
¼ Tsp. Pepper
1 Lb. Ground Beef
½ Lb. Ground Veal
½ Lb. Ground Pork
¾ Cup Sauterne
¾ Cup Water
1 Bay Leaf
4 Whole Cloves
4 Peppercorns

Sauce:
2 Tbs. All-purpose Flour
¼ Cup Cold Water
1 Lemon, sliced very thin
1 Tbs. Capers
¼ Tsp. Salt

Hot Cooked Noodles
Snipped Parsley

To desalt anchovies, soak in cold water to cover for about 20 minutes; drain well. Soak bread in milk. Cook onion in butter until tender but not brown. Combine the eggs, anchovies, bread mixture, onion, 1½ teaspoons salt, and pepper. Add the meats and mix well. Form into 24 large meatballs (klops).

In a very large skillet, combine wine, ¾ cup water, bay leaf, cloves and peppercorns. Add meatballs. Cover and simmer for 25 to 30 minutes. Remove meatballs and strain the liquid. Return liquid to skillet.

Blend flour and ¼ cup cold water until smooth. Stir into hot liquid; cook & stir until mixture thickens and bubbles. Add lemon slices, capers, and ¼ teaspoon salt. Cook 1 or 2 minutes longer. Arrange the meatballs on platter of hot cooked noodles. Pour sauce over all. Garnish with snipped parsley. Makes 8 servings.

BUTTER SAUCE
(For Vegetables)

½ Cup Butter or Margarine
2 Tbs. Lemon Juice
2 Tbs. Finely-cut Chives
2 Tbs. Finely-cut Watercress
1/16 Tsp. Cayenne

Melt butter or margarine in skillet. Heat until butter starts to brown. Stir in the lemon juice. Add chives, watercress and cayenne. Stir. Makes about ¾ cup of sauce. Serve hot over broccoli, green beans, asparagus, cauliflower, new potatoes, carrots, or other vegetables.

STUFFED GRAPE LEAVES
(A Favorite of Greece)

1 Lb. Lean Ground Beef
1 Egg, beaten
1 Medium Onion, finely chopped
½ Cup Raw Rice
¼ Cup Chopped Parsley
1 Tsp. Chopped Fresh Mint
    Leaves, or ½ Tsp. Dried Mint
2 Tbs. Olive Oil
1¾ Cups Water
Salt and Pepper to taste
Grape or Cabbage Leaves
1½ Cups Undiluted Canned Beef
    Bouillon

Mix beef with egg. Add onion, rice, parsley, mint, olive oil and ¼ cup water. Season to taste with salt and pepper. If using fresh grape leaves or cabbage, soak in hot water for 5 minutes to soften. (Remove core of cabbage and soak the whole head so that leaves may be peeled off without breaking.) If using canned grape leaves, rinse in warm water.

Place a spoonful of the meat mixture on a leaf. Be sure the shiny side is down if using grape leaves. Roll, folding ends in as you go to seal mixture in. Place, folded side down, in a saucepan, making more than 1 layer if necessary. Add bouillon and remaining water. Cover and simmer for 45 minutes. Makes 4 to 6 servings.

MATZO BALLS

2 Eggs
¼ Cup Chicken Fat or Shortening
1 Scant Cup Matzo Meal
¼ to ½ Cup Water (approximately)
1 Tsp. Salt
Dash of Ground Ginger or Cinnamon

Combine the eggs, fat and matzo meal and beat well. Add water and salt, stirring to make a stiff batter. Add seasoning; cover and chill in refrigerator for at least 2 hrs. About 30 minutes before serving, wet your hands with cold water to prevent sticking and form balls of the batter. Drop the dumplings into boiling salted water; cover and cook for 30 minutes. Drain and serve with clear soup or as a substitute for potatoes.

CONSOMME'

2 Lbs. Lean Beef
1½ Lb. Beef Knuckle
   (with bone)
Salt
2 Large Carrots
1 Turnip
1 Small Parsnip
2 Leeks
Stalk of Celery
Small onion, stuck with
   one clove
½ Clove Garlic
Sprig of Thyme
¼ Small Bay Leaf

Put the meat into a large stockpot with 8 pints of cold water. Bring to a boil and skim thoroughly. Add a tablespoonful of salt and all vegetables and herbs. Simmer for 5 hours. Remove fat and strain broth through a cloth wrung out in cold water. The consomme' can be served with many different garnishes and the meat and vegetables may be served separately. Chicken consomme' is made as above, with the addition of a small chicken, previously browned in the oven. Consomme' can be served cold. It should be very clear and strong enough to set into a jelly.

Garnishes for Consomme's:
Beef consomme' with sauerkraut and
   sausages cut into small rounds.
Beef consomme' with diced carrots,
   turnips and potatoes, sprinkled with
   chervil.
Beef consomme' with very fine cooked
   vermicelli added.
Beef consomme' with thin strips of vari-
   ous vegetables.

CHILI-CHEESE CASSEROLE

2 - 4 Oz. Cans Green Chili Peppers,
   drained
1 Lb. Monterey Jack Cheese,
   coarsely grated
1 Lb. Cheddar Cheese, coarsely grated
4 Egg Whites
4 Egg Yolks
2/3 Cup Canned Evaporated Milk,
   undiluted
1 Tbs. Flour
½ Tsp. Salt
1/8 Tsp. Pepper
2 Medium Tomatoes, sliced

Preheat oven to 325°F. Remove seeds from chili peppers and dice. In a large bowl, combine the grated cheese and green peppers. Turn into a well-buttered, shallow 2-quart casserole (12x8x2"). In a large bowl, with electric mixer at high speed, beat egg whites just until stiff peaks form when beater is slowly raised. In small bowl of electric mixer, combine egg yolks, milk, flour, salt and pepper; mix until well blended. Using a rubber scraper, gently fold beaten whites into egg-yolk mixture. Pour egg mixture over cheese mixture in casserole, and using a fork, "ooze" it through the cheese. Bake 30 minutes; remove from oven and arrange sliced tomatoes, overlapping, around the edge of casserole. Bake 30 minutes longer, or until a silver knife inserted in center comes out clean. Garnish with a sprinkling of chopped green chili peppers, if desired. Makes 6 to 8 servings.

TAMALE PIE

1 Onion, chopped
1 Garlic Clove, minced
½ Green Pepper, chopped
2 Tbs. Olive Oil
1 Lb. Ground Round Steak
1 - 1 Lb. 12 Oz. Can Tomatoes
   (about 3½ cups)
Salt
1 Dozen Ripe Olives, pitted
1 Tsp. Ground Coriander
1 to 2 Tbs. Chili Powder
1 Cup Yellow Cornmeal
1 Cup Cold Water
1 Qt. Well-seasoned Beef or
   Chicken Broth
Butter

Saute' onion, garlic and pepper in hot olive oil in a skillet. Add beef and saute' until meat loses red color, stirring with a fork to crumble meat. Add tomatoes, 1 tsp. salt, olives, coriander, and chili powder. Cook slowly for 20 minutes.

Meanwhile, mix the cornmeal and cold water in top part of double boiler. Add hot broth slowly and cook over boiling water until thickened, stirring occasionally. Line an oiled 2-quart casserole with half the mush mixture. Add meat mixture and top with remaining cornmeal mush. Let cool slightly and crisscross top with knife. Dot generously with butter. Bake in pre-heated oven (350°F.) for 45 minutes. Makes 6 servings.

CHEESE SOUP

2 Oz. Butter
1 Oz. Flour
3 Pints Chicken Stock
3 Oz. Grated Cheese
2 Oz. Cooked Noodles
1 Tbs. Chopped Chives
Salt and Pepper to taste

Make a roux with the butter and flour; stir in the stock. Simmer for 30 minutes and add grated cheese. Cook for another five minutes and stir in the noodles, cut small. Heat through and serve with some chives on top.

SWEDISH OMELETTE

4 Eggs
Salt and Pepper
1/8 Cup Butter
Asparagus Tips
1½ Cups Thick White Sauce
½ Cup Cream

Separate eggs; beat the yolks. Whip the whites separately to a stiff froth. Fold egg yolks and whites together and add 1 tsp. cold water and salt and pepper to taste. Melt the butter in a heated omelette pan and cook the omelette. Mix the asparagus tips with ½ cup of the sauce and fold this mixture into the omelette; put the omelette on a dish and leave it to get quite cold. Cool the remainder of the white sauce. Put the sauce through a sieve and then whisk in the whipped cream. Pour this sauce over the omelette and serve cold.

FROGS' LEGS SAUTE'

10 Cleaned Frogs' Legs
½ Cup Heavy Cream, or Undiluted
   Evaporated Milk
1 Tsp. Salt
½ Tsp. Pepper
¼ Cup Flour
3 Tbs. Olive Oil
1 Onion, peeled and cut fine
½ Small Eggplant, pared and cut fine
1 Tomato, peeled and cut fine
1 Clove Garlic
½ Tbs. Butter or Margarine
Lemon Quarters

Rinse frogs' legs and wipe dry. Dip each in cream. Sprinkle with seasoning and roll in flour. Fry legs in olive oil in large skillet until golden brown. Remove to pan and keep hot in oven (leave door of oven open).

Saute' onion, eggplant, and tomato together for 10 minutes in same skillet used to brown frogs' legs. Peel garlic and slice; cook in butter or margarine in small pan for 3 min. Add to vegetables and mix. Pour over the frogs' legs on warmed serving platter. Serve garnished with lemon quarters. Makes 3 to 4 servings.

STEAMED EGG-PARMESAN PUDDING

6 Eggs, separated
¼ Cup All-purpose Flour
1 Cup Milk
¼ Tsp. Salt
¼ Tsp. Pepper
1 Cup Coarsely-grated Parmesan Cheese
   (¼ pound)
Hot Tomato Sauce

Beat egg whites until stiff, but not dry. Set aside. Beat yolks until blended. Blend the flour with some of milk until smooth. Stir in remaining milk. Cook, stirring constantly, until thickened. Stir mixture into eggs; put back in saucepan & cook, stirring, for a few minutes longer. Remove from heat and stir in salt, pepper and cheese. Fold in egg whites. Pour into well-greased 1½-quart pudding mold. Grease lid and cover mold. Put on rack in kettle, and add enough boiling water to come half way up sides of mold. Cover kettle and steam for about 45 minutes. Unmold and serve with hot tomato sauce. Makes 4 servings.

GREEK EGG-AND-LEMON SOUP

2 Qts. Strong, Strained Chicken
   Broth
½ Cup Raw Rice
4 Eggs
Juice of 2 Lemons

Bring the broth to a boil and add the rice. Cook until the rice is tender, about 20 min. Remove the broth from the heat. Just before serving, beat the eggs with a rotary beater until they are light and frothy. Slowly beat in the lemon juice and dilute the mixture with two cups of the hot soup. Beat constantly until well mixed. Add the diluted egg-lemon mixture to the rest of the soup, beating constantly. Bring almost to the boiling point but do not boil or the soup will curdle. Serve immediately. Makes 6 to 8 servings.

VICHYSSOISE SOUP

4 Leeks
2 Oz. Butter
1 Onion, minced
Salt and Pepper to taste
2 Pints Chicken Stock
2 Potatoes
¼ Pint Cream
Chives or Parsley

Prepare the leeks; cut finely and add to hot butter with the onion and seasonings. Cover and cook slowly but do not brown. Add the stock and the thinly-cut potatoes and cook until the vegetables are tender. Put through a sieve. Add more seasonings if desired; stir in the cream and sprinkle with chives or parsley just before dishing up. Serve hot or cold.

FRANK AND BEEF ROLLS

1 Egg, beaten
¼ Cup Milk
1½ Cups Soft Bread Crumbs
2 Tbs. Finely-chopped Onion
1 Lb. Ground Beef
4 Frankfurters, or Fully-cooked
   Smoked Sausage Links
Dijon-style Mustard
2 Tbs. All-purpose Flour
2 Tbs. Shortening
Gravy

Combine first 4 ingredients with ½ teaspoon of salt and a dash of pepper. Add beef and mix well. Divide into 8 portions. Cut franks crosswise; spread generously with mustard. Shape meat around franks to form rolls, leaving ends of franks exposed. Coat with flour. Brown rolls in hot shortening. Cook, covered, over low heat for 15 minutes to 20 minutes, turning occasionally. Remove rolls; reserve pan juices.

Gravy: In skillet, blend 2 tablespoons of reserved pan juices with 2 tablespoons of all-purpose flour. Dissolve 1 beef bouillon cube in 1 cup boiling water; add to flour mixture with 1/3 cup light cream. Cook and stir until bubbly. Add ¼ teaspoon of salt. Heat through. Makes 4 servings.

DEVILED EGGS

8 Hard-cooked Eggs, shelled
¼ Cup Mayonnaise or Salad Dressing
1 Tsp. Salt
½ Tsp. Dry Mustard
¼ Tsp. Pepper
2 Tsp. Chopped Pimiento
1 - 6 Oz. Pkg. Process Gruyere
   Cheese, shredded
1 Cup Boiling Water
1 Envelope Instant Chicken Broth
¼ Cup Butter or Margarine
1 Medium Onion, chopped
   (about ½ cup)
¼ Cup Sifted All-purpose Flour
1½ Tsp. Curry Powder
¼ Tsp. Ground Ginger
1 Cup Milk
1 - 10 Oz. Pkg. Frozen Peas
4 Cups Hot Cooked Rice

Halve eggs lengthwise; remove yolks and press through a coarse sieve into a small bowl. Blend in mayonnaise or salad dressing, ½ teaspoon of salt, dry mustard, 1/8 teaspoon of pepper, chopped pimiento & ¼ cup shredded cheese. Pile evenly into egg-white halves. Cook the peas, following direction on the label; drain and reserve. Dissolve instant chicken broth in boiling water; reserve for next step. Melt butter or margarine in a medium saucepan; saute' onion until tender, about 5 minutes. Stir in flour, remaining ½ teaspoon of salt, remaining pepper, curry powder and ground ginger. Cook, stirring constantly, just until bubbly. Stir in dissolved chicken broth and milk; continue to cook and stir until sauce thickens and bubbles for 1 minute. Remove from heat; stir in remaining cheese until melted; add peas. Spoon hot cooked rice into a heated serving dish; spoon sauce over and arrange eggs around edge of dish. Makes 4 servings.

SWISS-CHEESE-AND-HAM PUFFED SANDWICH

2 Cups Ground Cooked Ham
   (about 1 lb.)
2 Cups Grated Swiss Cheese (½ lb.)
½ Cup Mayonnaise or Salad Dressing
1 Tsp. Prepared Mustard
12 Slices White Bread, toasted
6 Eggs
2¼ Cups Milk

Combine ham and cheese in a medium bowl. It helps if you put both the cheese and ham through a food chopper, using a coarse blade. Blend in mayonnaise or salad dressing and mustard. Spread on 6 toast slices and put together with the remaining slices to make sandwiches. Cut each diagonally into quarters; stand, crust edge down, in a buttered baking dish, 13x9x2". Beat eggs with milk in a medium bowl. Pour over the sandwiches. Cover and chill at least 4 hrs., or overnight. Bake in 325°F. oven for 35 minutes, or just until custard sets. Garnish with parsley. To serve, cut between sandwiches; lift onto serving plates with a wide spatula. Makes 6 to 8 servings.

PIZZA with HAMBURGER CRUST

1 Lb. Ground Beef Chuck or
   Ground Round
1 Small Garlic Clove, minced
1 - 8 Oz. Can Tomato Sauce
¼ Tsp. Garlic Salt
½ Tsp. Sugar
¼ Tsp. Italian Herb Seasoning
1 Sweet Onion, sliced thin
¼ Lb. Italian Salami, sliced thin
½ Lb. Mozzarella Cheese, sliced thin
1 - 6 Oz. Can Chopped Mushrooms,
   drained
¼ Tsp. Crumbled Dried Oregano
¼ Cup Grated Parmesan Cheese

Mix hamburger and garlic together and pat into a 12" pizza pan. Mix the next 4 ingredients and spread on beef. Arrange next 4 ingredients on beef in order given. Sprinkle with oregano and grated cheese. Bake in 450°F. oven for about 15 minutes, or until Mozzarella is bubbly. Makes 4 to 6 servings.

POLISH BIGOS

1 - 1 Lb. 13 Oz. Can Sauerkraut
   (about 3½ cups)
2 Cups Meat Stock
1 - 1 Lb. Can Tomatoes
   (about 2 cups)
1 Large Onion, chopped
1 Large Apple, peeled and chopped
1 Tbs. Bacon Fat
1 Lb. Kielbasa Sausage
2 Cups Diced Leftover Cooked Meat
Salt to taste
Dash of Black Pepper
Dash of Cayenne
1 Tbs. Sugar
1 Tbs. Flour
2 - 4 Oz. Cans Sliced Mushrooms,
   drained
Boiled Potatoes

Drain and rinse sauerkraut. Put into heavy
pot with stock and liquid from tomatoes;
simmer. Saute' tomatoes and onion with apple in fat for a few minutes. Cut kielbasa
into 1" pieces and add with meat to vegetables; simmer for 10 minutes. Add seasonings, sugar, and flour to vegetable-meat mixture; stir. Add mushrooms and stir; cook
until slightly thickened. Add to sauerkraut.
Simmer mixture for 1½ to 2 hours, adding
more stock if dry. Let stand in cool place
overnight. When ready to use, reheat slowly
and serve with hot boiled potatoes. Makes
6 to 8 servings.

BAKED EGGS WITH CHEESE

1 Cup Grated Sharp Cheese
6 Eggs
Salt
Pepper
½ Cup Light Cream

Sprinkle half of the cheese into a greased 9"
pie pan. Break each egg into a small cup;
slide on top of cheese, being careful not to
break yolk. Season with salt and pepper to
taste. Pour cream evenly over eggs and sprinkle remaining cheese on top. Bake in moderate oven, 350°F., for 15 minutes. Makes 6
servings.

CHILI SAUCE

12 Ripe, Medium Tomatoes
2 Medium Onions, chopped fine
2 Green Peppers, chopped fine
2 Cups Cider Vinegar
¾ Cup Sugar
2 Tsp. Ground Cinnamon
2 Tsp. Whole Cloves
2 Tsp. Salt
½ to 1 Tsp. Cayenne

Dip tomatoes into boiling water; core,
remove skins and cut into eighths. Add
remaining ingredients. Cook at slow bub-
ble until sauce is thick and vegetables
are tender. Pour mixture into hot sterilized jars. Seal, cool and store. Makes
about 2½ pints.

PICADILLO

2 Tbs. Cooking Oil
2 Large Garlic Cloves, minced
1 Large Onion, chopped coarsely
Salt and Pepper to taste
1 Lb. Lean Beef, ground
1/3 Cup Dry White Wine
2 Large Ripe Tomatoes, peeled
   and chopped
½ Cup Dark or Light Raisins,
   plumped up in hot water
1/3 Cup Pimiento-stuffed Olives,
   sliced into thirds
1 Green Pepper, seeded and chopped
   into ½" squares

In the oil, fry the garlic and onion for five
minutes, stirring frequently. Add the seasonings, meat and wine and stir again. Add
the tomatoes, raisins and olives; stir. Add
green pepper and cook only long enough for
it to get thoroughly hot. The pepper should
be crisp and retain its color. One of the
nice parts about this recipe is that all of the
chopping and slicing can be done in advance.
The cooking time required is only about 10
minutes. In Cuba, this dish is served with
plain white rice, usually served with the
Picadillo on top of the rice and the juices
trickling down. Makes enough for 3 to 5
people.

CAKES - BREADS

APRICOT DOBOSCHTORTE

Note: This recipe is shown on the cover of this book.

Cake:
6 Eggs, separated
Sugar
1 Cup Flour

Beat egg whites in large bowl until foamy. Gradually add 1/3 cup sugar, beating until stiff peaks form. Beat egg yolks with ½ cup of sugar until thick and pale yellow. Fold into egg whites. Gradually fold in the flour. Grease and flour bottoms of six 9" layer cake pans. Spread batter thinly over each one. Bake in 350°F. oven for 15 minutes, or until golden. Using a sharp knife, remove layers from pan and cool on racks.

Chocolate Butter Cream:
¾ Cup Sugar
3 Eggs
2 Egg Yolks
2 Oz. Semisweet Chocolate
1 Tsp. Instant Coffee Powder
1 Tsp. Vanilla
1 Cup Sweet Butter, softened

In top of double boiler, beat together the sugar, eggs, yolks, chocolate, coffee powder and vanilla; cook over simmering water 10 to 15 minutes or until thickened, stirring frequently. Cool completely. Beat butter until fluffy; gradually beat into the chocolate mixture.

Apricot Filling:
1 - 17 Oz. Can Apricot Halves, drained
¼ Cup Apricot Preserves

Quarter 3 apricot halves; chop remainder and mix with preserves.

To assemble:
Cake Layers
Chocolate Butter Cream
Apricot Filling
½ Cup Chopped, Toasted Filberts
Apricot Preserves
Chocolate Curls

Spread 3 cake layers with chocolate butter cream, using 1/3 cup of cream of each. Spread 2 cake layers with Apricot Filling. Stack together on serving plate. Leaving cream-topped layer on bottom and alternating fillings, invert remaining cake layer and place on top. Spread remaining butter cream over sides of cake; press in nuts. Spread preserves on top. Garnish with reserved apricot slices and chocolate curls. Chill 3 hours before serving. Makes 12 servings.

CHUCK WAGON PECAN BREAD

3½ Cups Sifted All-purpose Flour
1 Cup Sugar
1 Tsp. Salt
3 Tsp. Baking Powder
1 Cup Milk
2 Cups Chopped Pecans
¼ Cup Melted Lard
1 Egg

Combine all ingredients and stir well. Pour into a greased 9x5x3" baking pan. Bake in moderate oven (350°F.) for 1 hour. Turn out and cool on a rack. Keeps well, wrapped tightly.

CONFETTI CAKE

2¼ Cups Flour
4 Tsp. Baking Powder
¾ Tsp. Salt
1-1/3 Cups Sugar
½ Cup Shortening
¾ Cup Milk
1 Tsp. Vanilla
¼ Cup Decorator Beads

Preheat oven to 350°F. Grease two 8" round cake pans. Line bottoms with wax paper or dust lightly with flour. Sift together in a large mixing bowl the flour, baking powder, salt and sugar. Add the shortening, milk and vanilla. Beat 1 minute at low speed with electric mixer. Fold in ¼ cup decorator beads. Pour batter into prepared pans. Bake for 35 to 40 minutes. Cool for 5 minutes; remove from pans & cool on wire racks. Frost as desired. Makes one 8" round cake.

IRANIAN RAISIN CAKE

1 Cup Sifted All-purpose Flour
½ Cup Sugar
½ Tsp. Baking Powder
5 Medium Eggs
½ Tsp. Vanilla Extract
1 Cup Raisins
¼ Cup Sliced Blanched Almonds
¼ Cup Sliced Pistachio Nuts

Mix the flour, sugar and baking powder together thoroughly. Beat the eggs slightly, add vanilla, and combine with the dry ingredients. Add raisins and nuts. Pour into a greased 9¼x5¼x2¾" loaf pan and bake in a preheated 350°F. oven for about 30 to 35 minutes, or until firm. Cool thoroughly and cut into very thin slices.

ORANGE-MARMALADE COFFEE CAKE

1 Pkg. Active Dry Yeast, or
   1 cake compressed yeast
2 Tbs. Water
½ Cup Milk
2 Tbs. Sugar
½ Tsp. Salt
4 Tbs. Butter or Margarine
1½ Cups Sifted All-purpose Flour
1 Egg
½ Cup Orange Marmalade
¼ Cup Sugar
¼ Tsp. Powdered Cinnamon
Extra Flour
Extra Butter or Margarine

Sprinkle yeast in warm water, or use luke-warm water for compressed yeast. Heat milk until film forms over surface. Pour into mixing bowl. Add sugar, salt and butter or margarine. Stir. Beat ½ cup flour into milk mixture. Beat egg slightly. Stir into milk mixture with yeast. Add remaining 1 cup flour and beat hard. If a little more flour is needed, beat it in. It should not be more than 2 tablespoons extra.

Grease a large bowl. Turn dough into it. Turn dough around to grease surface and grease top lightly with softened butter or margarine. Cover bowl with a towel. Let stand in warm place about 1 hour, or until doubled in bulk.

Grease a 9" cake pan. Punch dough down in bowl and turn it out into prepared cake pan. Spread dough lightly. Drop spoonfuls of jam on top and swirl it into dough with a spoon. Sprinkle top with sugar and cinnamon. Cover pan lightly with towel. Let rise until doubled.

Bake in moderate oven (375°F.) for 20 to 30 minutes. It should be lightly browned around the edges. Remove from pan. Cool slightly. Serve warm or cold. Makes 6 to 8 servings.

CHEESE BREAD

1 Cup Milk
2 Tbs. Sugar
3 Tsp. Salt
1 Tbs. Butter or Margarine
1 Envelope Active Dry Yeast
1 Cup Warm Water
5 Cups Sifted All-purpose Flour
2 Cups Grated Swiss Cheese (8 oz.)

Scald milk with sugar, salt and butter or margarine in a small saucepan; cool just until warm. Sprinkle yeast into warm water in a large bowl (water should feel comfortably warm when dropped on wrist). Stir until yeast dissolves; stir in the cooled milk mixture. Beat in 2 cups of the flour to form a smooth soft dough. Beat in cheese; gradually beat in remaining 3 cups of flour to make a stiff dough. Turn out onto a lightly-floured pastry cloth or board; knead until smooth and elastic, adding only enough extra flour to keep dough from sticking.

Place in a greased bowl; turn to coat all over with shortening; cover with a clean towel and let rise in warm place, away from drafts, for about 1 hour, or until double in bulk. Punch dough down and divide in half. Knead each a few times. Shape each into a ball. Place in a greased 8" round layer-cake pan. Cover and let rise again in warm place, away from draft, for about 1 hour, or until double in bulk. Bake in moderate oven (350°F.) for 50 minutes, or until bread gives a hollow sound when tapped. Remove from pans and cool on wire racks. Slice in wedges. Makes two 8-inch round loaves.

SWEET-POTATO BISCUITS

1 Small Sweet Potato, baked
2 Tbs. Shortening
1 Cup Sifted All-purpose Flour
1 Tsp. Baking Powder
¼ Tsp. Salt
2 to 3 Tbs. Milk

Peel and dice sweet potato. Cut potato and shortening into flour which has been sifted with baking powder and salt; add milk and stir until mixed. Turn onto floured board and knead gently. Roll to ½" thickness and cut. Bake on a greased cookie sheet in preheated 400° F. oven for about 12 minutes. Makes 10 to 12 two-inch biscuits.

COCONUT CAKE

3 Cups Sifted Cake Flour
4 Tsp. Baking Powder
1 Tsp. Salt
¾ Cup Vegetable Shortening
1¾ Cups Sugar
3 Eggs
1 Tsp. Vanilla
½ Tsp. Lemon Extract
1¼ Cups Milk
1 Recipe Lemon Filling
   (your favorite)
1 - 3½ Oz. Can Flaked Coconut
Sugar-Candy Flowers (if desired)

Grease bottoms of three 9x1½" layer-cake pans; line pans with wax paper. Grease the paper. Sift cake flour, baking powder and salt into a bowl. In a large bowl, cream shortening with sugar until fluffy (with electric mixer at medium speed). Beat in eggs, one at a time, beating well after each addition. Beat in vanilla and lemon extract. Add the sifted dry ingredients, a third at a time, alternately with the milk; stir with a spoon or beat with mixer at low speed just until blended. Pour into prepared pans. Bake in a preheated 350°F. oven for 30 min., or until centers spring back when lightly touched with fingertip. Cool on wire racks for 5 minutes; loosen around edges with knife and turn the layers out on racks. Peel off wax paper and cool layers completely. Put layers together with lemon filling and frost top and sides with seven-minute frosting. Sprinkle coconut around sides and over top. Arrange sugar-candy flowers to form a bouquet on top if desired. Makes one 9" triple-layer cake.

CRANBERRY ORANGE BREAD

2 Cups Flour
1 Cup Sugar
½ Tsp. Soda
1 Tsp. Baking Powder
½ Tsp. Salt
½ Cup Chopped Nuts
½ Cup Raisins
1 Cup Cranberries, chopped
2 Tbs. Butter
1 Orange (juice and rind)
1 Egg

Sift the dry ingredients together. Grind the orange. Put the ground orange and rind into a cup and add boiling water to make ¾ cup of liquid. Add this, together with butter & egg, to the dry ingredients. Beat well. Add nuts, raisins and cranberries. Put batter into a greased loaf pan and bake for 1 hour at 325°F. Store for 24 hours before using, to allow the flavors to mellow. Makes 1 loaf.

CARAMEL FROSTING

2 Tbs. Butter or Margarine
1/3 Cup Heavy Cream
2/3 Cup Brown Sugar, firmly
   packed
1/8 Tsp. Salt
3 Cups Sifted Confectioners'
   Sugar

Mix butter, cream, brown sugar and salt in a saucepan. Bring to a boil, stirring constantly. Remove from heat; add vanilla & then gradually add enough powdered sugar to make frosting of spreading consistency.

CHERRY CAKE

1½ Cups Milk
4 Eggs
½ Cup All-purpose Flour
¼ Cup Sugar
2 Tsp. Vanilla Extract
2 to 3 Cups Fresh Black Sweet
   Cherries, pitted (or use drained,
   canned, pitted Bing cherries, or
   frozen sweet cherries, thawed
   and drained
Confectioners' Sugar

Combine flour and eggs together in a large mixing bowl; slowly stir in the milk, sugar and vanilla extract. Beat with electric beater until smooth. Pat the cherries completely dry with paper towels. Spread them evenly in a shallow, buttered baking dish or pan that holds 5 to 6 cups and is about 2" deep. Pour in the batter. Bake on middle shelf of oven for 1½ hours, at 350°F., or until top is golden brown and firm to the touch. Dust lightly with confectioners' sugar and serve while it is still warm.

CHOCOLATE POUNDCAKE

1 Cup Soft Butter or Margarine
1¼ Cups Sugar
1 Tsp. Vanilla Extract
5 Eggs, separated
2 Oz. Unsweetened Chocolate, melted
   (2 squares)
2 Cups Sifted All-purpose Flour
½ Tsp. Baking Powder
½ Tsp. Salt

Cream the butter or margarine until light and fluffy. Add 1 cup sugar gradually, beating until light and fluffy. Add vanilla, then egg yolks, one at a time, beating well after each addition. Blend in cooled chocolate. Add the sifted flour, baking powder and salt; beat until smooth. Beat the egg whites until stiff but not dry. Gradually beat in ¼ cup sugar. Fold into the first mixture. Pour into a 9x5x3" loaf pan which has been lined on the bottom with waxed paper (greased). Bake in 300°F. oven for about 1¾ hours. Cool for 5 min. Turn out on rack and peel off paper. When cool, sift confectioners' sugar over the top if desired.

SWISS HOLIDAY BREAD

1 Pkg. Dry Yeast
1 Cup Milk
¼ Cup Sugar
¼ Cup Butter
1 Tsp. Salt
1 Egg
Flour
1/3 Cup Diced, Preserved Citron
1 Cup Chopped, Seeded Raisins
½ Cup Unblanched Almonds,
   chopped
¼ Cup Mixed Red and Green
   Maraschino Cherries, drained
   and halved
½ Tsp. Grated Lemon Rind
1 Beaten Egg, for glaze

Sprinkle the yeast into ¼ cup warm water. Stir until dissolved. Put the scalded milk in a bowl and stir in the sugar, butter & salt; let sit until lukewarm. Beat in 2 cups of flour, then the yeast, egg and enough extra flour to make a soft dough (1½ to 1¾ cups). Turn the dough out on a lightly-floured surface, cover with bowl and let it stand for 10 minutes. Knead until smooth--about 10 minutes. Place in a lightly-greased bowl, turning it once to grease the whole surface. Cover and leave to rise in a warm place (80° to 85°F.), until doubled in bulk--about 1½ hours.

Punch down the dough and let it rise again until it doubles in size. Punch it down and, using hands, work in the citron, raisins, almonds, cherries and lemon rind. Divide the dough in half; shape into two loaves, and put into greased 9x5x3" loaf pans. Let rise until almost doubled in bulk--about 30 to 40 minutes.

Preheat oven to 350°F. Brush loaves with beaten egg, then bake loaves for 25 to 30 minutes, or until they sound hollow when tapped with the finger. Remove from the tins and cool on a rack.

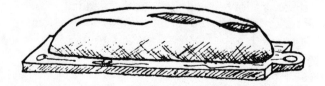

BLACK WALNUT CAKE

2 Cups Sifted Flour
1½ Cups Sugar
1 Tbs. Baking Powder
1 Tsp. Salt
1 Tsp. Ground Cinnamon
½ Tsp. Ground Nutmeg
½ Tsp. Ground Allspice
½ Tsp. Ground Cloves
7 Eggs, separated
2 Tbs. Caraway Seeds
½ Cup Salad Oil
¾ Cup Ice Water
½ Tsp. Cream of Tartar

Sift the flour, sugar, baking powder, salt & spices together several times. Combine egg yolks, caraway seeds, oil and water in large bowl. Add dry ingredients. Beat about 30 seconds at low speed on mixer, or 75 strokes by hand. Add cream of tartar to egg whites. Beat until stiff peaks form. Gradually pour egg yolk mixture over the beaten whites; gently fold in. Pour into an ungreased 10" tube pan. Bake in slow oven, 325°F., for 55 minutes, then increase heat to 350°F. and bake 10 to 15 minutes longer. Invert pan on rack to cool cake. When completely cool, spread Rocky Mountain Frosting over top & sides of cake.

Rocky Mountain Frosting:
½ Cup Butter
2½ Tbs. Flour
¼ Tsp. Salt
½ Cup Milk
½ Cup Brown Sugar, firmly
   packed
2 Cups Confectioners' Sugar
1 Tsp. Vanilla
1 Cup Chopped Black Walnuts

In saucepan, blend butter with flour & salt. Cook 1 minute; do not allow to brown. Add milk; cook until thick. While hot, add brown sugar and beat well. Add sifted confectioners' sugar and beat until thick and creamy. Add vanilla and black walnuts and spread over top and sides of cake.

LOUISIANA PECAN CAKE

1½ Pkgs. Seeded Raisins, cut
   into halves
1 Cup Whiskey
1 Cup Butter or Margarine, softened
2¼ Cups Granulated Sugar
1 Nutmeg, grated
6 Eggs, well beaten
4½ Cups Sifted All-purpose Flour
3½ Cups Coarsely-chopped Pecans
2 Tsp. Baking Powder
1 Tsp. Salt
Confectioners' Sugar

Soak raisins in whiskey overnight. Cream butter and granulated sugar. Add the nutmeg and eggs and beat thoroughly. Mix 1 cup of the flour with the nuts. Sift together remaining flour, baking powder and salt. Add dry ingredients to creamed mixture. Fold in nuts, then raisins. Mix lightly and pour into a well-greased and floured 10-inch tube pan. Bake in 325°F. oven for 1¼ hours, or until top seems firm and sides of cake begin to shrink away from pan. Do not overbake. Let cool in pan for 5 min. Turn out and cool on a cake rack. Sprinkle with confectioners' sugar.

COCONUT DOUGHNUTS

2-1/3 Cups All-purpose Flour
2 Tsp. Baking Powder
2 Eggs, beaten
½ Cup Sugar
¼ Cup Milk
2 Tbs. Shortening, melted
¾ Cup Flaked Coconut
Fat, for frying

Stir together the flour, baking powder and ½ tsp. salt. Beat eggs and sugar together till thick and lemon-colored. Stir in the milk and cooled shortening. Add dry ingredients and coconut to egg mixture, stirring just until blended. Cover and chill several hours. Roll out on a lightly-floured surface to ½" thickness. Cut with floured 2½" doughnut cutter. Fry in deep hot fat (375° F.) about 1 minute per side, turning once. Drain on paper towels. Dust with sugar, if desired. Makes 12 doughnuts.

LEMON BUTTERCUP FILLING

½ Cup Sugar
3 Tbs. Cornstarch
¼ Tsp. Salt
2 Egg Yolks
¾ Cup Water
1/3 Cup Lemon Juice
2 Tbs. Butter or Margarine

Mix sugar, cornstarch, and salt in medium-size saucepan. Stir in egg yolks and water. Cook, stirring constantly, until mixture thickens and boils. Boil for 3 minutes; remove from heat and stir in lemon juice & butter or margarine. Stir until well-blended. Cool completely. Makes enough filling for one 9" triple-layer cake.

LEMON CRUNCH CAKE

1½ Cups Sugar
1/3 Cup Water
¼ Cup Light Corn Syrup
1 Tbs. Sifted Baking Soda
1/8 Tsp. Oil of Lemon
1 - 10" Sponge or Chiffon Cake
1 Pint Whipping Cream (2 cups)
¼ Cup Powdered Sugar
1/8 Tsp. Lemon Extract

Combine sugar, water and corn syrup in a heavy saucepan. Cook over moderate heat, stirring occasionally, until syrup reaches very hard-crack stage (300° on candy thermometer). Remove from heat at once and quickly stir in soda and oil of lemon. Stir until blended and turn out onto a buttered 8x12" shallow baking pan. Let cool. Crush into crumbs.

Split cake into 4 layers. Whip cream until stiff. Flavor with powdered sugar and lemon extract. Spread half the cream between the layers and the remainder on top and sides. Sprinkle crushed candy generously on top and sides. Serves 14 to 16.

For Coffee Crunch Cake, add 3 teaspoons instant coffee to syrup mixture before cooking, and flavor whipped cream with 1 teaspoon of instant coffee.

OLD-FASHIONED SPICE CAKE

2 Cups Sifted All-purpose Flour
1 Tsp. Baking Powder
1 Tsp. Baking Soda
1 Tsp. Ground Cinnamon
¼ Tsp. Ground Nutmeg
¼ Tsp. Salt
4 Tbs. Butter or Margarine
1 Cup Sugar
1 Egg
1 - 10¾ Oz. Can Condensed Tomato
   Soup
½ Cup Chopped Walnuts
½ Cup Golden Raisins

Sift flour, baking powder, soda, cinnamon, nutmeg and salt into a bowl. In a large bowl, cream butter or margarine with sugar until fluffy; beat in egg. Beat in flour mixture, half at a time, alternately with tomato soup, beating just until blended. Stir in the walnuts and raisins. Pour into two greased and floured 8x1½" round layer cake pans. Bake in 350°F. oven for 30 minutes or until cake tests done. Cool in pans, on wire racks, for 10 minutes. Loosen around edges with a knife; turn out onto racks and cool completely. Fill and frost with your favorite icing. Makes one 8-inch double-layer cake.

CHOCOLATE NUT CAKE

1/3 Cup Soft Butter, or other
   shortening
¾ Cup Sugar
1 Egg
2 Oz. Unsweetened Chocolate
   (2 squares), melted and cooled
1-1/3 Cups Sifted Cake Flour
¾ Tsp. Baking Soda
½ Tsp. Salt
¾ Cup Buttermilk
1 Tsp. Vanilla Extract
1 Cup Coarsely Chopped Pecans
   or Walnuts

Cream butter and sugar. Add egg and beat until light. Blend in cooled chocolate. Sift dry ingredients; add alternately with buttermilk. Add vanilla and nuts. Pour into a greased 8" tube pan 3" deep. Bake in preheated moderate oven (350°F.) for about 1 hour. Cool and frost as desired.

APPLE GINGERBREAD

½ Cup Whole Bran Cereal
½ Cup Light Molasses
¼ Cup Softened Shortening
¼ Cup Boiling Water
1 Egg
1 Cup Sifted Flour
½ Tsp. Baking Soda
½ Tsp. Baking Powder
½ Tsp. Ground Ginger
¼ Tsp. Ground Cloves
¼ Tsp. Salt
6 Cups Peeled, Thin Apple
    Slices
¼ Cup Melted Butter
¼ Cup Light Corn Syrup
Milk

Mix bran, molasses, shortening and water.
Add the egg and beat mixture with a rotary
beater; let stand 5 minutes. Sift together
the flour, soda, baking powder, spices and
salt; add to bran mixture and stir only until
blended. Pour into greased 8" square pan.
Bake in moderate oven, 350°F., for 20 min.

Arrange apple slices in layers over the top.
Brush with mixture of butter and corn
syrup. Bake 10 minutes longer, or until the
apples are tender. Remove from the oven,
brush apples with milk and broil just a few
minutes to brown edges of apple slices.
Serve warm. Makes 12 servings.

DIPLOMAT CAKE

1-1/3 Cups Orange Marmalade
2/3 Cup Dark Rum
3 Pkgs. Ladyfingers
1 Cup Heavy Cream, whipped
Chocolate Curls

Line a 1½-quart decorative mold with
plastic film. In small bowl, combine the
orange marmalade with 1/3 cup rum; mix
well. Set aside ¼ cup of mixture and refrigerate for later use. Split ladyfingers;
brush cut sides with remaining 1/3 cup
of rum. In bottom of mold, arrange two
layers of split ladyfingers, cut side up.
Spread with 2 tablespoons of marmalade
mixture. Repeat layers of ladyfingers,
cut side up, and spread with 2 tablespoons of marmalade mixture.

Around side of mold, arrange a row of
split ladyfingers, vertically, rounded side
against mold. Continue layering ladyfingers and marmalade mixture to fill
center of mold, ending with ladyfingers.
Cover top with plastic film; refrigerate
several hours or overnight. To unmold,
remove plastic film from top; invert
mold onto serving plate and gently remove mold and film. Spoon reserved
¼ cup marmalade-rum mixture over top
of cake, letting it drizzle down sides.
Using pastry tube with a number 5 star
tip, make rosettes of whipped cream
around base of cake and on top. Arrange chocolate curls on top of rosettes.
Refrigerate. Makes 8 servings.

BLUEBERRY-ORANGE BREAD

2 Tbs. Butter
¼ Cup Boiling Water
2/3 Cup Orange Juice (approximate)
4 Tsp. Grated Orange Rind
1 Egg
1 Cup Sugar
2 Cups Sifted All-purpose Flour
1 Tsp. Baking Powder
¼ Tsp. Baking Soda
½ Tsp. Salt
1 Cup Fresh Blueberries, washed and
    drained (or use frozen berries which
    have been thawed and drained)
2 Tbs. Honey

Melt butter in boiling water in small bowl.
Add ½ cup orange juice and 3 teaspoons
rind. Beat egg with sugar until light and
fluffy. Add sifted dry ingredients alternately with orange liquid, beating until
smooth. Fold in berries. Bake in greased
fancy 1½-quart baking dish or loaf pan
(9x5x3") in preheated 325°F. oven for
about 1 hour and 10 minutes. Turn out
on rack or tray. Mix 2 tablespoons of
orange juice, 1 teaspoon rind, and honey;
spoon over hot loaf. Let stand until cold.
Makes 1 loaf.

ARMENIAN BREAD

2 Envelopes Active Dry Yeast
2¼ Cups Very Warm Water
   (105°F. to 115°F.)
¾ Cup Nonfat Dry Milk
3 Tbs. Sugar
2 Tsp. Salt
3 Tbs. Olive Oil or Vegetable Oil
6½ Cups Sifted All-purpose Flour
¼ Cup Sesame Seeds
1 Egg, beaten

Sprinkle yeast into very warm water in a large bowl. Stir until yeast dissolves, then stir in dry milk, sugar, salt and oil. Beat in 2 cups of the flour until smooth. Beat in enough of the remaining flour to make a soft dough. Turn out onto lightly-floured pastry board. Knead until smooth and elastic, about 10 minutes, using only as much flour as needed to keep dough from sticking. Invert a large bowl over dough & allow to rest for 20 minutes.

Divide dough into 4 pieces. Divide one of these pieces into 3 pieces. Grease three cooky sheets with oil. Pat out one of the large pieces of dough to make a 9" round on one of the cooky sheets. Make a 3" hole in center of round by pulling dough back with fingers. Pat a small piece of dough into a 3" round and place in hole. Repeat steps to make 3 loaves. Cover each loaf with plastic wrap and chill for 2 hrs., or to a maximum of 6 hours. Remove the breads from the refrigerator and remove the plastic wrap. Allow dough to stand at room temperature for 10 minutes. Sprinkle the sesame seeds on a shallow baking pan. Toast in a 350°F. oven for 5 minutes, or just until golden. Brush breads with beaten egg and sprinkle with toasted sesame seeds. Bake in 350°F. oven for 30 minutes, or until breads are golden and give a hollow sound when tapped. Remove from cooky sheets to wire racks and allow to cool completely. Makes three 15-inch rounds.

GRANGE RAISIN CAKE

2 Eggs
1½ Cups Sugar
½ Cup Butter, melted
2½ Cups All-purpose Flour, unsifted
1 Tsp. Baking Soda
1 Tsp. Salt
¼ Tsp. Ground Nutmeg
½ Cup Buttermilk
1 Cup Raisins, chopped
1 Large Unpeeled Orange, ground

Break eggs into mixing bowl and beat until frothy. Beat in sugar and melted butter. Sift dry ingredients and add alternately with buttermilk to first mixture. Fold in raisins and orange. Pour into well-greased pan (9x9x2") and bake in a preheated 350°F. oven for 50 to 55 minutes. This cake is so rich that it needs no frosting. Makes nine 3-inch squares.

TOMATO-SOUP SPICE CAKE

2 Cups Sifted All-purpose Flour
1 Tsp. Baking Powder
1 Tsp. Baking Soda
1 Tsp. Ground Cinnamon
¼ Tsp. Ground Nutmeg
¼ Tsp. Salt
4 Tbs. Butter or Margarine
1 Cup Sugar
1 Egg
1 - 10¾ Oz. Can Condensed
   Tomato Soup
½ Cup Chopped Walnuts
½ Cup Golden Raisins

Grease two 8-inch round layer cake pans; flour lightly. Sift flour, baking powder, soda, cinnamon, nutmeg and salt into a small bowl. Cream butter or margarine with sugar until fluffy in a large bowl; beat in egg. Beat in flour mixture, half at a time, alternately with the tomato soup, beating just until blended. Stir in walnuts and raisins. Pour into the prepared pans. Bake in 350°F. oven for 30 minutes, or until cake tests done. Cool in pans on wire racks for 10 minutes. Loosen around edges with a knife; turn out onto racks and cool completely. Fill and frost with cream cheese frosting.

SWEDISH RYE BREAD

1 Pkg. Active Dry Yeast (or
   1 cake compressed yeast)
¼ Cup Lukewarm Water
2 Cups Milk or Water
1/3 Cup Butter
¼ Cup Molasses
¼ Cup Brown Sugar
2 Tsp. Salt
2 Cups Rye Flour
1 Tsp. Caraway Seeds (or
   2 Tsp. Pounded Fennel or
   Aniseeds)
4 Cups Sifted All-purpose Flour

Sprinkle dry yeast into warm water. Use very warm water for dry yeast (105°F. to 115°F.) and use lukewarm water (80°F. to 90°F.) for compressed yeast. Let stand for a few minutes, then stir until dissolved. Scald milk; add butter, molasses, brown sugar, salt and rye flour. Beat until smooth. Cool to lukewarm; add caraway seeds and yeast. Add flour gradually to make a stiff dough. Knead until smooth and elastic to the touch, about 8 to 10 minutes. Cover, and let rise in a warm place until almost double in bulk. Toss on lightly-floured board and divide into 2 equal parts. Form each into a flat round loaf. Cut a small hole in the center. Place on buttered cookie sheet, prick with fork, cover and let rise until light. Bake in 375°F. oven (preheated) for 35 minutes. Brush with warm water when half done and again when bread is taken from the oven.

DANISH KRINGLE

1 Tbs. Sugar
1 Tsp. Salt
2 Cups Sifted All-purpose Flour
½ Cup Butter or Margarine
1 Pkg. Active Dry Yeast
¼ Cup Very Warm Water
1 Egg
¼ Cup Cold Milk
Filling (see recipe below)
Confectioners' Icing
Chopped Dates, Prunes, Pecans
   or Almond Paste

Sift together sugar, salt and flour; cut in the butter until mixture resembles coarse cornmeal. Sprinkle dry yeast into very warm water (105° to 115°F.). Let stand for a few minutes, then stir until dissolved. Beat egg until thick and lemon colored. Using a fork, stir egg, milk, and yeast mixture lightly into flour mixture. Refrigerate overnight. Turn out on a lightly-floured board. Divide into thirds. Cover and let stand for 10 minutes. Roll each part into a rectangle 9″ wide and as long as it will roll without breaking; the dough should be thin. Spread one-third of filling mixture down the center of each rectangle of dough. Top this with a thin layer of dates, prunes, chopped pecans, or almond paste. Fold one edge of dough over the filling and top this with the other edge of dough. Seal all edges well. Place on buttered cookie sheet in form of an oval or horseshoe. Let rise in a warm place for 1 hour. Bake in preheated 375°F. oven for 20 to 25 minutes. Frost with confectioners' icing while hot. Makes 3 loaves.

For filling: Cream together ½ cup butter or margarine, ¾ cup sugar and 1 teaspoon of ground cinnamon.

PICNIC CAKE with POLKA DOTS

1¼ Cups Chopped Dates
1 Cup Sugar
¾ Cup Butter or Margarine
1 Cup Sugar
2 Eggs
2 Cups Sifted All-purpose Flour
1 Tsp. Baking Soda
½ Tsp. Salt
1 Tsp. Vanilla
1 - 6 Oz. Pkg. Semisweet Chocolate
   Pieces
½ Cup Chopped Nuts

Mix chopped dates and hot water; set aside to cool. Cream together butter and sugar. Add eggs and beat until fluffy. Sift together flour, soda and salt. Add to creamed mixture alternately with date mixture. Mix well after each addition. Stir in vanilla and ½ cup chocolate pieces. Spread batter in a greased 13x9x2″ pan. Top with remaining chocolate pieces and nuts. Bake in 350°F. oven for about 35 minutes.

ITALIAN ORANGE-RUM CAKE

3 Eggs
1 Cup Sugar
3 Tbs. Fresh Orange Juice
2 Tsp. Grated Orange Rind
1 Cup Sifted All-purpose Flour
2 Tsp. Baking Powder
Orange-Rum Topping (see recipe
  below)
Orange Slices, Candied Cherries
  and Whipped Cream Rosettes

Beat eggs until light. Gradually beat in
the sugar and continue to beat until the
mixture is thick and lemon-colored. Use
an electric mixer if possible, and beat at
high speed for about 5 minutes. Stir in
orange juice and rind. Sift flour with
baking powder 3 times and fold into the
batter. Pour into buttered & floured 9''
springform pan. Bake in preheated 350°
F. oven for 30 minutes, or until cake
tests done. Cool in pan. Pour the topping over cooled cake and chill until
serving time. Remove from pan and
decorate with oranges, cherries and the
whipped-cream rosettes.

Orange-Rum Topping:
1 Envelope Unflavored Gelatin
¼ Cup Cold Water
2 Cups Hot Milk
¾ Cup Sugar
4 Egg Yolks, lightly beaten
1/3 Cup Dark Rum
1 Large Orange, peeled and sectioned
1 Cup Heavy Cream, whipped

Soften gelatin in cold water. Stir in hot
milk and sugar. Cook over low heat until mixture is hot. Do not boil. Gradually pour over egg yolks, stirring constantly. Add rum. Set pan in a bowl
of cracked ice and stir constantly until
cool and beginning to set. Fold in the
orange sections and whipped cream.

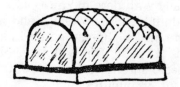

GRAHAM MUFFINS

2 Cups Graham Flour
2 Tbs. Sugar
½ Tsp. Salt
1 Egg
¾ Tsp. Soda
1½ Cups Sour Milk
½ Tbs. Shortening
1 Tsp. Baking Powder

Sift the flour with the other dry ingredients
and turn the bran back into it. Add the
milk gradually, the well-beaten egg and the
melted shortening. Fill well-greased muffin
tins about 2/3 full and bake in a hot oven
(400-425 degrees F.) from 20 to 25 minutes.

LEMON LOAF

3 Cups Sifted All-purpose Flour
¾ Cup Granulated Sugar (for bread)
3 Tsp. Baking Powder
1 Tsp. Salt
¼ Tsp. Baking Soda
¼ Tsp. Ground Nutmeg
½ Cup Finely-chopped Walnuts
¼ Cup Brown Sugar, firmly packed
1 Tbs. Grated Lemon Peel
1 Egg
1¼ Cups Milk
4 Tbs. Butter or Margarine,
  melted
1 Tbs. Granulated Sugar (for
  topping)
1 Tbs. Lemon Juice

Sift the flour, ¾ cup granulated sugar, baking powder, salt, soda and nutmeg into a
large bowl; stir in walnuts, brown sugar and
lemon peel. Beat egg slightly with milk in
a small bowl; stir in melted butter or margarine. Pour, all at once, into flour mixture.
Stir about 30 strokes, or just until all of batter is moist. Spoon into a well-greased 9x5x
3'' loaf pan. Let stand 20 minutes. Bake in
350°F. oven for 1 hour and 15 minutes, or
until a wooden pick inserted in center comes
out clean. Cool in pan on wire rack for 5
minutes, then turn out on rack. Mix the 1
tablespoon granulated sugar and lemon juice
in a cup; brush over the top of the loaf
several times to glaze. Cool loaf completely.
Wrap and store for at least a day before
slicing. Makes 1 loaf.

POUND CAKE

2-1/3 Cups Sifted Cake Flour
1 Tsp. Baking Powder
½ Tsp. Salt
2/3 Cup Butter or Margarine, softened
1¼ Cups Sugar
3 Eggs
½ Cup Milk
1 Tsp. Grated Lemon Rind
1 Tbs. Lemon Juice

Preheat oven to 350°F. Grease a 9" tube pan and dust lightly with flour, tapping out any excess flour.

Sift flour, baking powder and salt. Combine butter or margarine, sugar and eggs in a large bowl of mixer; beat at high speed for 3 min. Remove bowl from mixer. Combine milk, lemon rind and juice in a cup. Stir flour mixture into creamed mixture alternately with milk mixture, beating after each addition until batter is smooth. Pour into prepared pan. Bake 60 minutes, or until center springs back when lightly pressed with fingertip. Cool 10 minutes on wire rack; loosen around edge and tube with a knife. Turn out onto wire rack; cool completely.

HOLIDAY RIBBON CAKE

4 Cups Sifted Cake Flour
4 Tsp. Baking Powder
½ Tsp. Salt
½ Tsp. Ground Mace
½ Tsp. Ground Ginger
1 Cup Butter or Margarine
2 Cups Sugar
4 Eggs
2 Tsp. Vanilla
1 Cup Milk
1 Cup Chopped Pecans
½ Cup Candied Red Cherries,
  halved
½ Cup Chopped Candied Orange
  Peel
½ Cup Golden Raisins
Lemon-Coconut Filling (see recipe
  below)
7-Minute Icing

Grease and flour three 9x1½" layer cake pans, tapping out any excess flour. Preheat oven to 350°F.

Sift flour, baking powder, salt, mace and ginger into a small bowl. Cream butter or margarine with sugar until light and fluffy; beat in eggs, one at a time; add vanilla. Beat in flour mixture, alternately with the milk, until well blended. Measure 2 cups of the batter into a medium bowl; stir in pecans, cherries, orange peel and raisins. Pour into one of the prepared pans. Pour remaining batter evenly into the other two pans. Bake in 350°F. oven for 25 minutes, or until cake tests done. The fruit layer may need an additional 5 minutes of baking time. Cool cakes in pans for 10 minutes on wire racks. Loosen around edges with a knife; turn out onto racks and cool completely. Prepare filling.

Lemon-Coconut Filling:
1/3 Cup Sugar
2 Tbs. Cornstarch
¾ Cup Water
1 Egg Yolk
1 Tbs. Butter or Margarine
1 Tsp. Grated Lemon Rind
3 Tbs. Lemon Juice
½ Cup Flaked Coconut

Mix sugar and cornstarch in a medium-size saucepan; stir in water. Cook, stirring constantly, until mixture thickens and boils 3 minutes. Beat egg yolk slightly in a small bowl; slowly beat in about half of the hot mixture, then stir back into saucepan. Cook, stirring constantly, 1 minute longer. Remove from heat. Stir in butter or margarine, the grated lemon rind, lemon juice and coconut. Cool. Makes about 1½ cups of filling.

Spread filling over fruit layer and one of the plain layers. Stack layers on a serving plate, putting the fruit layer in the middle. Prepare 7-minute icing from your favorite recipe. Spread over sides and top of cake. Decorate top with red cherries and leaves cut from angelica, if you wish. Makes one 9" triple-layer cake.

RAISIN BREAD with ORANGE/NUT GLAZE

1 Cup Milk
1½ Tsp. Salt
½ Cup Sugar
½ Cup Soft Butter or Margarine
   (or shortening)
2 Pkgs. Active Dry Yeast
¼ Cup Warm Water (110 to 115°F.)
5¼ to 5¾ Cups Sifted All-purpose
   Flour
2 Eggs
1 Tsp. Grated Orange Peel
1 Tsp. Ground Ginger
1½ Cups Raisins

Scald milk; pour over the salt, sugar and butter in a large bowl. Blend and cool to lukewarm. Sprinkle yeast on warm water; stir to dissolve. Add to milk mixture with 2½ cups of flour. Beat 2 minutes with electric mixer at medium speed, scraping bowl occasionally (or beat with spoon until smooth, about 100 strokes). Beat in eggs, orange peel, ginger, raisins and ½ cup flour, a little at a time, first with a spoon and then with hands, to make a soft dough that leaves sides of bowl.

Turn onto a lightly-floured board and knead just until smooth, about 50 strokes. Round up in a ball; place in a lightly-greased bowl and turn the dough over to grease the top. Cover and let rise in a warm place, free from drafts, until doubled--1 to 1½ hours. Punch down and let rest for 15 minutes. Divide in half. Shape into loaves and place in 2 greased 8½x4½x2½ loaf pans. Make 3 diagonal slashes ¼" deep across top of each loaf. Cover and let rise in a warm place, free from drafts, only until doubled, about 1 hour. Bake in 375°F. oven for 40 to 50 minutes. Cover with sheet of foil after the first 20 minutes of baking if loaves are browning too fast. Remove loaves from pans; place on wire racks. Spread with glaze, then cool. Makes 2 loaves.

Orange/Nut Glaze: Blend 1 cup sifted confectioners' sugar, 2 tsp. soft butter and ½ cup finely-chopped walnuts; add 2 to 4 tbs. orange juice to make glaze of spreading consistency.

CRANBERRY MUFFINS

1 Cup Chopped Raw Cranberries
½ Cup Sugar
2 Cups All-purpose Flour
3 Tsp. Baking Powder (Double-Acting)
½ Tsp. Salt
2 Tbs. Sugar
1 Egg
1 Cup Milk
¼ Cup Melted Shortening

Combine chopped cranberries and ½ cup of sugar. Sift flour, measuring and then resifting with baking powder, salt and 2 tablespoons of sugar. Beat egg; add milk & beat well. Add melted shortening and immediately add all at once to dry ingredients, mixing until dry ingredients are just dampened. Batter is not smooth. Stir in cranberries with the last few stirs until just distributed, and quickly put batter into well-greased muffin pans, filling 2/3 full. Bake in 400°F. oven for 20 to 25 minutes. Makes 12 large or 16 medium muffins.

BRANDY NUT CAKES

4 Egg Yolks
2/3 Cup Granulated Sugar
1-1/3 Cups Nuts, chopped medium fine
1/8 Tsp. Salt
1/8 Tsp. Ground Cloves
1/8 Tsp. Cinnamon
1/3 Cup Cracker Meal
2 Tbs. Brandy
¼ Cup Butter or Margarine, melted
Confectioners' Sugar
Candied Cherries
Angelica

Beat the egg yolks until thick and lemon-colored. Gradually beat in granulated sugar. Add remaining ingredients except for the last 3, and mix well. Pour into a greased and floured pan (9x9x2"). Bake in a preheated moderate oven (375°F.) for about 25 minutes. Cool in pan.

Turn out and cut into 1½" diamonds. Sprinkle with confectioners' sugar and decorate with cherries and angelica. Makes about 3 dozen.

PUMPKIN-PRUNE CAKE

2/3 Cup Soft Shortening
2½ Cups Sifted Cake Flour
4 Tsp. Baking Powder
1 Tsp. Salt
1 Tsp. Ground Cloves
1 Tsp. Ground Ginger
2 Tsp. Ground Cinnamon
1½ Cups Sugar
¾ Cup Milk
1 Cup Canned Pumpkin
1 Cup Chopped Cooked Dried Prunes
2 Eggs

Put shortening in a mixing bowl. Add the sifted dry ingredients, ½ cup milk, pumpkin and prunes. Beat for 2 minutes. Scrape the bowl frequently during beating. Add eggs and remaining milk; beat for 2 minutes longer. Pour batter into two 8-inch square cake pans, greased and floured. Bake in a 375°F. oven for about 40 minutes. Let stand for 5 minutes; turn out on racks to cool. Frost if desired. Makes two 8-inch squares.

DUTCH HONEY CAKE

½ Cup Dark Brown Sugar, firmly packed
1 Egg
½ Cup Honey
3 Tbs. Dark Molasses
1 Tsp. Baking Soda
½ Tsp. Baking Powder
¼ Tsp. Pepper
¼ Tsp. Ground Allspice
¼ Tsp. Cinnamon
¼ Tsp. Nutmeg
¼ Tsp. Mace
3 Tbs. Butter, melted
1½ Cups Sifted All-purpose Flour

Beat together sugar and egg. Beat in honey and molasses. Soften baking soda in 2 tsp. water and stir into mixture. Combine baking powder, spices and melted butter. Beat into mixture. Gradually beat in flour, a little at a time. Thoroughly grease & flour a loaf pan (9¼x5¼x2¾"). Pour mixture into it. Bake in preheated moderate oven (350°F.) for 30 to 45 minutes, or until knife blade inserted in center comes out clean. Cool in pan for 5 minutes. Remove and cool on wire rack.

STRAWBERRY RIBBON CAKE

3 Cups Sifted Cake Flour
2½ Tsp. Baking Powder
½ Tsp. Salt
1 Cup Butter or Margarine
2 Cups Sugar
4 Eggs
1 Tsp. Vanilla
½ Tsp. Almond Extract
¾ Cup Milk
1/8 Tsp. Red Food Coloring
Strawberry Butter Cream (see
   recipe below)

Grease and flour two 8x8x2" baking pans. Sift cake flour, baking powder and salt into a bowl. Cream butter or margarine until soft in a large bowl; beat in sugar gradually until fluffy. Beat in eggs, one at a time, until fluffy again, then add flavorings. Stir in flour mixture, alternately with milk, and stir just until blended. Spoon half the batter into one pan; stir food coloring into remaining batter and pour into second pan. Bake in 375°F. oven for 35 minutes, or until cake tests done. Cool layers in pans on wire racks for 10 minutes; turn out onto racks & cool completely. Split each cooled layer; put together, alternating pink and yellow, with part of the strawberry butter cream. Frost sides and top with the remaining frosting.

Strawberry Butter Cream:
1 - 3 or 4 Oz. Pkg. Cream Cheese
4 Tbs. Butter or Margarine
1/3 Cup Mashed Fresh Strawberries
1 - 1 Lb. Pkg. Confectioners' Sugar

Blend cream cheese with butter or margarine until fluffy (use medium-size bowl). Beat in strawberries. Stir in 2 cups of the confectioners' sugar until smooth. Measure out 1½ cups of the mixture for filling. Beat remaining confectioners' sugar into remaining mixture in bowl for frosting.

MARSHMALLOW SURPRISE APPLESAUCE CAKE

2¾ Cups Flour
2 Cups Sugar
1½ Tsp. Baking Soda
1½ Tsp. Salt
¼ Tsp. Baking Powder
1 Tsp. Ground Cinnamon
½ Tsp. Ground Cloves
½ Tsp. Ground Allspice
½ Cup Shortening
2 Eggs
2 Cups Unsweetened Applesauce
1 Cup Walnut Halves
20 Large Marshmallows

Sift together flour, sugar, soda, salt, baking powder and spices. Add shortening, eggs and applesauce. Beat until blended and smooth. Stir in the walnuts. Pour into a greased and floured 13x9x2" pan. Press whole marshmallows into batter to bottom of the pan, in 4 rows with 5 in each row. Bake in moderate oven, 350°F., for about 50 minutes. Cool on a rack.

SPICY POTATO DOUGHNUTS

4 Cups All-purpose Flour
2 Tbs. Baking Powder
½ Tsp. Ground Cloves
½ Tsp. Ground Cinnamon
3 Eggs, beaten
1 Cup Brown Sugar, packed
1½ Cups Mashed, Cooked Potatoes
2 Tbs. Shortening, melted and cooled
1 - 5-1/3 Oz. Can Evaporated Milk
Fat, for frying

Stir together the first 4 ingredients and 1 teaspoon of salt. Beat eggs and sugar until thick. Stir in cooled potatoes, shortening and milk. Gradually add dry ingredients to potato mixture, stirring until combined. Chill for at least 3 hours. Roll the dough on a well-floured surface, half at a time, to 3/8" thickness. Cut with floured doughnut cutter; chill 15 minutes. Fry in deep hot fat (365°F.) for 1 to 1½ minutes per side, turning once. Drain on paper towels. Makes 36 doughnuts.

SWEDISH LIMPA BREAD

2½ Cups Warm Water (105° to 115°F.)
2 Pkgs. Active Dry Yeast
1 Tbs. Salt
¼ Cup Light or Dark Molasses
½ Cup Light Brown Sugar, packed
¼ Cup Soft Butter or Margarine
2 Tbs. Grated Orange Peel
1 Tsp. Anise Seed
4 Cups Unsifted Rye Flour
4½ Cups Unsifted All-purpose Flour
Cornmeal
2 Tbs. Butter or Margarine, melted

Sprinkle yeast over water in large bowl, stirring until dissolved. If possible, check the temperature of the water first with a thermometer. Add salt, molasses, brown sugar, ¼ cup butter, the orange peel, anise seed & rye flour. Beat vigorously with a wooden spoon until smooth. Gradually add all-purpose flour; mix in with hand until dough leaves the side of the bowl. Dough will be stiff. Turn dough out onto lightly-floured pastry cloth or board. Knead until smooth and elastic--about 10 minutes. Place in a lightly-greased large bowl; turn dough to bring up greased side. Cover with a towel and let rise in warm place (85°F.), free from drafts, until double in bulk--about 1½ hours.

Grease a large cookie sheet and sprinkle it lightly with cornmeal. Punch down dough. Turn out onto lightly floured pastry cloth or board and divide dough in half. Shape each half into a smooth ball, 6 inches in diameter; tuck edges under. Place on opposite ends of cookie sheet. (Or make oval loaves by shaping into a loaf 8 inches long, tapering ends.) With a sharp knife, cut 3 diagonal slashes on top of loaf-- about ¼ inch deep. Cover with towel & let rise in a draft-free warm place until double in bulk--1 to 1½ hours. Preheat oven to 375°F. Bake on middle shelf of oven for 30 to 35 minutes, covering with foil or brown paper the last 10 minutes. Remove to rack; brush with melted butter. Serve slightly warm, or let cool completely. Makes 2 loaves.

ORANGE BUTTER CREAM FROSTING

½ Cup Butter or Margarine, softened
2 Tsp. Grated Orange Rind
1/8 Tsp. Salt
1 Egg Yolk
1 - 1 Lb. Pkg. Confectioners' Sugar,
    sifted
¼ Cup Orange Juice

Combine butter or margarine, orange rind, salt and egg yolk in small bowl of mixer. Beat at medium speed until thoroughly blended. Add sugar alternately with the orange juice, beating until mixture is of good spreading consistency. Makes enough frosting to fill and frost two 9" layers.

GUMDROP ORANGE-DATE BREAD

1 Cup Hot Water
1½ Cups Pitted Fresh Dates,
    cut into small pieces
¾ Cup Granulated Sugar
¾ Cup Brown Sugar, firmly
    packed
½ Cup Butter or Margarine,
    softened
2 Eggs
1 Cup Orange Juice
2 Cups Cut-up Orange Gumdrops
1 Tsp. Grated Orange Peel
4 Cups Regular All-purpose Flour
2 Tsp. Baking Powder
2 Tsp. Soda
1 Tsp. Salt

Pour hot water over dates and allow to stand for 15 minutes. In a large mixing bowl, cream together thoroughly the granulated sugar, brown sugar, and butter or margarine. Beat in eggs, one at a time. Add the orange juice. Stir in dates (including water), gumdrops, and grated orange peel. Sift flour into mixing bowl along with baking powder, soda, and salt. Stir to combine thoroughly. Divide mixture evenly into 2 well-greased 9x5" loaf pans. Bake in 350°F. oven for 1 hour or until a toothpick inserted in center comes out clean. Cool loaves in pans for about 3 minutes, then turn out on a wire rack to continue cooling. Makes 2 loaves.

WHEAT GERM MUFFINS

1½ Cups Sifted All-purpose Flour
¼ Cup Sugar
2 Tsp. Baking Powder
1 Tsp. Salt
1 Cup Wheat Germ
1 Egg, well beaten
¾ Cup Milk
4 Tbs. Butter or Margarine, melted
¼ Cup Molasses

Sift flour, sugar, baking powder and salt into a medium-size bowl. Stir in the wheat germ. Combine egg, milk, melted butter or margarine, and molasses in a small bowl; add all at once to flour mixture and stir lightly just until liquid is absorbed. The batter will be lumpy. Spoon into 12 greased medium-size muffin cups (fill 2/3 full). Bake in 400°F. oven for 30 minutes, or until richly browned. Remove from pan at once. Serve hot with butter or margarine and your favorite jelly, jam or marmalade. Makes 12 medium muffins.

BANANA AMBROSIA RING

½ Cup Flaked Coconut
1/3 Cup Maple-flavored Syrup
2 Tbs. Butter or Margarine, melted
2 Cups Packaged Biscuit Mix
3 Tbs. Sugar
½ Cup Mashed Ripe Banana
1 Slightly-beaten Egg
3 Tbs. Butter or Margarine, melted
2 Tbs. Sugar
1 Tsp. Cinnamon
2 Tbs. Butter or Margarine

Mix coconut with the maple syrup and 2 tablespoons of melted butter and spread over the bottom of a 5-cup ring mold. Combine biscuit mix with 3 tablespoons of sugar. Stir in banana, egg, and 3 tablespoons of melted butter. Beat mixture vigorously for 1 minute ; spoon half of batter over the coconut in the mold. Mix 2 tablespoons of sugar with the cinnamon; sprinkle over batter. Dot with butter. Cover with the remaining batter. Bake at 375°F. for 20 minutes, or until it tests done. Invert to unmold. Serve warm.

YUMMY YAM CAKE

1¾ Cups Sugar
1 Cup Cooked, Mashed Yams
   (cold)
¾ Cup Soft Shortening
1 Tsp. Cinnamon
½ Tsp. Salt
3 Eggs, unbeaten
1 Tsp. Baking Soda
1 Cup Buttermilk
2 Cups Sifted Flour
¾ Cup Chopped Pecans

Combine sugar, yams, shortening, cinnamon and salt. Cream well. Add eggs, beating until blended. Combine baking soda and buttermilk. Add alternately with flour to the creamed mixture, beginning and ending with the flour. Coat the pecans with 2 tsp. of flour, stir into the batter. Turn into greased and floured 13x9x2" baking pan and bake at 350°F. for 50 to 60 minutes. Cool and frost as desired.

PASSOVER NUT CAKE

6 Eggs
6 Tbs. Sugar
6 Tbs. Matzo Cake Meal
1 Tbs. Fresh Lemon Juice
2/3 Cup Finely-chopped Almonds or
   Walnuts
1/8 Tsp. Salt
Confectioners' Sugar

Separate eggs and beat egg yolks until thick and lemon-colored. Beat in sugar and continue beating until thick and creamy. Gradually stir in matzo cake meal. Stir in lemon juice and nuts. Beat egg whites with salt until stiff but not dry and fold them into cake batter. Pour mixture into an ungreased tube pan (9x3") and bake in a preheated oven (300°F.) for 45 minutes. Increase heat to 325°F. and bake for 15 minutes more, or until top of cake springs back when lightly touched. Remove from the oven and invert pan. Cool thoroughly & then cut out of pan. Sprinkle with confectioners' sugar. Makes one 9" cake.

BANANA-NUT CAKE

2-1/3 Cups Sifted Cake Flour
2½ Tsp. Baking Powder
½ Tsp. Baking Soda
½ Tsp. Salt
½ Tsp. Ground Cinnamon
1 Cup Mashed Ripe Bananas
   (2 medium)
½ Cup Buttermilk
½ Cup Butter or Margarine
1¼ Cups Sugar
2 Eggs
¼ Tsp. Vanilla
¾ Cup Chopped Walnuts

Grease two 9" round layer-cake pans; dust lightly with flour and tap out any excess. Sift flour, baking powder, baking soda, salt, and cinnamon onto wax paper and set aside. Stir buttermilk into mashed banana in a small bowl; set aside. Beat butter or margarine, sugar and eggs in large bowl of mixer at high speed for 3 minutes. Remove bowl from mixer. Stir in flour mixture alternately with banana mixture, beating after each addition until batter is smooth. Stir in vanilla and ¼ cup chopped nuts; pour batter into prepared pans and bake in 350°F. oven for 30 minutes. Cool layers in pans on wire racks for 10 minutes; loosen around edges with a knife and turn layers out onto wire racks. Cool completely. Put layers together with Rum Butter Cream Frosting; frost sides and top and press the remaining ½ cup chopped nuts on sides of cake. Dip banana slices in orange or pineapple juice (to keep them from getting dark); garnish top of cake with banana slices.

Rum Butter Cream Frosting:

1/3 Cup Butter or Margarine
3½ Cups Sifted Confectioners' Sugar
¼ Cup Milk
1½ Tsp. Rum Extract

Beat butter or margarine in a medium bowl until soft. Add confectioners' sugar alternately with rum extract and milk and beat until creamy-smooth.

LADY BALTIMORE CAKE

2-2/3 Cups Sifted Cake Flour
1½ Cups Sugar
4 Tsp. Baking Powder
1 Tsp. Salt
2/3 Cup Vegetable Shortening
1¼ Cups Milk
1 Tsp. Vanilla
4 Egg Whites

Grease bottom of two 9x1½" round layer-cake pans and line the pans with waxed paper. Grease and flour the paper.

Combine flour, sugar, baking powder, salt, shortening, ¾ cup of milk and the vanilla in a large bowl. Beat at low speed with electric mixer until blended, then beat at high speed for 2 minutes. Add the remaining ½ cup milk and the egg whites; continue beating at high speed 2 minutes longer, scraping down side of bowl often. Pour the cake batter into the prepared pans.

Bake in 350°F. oven for 30 minutes, or until cake tests done. Cool layers in pans on wire racks for 10 minutes; loosen around edges with a knife; turn out onto wire racks and remove wax paper. Cool completely; fill and frost as desired. Makes one 9-inch double-layer cake.

APPLE PUDDING CAKE

½ Cup Butter or Margarine
1 Cup Sugar
1½ Cups Grated Peeled Apples
2 Cups Flour
1 Tsp. Baking Soda
1 Tsp. Ground Cinnamon
1 Tsp. Ground Allspice
1 Tsp. Salt
1 Cup Walnuts, chopped
1 Cup Raisins
1 Tbs. Butter
½ Cup Sugar
Grated Peel and Juice of 1 Orange

Cream ½ cup butter and 1 cup sugar until light and fluffy. Blend in grated apples. Sift dry ingredients together and stir into the apple mixture. Stir in nuts & raisins. Spread batter in a lightly greased and floured 13x9x2" pan. Bake in 350°F. oven for 40 minutes. Combine 1 tbs. butter, ½ cup sugar, the orange peel and orange juice; bring to a boil over moderate heat. Reduce heat and simmer until sugar is dissolved. Pour hot topping over cake when it comes from the oven. Cut in individual servings. Makes 12 servings.

GOLDEN DATE CAKE

2 Cups + 2 Tbs. Sifted All-
   purpose Flour
1½ Cups Sugar
3 Tsp. Baking Powder
1 Tsp. Salt
½ Cup Soft Shortening
1 Cup Milk
1½ Tsp. Vanilla
1/3 to ½ Cup Unbeaten
   Eggs (2 medium)
1 Cup Pitted Dates, cut up
½ Cup Coarsely-chopped Nuts

Heat oven to 350°F. Grease and flour 2 8" or 9" round layer cake pans, or 1 oblong pan, 13x9x2".

Sift flour, sugar, baking powder and salt together into a bowl. Add shortening, milk, vanilla. Beat 2 minutes at medium speed on mixer, or 300 vigorous strokes by hand. Scrape sides and bottom of bowl constantly. Add eggs and dates. Beat 2 minutes more, scraping bowl constantly. Fold in nuts. Pour into prepared pans & bake layers 35 to 45 minutes, oblong 40 to 45 minutes. Cool and frost with an orange butter icing.

BLACKBERRY JAM CAKE

1 Cup Raisins
1 - 8½ Oz. Can Crushed Pineapple
1 Cup Butter
1 Cup Sugar
5 Eggs
1 Cup Blackberry Jam
2½ Cups Sifted Flour
1 Tsp. Baking Soda
1 Tsp. Ground Cinnamon
1 Tsp. Ground Nutmeg
½ Tsp. Ground Cloves
2/3 Cup Buttermilk
1 Cup Chopped Pecans

Soak raisins for several hours or overnight in pineapple and juice. Cream butter and sugar until light and fluffy. Add eggs, one at a time, beating well after each addition. Stir in jam. Sift dry ingredients together & add alternately to creamed mixture with the buttermilk. Stir in fruit and pecans. Pour batter into a paper-lined 13x9x2" pan. Bake in 350°F. oven for 50 to 55 minutes; cool on a rack. Dust with confectioners' sugar before serving.

ZUCCHINI NUT LOAF

1 Cup Grated Unpeeled Zucchini
1 Cup Sugar
1 Egg
½ Cup Cooking Oil
1½ Cups All-purpose Flour
1 Tsp. Ground Cinnamon
½ Tsp. Salt
½ Tsp. Baking Soda
½ Tsp. Ground Nutmeg
¼ Tsp. Baking Powder
¼ Tsp. Grated Lemon Peel
½ Cup Chopped Walnuts

In mixing bowl, beat grated zucchini, sugar and egg together. Add oil and mix well. Stir together the flour, cinnamon, salt, soda, nutmeg, baking powder and lemon peel. Stir into zucchini mixture. Fold in nuts. Pour into a greased 8½x4½x2½" loaf pan. Bake at 325°F. for 60 to 65 minutes, or until loaf tests done. Cool in pan for 10 minutes; remove from pan and cool loaf thoroughly on wire rack. Wrap and store loaf overnight before slicing. Makes 1 loaf.

OLD—FASHIONED GINGERBREAD

½ Cup Granulated Sugar
½ Cup Shortening
2½ Cups Sifted All-purpose Flour
1 Egg
1 Cup Molasses
1½ Tsp. Soda
1 Tsp. Cinnamon
1 Tsp. Ginger
½ Tsp. Cloves
½ Tsp. Salt
1 Cup Hot Water

Cream shortening and sugar; add beaten egg and molasses, then dry ingredients which have been sifted together. Add the water last. Beat until smooth. Bake in a greased shallow pan for 35 minutes, in 350°F. oven. Use a 9" square pan.

NO-KNEAD DROP ROLLS

2/3 Cup Sugar
¼ Cup Lukewarm Water
1 Pkg. Dry Granular Yeast
1 Cup Milk, scalded and cooled
3½ Cups Sifted All-purpose Flour
1/3 Cup Shortening
1 Tsp. Salt
3 Eggs, beaten
1 Tsp. Vanilla

Stir 1 teaspoon of the sugar into water; add yeast and let stand 10 minutes. Stir yeast mixture and add lukewarm milk and blend well. Add 1½ cups of the flour and beat until smooth. Cover and let batter rise in a warm place (about 86°F.) until light, about 45 minutes. Cream shortening with salt and remaining sugar and add yeast batter gradually stirring to mix well. Add eggs and vanilla and beat thoroughly. Add remaining flour and beat until thoroughly mixed. Drop batter into well-greased muffin pans filling about 1/3 full. Cover and allow to rise in a warm place (86°F.) until light, about 1 hour. Brush lightly with melted butter and sprinkle with a mixture of 3 tablespoons of sugar and 1 teaspoon of cinnamon. Bake in a moderately hot oven (400°F.) for about 18 minutes. Makes about 2 dozen rolls.

BRAZILIAN ORANGE CAKE

2/3 Cup Butter
2 Cups Sugar
Grated Rind of 2 Oranges
3 Egg Yolks, well beaten
Juice of 2 Oranges + Water to
    equal 1 cup liquid
3 Cups Sifted Cake Flour
3 Tsp. Baking Powder
½ Tsp. Salt
3 Egg Whites, stiffly beaten
Orange Boiled Frosting (see
    recipe below)

Cream butter; add sugar and beat until fluffy. Add rind and beat in egg yolks, one at a time. Add orange juice and water alternately with mixed and sifted dry ingredients. Fold in egg whites. Spoon into 2 greased, paper-lined, 9" layer cake pans. Bake in preheated 375°F. oven for 25 minutes. Turn out on racks and cool. Spread frosting between the layers and on top and sides of cake. Makes 8 to 10 servings.

Orange Boiled Frosting:

1½ Cups Sugar
1 Tbs. Light Corn Syrup
2/3 Cup Boiling Water
¼ Tsp. Salt
2 Egg Whites, stiffly beaten
Grated Rind of 1 Orange

Cook sugar, corn syrup and water together until a small amount of syrup forms a soft ball in cold water, or until it reaches 242°F. on a candy thermometer. Pour syrup gradually over salted egg whites, beating constantly until frosting has right consistency to spread. Fold in orange rind.

SAVORY CORN MUFFINS

1 Cup Sifted All-purpose Flour
¾ Tsp. Salt
¼ Tsp. Baking Soda
2 Tsp. Baking Powder
1 Cup Yellow Cornmeal
1 Tbs. Sugar
1 Cup Buttermilk, or Sour Milk
1 Small Onion, grated
½ Tsp. Poultry Seasoning
¼ Cup Melted Pork Drippings
¼ Cup Fried-out Pieces of
    Pork Fat

Sift the dry ingredients together; stir in buttermilk, onion, poultry seasoning, drippings and fat. Turn into well-greased muffin pans and bake in preheated 400° F. oven for about 30 minutes. Makes 8 muffins.

APRICOT-PINEAPPLE-NUT LOAF

2¾ Cups Sifted All-purpose Flour
3 Tsp. Baking Powder
¼ Tsp. Baking Soda
¼ Tsp. Salt
¾ Cup Sugar
1/3 Cup Butter, melted
1 Egg
1/3 Cup Milk
1 Cup Canned Crushed Pineapple,
    undrained
1/3 Cup Chopped Dried Apricots
¼ Cup Light Raisins
1 Tbs. Chopped Candied Green
    Cherries or Citron
1 Cup Chopped Walnuts

In large bowl, combine sugar, melted butter and egg. Using a wooden spoon, beat all ingredients until well blended. Add milk, pineapple, apricots, raisins and cherries; blend well. Sift flour with baking powder, soda and salt. Add flour mixture and beat just until combined. Stir in nuts. Turn into prepared pan (a greased and floured 9x5x3" loaf pan). Bake in preheated 350°F. oven for 1¼ hours, or until cake tester inserted in center comes out clean. Let cool in the pan for 10 minutes. Remove from pan; let cool completely on wire rack. Makes 1 loaf.

BABKA

1 Cup Milk
¼ Cup Warm Water (105° to 115°F.)
2 Pkgs. Active Dry Yeast
½ Cup Sugar
1 Tsp. Salt
½ Cup Butter or Margarine, softened
4 Eggs
1 Egg Yolk
4½ Cups Unsifted All-purpose Flour
½ Cup Seedless Raisins

Topping:

1 Egg White
2 Tbs. Flour
2 Tbs. Sugar
¼ Tsp. Cinnamon
2 Tbs. Butter or Margarine

In small saucepan, heat milk until bubbles form around edge. Remove from heat & cool to lukewarm. If possible, check the temperature of warm water with thermometer. In large bowl, sprinkle yeast over water, stirring until dissolved. Add lukewarm milk, ½ cup sugar, the salt, ½ cup butter, the eggs, egg yolk, and 3 cups of flour. With electric mixer at medium speed, beat until smooth and blended. With wooden spoon, stir in 1½ cups of flour, beat vigorously 2 minutes, or until dough leaves side of bowl. Mix in raisins. Cover with towel; let rise in a warm place (85°F.) free from drafts, until double in bulk--about 1 hour. Grease and flour a 9" springform pan. Turn dough into prepared pan. Cover with a towel and let rise in warm place (85°F.), free from drafts, until dough is ½" from top of pan--about 1 hour. Preheat oven to 350°F. Make topping. Beat egg white with 1 tablespoon water; use to brush top of babka. Mix flour, sugar, cinnamon and butter; sprinkle on babka. Bake 60 minutes, or until cake tester inserted in center comes out clean. Cool in pan on wire rack 15 minutes. To serve, remove side and bottom of springform pan. Cut babka into wedges and serve warm. Makes 16 servings.

MAPLE DATE-NUT BREAD

1 Cup Boiling Water
1 Cup Chopped Dates
1 Egg
½ Cup Brown or Maple Sugar
1 Cup Sifted Cake Flour
1 Tsp. Baking Powder
½ Tsp. Baking Soda
1 Tsp. Salt
1 Cup Whole-wheat Flour
1 Tbs. Melted Butter
½ Cup Chopped Nuts
2 Tbs. Maple Syrup

Pour boiling water over dates; cool. Add egg and sugar. Sift cake flour, baking powder, baking soda, and salt together; combine with whole-wheat flour and add to first mixture. Fold in butter and nuts. Mix only until ingredients are blended. Pour into a greased pan (9½x5½x2¾") and bake in a preheated 350°F. oven for 50 to 60 minutes. Remove bread from pan. While hot, brush top with maple syrup.

FRENCH CRULLERS

¼ Cup Sugar
½ Tsp. Salt
¼ Cup Shortening
1 Cup Boiling Water
1 Cup Sifted All-purpose Flour
3 Eggs
1 Tsp. Vanilla Extract
Fat for Deep Frying
Confectioners' Sugar Frosting

Combine sugar, salt, shortening, and boiling water in a saucepan. Mix and bring to a rapid boil. Add flour all at once and mix and cook until thickened, stirring constantly. Remove from heat. Add eggs, one at a time, beating thoroughly after each addition. Add vanilla. Force mixture through pastry tube onto greased paper, forming circles. Heat deep fat to 375°F. on frying thermometer. Carefully turn paper upside down so crullers will drop into fat. Fry until golden brown. Spread with thin confectioners' sugar frosting. Makes about 1 dozen.

PINK SWIRL CAKE

½ Cup Chopped Nuts
1½ Cups All-purpose Flour
2 Tsp. Baking Powder
½ Tsp. Salt
½ Cup Butter
1 Cup Granulated Sugar
2 Eggs
1 Tsp. Vanilla
¾ Cup Milk
1/3 Cup Red Currant Jelly
1 Tbs. Water

Grease a 9" square cake pan and sprinkle bottom with the chopped nuts. Sift together the flour, baking powder and salt; set aside. Cream the butter; beat in the granulated sugar. Blend in the eggs and vanilla and beat until light and fluffy. Add sifted dry ingredients to creamed mixture alternately with the milk, beginning & ending with the dry ingredients. Turn into pan. Melt together and swirl on the batter the currant jelly and water. Bake in a preheated 350°F. oven for 45 to 50 minutes, or until cake tests done. Cool 5 minutes, invert on greased wax paper. Remove pan and quickly reinvert on serving plate, nutside down. Makes 9 servings.

BURNT-SUGAR CAKE

1¾ Cups Sugar
¾ Cup Boiling Water
2/3 Cup Soft Butter or Margarine
1 Tsp. Vanilla
2 Eggs, separated
3 Cups Sifted Cake Flour
3 Tsp. Baking Powder
½ Tsp. Salt
¾ Cup Milk

In a small, heavy skillet or saucepan heat ¾ cup sugar, stirring, until a brown syrup forms and mixture begins to smoke.

Very gradually stir in boiling water and remove from heat. Stir and blend well. Cool thoroughly. Cream butter and 1 cup sugar until light. Gradually beat in ½ cup burnt-sugar syrup. (Save the rest of the syrup for the frosting.)

Add vanilla, then egg yolks, one at a time, beating well after each addition. Add the sifted flour, baking powder, and salt alternately with milk, beating until smooth, beginning and ending with dry ingredients.

Fold in stiffly-beaten egg whites. Pour the batter into two 8" layer pans lined on the bottom with greased waxed paper. Bake in preheated 375°F. oven for about 25 min. Cool and frost.

Burnt-Sugar Frosting:

1/3 Cup Butter or Margarine
1 Lb. Confectioners' Sugar
½ Tsp. Salt
1 Tsp. Vanilla
Remaining Burnt-Sugar Syrup
Cream or Undiluted Evaporated Milk
    (about 2 tbs. or enough to give
    spreading consistency)

Cream the butter or margarine. Beat in the confectioners' sugar, salt and vanilla. Beat in the burnt-sugar syrup. Add enough cream or evaporated milk to give spreading consistency. Decorate top of cake with nut halves if desired.

HOT-MILK SPONGE CAKE

1 Cup Sifted Cake Flour
1 Tsp. Baking Powder
¼ Tsp. Salt
3 Eggs
1 Cup Sugar
¼ Cup Hot Milk
1 Tsp. Vanilla

Sift flour, baking powder and salt into a bowl. In large bowl of electric mixer, at high speed, beat eggs until fluffy and thick. Slowly beat in sugar until mixture almost doubles in volume and is very thick. Turn speed to low and beat in hot milk and vanilla. Fold in flour mixture, a third at a time, just until blended. Pour in two 8" layer cake pans which have been greased and floured. Bake in moderate oven (350° F.) for 25 minutes. Cool 10 minutes in pans on wire racks; loosen carefully around edges with a knife and turn out onto racks. Cool completely.

MINI WHITE FRUITCAKES

1 Cup Shortening
1 Cup Sugar
5 Eggs
2 Cups Sifted All-purpose Flour
1 Tsp. Salt
1½ Tsp. Baking Powder
¼ Cup Pineapple Juice
½ Cup Chopped Candied Cherries
½ Cup Finely-cut Citron
½ Cup Finely-cut Orange Peel
½ Cup Finely-cut Lemon Peel
½ Cup Chopped Pitted Dates
½ Cup Chopped Dried Figs
½ Cup Chopped Dried Apricots
1¼ Cups Chopped Candied Pineapple
1 Cup Golden Raisins
2 Cups Flaked Coconut
2 Cups Sliced Blanched Almonds

Cream the shortening and sugar until light. Add eggs, one at a time, beating well after each addition. Sift 1½ cups flour, salt and baking powder. Add alternately with pineapple juice to first mixture. Dust fruits with remaining flour. Add fruits, coconut and almonds to batter. Mix only until well blended. Pour into paper baking cups in muffin pans and bake in preheated very slow oven (275°F.) for 50 minutes. Store airtight. Makes thirty-two 2" cakes.

FLUFFY FROSTING

2 Egg Whites
¼ Tsp. Cream of Tartar
2 Tbs. Light Corn Syrup
2½ Tbs. Water
1½ Tsp. Vanilla
½ Tsp. Lemon Extract
1 Lb. Confectioners' Sugar, sifted

Combine egg whites and cream of tartar in a medium-size bowl; beat until egg whites stand in firm peaks. Combine the light corn syrup, water, vanilla, and lemon extract in a cup. Add alternately with the powdered sugar to egg-white mixture, beating well after each addition. Beat until frosting is creamy-stiff and easy to spread. Makes enough to frost top and sides of one 9" triple-layer cake.

FRENCH BREAKFAST PUFFS

1/3 Cup Soft Shortening
½ Cup Sugar
1 Egg
1½ Cups Sifted All-purpose Flour
1½ Tsp. Baking Powder
½ Tsp. Salt
¼ Tsp. Nutmeg
½ Cup Milk
6 Tbs. Butter, melted
½ Cup Sugar
1 Tsp. Cinnamon

Heat oven to 350°F. Mix the shortening, ½ cup sugar and egg together. Sift flour, baking powder, salt and nutmeg together and stir into egg mixture alternately with milk. Fill greased muffin cups 2/3 full & bake 20 to 25 minutes, until golden brown. Immediately roll in melted butter, then in a mixture of sugar and cinnamon. Makes 12 medium puffs.

ZEPPOLE
(Fried Bread)

1 Tsp. Active Dry Yeast
¾ Cup Warm Water
1 Egg
2 Cups All-purpose Flour
½ Tsp. Salt
Oil, for frying

Sprinkle yeast into water. Let stand for a few minutes, then stir until dissolved. Beat in egg, flour and salt. When smooth, cover and let stand in a warm place until doubled in bulk. Beat down and let rise again until doubled. Drop by tablespoonfuls into 1" of hot oil (375°F. on frying thermometer). When browned on one side, turn and brown on the other. Drain on absorbent paper. Serve as a bread with butter, or sprinkled with sugar and cinnamon as a dessert. These are also good dipped in honey or syrup. Makes about 20.

Note: For variety, flour hands and shape tablespoonfuls of dough around a small piece of cooked cauliflower or an anchovy before frying. Cubes of Mozzarella or a teaspoonful of Ricotta can be used in the same way.

CHOCOLATE CAKE FROM WISCONSIN

¾ Cup Cocoa
1¾ Cups Sugar
4 Eggs
½ Cup Milk
½ Cup Butter or Margarine
2 Cups Sifted All-purpose Flour
1 Tsp. Baking Powder
1 Tsp. Baking Soda
½ Tsp. Salt
1 Cup Dairy Sour Cream
1 Tsp. Vanilla Extract
Glossy Chocolate Frosting (see recipe
    below)

Combine cocoa, ¾ cup sugar, 1 egg yolk
and the milk; cook until thick, stirring constantly to prevent sticking. Cool mixture.

Cream butter until soft. Gradually add remaining 1 cup of sugar, beating until well
blended. Add 1 whole egg and 2 egg yolks.
Mix well. Stir in sifted dry ingredients alternately with sour cream. Add vanilla
and cocoa mixture. Fold in egg whites
which have been beaten until stiff but not
dry. Pour into three 8" layer pans, lined
on the bottom with waxed paper. Bake
in a preheated moderate oven (350°F.)
for 30 to 35 minutes. Turn out on racks
and peel off paper. Cool, and thinly frost
top and sides of cake with frosting.

Frosting:

Melt 6 ounces (6 squares) of unsweetened
chocolate. Add 1½ cups sifted confectioners'
sugar and 5 tablespoons hot water; beat well
and add 1½ cups more sugar. Gradually
beat in 6 egg yolks. When smooth and
blended, beat in ½ cup soft butter or margarine. Makes enough frosting for tops and
sides of three 9" layers.

CURRANT SCONES

2 Cups Unsifted All-purpose Flour
1½ Tsp. Cream of Tartar
¾ Tsp. Baking Soda
1 Tsp. Salt
½ Cup Butter or Margarine,
    softened
½ Cup Dried Currants
1 Egg
1 Cup Buttermilk (approximate)
1 Egg Yolk
Sugar

Sift flour, cream of tartar, soda and salt
into bowl. Cut in butter. Add currants,
whole egg, and enough buttermilk to make
a soft dough. Mix and turn out on well-
floured board. Knead a few times, then
roll to ½" thickness. Cut into 2-inch
diamonds. Put on cookie sheets and prick
tops several times with a fork. Beat egg
yolk with a little cold water and brush
on scones. Sprinkle with sugar. Bake in
preheated oven (425°F.) for about 15
minutes. Makes about 2 dozen.

CINNAMON BREAD

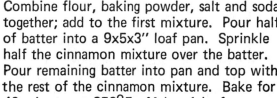

3 Tbs. Brown Sugar
1 Tbs. Cinnamon
¼ Cup Shortening
1 Cup Granulated Sugar
2 Eggs
1 Cup Milk, soured with
    2 tsp. vinegar
½ Tsp. Soda
½ Tsp. Salt
1 Tsp. Baking Powder
2 Tsp. Vanilla
2 Cups Flour

Mix the brown sugar and cinnamon together
and set aside. Mix shortening and sugar together; add eggs, then sour milk and vanilla.
Combine flour, baking powder, salt and soda
together; add to the first mixture. Pour half
of batter into a 9x5x3" loaf pan. Sprinkle
half the cinnamon mixture over the batter.
Pour remaining batter into pan and top with
the rest of the cinnamon mixture. Bake for
40 minutes at 350°F. Makes 1 loaf.

ITALIAN CREAM CAKE

½ Cup Margarine
1 Tsp. Vanilla
2 Cups Granulated Sugar
5 Eggs, separated
2 Cups Flour
1 Tsp. Soda
½ Cup Vegetable Shortening
1 Cup Buttermilk
1 Small Can Coconut
1 Cup Nuts, chopped

Cream the margarine, shortening and sugar; beat until mixture is smooth. Add egg yolks and beat well. Combine flour & soda. Add to creamed mixture alternately with buttermilk. Stir in the vanilla. Add the coconut and chopped nuts. Beat egg whites until stiff and fold into the first mixture. Pour batter into 3 greased and floured 8" cake pans. Bake at 350°F. for 25 minutes or until cake tests done. Cool and frost with cream cheese frosting.

Cream Cheese Frosting:
1 - 8 Oz. Pkg. Cream Cheese, softened
1 Tsp. Vanilla
¼ Cup Margarine
1 Box Powdered Sugar
Pecan Halves

Beat cream cheese and margarine until smooth. Add sugar and mix well. Add vanilla and beat until smooth. Spread layers, top and sides of cake with icing. Sprinkle with pecans.

DAFFODIL RING CAKE

¾ Cup Sifted Cake Flour
½ Tsp. Salt
3 Eggs, separated
½ Tsp. Cream of Tartar
2/3 Cup Sugar
1 Tsp. Vanilla
3 Tbs. Hot Water
1 Tsp. Orange Extract
1 Tbs. Confectioners' Sugar

Sift flour and salt into a small bowl. Beat egg whites with cream of tartar until foamy and double in volume (use large bowl). Sprinkle in 1/3 cup of the granulated sugar

very slowly, 1 tablespoon at a time, beating all the time until meringue stands in firm peaks. Beat in vanilla. Reserve remaining 1/3 cup sugar for use later. Sprinkle 2 tablespoons of the flour mixture over top of meringue; fold in completely. Repeat with 4 additional tablespoons of flour mixture. Reserve remaining flour for use later.

Beat egg yolks with hot (not boiling) water until very thick and light lemon color in a medium bowl. Sprinkle reserved 1/3 cup granulated sugar, 1 tablespoon at a time, into the egg yolks, beating all the time, until mixture is creamy and thick. Beat in orange extract. Sprinkle 2 tablespoons of the remaining flour mixture over the top of the egg-yolk mixture; fold in completely. Repeat with remaining flour mixture.

Spoon the batters, alternating spoonfuls of white and yellow, into an ungreased 9-inch ring mold (do not mix batters in the pan). Bake in 325°F. oven for 30 minutes, or until golden. Turn cake, in pan, upside down on a wire rack and cool completely. When completely cooled, loosen around edge and center with a sharp knife and invert the cake onto a serving plate. Sprinkle confectioners' sugar over top. Slice into 10 even-size wedges to serve plain. Makes one 9" ring cake.

HAWAIIAN PINEAPPLE MUFFINS

4 Cups Sifted All-purpose Flour
2 Tbs. Baking Powder
½ Cup Sugar
1 Tsp. Salt
4 Eggs, beaten
1½ Cups Milk
½ Cup Butter or Margarine, melted
1½ Cups Drained Crushed Pineapple

Sift dry ingredients. Add eggs, milk and butter. Stir until smooth. Add pineapple and mix well. Spoon into greased 3-inch muffin pans. Fill the muffin cups three-quarters full. Bake in a preheated hot oven (425°F.) for 20 to 25 minutes. Makes 2 dozen.

QUICK COFFEECAKE

1½ Cups Sugar
½ Cup Chopped Nuts
1 Tbs. Ground Cinnamon
½ Cup Butter
2 Eggs
1 Tsp. Vanilla Extract
1 Tbs. Fresh Lemon Juice
2 Cups Sifted All-purpose Flour
½ Tsp. Baking Powder
1 Tsp. Baking Soda
1 Tsp. Salt
½ Pint Dairy Sour Cream

Mix and set aside ½ cup of the sugar, the chopped nuts, and cinnamon. Cream the butter; beat in remaining 1 cup of sugar and the eggs. Add the vanilla and lemon juice. Sift the dry ingredients together and add alternately to the butter mixture with the sour cream. Pour half of the batter into a buttered 9x9x2" pan. Sprinkle with some of the cinnamon mixture. Spread the rest of the batter over this and sprinkle with the remaining topping. Bake in a moderate oven (350°F.) for 35 minutes. Serve hot.

SAFFRON BREAD

½ Cup Boiling Water
1 Tsp. Saffron Shreds
3 Cups Sifted All-purpose Flour
½ Tsp. Salt
3 Tsp. Baking Powder
½ Tsp. Baking Soda
½ Cup Shortening
1 Cup Sugar
2 Eggs, beaten
½ Cup Fresh Lemon Juice
½ Cup Shredded Fresh Lemon Peel

Add boiling water to saffron and steep for 30 minutes. Sift dry ingredients together. Cream the shortening and sugar until light and fluffy. Add the eggs and beat well. Combine saffron and water with lemon juice and lemon peel. Add with dry ingredients to creamed mixture, stirring just enough to moisten. Turn into two greased and floured loaf pans (7½x3½x2¼"). Bake in preheated moderate oven (350° F.) for 40 to 45 minutes.

HONEY GINGERBREAD

½ Cup Soft Butter or Margarine
½ Cup Sugar
1 Cup Honey
1 Egg
2½ Cups Sifted Cake Flour
1 Tsp. Salt
1 Tsp. Baking Soda
½ Tsp. Baking Powder
1 Tsp. Ground Cinnamon
1 Tsp. Ground Ginger
1 Cup Buttermilk

Cream butter and sugar; add honey and cream until light. Add egg and beat well. Sift dry ingredients together and add alternately with buttermilk, beating until smooth. Pour into greased pan (13x9x2") lined on the bottom with wax paper. Bake in preheated oven (350°F.) for about 45 minutes. Turn out on rack and peel off paper. Cut into squares & serve warm or cold. Makes 12 to 15 servings.

TEXAS CHOCOLATE CAKE

1 Cup Sliced Dates
1 Tsp. Soda
1 Cup Boiling Water
½ Lb. Butter or Margarine
1 Cup Sugar
2 Eggs
1¾ Cups Sifted All-purpose Flour
3 Tbs. Powdered Cocoa
1 Tsp. Salt
1 Tsp. Vanilla
1 - 6 Oz. Pkg. Chocolate Morsels
Powdered Sugar

Sprinkle soda over dates in small saucepan. Add boiling water; bring to a boil over direct heat and let boil for 1 or 2 minutes. Set aside to cool. Cream butter or margarine in mixing bowl. Beat in sugar; add eggs, one at a time, beating well after each addition. Sift flour, cocoa and salt together. Add alternately with date mixture to butter mixture. Add vanilla. Pour into a greased 6½x10½" pan. Cover top with chocolate morsels. Bake 45 minutes in a preheated 350°F. oven. Remove pan from oven. While cake is still warm, sprinkle with confectioners' sugar. Makes 12 squares.

SWEET POTATO/NUT BREAD

½ Cup Butter or Margarine, softened
½ Cup Shortening
2-2/3 Cup Sugar
4 Eggs
2 Cups Cold, Mashed Sweet Potatoes
3½ Cups Sifted Flour
1 Tsp. Salt
1 Tsp. Ground Cinnamon
1½ Tsp. Ground Nutmeg
2 Tsp. Baking Soda
1 Cup Chopped Walnuts
2/3 Cup Cold, Strong Black Coffee

Cream butter, shortening and sugar. Add the eggs, one at a time, mixing well after each addition. Blend in sweet potatoes. Sift together dry ingredients; add nuts. Stir into creamed mixture alternately with cold coffee. Pour batter into 2 greased 9x5x3" loaf pans and 8 greased muffin-pan cups & bake in a moderate oven, 375°F., for 1 hr. for loaves and 25 minutes for muffins, or until they test done in the center. Cool for 10 minutes; remove from pans and cool completely. Makes 2 loaves plus 8 muffins.

BLACK FRUITCAKE (Canada)

4 Oz. Candied Citron, coarsely
    chopped
2 Oz. Candied Lemon Peel,
    coarsely chopped
2 Oz. Candied Orange Peel,
    coarsely chopped
½ Lb. Candied Cherries, halved
1 Lb. Candied Pineapple, shredded
1 Lb. Golden Raisins
½ Lb. Seeded Raisins
4 Oz. Currants
½ Cup Dark Rum, Cognac or Sherry
4 Oz. Almonds, blanched and
    shredded
4 Oz. Walnuts or Pecans, coarsely
chopped
2 Cups Sifted All-purpose Flour
½ Tsp. Mace
½ Tsp. Cinnamon
½ Tsp. Baking Powder
1 Tbs. Milk
1 Tsp. Almond Extract
½ Cup Butter
1 Cup Granulated Sugar
1 Cup Brown Sugar, packed
5 Eggs

Almond Paste:
1 Lb. Almonds, blanched
1 Lb. Sifted Confectioners' Sugar
3 Egg Whites, lightly beaten
1 Tsp. Almond Extract

Milk Frosting:
1 Tsp. Butter
1½ Cups Sugar
1 Tbs. Light Corn Syrup
½ Cup Milk
½ Tsp. Almond Extract

Prepare the cake. Mix the fruits; add rum and cover. Let stand overnight. Preheat oven to 275°F. Grease one 10-inch tube pan or two 9x5x3" loaf pans. Line with waxed paper and grease the paper. Combine the fruits, the nuts and ½ cup flour. Sift together the remaining flour, mace, cinnamon and baking powder. Mix the milk with the almond extract. Cream the butter until smooth, adding sugars gradually. Add the eggs, mix well and add the milk mixture. Add flour mixture and mix well. Pour the batter over the fruits and nuts and mix thoroughly. Fill the pans and press batter down firmly. Bake tube cake about 4 hrs., loaves about 3 hrs.; let cakes stand for 30 minutes and then turn out on a rack and peel off the paper. Wrap cooled cakes in cheesecloth soaked in rum, cognac or sherry. Place in a crock or deep kettle & cover tightly. As the cloth dries, dribble a little of the same liquor over it. Let ripen about 1 month before frosting with a layer of each of the frostings above.

Almond Paste: Grind the almonds fine. Add remaining ingredients; mix thoroughly. Spread over the cake and let dry.

Milk Frosting: Cook the butter, sugar, corn syrup and milk to 234°F., stirring constantly. Cool. Add the almond extract and beat until a soft fudge consistency. Spread over almond paste & let dry. When the milk frosting is dry, spread it evenly with a confectioners' icing.

CHERRY-PINEAPPLE BREAD

3 Cups Sifted All-purpose Flour
4 Tsp. Baking Powder
¾ Cup Sugar
1 Tsp. Salt
1 Cup Chopped Walnuts
½ Cup Candied Cherries, halved
1 Egg
1 - 9 Oz. Can Crushed Pineapple
½ Cup Milk
¼ Cup Vegetable Oil

Sift flour, baking powder, sugar and salt into a large bowl; stir in walnuts and cherries. Beat egg well in a medium-size bowl; stir in pineapple and syrup, milk & vegetable oil. Add all at once to flour mixture; stir just until evenly moist. Spoon batter into a greased 9x5x3" loaf pan; spread top even. Bake in 350°F. oven for 1 hr. and 15 min., or until a wooden pick inserted in center comes out clean. Cool in pan on a wire rack for about 10 minutes. Loosen around edges with a knife; turn out onto rack and cool completely. Wrap loaf in waxed paper or foil and store overnight to blend the flavors. Makes 1 loaf.

COCOA CAKE WITH BANANA-CREAM FILLING

Cake:

½ Cup Cake Flour
¼ Cup Cocoa
¾ Tsp. Baking Powder
¼ Tsp. Salt
2 Tbs. Water
½ Tsp. Vanilla
3 Eggs, separated
¾ Cup Sugar

Sift flour, measure and resift with cocoa, baking powder and salt. Add water and vanilla to egg yolks and beat until thick, adding half of the sugar while beating. Beat egg whites until stiff; add remaining sugar gradually and continue beating until all is added. Fold yolk mixture into stiffly-beaten whites, then fold in flour mixture lightly but thoroughly. Spread in a shallow baking pan (about 9x13") lined with thin, plain paper on bottom,

and bake in a 375°F. oven for 12 min., or until cake tests done. Loosen edges and turn out on a cake rack. When cool, cut in half. Spread one half with cream filling and slice bananas on it. Cover with other half and sprinkle with powdered sugar. Cut in desired sizes for serving. Top with whipped cream, if desired. Makes 5 to 8 servings.

Banana-Cream Filling:

¾ Cup Sugar
6 Tbs. Cornstarch
½ Tsp. Salt
2 Cups Milk, scalded
2 Eggs, slightly beaten
2 Tbs. Butter
½ Tsp. Vanilla
2 or 3 Bananas

Mix sugar, cornstarch and salt. Gradually add scalded milk and cook in double boiler until thick. Add small amount of hot mixture to beaten eggs; mix well and return to the remaining hot mixture, stirring to blend thoroughly. Cook, covered, over boiling water for about 15 minutes, stirring occasionally. Remove from heat; stir in butter and vanilla and cool.

UPSIDE-DOWN CAKE

1/3 Cup Butter or Margarine
¾ Cup Firmly-packed Light Brown Sugar
6 Slices of Canned Pineapple
1 Pkg. Cake Mix (yellow, orange or orange-coconut)
1 - 11 Oz. Can Mandarin Oranges
Coconut
6 Maraschino Cherries

Melt the butter in a 13x9x2" pan. Sprinkle with brown sugar. Arrange the slices of pineapple on sugar. Prepare the cake mix as directed on the label. Pour batter over the pineapple slices and bake as directed for pan size. Turn out on rack and cut into 6 serving pieces. Drain the mandarin oranges. Arrange sections around each cake serving and sprinkle with coconut. Put a maraschino cherry in each pineapple ring. Makes 6 large servings.

SWEET POTATO SPICECAKE

2 Cups Sifted Cake Flour
¾ Tsp. Salt
2 Tsp. Baking Powder
¼ Tsp. Baking Soda
1 Tsp. Ground Cinnamon
1 Tsp. Ground Nutmeg
1/8 Tsp. Ground Cloves
½ Cup Butter or Margarine,
  softened
¾ Cup Sugar
2 Eggs
1¼ Cups Cold Mashed Cooked or
  Canned Yams
½ Cup Milk
Fluffy White Frosting
¼ Cup Coarsely Chopped Nuts

Sift the first seven ingredients. Cream the
butter; add sugar and cream until light and
fluffy. Add the eggs, one at a time, beating thoroughly after each addition. Beat
in the yams. Add the sifted dry ingredients
and the milk, beating only until smooth.

Line two 8-inch layer cake pans with wax
paper. Pour batter into the pans. Bake in
a preheated 350°F. oven for about 35 min.
Turn out on racks and peel off paper.
Cool and frost. Top with nuts.

FILLED CRESCENTS

½ Cup Butter
1 Tbs. Lard
2 Cups Sifted All-purpose Flour
¼ Tsp. Salt
2 Small Egg Yolks
½ Cup Sour Cream
½ Cup Stiff, Tart Jelly (approximate)

With a pastry blender cut butter, lard
flour and salt together (or work with finger-
tips till consistency of cornmeal). Drop in
the egg yolks; add cream and mix thoroughly.
Shape into a patty, wrap in waxed paper and
chill overnight.

Roll on lightly-floured board to 1/8" thickness. Cut into rounds 3" in diameter. Place
about ½ teaspoon jelly off center on each
round. Fold edge near jelly, completely
covering jelly. Press down to seal, then roll

up jelly-roll fashion, turn and shape into
crescents. Brush with egg and milk (1 egg
yolk beaten with 3 tablespoons of milk).

Place on baking sheet and bake in moderately
hot oven (400°F.) for 10 to 12 minutes. Remove from pan while warm. Sprinkle with
powdered sugar when cool. Makes about
2 dozen.

MOCHA CAKE

4 Oz. Unsweetened Chocolate
  (4 squares)
2/3 Cup Hot Water
1 Cup Soft Butter or Margarine
2¼ Cups Sugar
1½ Tsp. Vanilla Extract
4 Eggs
3 Cups Sifted All-purpose Flour
3 Tsp. Baking Powder
¾ Tsp. Salt
2 Tsp. Instant Coffee
¾ Cup Milk

Melt the chocolate and stir in hot water;
cool. Cream butter, sugar, and vanilla.
Add eggs, one at a time, beating thoroughly after each addition. Add chocolate mixture and blend. Sift dry ingredients and add alternately with milk. Beat
until smooth. Pour into three 9" layer-
cake pans lined on bottom with greased
waxed paper. Bake in 375°F. oven, preheated, for about 30 minutes. Cool and
frost.

Mocha Frosting:

½ Cup Butter or Margarine, softened
¼ Cup Cocoa
4 Tsp. Instant Coffee
½ Tsp. Ground Cinnamon
4 Cups Confectioners' Sugar
¼ Cup Undiluted Evaporated Milk
  (or enough to make frosting of
  spreading consistency)
1 Tsp. Vanilla Extract

Cream butter, cocoa, instant coffee and
cinnamon until fluffy. Add confectioners'
sugar alternately with evaporated milk.
Add vanilla extract.

BROWN-AND-GOLD PINWHEEL LOAF

½ Cup Milk
4 Tbs. Butter or Margarine
¼ Cup Sugar
1 Tsp. Salt
1 Pkg. Active Dry Yeast
¼ Cup Very Warm Water
2 Eggs, beaten
3 Cups Sifted All-purpose Flour
1 Square Unsweetened Chocolate,
   melted
½ Tsp. Cinnamon
Syrup Glaze (see recipe below)

Scald milk with butter or margarine in small saucepan. Stir in the sugar and salt and cool mixture to lukewarm. Dissolve yeast in very warm water in a large bowl (water should feel comfortably warm when dropped on wrist). Stir in cooled milk mixture and the beaten eggs. Stir in 2 cups of flour and beat until smooth. Gradually stir in enough of remaining flour to make a stiff dough.

Divide dough in half; turn out one half onto lightly-floured pastry cloth or board. Leave remaining half of dough in bowl for mixing with chocolate and cinnamon later. Knead dough until smooth and elastic, adding only enough flour to keep from sticking.

Place dough in greased medium-size bowl; cover with clean towel and let rise in warm place, away from drafts, for 1 hour, or until double in bulk.

Stir melted chocolate and cinnamon into remaining dough (do not worry if it is marbled, the chocolate will melt during baking). Knead and let rise as above. Punch down both doughs; roll out half of plain dough to 1/8" thickness on lightly-floured pastry cloth or board. Cut into a rectangle 10x8" and lay it on a sheet of wax paper. Save dough cuttings for later.

Roll out half of the chocolate dough and cut the same as plain dough; place rectangle on top of plain dough. Save the cuttings for later. Repeat with other halves of plain and chocolate doughs to make a total of 4 layers, ending with the chocolate layer.

Roll chocolate cuttings into a rope, 8" long. Roll plain cuttings into a rectangle 8x4" and wrap around the chocolate rope. Place on one end of stacked layers. Roll up as for a jelly roll, starting at rope end. Place, seam side down, in greased loaf pan, 9x5x3". Make 4 shallow diagonal cuts in top of loaf. Cover with clean towel; let rise in warm place, away from drafts, for 1 hour, or until double in bulk. Bake in 375°F. oven for 30 min., or until loaf is golden brown and gives a hollow sound when tapped. Remove from pan and brush with syrup glaze. Cool on a wire rack.

Syrup Glaze: Combine ½ cup light corn syrup and ¼ cup water in a small heavy saucepan; heat slowly to a rolling boil & boil for 1 minute. Store any remaining glaze in covered jar. Heat just before using. Makes ½ cup.

STRAWBERRY CIRCLE CAKE

1/3 Cup Butter
Sugar
1 Egg
½ Tsp. Vanilla Extract
1¼ Cups Sifted Cake Flour
1 Tsp. Baking Powder
½ Tsp. Salt
1/3 Cup Milk
3 Cups Fresh Strawberries, hulled
1/8 Tsp. Red Food Coloring
1 Tbs. Cornstarch
1 Cup Heavy Cream, whipped and
   sweetened

Cream butter and 2/3 cup sugar. Beat in egg and vanilla. Add sifted dry ingredients alternately with milk, beating until smooth. Pour into 8" layer pan, lined on the bottom with wax paper. Bake in 350°F. oven for 25 to 30 minutes. Cool; turn out on a plate.

Heat berries, ¼ cup sugar, and red food coloring until juice begins to flow. Spoon out berries and put on cake. Blend cornstarch into juice and cook, stirring, until thickened. Cool slightly; pour over cake and chill until set. Decorate with whipped cream.

OATMEAL CAKE

1 Cup Uncooked Quick Oats
1¼ Cups Boiling Water
1 Cup Brown Sugar, packed
1 Cup Granulated Sugar
2 Eggs
½ Tsp. Salt
½ Cup Margarine
1¼ Cups All-purpose Flour
1 Tsp. Soda
1 Tsp. Cinnamon

Mix oats, boiling water and margarine and let stand for 20 minutes. Mix the remaining ingredients together. Add to the oatmeal mixture and beat well. Bake at 350° F. for 35 min. Use a 13x9x2" pan.

Icing:
1 Small Can Condensed Milk
½ Cup Sugar
1 Cup Pecans
½ Tsp. Vanilla
½ Cup Margarine
1 Cup Flaked Coconut

Mix milk, sugar, margarine and coconut in a small saucepan. Boil 3 to 5 minutes. Remove from heat and stir in vanilla and pecans. Spread on cake. Put under the broiler and brown. Watch carefully as this icing burns easily.

ALMOND LOAVES

¾ Cup Milk
1 Cup Sugar
1 Tsp. Salt
¾ Cup Butter or Margarine
2 Envelopes Active Dry Yeast
¼ Cup Very Warm Water
2 Eggs, beaten
5¼ Cups Sifted All-purpose Flour
1½ Cups Golden Raisins
1 - 8 Oz. Container Candied Red
    Cherries, halved
1 Tsp. Grated Orange Rind
1 - 8 Oz. Can Almond Paste
1 Egg White, slightly beaten
Confectioners' Sugar

Combine milk, ½ cup granulated sugar, salt and ½ cup of butter or margarine in small saucepan. Heat slowly until butter or margarine melts; cool to lukewarm. Sprinkle yeast into very warm water in a large bowl. Stir until yeast dissolves, then stir in milk mixture and eggs. Beat in 2 cups of flour until smooth; stir in raisins, cherries and orange rind. Beat in 3 more cups of flour to make a stiff dough.

Turn dough out onto a lightly-floured pastry cloth or board; knead until smooth and elastic, adding only enough of the remaining ¼ cup flour to keep dough from sticking. Place in a greased large bowl & turn to coat all over with shortening. Cover with a clean towel. Let rise in a warm place, away from drafts, for 2 hrs., or until double in bulk.

While dough rises, crumble almond paste into a small bowl. Stir in egg white and remaining ½ cup granulated sugar until smooth.

Punch dough down; knead a few times & divide into 12 even pieces. Pat each into an oval, 6x4", on a lightly-floured pastry cloth or board. Place, 2" apart, on greased cooky sheets. Melt remaining ¼ cup butter or margarine in a small frying pan; brush over ovals. Divide almond mixture into 12 equal parts. With palms of hands, roll each into a 5'' long log. Place one lengthwise on half of each oval of dough. Flatten slightly. Fold dough in half. Press edges lightly to seal; cover and let rise again for 1 hour, or until double in bulk. Brush with part of the remaining melted butter or margarine. Bake in a moderate oven (350°F.) for about 20 minutes, or until golden brown. Makes 12 small loaves.

PANETTONE

½ Cup Milk
2 Tsp. Anise Seeds
½ Cup Sugar
1 Tsp. Salt
1 Envelope Active Dry Yeast
¼ Cup Very Warm Water
   (105°F. to 115°F.)
2 Eggs, beaten
2 Tsp. Grated Lemon Rind
3 Cups Sifted All-purpose Flour
½ Cup Butter or Margarine, melted
   and cooled
1 - 8 Oz. Jar Mixed Candied Fruits
   (1 cup), chopped fine
½ Cup Seedless Raisins

Scald milk with anise seeds in small sauce-pan; remove from heat. Let stand for 5 minutes, then strain into a cup, discarding seeds. Stir in ¼ cup sugar and salt. Reserve remaining sugar. Cool milk mixture just until warm. Sprinkle yeast into very warm water in a large bowl. Stir until dissolved. Stir in cooled milk mixture, eggs, lemon rind and flour. Beat vigorously, scraping down side of bowl. Continue to beat with a spoon 100 times, or until dough is elastic and forms a ball. (This will take about 5 minutes.) Stir in cooled melted butter or margarine. The dough will become stringy, so beat it again until it forms a ball. Place in greased bowl; cover with clean towel. Let rise in warm place, away from drafts, for 1 hour, or until double in bulk.

While dough rises, prepare a 6" spring-form pan or 6-cup straight-sided baking dish as follows: Cut a piece of foil, long enough to wrap around pan and overlap slightly; fold in quarters lengthwise. Grease the pan and foil strip, then wrap the strip around the top of the pan to make a 2" stand-up collar; hold in place with a paper clip and string.

Sprinkle saved ¼ cup sugar over raised dough; stir down and work in candied fruits and raisins. Place in pan. Cover with a clean towel; let rise in a warm place, away from drafts, for 1½ hours, or until double in bulk. Bake in 375° F. oven for 1 hour 15 minutes, or until a deep rich brown and loaf gives a hol-

low sound when tapped. Cool 5 minutes on wire rack. Remove foil collar, then remove bread from pan. Cool completely. Makes 1 large round loaf.

ORANGE BREAD

1 Cup Granulated Sugar
2 Tbs. Butter
1 Egg
½ Cup Orange Juice
1 Tsp. Vanilla
2 Cups All-purpose Flour
1 Tsp. Baking Soda
¼ Tsp. Salt
1 Cup Seedless Raisins

Pour ½ cup boiling water over the raisins and grated rind of 1 orange; let cool. Mix together butter and sugar; cream until fluffy. Add egg and dry ingredients and blend. Stir in cooled raisin mixture. Pour into a prepared bread pan and bake 1 hr. at 350°F. Makes one loaf.

SPICED BREAD

1¼ Cups Boiling Water
1 Tsp. Aniseed
1 Cup Honey
1¼ Cups Sugar
½ Tsp. Baking Soda
¼ Cup Rum
4 Cups Sifted All-purpose Flour
2½ Tsp. Baking Powder
1 Tsp. Cinnamon
½ Tsp. Ginger
¼ Tsp. Salt
¼ Cup Chopped Candied Citron
¼ Cup Chopped Candied Orange Peel
½ Tsp. Grated Orange Rind
¼ Cup Chopped Almonds

Bring water to a boil with aniseed. Add the honey and sugar and stir until dissolved. Remove from heat; stir in soda & rum. Strain. Add slowly to the flour which has been sifted with baking powder, spices and salt. Beat until smooth. Add fruit and nuts. Pour into buttered loaf pan (9x5x3") and bake in preheated 350°F. oven for 1 hour, or until done.

APPLE UPSIDE-DOWN CAKE

¼ Cup Butter
¾ Cup Brown Sugar
3 Apples
¼ Cup Shortening
1/3 Cup Granulated Sugar
1 Egg
¼ Cup Molasses
1 Cup Sifted All-purpose Flour
1 Tsp. Baking Powder
½ Tsp. Soda
1/8 Tsp. Salt
1 Tsp. Ginger
½ Tsp. Cinnamon
1/3 Cup Boiling Water

Melt the ¼ cup butter in a baking dish; add the brown sugar and blend together. Pare and core apples. Cut each apple in half to make two thick rings. Arrange rings of apples in butter and sugar mixture. Cream the shortening; add granulated sugar and cream together well. Add well-beaten egg and molasses. Beat thoroughly. Mix and sift dry ingredients and add to mixture. Lastly add boiling water, mixing quickly. Pour over apples in baking dish and bake in a moderately slow oven, 325°F., for 40 minutes. Makes 6 servings.

RYE TWIST

4 Cups Sifted All-purpose Flour
4 Cups Whole-rye Flour
2 Envelopes Active Dry Yeast
2½ Cups Very Warm Water
¼ Cup Butter or Margarine, melted
1/3 Cup Dark Molasses
3 Tsp. Salt
2 Tsp. Caraway Seeds, crushed
1 Cup Whole-bran Cereal
¼ Cup Dry Cocoa (not a mix)
2 Tsp. Instant Coffee
Corn Meal
Butter or Margarine, melted
1 Tsp. Cornstarch
½ Cup Cold Water

Combine 3 cups all-purpose flour with the rye flour in a medium-size bowl; blend well. Set aside. Sprinkle yeast into very warm water in a large bowl. Stir until yeast dissolves; stir in butter or margarine, molasses, salt and caraway. Pour one half of mixture into a second large bowl.

To one half of the yeast mixture, add the bran, cocoa and coffee, stirring to mix well. Stir in enough of the rye-flour mixture to make a soft dough (about 3 cups). Turn dough out onto a lightly floured pastry board. Knead until smooth and elastic, about 5 minutes, using only as much of the remaining all-purpose flour as needed to keep dough from sticking. Place dough in a greased medium-size bowl; turn to coat all over with shortening. Cover with a clean towel. Let rise in a warm place, away from draft, 45 minutes, or until double in bulk.

To the remaining half of yeast mixture, stir in enough rye-flour mixture, a little at a time, to make a soft dough (about 3½ cups). Turn out onto lightly-floured board. Knead until smooth and elastic, about 5 minutes, adding only as much of the remaining all-purpose flour as needed to keep dough from sticking. Let rise as above. Grease two large cooky sheets & sprinkle with cornmeal.

When both doughs have doubled, punch down; knead each a few times. Divide each in half. Roll each of the four pieces on board with hands to form a thick rope 18 inches long. For each loaf, twist light and dark rope together; pinch together at ends. Place loaf on cooky sheet; repeat with remaining 2 ropes. Let rise again in a warm place away from draft for 45 min., or until double in bulk. Brush lightly with melted butter or margarine. Bake in 350° F. oven for 45 minutes, or until loaves give a hollow sound when tapped.

While loaves are baking, combine cornstarch with cold water in small saucepan; stir until smooth. Cook, stirring constantly, until mixture thickens and boils 1 minute. Brush over baked loaves; return to oven and bake another 5 minutes. Remove from cooky sheets to wire racks and cool completely. Makes two 20-ounce loaves.

JEWISH ALMOND BREAD

1½ Cups Sifted All-purpose Flour
¼ Tsp. Salt
1 Tsp. Baking Powder
4 Eggs
1 Cup Sugar
3 Tbs. Cooking Oil
1 Tsp. Vanilla Extract
1 Cup Chopped Blanched Almonds
1 Tbs. Ground Cinnamon

Sift flour with salt and baking powder. Beat eggs until they are thick and lemon-colored. Gradually beat in sugar. Stir in oil and the vanilla. Stir in flour and almonds. Grease and flour two loaf pans (9x5x3"). Cover the bottoms of the pans with batter. Sprinkle with cinnamon. Add another layer of batter and cinnamon and continue layering until all cinnamon and batter are used.

Bake in preheated 350°F. oven for 25 min., or until cake is golden brown. The breads will only be 2½ inches high. Remove from pans, and cool. With a sharp knife, cut the breads into ½" slices. Place slices on a greased cookie sheet and brown in preheated 400°F. oven for 5 to 6 minutes.

BANANA BREAD

1¾ Cups Sifted All-purpose Flour
2/3 Cup Sugar
3 Tsp. Baking Powder
½ Tsp. Salt
¼ Tsp. Baking Soda
1/3 Cup Regular Margarine
1 Cup Mashed Very-ripe Banana
   (2 or 3 bananas)
2 Eggs
½ Cup Chopped Walnuts
¼ Cup Chopped Candied Citron
¼ Cup Chopped Candied Orange Peel
¼ Cup Chopped Candied Cherries
¼ Cup Chopped Candied Pineapple
¼ Cup Dark Raisins

Sift flour before measuring. Preheat oven to 350°F. Grease a 9x5x3" loaf pan.

Sift flour, sugar, baking powder, salt and soda into a large bowl. With pastry blender cut in margarine until mixture resembles coarse crumbs. Add banana and eggs and beat with electric mixer at low speed for 2 minutes. Add nuts, candied fruit and raisins; beat until well blended. Turn into prepared pan. Bake 1 hr. and 10 min., or until cake tester inserted in center comes out clean. Let cool in pan on wire rack for 10 minutes. Remove from pan and let cool completely on wire rack. Wrap with plastic film, then in foil, and store overnight before serving. Makes 1 loaf.

ANADAMA BREAD

2 Cups Cold Milk
½ Cup Yellow Cornmeal
1½ Tsp. Salt
½ Cup Light Molasses
3 Tbs. Shortening
1 Tsp. Sugar
¼ Cup Lukewarm Water
1 Pkg. Dry Yeast (or 1 cake
   compressed yeast)
4½ Cups Sifted All-purpose Flour

Combine milk, cornmeal and salt in a sauce-pan; heat to boiling, stirring constantly. Reduce to low heat and continue to stir for 5 minutes more. Remove from heat. Add molasses and shortening and blend. Cool to lukewarm. Meanwhile, stir sugar into water. Add yeast and let stand for 10 minutes. Stir yeast mixture to blend and add cooled cornmeal mixture. Stir well. Add flour gradually and mix thoroughly. Turn out onto lightly floured board and knead lightly but thoroughly for 10 minutes. Place dough in a clean, greased bowl. Turn once to bring greased side up. Cover; set in warm place (86°F.) away from drafts until doubled in bulk, about 1 hour.

Turn dough out again onto lightly floured board and divide in half. Round up each portion, cover and let rest for 10 minutes. Shape into loaves and place in greased pans (8¼x4½x2¾"). Lightly grease tops of loaves, cover and set in warm place until doubled in bulk (about 1¼ hours). Bake in a moderately hot oven (400°F.) for 45 to 50 minutes. Remove from pans, cool on a rack, uncovered and away from drafts. Makes 2 loaves.

CALIFORNIA BREAKFAST PASTRY

1 Pkg. Active Dry Yeast, or 1 Cake
   Compressed Yeast
¼ Cup Water
1 Cup Milk
½ Cup Butter or Margarine
2 Eggs
½ Cup Sugar
Juice and Peel of ½ Lemon
½ Tsp. Vanilla
½ Tsp. Salt
4 Cups Sifted All-purpose Flour

Filling:

1 Lb. California Walnut Meats
   (about 4 cups)
1 Egg
1/3 Cup Milk
½ Cup Sugar
½ Tsp. Powdered Cinnamon
¼ Tsp. Powdered Ginger
Juice and Peel of 1 Lemon
Melted Butter or Margarine

Sprinkle yeast into warm water to soften, or use lukewarm water for compressed yeast. Heat milk until film wrinkles over the top. Pour into mixing bowl. Stir butter or margarine in; mix and let cool to lukewarm. Beat eggs with sugar until smooth. Stir into milk mixture with juice and peel from half a lemon, the vanilla, salt and yeast. Beat flour in gradually. Cover with folded kitchen towel; set bowl in warm, not hot, place until dough has doubled.

To make filling, chop walnuts with finest blade of food chopper. Beat egg and milk together. Stir into nuts with sugar, spices, peel and juice of 1 lemon. Add a little more milk if too thick for spreading.

Grease two 11x7x1½" baking pans. If dough is too soft to handle, chill for a few minutes. Turn dough out onto floured board. Cut in half. Flour hands and pat one piece into a 12" square. Spread with half of the nut filling; roll up as for jelly roll. Moisten edge and press to seal. Place roll in baking pan. Do the same with the remaining piece of dough and filling. Cover pans with folded kitchen towel. Let rise in warm, but not hot, place until doubled. Bake in moderate oven (350°F.) for 45 to 50 minutes. Brush tops with melted butter or margarine while still warm. Makes 8 or more servings in each loaf. Serve warm for brunch, buffet luncheon or supper.

FINNISH COFFEE BRAID

½ Cup Butter
1 Pkg. Active Dry Yeast
3 Tbs. Warm Water
2 Egg, beaten
1 Cup Milk, scalded and cooled
½ Cup Sugar
½ Tsp. Salt
½ Tsp. Fresh Ground Cardamom
Grated Peel of 1 Orange (optional)
5 Cups (approximate) Unsifted
   All-purpose Flour
1 Egg Yolk
1 Tbs. Milk

Melt butter and set aside to cool. Dissolve yeast in the warm water. In a large mixing bowl, combine beaten eggs, milk, sugar, salt, cardamom, grated orange peel, yeast mixture, and butter. Stir in enough flour to make a fairly stiff dough. Turn onto a floured board and knead until dough is smooth. Shape into a ball and place in a greased bowl; cover and put in a warm place, free from drafts, and allow dough to rise until almost doubled in bulk, about 2 hours. Punch down and divide into two equal portions, then divide each portion into thirds. Roll each third between hands to form strands 18 to 24 inches long (all strands should be the same length), rolling from center. Place 3 strands on a board, crossing in the center, and braid out to each end. Form braid into a ring and pinch the ends together. Place on a greased baking sheet. Repeat process to make the second braid. Cover lightly with waxed paper and let rise in a warm place until almost doubled, from 2 to 2½ hours.

Paint each braid with a mixture of egg yolk beaten with the 1 tablespoon of milk. Bake in a moderate oven (350°F.) for about 45 minutes, or until a medium brown. Let cool on wire racks (or serve warm). Decorate if desired. Wrap airtight. Slice to serve. Makes 2 large loaves.

MARBLE CAKE

2 Cups Flour
2 Tsp. Baking Powder
½ Tsp. Salt
½ Cup Shortening
¾ Cup Sugar
2 Eggs, well beaten
½ Cup Milk
1 Tsp. Cinnamon
½ Tsp. Cloves
½ Tsp. Nutmeg
2 Tbs. Molasses

Cream shortening thoroughly; add sugar gradually and cream until light and fluffy. Add well beaten eggs. Mix and sift flour, baking powder and salt; add alternately with·milk. Mix well. Divide batter into two parts. To one part add spices and the molasses. Place the light and dark batters, alternately, a tablespoonful at a time, in a greased 8x8" pan. Bake in 350°F. oven for 50 to 60 minutes.

PUMPKIN CAKE

½ Cup Shortening
1 Cup Sugar
1 Cup Brown Sugar, firmly packed
2 Eggs, beaten
1 Cup Cooked, Mashed Pumpkin
   or Winter Squash
3 Cups Sifted Cake Flour
4 Tsp. Baking Powder
¼ Tsp. Baking Soda
½ Cup Milk
1 Cup Chopped Walnuts
1 Tsp. Maple Flavoring
Harvest Moon Frosting (recipe
   below)

Cream shortening and slowly add sugars, eggs and pumpkin. Sift together flour, baking powder and soda; add alternately with milk to creamed mixture. Fold in walnuts and maple flavoring. Pour into 3 greased 8" round layer cake pans. Bake in 350°F. oven for 30 minutes. Cool on racks. Put cake layers together with Harvest Moon Frosting. Frost sides, bringing frosting slightly over top edge, then frost top.

Harvest Moon Frosting:
3 Egg Whites
1½ Cups Brown Sugar, firmly packed
Dash of Salt
6 Tbs. Water
1 Tsp. Vanilla

Combine in double boiler the 3 egg whites, brown sugar, salt and water. Beat well; place over rapidly boiling water and cook 7 minutes, beating constantly, or until frosting will stand in peaks. Remove from boiling water and add vanilla. Beat until thick enough to spread. Makes enough frosting for a 3-layer cake.

SPICED NUT CORN BREAD

½ Cup Sifted All-purpose Flour
2 Tsp. Baking Powder
¼ Tsp. Salt
¼ Cup Sugar
½ Tsp. Ground Cinnamon
¼ Tsp. Ground Allspice
¼ Tsp. Ground Nutmeg
½ Cup White Cornmeal
½ Cup Finely Chopped Pecans
1 Egg, beaten
½ Cup Milk
2 Tbs. Melted Butter

Sift first seven ingredients. Add the cornmeal and nuts; stir well. Add egg, milk, and 1 tablespoon melted butter. Blend to make a batter. Put 1 tablespoon butter in a 7" iron skillet. Heat the skillet in preheated hot oven (400°F.), then brush heated butter on sides and bottom of pan. Add batter and return to oven at once. Bake for 30 minutes, or until corn bread tests done. Cut into 6 wedges and serve immediately. Makes 6 servings.

BAGELS

3 Cups Sifted All-purpose Flour
1½ Tsp. Salt
2 Tbs. Sugar
1 Pkg. Active Dry Yeast (or 1 Cake
    Compressed Yeast)*
2/3 Cup Water
3 Tbs. Salad Oil or Shortening
1 Egg
4 Qts. Boiling Water
2 Tbs. Sugar

Sift dry ingredients together into a deep mixing bowl. Dissolve yeast in one third of the water. Sprinkle dry yeast or crumble cake into water. Let stand for a few minutes, then stir until dissolved.

Add oil or melted shortening to the remainder of warm water and stir into dissolved yeast. Make a well in the center of flour mixture and stir in the liquid, adding the slightly-beaten egg when half the liquid has been used. Stir briskly to form a ball of dough and knead on a lightly floured board for 2 minutes. Return dough to mixing bowl, smooth side up, and punch down 3 times. Cover and let rise at room temperature for 30 to 45 minutes, or until the dough has come to the top of the bowl.

Knead again on board until smooth and elastic as for rolls. Divide dough into 12 equal portions. Form into lengths not more than ¾" thick, pinching ends together. Place on a floured cookie sheet and slip under broiler for 3 minutes. Drop each bagel into rapidly boiling water, in a deep kettle (2 tbs. sugar should be added to the boiling water). Do only a few at a time so they will not touch each other. Cook over moderate heat for 15 to 20 minutes. Skim out and place on a cookie sheet. Bake in 375°F. oven for 15 min., then increase heat to 400°F. for 10 min., or until bagels are browned and crust is golden brown and crisp. Makes 1 dozen.

Note: Use very warm water (105°F. to 115°F.) for dry yeast. Use lukewarm (80°F. to 90°F.) for compressed yeast.

CRUNCHY ORANGE MUFFINS

1 Egg, slightly beaten
¼ Cup Sugar
½ Cup Orange Juice
2 Tbs. Salad Oil or Melted
    Shortening
2 Cups Packaged Biscuit Mix
½ Cup Orange Marmalade
½ Cup Chopped Pecans
¼ Cup Sugar
1½ Tbs. All-purpose Flour
½ Tsp. Cinnamon
¼ Tsp. Nutmeg
1 Tbs. Butter or Margarine

Combine first 4 ingredients; add biscuit mix and beat vigorously for 30 seconds. Stir in the marmalade and pecans. Grease muffin pans or line with paper bake cups; fill 2/3 full. Combine sugar, flour, cinnamon and nutmeg; cut in butter until crumbly. Sprinkle over batter. Bake at 400°F. for 20 to 25 minutes. Makes 1 dozen muffins.

DUTCH APPLE CAKE

1¼ Cups Sifted All-purpose Flour
½ Tsp. Salt
1 Tsp. Sugar
1 Tsp. Baking Powder
½ Cup Butter or Margarine
1 Egg Yolk
2 Tbs. Brandy or Milk
Apples
Dried Currants
Cinnamon Topping

Sift the dry ingredients together; blend in butter. Add egg yolk and brandy. Press dough with fingers into a 9-inch layer-cake pan. Cover with apples that have been peeled, cored and cut into eighths. Sprinkle with a few currants. Cover with Cinnamon Topping. Bake in moderate oven (350°F.) for 45 min. Makes 6 to 8 servings.

Cinnamon Topping:

Blend together ¾ cup sugar, 1½ tablespoons all-purpose flour, 2 tablespoons of butter and ½ teaspoon ground cinnamon.

GOLDEN GLOW CAKE

1 Cup Shortening
5 Cups Sifted Cake Flour
3 Cups Sugar
6 Tsp. Baking Powder
2 Tsp. Salt
2 Cups Milk
2 Tsp. Vanilla Extract
4 Eggs
Confectioners' Sugar

Put shortening in bowl. Sift the flour, sugar, baking powder and salt into the bowl with the shortening. Add 1-1/3 cups of milk and the vanilla. Mix just until dry ingredients are moistened, then beat for 2 minutes at medium speed with electric mixer (or 300 strokes by hand). Add remaining milk and eggs; blend and beat for 2 minutes at medium speed (or 300 strokes by hand), scraping bowl and beaters thoroughly. Divide batter into two pans (13x9x2") lined on the bottom with waxed paper. Bake in preheated 375°F. oven for approximately 30 min. Cool slightly before turning out on racks; peel off the waxed paper. This may be sprinkled with confectioners' sugar or may be served with fudge sauce or butterscotch sauce or ice cream.

NO-BAKE FRUITCAKE

1 Cup Grape Juice
1 Cup Thick Raspberry Juice
4 Whole Cloves
2 Inches Stick Cinnamon
2 Allspice Berries
¼ Tsp. Nutmeg
2 Cups Toasted Rolled Oats
1½ Cups Crumbled Wheat Biscuits
1¼ Lbs. Dates
1¼ Lbs. Seeded Raisins
½ Lb. Currants
½ Lb. Candied Peel
¼ Lb. Glace Pineapple
¼ Lb. Red Glace Cherries
¾ Lb. Nutmeats (walnuts or pecans)
¼ Cup Olive Oil
¾ Cup Strained Clover Honey

Tie spices in cheesecloth and simmer in the fruit juices to flavor well. Lift out spice bag and pour boiling juice over the well-mixed toasted oats and crumbled wheat biscuits. Let stand overnight. The next day, add the oil and honey. Pit and cut up dates, chop the raisins, wash the currants and dry well. Shape peel thinly and cut up the glace fruit. Break nutmeats and mix with the fruits; add to mixture, using hands to blend. Line a pan with heavy white paper brushed with olive oil. Press the mixture closely into the pan, packing it well to make a solid mass. Press glace fruits and nutmeats into the top. Cover with another oiled paper and place in a covered crock or tin to ripen. A few days before cutting, take from pan and wrap in a cloth kept moist with fruit juice.

MARMALADE SWEET ROLLS

Batter:
¼ Cup Butter
¼ Cup Sugar
2 Eggs
2¼ Cups Flour
2 Tsp. Baking Powder
½ Tsp. Baking Soda
½ Tsp. Salt
1 Cup Buttermilk or Sour Milk

Filling:
¼ Cup Orange Marmalade
1 Tsp. Grated Orange Rind
¼ Tsp. Cinnamon
1/8 Tsp. Nutmeg

In a small bowl, mix the marmalade, orange rind, cinnamon and nutmeg. Set aside.

In a medium-size bowl, cream butter with sugar until light and creamy. Add eggs, one at a time, beating well after each addition. Sift flour with baking powder, baking soda and salt. Add gradually to egg and butter mixture. Add buttermilk gradually, mixing well each time.

Grease a 12-cup muffin pan. Place 2 tbs. of batter in each mold. Next place 1 level tsp. of filling in center of each. Continue to fill with remainder of batter until molds are 2/3 full. Bake in a preheated 400°F. oven for 20 to 25 minutes or until golden. Makes 12 rolls.

CHOCOLATE-SUNDAE CAKE

1½ - ¼ Lb. Bars Sweet Baking
  Chocolate
3 Tbs. Water
3 Tbs. Light Cream
4½ Cups Sifted All-purpose Flour
4½ Tsp. Double-acting Baking
  Powder
1½ Tsp. Salt
¾ Cup Butter or Margarine
¾ Cup Soft Vegetable Shortening
2¼ Cups Granulated Sugar
6 Eggs, unbeaten
1½ Cups Milk
1½ Tsp. Vanilla Extract
Chocolate Glaze (see recipe below)

Early in the day, preheat oven to 350°F.
Grease, then flour bottom only of a 10-inch
tube cake pan. In a double boiler, over hot,
not boiling, water, melt the chocolate with
the 3 tablespoons of water until very smooth,
stirring occasionally. Remove from heat &
blend in cream.

Sift flour with baking powder and salt. In
a large bowl, with mixer at medium speed,
cream butter with shortening until blended;
gradually add sugar, beating until light and
fluffy--about 5 minutes. Now beat in eggs,
one at a time, beating 1 minute after each
addition.

Combine milk and vanilla. With mixer at
low speed, alternately beat in flour mixture
and milk, starting and ending with flour, &
beating thoroughly after each addition. Batter will be quite thick. Now turn about ¼
of batter into prepared tube pan; drizzle it
with about 1/3 of melted chocolate mixture. Repeat with 2 more alternating layers
of batter and chocolate mixture; top with
remaining batter. Bake 70 to 80 minutes,
or until cake tester, inserted in center,
comes out clean. Cool in pan 15 minutes,
then remove from pan to wire rack to
finish cooling (a crack on top is normal,
so don't worry). Make up Chocolate
Glaze. When cake is cool, spoon glaze
along top edge of cake, letting it run over
sides. Makes 10 to 12 servings.

Chocolate Glaze: In double boiler, over
hot, not boiling, water, melt one and one-
half ¼-pound bars of sweet baking chocolate with 2 tsp. vegetable shortening, stirring until smooth.

HIGH-RISING YEAST BREAD

¾ Cup Milk
1/3 Cup Granulated Sugar
1 Tsp. Salt
½ Cup Butter or Margarine
1 Envelope Active Dry Yeast
¼ Cup Very Warm Water
  (105°F. to 115°F.)
3 Eggs, well beaten
1 Tsp. Grated Lemon Rind
½ Tsp. Ground Mace
4 Cups Sifted All-purpose Flour
Confectioners' Sugar

Scald milk with granulated sugar, salt and
butter or margarine in a small saucepan;
cool to lukewarm. Sprinkle yeast into very
warm water in a large bowl; stir until the
yeast dissolves. Stir in cooled milk mixture,
eggs, lemon rind and mace. Stir in flour
until well blended, then beat vigorously with
a wooden spoon, scraping down side of bowl
often, 100 strokes, or until dough is shiny
and elastic; cover with a towel. Let rise in
a warm place, away from drafts, for 1 hour,
or until double in bulk. Stir dough down;
spoon into a greased 12-cup tube pan or
10" angelfood cake pan; cover and let rise
again for 1 hour, or until not quite double
in bulk. Bake in 350°F. oven for 45 min.,
or until bread is golden and gives a hollow
sound when tapped. Remove from pan;
cool on a wire rack. Sprinkle lightly with
confectioners' sugar. Makes 1 ten-inch
round coffeecake.

SAVARIN CAKE

1 Pkg. Active Dry Yeast (or 1 cake
   compressed yeast)
¼ Cup Water
¼ Cup Milk, scalded and cooled
2 Cups Sifted All-purpose Flour
2 Tbs. Sugar
½ Tsp. Salt
4 Eggs, slightly beaten
2/3 Cup Butter or Margarine,
   softened
1 Tsp. Grated Lemon Rind
Rum Syrup (see recipe below)
Whipped Cream

Sprinkle dry yeast or crumble cake yeast
into water. Let stand for a few minutes;
then stir until dissolved. Put milk and
flour into a mixing bowl. Add the yeast
mixture, sugar, salt and eggs. Beat with
spoon or in electric mixer until a soft,
sticky dough is formed. When thoroughly
mixed, beat for 2 minutes with hands,
pulling up the dough and letting it slap
back hard into the bowl. Then cover and
let stand in a warm place for 45 minutes,
or until the dough is doubled in bulk.
Stir down and add butter in small pieces.
Beat with hands for about 4 minutes.
Add lemon rind. Pour into a well-buttered
9" ring mold and let rise to the top of the
pan, about 1 hour. Bake in preheated hot
oven (400°F.) for 30 to 35 minutes. Turn
out of mold and spoon hot Rum Syrup
over cake until well saturated. Serve warm
with the center filled with whipped cream.
Makes 8 to 10 servings.

Rum Syrup: In saucepan combine 1 Cup
sugar, 1½ cups water, and ½ cup rum.
Bring to a boil and simmer for 35 to 40
minutes.

ALMOND-FILLED COFFEE RING

1 Pkg. Active Dry Yeast (or 1 cake
   compressed yeast)
2 Tbs. Very Warm Water
¼ Cup Sugar
½ Tsp. Salt
½ Cup Milk
1 Egg, beaten
2 Cups Sifted All-purpose Flour (approx.)
¾ Cup Butter or Margarine
Almond Filling (see recipe below)
½ Cup Chopped Candied Cherries
Confectioners' Sugar Frosting
Whole Candied Cherries
Angelica

Sprinkle or crumble yeast into water. Let
stand a few minutes, then stir until dissolved.
Stir in sugar, salt, milk and egg. Add 1½
cups sifted flour and beat until smooth. Stir
in enough more flour (about ½ cup) to make
a very stiff dough. Turn out on well-floured
board and sprinkle with flour. Roll to ¼"
thickness. Spread ½ cup softened butter on
upper 2/3 of dough and fold lower third
over middle third. Fold top third over that.
Turn and roll again to ¼" thickness. Fold
in thirds. Put on cookie sheet and chill
about 30 minutes. Repeat rolling, folding
and chilling three times.

Divide dough in half. Roll each into rectangle about 8" long. Brush with ¼ cup
melted butter and spread each with Almond
Filling. Sprinkle with chopped cherries.
Roll up like jelly roll. Form into rings.
With a scissors, cut through rings, almost
to center, in slices about 1" thick. Turn
each slice slightly. Put each ring on greased
cookie sheet. Let rise in warm place until
light (about 25 minutes) Bake in preheated
350°F. oven for about 30 minutes. Cool
and frost and decorate with whole cherries
and angelica. Makes two 9" coffee rings.

Almond Filling:

1 Cup Blanched Almonds
½ Cup Fine Dry Bread Crumbs
¾ Cup Sugar
2 Tbs. Melted Butter
1 Well-beaten Egg

Force almonds through fine blade of food
chopper. Blend in bread crumbs, sugar and
melted butter. Add egg and mix thoroughly.

PUEBLO INDIAN BREAD

1½ Cups Water
3 Tbs. Butter or Margarine
1 Tbs. Sugar
3 Tsp. Salt
2 Envelopes Active Dry Yeast
½ Cup Very Warm Water
   (105°F. to 115°F.)
6½ Cups Sifted All-purpose Flour

Combine water, butter or margarine, sugar and salt in a small saucepan. Heat slowly until butter or margarine melts; cool to lukewarm. Sprinkle yeast into very warm water in a large bowl. Stir until yeast dissolves, then stir in butter mixture. Beat in 4 cups of flour until smooth. Beat in enough remaining flour to make a soft dough. Turn out onto a lightly-floured board and knead until smooth and elastic, about 5 minutes. Use only as much flour as you need to keep dough from sticking.

Place in a greased large bowl; turn to coat all of dough with shortening; cover with a clean cloth and let rise in a warm place, free from drafts, for 1½ hours, or until double in bulk. Punch dough down; turn out onto board. Knead dough a few times, divide into 3 equal pieces, and shape each piece into a ball. Cover with a towel and let rest 10 minutes.

On the board, roll each ball into a 9-inch circle. Fold each circle almost in half. Top circular edge should be about 1" from bottom circular edge. Place on greased cooky sheet. With kitchen scissors, make about 6 gashes in the dough, cutting from the circular edge about 2/3 of the way inward to the folded edge. Spread the fingers of the dough apart so they will not touch each other while baking. Do the same with the remaining 2 balls of dough. Let rise again in a warm place, free from drafts, for 1 hour, or until double in bulk. Bake in 350° F. oven for 50 minutes, or until breads are golden and give a hollow sound when tapped. Remove from cooky sheet to wire racks and cool completely. Makes three loaves.

ALABAMA FRUITCAKE

2 Cups Butter (1 lb.)
2 Cups Sugar (1 lb.)
12 Eggs
1 Cup Molasses
1 Cup Brandy, Rum or Bourbon
1 Cup Rosewater
4 Cups (1 lb.) sifted All-purpose Flour
¼ Lb. Candied Orange Peel, chopped
2 Lbs. Currants
2 Lbs. Raisins
2 Lbs. Candied Citron
1 Lb. Shelled Almonds, blanched
   and cut into small pieces
1 Tbs. Ground Nutmeg

Cream butter until light. Gradually beat in sugar, a little at a time. Add eggs, one by one, beating well after each addition. Stir in molasses, brandy and rosewater. Sprinkle flour over fruits and nuts and add nutmeg. With hands, mix fruits and flour so that fruits are well coated with flour. Add floured fruits to batter and mix thoroughly. Grease two 10" angel food cake pans, or four loaf pans (9x5x3"). Line pans with heavy unglazed brown paper and grease the paper. Spread batter into pans. Bake in preheated very slow oven (250°F.) for about 3 hours, or steam first for 1 hour & bake for remaining time. Cake will be crumbly. Cool cake in pans overnight to set. Let cake get very cold. If at all possible, ripen from 1 week to 3 months before using. Makes about 12 pounds of rich dark fruitcake. The flavor of this fruitcake will vary, depending upon whether you use brandy, rum, or bourbon. Rosewater can be purchased at a gourmet food store. Do not omit this as it adds a subtle taste to the cake.

IRISH SODA BREAD

3 Cups Sifted All-purpose Flour
3 Tbs. Sugar (for dough)
3 Tsp. Baking Powder
½ Tsp. Baking Soda
½ Tsp. Salt
1 Cup Dried Currants
1-1/3 Cups Buttermilk
2 Tbs. Sugar (for glaze)
2 Tbs. Hot Water

Sift flour, 3 tablespoons of sugar, baking powder, soda and salt into a medium-size bowl. Stir in currants, then buttermilk. Stir until blended (dough will be sticky). Turn out onto a lightly-floured pastry cloth or board and knead about 10 times. Shape into an 8″ round loaf; place on un-greased cooky sheet. Cut a cross in top of dough with a sharp knife. Bake in a moderate oven (375°F.) for 45 minutes. Remove from oven. Dissolve 2 table-spoons sugar in hot water in a cup and brush generously over hot loaf. Bake 10 minutes longer, or until richly golden. Serve warm. Makes 1 round loaf.

BUTTERSCOTCH APPLE CAKE

2 Large Baking Apples
¼ Cup Red Cinnamon Candies
Water
½ Cup Butter or Margarine
1 Cup Light Brown Sugar
   (firmly packed)
8 Maraschino Cherries
1/3 Cup Chopped Pecans
1 Pkg. Yellow Cake Mix
Eggs
Whipped Cream

Core apples, but do not pare. Cut each into 4 thick rings. Combine cinnamon candies and ½ cup water in a large frying pan. Heat, stirring constantly, until the candies melt. Add apple rings. Simmer, turning once, for 3 minutes. Remove with a slotted spoon and drain on paper toweling.

Melt butter or margarine in a baking pan. Use 13x9x2″ size. Stir in brown sugar. Place apple rings in two rows over the sugar mixture; top each with a maraschino cherry. Sprinkle pecans between apples. Prepare cake mix with eggs and water, following label directions. Pour batter evenly over apples in pan. Bake in 350° F. oven for 45 minutes, or until golden and cake tests done. Cool in pan on a wire rack 10 minutes. Loosen around edges with a knife; invert onto a large serving plate. Let stand for 5 minutes, then carefully lift off pan. Serve warm with whipped cream. Makes 12 servings.

SPANISH DOUGHNUTS

4 Tbs. Butter or Margarine, cut
   into small pieces
1/8 Tsp. Salt
1¼ Cups Sifted All-purpose Flour
3 Eggs
¼ Tsp. Vanilla Extract
Salad Oil for deep frying
½ Tsp. Cinnamon
½ Cup Sugar

In a medium saucepan, combine butter with ½ cup water; cook over low heat, stirring, until butter is melted & mixture just comes to a boil. Add salt and remove from heat.

Add flour all at once; beat very hard with a wooden spoon. Return to low heat and beat until very smooth--about 2 minutes. Remove from heat and let cool slightly. Beat in eggs, one at a time, beating well after each addition. Add vanilla. Continue beating until mixture has satinlike sheen. Meanwhile, in deep skillet or deep-fat fryer, slowly heat oil (at least 1½″) to 380°F. on deep-frying thermometer. Press doughnut mixture through a large pastry bag with a large, fluted tip, ½″ wide. With wet scissors, cut batter into 2″ lengths as it drops into hot oil.

Deep fry a few at a time, 2 minutes on a side, or until golden brown. Lift out of fat with a slotted spoon; drain well on paper towels.

Combine cinnamon and sugar in medium bowl. Add doughnuts, a few at a time, and toss to coat well. Serve warm. Makes about 2½ dozen.

CARROT-PINEAPPLE MUFFINS

1 - 8¼ Oz. Can Crushed Pineapple
Milk
2 Cups All-purpose Flour
1/3 Cup Brown Sugar, packed
1 Tbs. Baking Powder
½ Tsp. Salt
1 Egg, beaten
¾ Cup Finely-shredded Carrot
1/3 Cup Cooking Oil
½ Tsp. Vanilla
2 Tbs. Granulated Sugar
½ Tsp. Ground Cinnamon

Drain the pineapple, reserving the syrup.
Add milk to the syrup to equal ¾ cup of
liquid. Stir together the flour, brown sugar,
baking powder and salt. Combine egg, carrot, milk-syrup mixture, drained pineapple,
oil and vanilla. Add all at once to the dry
ingredients, stirring just until moistened.
Fill greased or paper-cup lined muffin pans
2/3 full. Sprinkle tops with a mixture of
the granulated sugar and cinnamon. Bake
at 400°F. for 20 to 25 minutes. Makes
12 muffins.

PINEAPPLE-CHERRY BREAD

3 Cups Sifted All-purpose Flour
4 Tsp. Baking Powder
¾ Cup Sugar
1 Tsp. Salt
1 Cup Chopped Walnuts
½ Cup Candied Cherries, cut
   in half
1 Egg
1 - 9 Oz. Can Crushed Pineapple
½ Cup Milk
¼ Cup Vegetable Oil

Sift flour, baking powder, sugar and salt
into a large bowl; stir in walnuts & cherries. Beat egg well in a medium bowl; stir
in pineapple and syrup, milk and vegetable
oil. Add all at once to flour mixture; stir
just until evenly moist. Spoon into a
greased 9x5x3″ pan. Bake in 350°F.
oven for 1 hour 15 minutes, or until a
wooden pick inserted in center comes
out clean. Cool in pan on a wire rack

for 10 minutes. Loosen around edges
with a knife; turn out onto rack. Cool
completely. Wrap loaf in wax paper,
foil or transparent wrap. Store overnight to blend flavors. Makes 1 loaf.

JEWELED POUND CAKE

¼ Cup Candied Cherries
¼ Cup Candied Orange Peel
¼ Cup Citron
¼ Cup Candied Pineapple
6 Tbs. Light Corn Syrup
2 Cups Butter (1 lb.)
1¼ Cups Sugar
2 Tsp. Vanilla
½ Tsp. Salt
10 Eggs, separated
4 Cups Sifted Cake Flour
1¼ Cups Sugar

Chop the fruits. Grease three 9x5x3″ loaf
pans. Pour 2 tbs. syrup into the bottom of
each pan and sprinkle an equal quantity of
fruits into each pan.

Cream butter until fluffy. Add 1¼ cups of
sugar, the vanilla and salt gradually, while
beating. Continue beating with an electric
mixer until mixture is light and fluffy and
no sugar particles remain, about 5 to 7
minutes. If beating by hand, cream until
very light and fluffy. Beat egg yolks until
light and lemon-colored; combine with the
creamed mixture. Blend in flour. Beat egg
whites until soft peaks form. Gradually
add remaining 1¼ cups sugar, beating constantly. Continue beating until whites
stand in stiff peaks. Fold meringue into
cake batter; blend well but do not beat.
Pour into prepared loaf pans over fruit.
Bake in 325°F. oven for 80 minutes for
metal pans, 10 minutes less for glass pans.
Turn loaves out of pans and cool upside
down on racks. Makes 3 loaves.

CHRISTMAS COFFEE RING

2 Pkgs. Active Dry Yeast
½ Cup Warm Water
1 Cup Lukewarm Milk
5 Cups Unsifted All-purpose Flour
Sugar
½ Cup Butter or Margarine
¼ Tsp. Mace
¼ Tsp. Cinnamon
¼ Tsp. Nutmeg
¾ Tsp. Salt
2 Eggs
1 Cup Coarsely-chopped Nuts
1 Cup Seedless Raisins
½ Cup Candied Cherries, halved
¼ Cup Chopped Citron
¾ Cup Mixed Candied Fruit

Dissolve yeast in water; let stand a few minutes. Add lukewarm milk, 2 cups of flour & 1 tablespoon of sugar. Beat until smooth. Let stand in warm place until bubbly and double in bulk. Cream butter and beat in ¾ cup sugar, spices and salt. Beat in eggs. Stir down yeast mixture and add butter mixture. Beat in 2 cups of flour; add nuts and fruit and enough flour to make a fairly stiff dough. Turn out on floured board & knead well. Put in greased bowl and let stand in warm place until double in bulk. Punch down in bowl and work dough well with hand for a few minutes. Pack into a large well-buttered 3½-quart mold with hold in center. Let stand in warm place until double in bulk. Bake in preheated 375°F. oven for about 35 minutes. Let stand a few minutes. Turn out and cool. If desired, frost with confectioners' sugar mixed with a little milk. Decorate with candied fruit.

BANANA PUFFS

2 Cups Flour
2 Tsp. Sugar
½ Tsp. Salt
½ Cup Butter
½ Cup Buttermilk
1 Large Ripe Banana, cut into
    ½" cubes
¼ Cup Flaked Coconut
1 Tsp. Lime Juice
1 Egg White, lightly beaten

Sift flour, sugar and salt into a bowl. Cut in butter, then blend in buttermilk and knead lightly. Cut the banana into ½" cubes and toss with the coconut and lime juice. Put the dough on a lightly-floured surface and roll out about ¼" thick. Using a 2¾" cutter, cut into about 24 rounds. On half of the rounds, put about 1 tbs. of the banana mixture; brush the edges of the pastry with lightly-beaten egg white, then top each with a second round. Press the edges together with a fork. Heat 1½" of salad oil in a large pan to 360°F., then fry 5 or 6 puffs at a time until golden, turning them once. Drain on paper towels. Serve warm or cold. Makes 12 puffs.

SPICED-APPLE LOAF

1 - 14 Oz. Jar Spiced Apple Rings
¼ Cup Brown Sugar, packed
¼ Tsp. Cinnamon
¼ Tsp. Ground Nutmeg
¼ Tsp. Ground Ginger
¼ Cup Butter or Margarine
1 Cup Granulated Sugar
2 Eggs
1 Tsp. Vanilla
2½ Cups All-purpose Flour
1 Tbs. Baking Powder
1 Tsp. Salt
1 Tsp. Ground Cinnamon
¾ Cup Milk
½ Cup Chopped Walnuts

Peel apple rings; mash apple with a fork. Add brown sugar and next 3 spices; set aside. In a bowl, cream the butter and granulated sugar together well. Beat in eggs and vanilla. Thoroughly stir together the flour, baking powder, salt and 1 tsp. cinnamon. Add alternately to creamed mixture with milk. Fold in nuts. Spread a third of the batter into a greased and floured 9x5x2" loaf pan. Drop a third of the apple mixture by tablespoons onto batter. Repeat layers to make 3 layers of each, ending with apple mixture. Bake at 350°F. about 60 minutes. Cool in pan 10 minutes; remove from pan and finish cooling on a rack. Cool thoroughly before slicing. Makes 1 loaf.

PISTACHIO-MINCE FRUITCAKE

2½ Cups Sifted All-purpose Flour
1 Tsp. Baking Soda
2 Eggs
1 - 1 Lb. 12 Oz. Jar Prepared
    Mincemeat
1 - 14 Oz. Can Sweetened Condensed
    Milk
1 - 8 Oz. Jar Chopped Candied
    Pineapple
1 - 8 Oz. Jar Chopped Candied Citron
½ Cup Coarsely-chopped Pistachio Nuts
½ Cup Confectioners' Sugar
1 Tbs. Water
Pistachio Nuts, finely chopped

Line bottom and sides of a greased 9" angel-cake pan. Use a double thickness of brown paper; grease the paper. Sift flour and soda together into a small bowl. Beat eggs slightly in a large bowl; stir in mincemeat, condensed milk, candied pineapple, citron and coarsely-chopped pistachio nuts. Fold in the flour mixture. Spoon batter into prepared pan and bake at 300°F. for 2 hours, or until firm on top. Cool cake completely in pan on a wire rack. Loosen around edge and tube with a knife; turn cake out onto rack. Peel off the paper and turn the cake right-side up. To store, place cake in a plastic bag and seal. It will keep in the refrigerator about 8 weeks, or in the freezer for 3 months. When ready to serve, make a glaze of confectioners' sugar and a little water and drizzle it over the cake, letting it drip down the side. Sprinkle top with additional finely-chopped pistachio nuts. Makes one 9" round cake.

ALMOND TWISTS

½ Cup Blanched Almonds
1 Egg
1 Tbs. Water
¼ Cup Sugar
2 Cups Sifted All-purpose Flour
1 Tsp. Salt
¼ Tsp. Ground Cardamom
2/3 Cup Vegetable Shortening
4 to 5 Tbs. Water

Put almonds through food chopper, using fine blade, or chop fine in an electric blender. Beat egg in a small bowl; measure 1 tbs. into a custard cup; stir in 1 tbs. water. Save to brush on top of twists. Stir almonds and sugar into the egg remaining in the bowl. Sift flour, salt and cardamom into medium bowl; cut in shortening with pastry blender until mixture is crumbly. Stir in 4 to 5 tablespoons of water with a fork just until dough holds together. Roll out, half at a time, to rectangle 12x8" on lightly-floured pastry cloth or board. Cut in half lengthwise. Spread one half evenly with half of filling; then top with other half of dough; press layers together lightly with rolling pin; trim edges, if needed. Rectangle should measure about 12x4". Cut crosswise into 24 half-inch-wide strips with a sharp knife. Carefully twist each strip and place, one-inch apart, on a greased cookie sheet. Repeat with remaining dough and filling to make 48 twists. Brush reserved egg mixture lightly over twists. Bake in 375°F. oven for 20 minutes, or until the twists are golden. Remove at once to wire racks with a spatula; let cool completely. Makes 4 dozen.

RAISED DOUGHNUTS

1 Cup Scalded Milk
1 Tsp. Salt
¾ Cup Sugar
2 Tbsp. Shortening
1 Yeast Cake softened in ¼ cup
    lukewarm water
3½ to 4 Cups Flour
1 Egg
½ Tsp. Grated Nutmeg

Add scalded milk to salt, sugar and fat. When lukewarm, add the softened yeast. Add 1½ cups flour. Allow the sponge to stand in a warm place until it is so light that it will fall at the slightest touch. Add the egg, nutmeg and remainder of the flour and knead. The dough should be softer than bread dough. Cover and set in a warm place to raise. Toss on a lightly floured board and roll until ¾ inch thick. Cut with a doughnut cutter and let raise. Fry in deep fat (360-370 degrees F.) 2 to 3 minutes. When frying put the raised side of the doughnut down in the fat. The heat will cause the top side to raise by the time the doughnut is ready to turn.

MINCEMEAT TEA LOAF

2 Cups Sifted All-purpose Flour
½ Tsp. Salt
½ Tsp. Baking Soda
1 Tsp. Baking Powder
¼ Cup Butter or Margarine
2/3 Cup Light Brown Sugar,
    firmly packed
2 Eggs
3 Tbs. Dairy Sour Cream
1 Cup Mincemeat
½ Cup Coarsely-chopped Pecans
    or Walnuts

Sift first 4 ingredients and set aside. Cream softened butter or margarine and sugar with an electric mixer. Add eggs, one at a time, beating well. Add sour cream. Fold into dry ingredients by hand, but do not overmix. This will be a stiff batter. Fold in mincemeat and nuts. Place batter in lightly buttered loaf pan (9x5x3"). Press batter with back of spoon to pack solidly and to even it. Bake in preheated 350°F. oven for 50 to 60 minutes, or until bread tests done. Loosen edges of loaf with knife; turn out on rack and let cool before slicing. This will slice beautifully the same day it is made.

RASPBERRY CHIFFON CAKE

1 - 15 Oz. Pkg. Frozen Raspberries
    (40% sugar)
1½ Cups All-purpose Flour
3 Tsp. Baking Powder
1 Tsp. Salt
1/3 Cup Granulated Sugar
½ Cup Vegetable Oil
6 Egg Yolks
½ Cup Raspberry Juice
2/3 Cup Drained, Mashed Raspberries
2 Tbs. Lemon Juice
6 Egg Whites
½ Tsp. Cream of Tartar
½ Cup Granulated Sugar

Thaw and drain the raspberries, reserving the juice. Sift together into a large bowl the flour, baking powder, salt and sugar. Add the vegetable oil, egg yolks, ½ cup of raspberry juice, 2/3 cup drained mashed

raspberries and the lemon juice and beat until smooth, about ½ minute with mixer.

Beat egg whites and cream of tartar together until soft peaks are formed. Gradually beat in the granulated sugar. Continue beating until very stiff and shiny. Fold egg yolk mixture into meringue until blended. Turn into an ungreased 10-inch tube pan and bake in a preheated 350°F. oven for 55 to 65 minutes, or until cake tests done. Invert and cool in pan. When cool, loosen edges and remove cake from pan.

JEWISH CHALLAH

1 Pkg. Active Dry Yeast (or 1 cake
    compressed yeast)
2 Tbs. Sugar
1½ Cups Lukewarm Water
5 Cups Sifted All-purpose Flour
    (approximate)
2 Tsp. Salt
2 Eggs
2 Tbs. Oil
1 Egg Yolk
2 Tbs. Poppy Seeds

Note: Use warm water 105°F. to 115°F. for dry yeast; use lukewarm water -- 80°F. to 90°F. -- for compressed yeast.

Combine yeast, sugar and ¼ cup water. Let stand for 5 minutes. Sift flour and salt into a large bowl. Make a well in the center and drop in eggs, oil, remaining warm water, and the yeast mixture. Work the liquids into the flour. Knead on a floured board until dough is smooth and elastic. Place in a bowl, brush top with oil, cover with a towel, and let stand in a warm place to rise for 1 hour.

Punch dough down, cover and let rise to double in bulk. Divide dough into 3 equal parts. Between lightly floured hands, roll dough into 3 strips of even length. Braid these and place on a greased cookie sheet. Cover and let rise to double in bulk. Brush with egg yolk and sprinkle with poppy seeds. Bake in preheated moderate oven (375°F.) for 45 to 50 minutes, or until golden brown. This makes 1 very large loaf or 2 smaller loaves.

WALNUT ROLL
(From Hungary)

1 Pkg. Active Dry Yeast
½ Cup Warm Water
4 Cups Sifted All-purpose Flour
½ Tsp. Salt
6 Egg Yolks
¾ Cup Warm Milk
Filling
1 Cup Chopped Walnuts
1/3 Cup Milk, scalded
2 Tbs. Sugar
1 Small Vanilla Bean, grated

Sprinkle dry yeast into warm water (105° F. to 115°F.); let stand for a few minutes. Stir until dissolved. Place sifted flour and salt into a large mixing bowl; form a well in the center and place in it the yeast, egg yolks and milk. Gradually blend the flour into the other ingredients; knead in bowl until the mixture is smooth. Cover and let rest while preparing filling. Roll out dough to a rectangle ½" thick; spread with filling and sprinkle with 1 cup chopped walnuts. Roll as for a jelly roll. Cut into 1½" pieces and place, cut side up, in a buttered ring mold or tube pan. It may be necessary to make 2 layers. Let rise in a warm place until doubled in bulk. Bake in preheated moderate oven (350°F.) for 25 minutes. Remove from oven and pour over 1/3 cup scalded milk mixed with 2 tablespoons sugar and 1 small vanilla bean, grated. Return to oven for 15 minutes longer. Remove from oven and cool on a rack.

Filling: Cream together ¾ cup sugar and ¾ cup sweet butter; add 1½" piece of vanilla bean, grated.

VELVET WHITE CAKE

1/3 Cup Salad Oil or Butter
1 Cup Sugar
1 Tbs. Orange Juice
½ Tbs. Lemon Juice
Grated Rind of 1 Lemon
¼ Tsp. Salt
2/3 Cup Milk
½ Cup Cornstarch
1½ Cups Flour
3 Tsp. Baking Powder
3 Egg Whites

Pour salad oil in bowl; add sugar, juices and rind. Beat until creamy. Sift dry ingredients. Add alternately with milk. Add beaten egg whites last; fold until mixed. Bake in well-greased and floured pans at 350 degrees about 35 minutes, or until done. Ice with marshmallow frosting and garnish with candied orange peel, cut fine.

ORANGE-NUT BREAD

¾ Cup Boiling Water
2 Tbs. Butter or Margarine
1/3 Cup Orange Juice
1 Tbs. Grated Orange Rind, lightly packed
1 Cup Ground Figs (6 Oz.)
½ Tsp. Vanilla
1 Egg, well beaten
2 Cups All-purpose Flour
½ Cup Sugar
½ Tsp. Salt
2 Tsp. Baking Powder
¼ Tsp. Soda
½ Cup Chopped Nuts

Combine first 6 ingredients and let stand for 20 minutes. Add the egg and beat thoroughly. Sift flour, then remeasure and sift with sugar, salt, baking powder and soda. Add the sifted dry ingredients all at once to the liquid and beat well. Fold in the nuts. Turn into a well-greased loaf pan (8x4x2½"), pushing well into the corners. Bake in a 350°F. oven for 1 hr. 15 min., or until bread tests done. Cool before slicing. Makes 1 loaf.

HOT CROSS BUNS

2 Envelopes Active Dry Yeast
½ Cup Very Warm Water
½ Cup Butter or Margarine
2/3 Cup Evaporated Milk
½ Cup Sugar
1 Tsp. Salt
2 Eggs
1 Cup Dried Currants
4½ Cups Sifted All-purpose Flour
¼ Tsp. Cinnamon
¼ Tsp. Nutmeg
Lemon Icing (see recipe below)

Sprinkle yeast into very warm water in large bowl. Stir until yeast dissolves. Melt butter or margarine in small saucepan; remove from heat. Add evaporated milk, sugar, and salt, stirring until sugar dissolves. Stir into yeast mixture. Beat eggs in small bowl, measure 2 tablespoons into a cup and set aside for brushing on top of buns later. Stir remaining eggs into yeast mixture, then stir in currants. Sift 2 cups of the flour, together with cinnamon and nutmeg, over yeast mixture. Beat until smooth, then stir in just enough of remaining flour to make a soft dough; turn out onto a lightly-floured pastry cloth or board and knead until smooth and elastic, adding only enough flour to keep dough from sticking. Place in greased bowl; brush top lightly with butter or margarine and cover with a clean towel. Let rise in a warm place, away from drafts, for 1 hour, or until double in bulk.

Punch dough down; turn out onto lightly-floured pastry cloth or board; divide in half. Cut each half into 16 equal pieces and shape each lightly into a ball. Place the 16 balls into a greased 9x9x2" baking pan. Cover with clean towel and let rise in a warm place, away from drafts, for 45 minutes, or until double in bulk. Brush top of buns lightly with saved egg. Bake in moderate oven (350°F.) for 30 min., or until golden brown. Remove from pans and cool on wire racks. Drizzle lemon icing from tip of teaspoon onto top of buns, making crosses with icing.

Lemon Icing: Blend 1 cup unsifted confectioners' sugar with 4 teaspoons milk, ¼ teaspoon vanilla, and ¼ teaspoon lemon extract until smooth in small bowl. Makes about ½ cup.

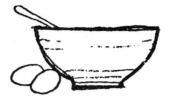

CHRISTMAS TREE BREAD
(Tannenbaum Brot)

2 Pkgs. Active Dry Yeast (or 2 Cakes
   Compressed Yeast)
¼ Cup Lukewarm Water
2 Tsp. Salt
½ Cup Sugar
1½ Cups Milk, scalded and cooled
½ Cup Melted Butter
2 Eggs
6 Cups Sifted All-purpose Flour
   (approximate)
½ Tsp. Ground Nutmeg
½ Tsp. Ground Cinnamon
½ Cup Raisins
½ Cup Candied Cherries, cut up
½ Cup Chopped Nuts
Confectioners' Sugar

Sprinkle dry yeast into warm water (105° F. to 115°F.). If using compressed yeast, use lukewarm water (80°F. to 90°F.). Let stand for a few minutes, then stir until dissolved. Now add the salt, sugar, cooled milk, butter, eggs and 4 cups of the flour. Beat with a spoon until thoroughly mixed. Stir in remaining flour and the rest of the ingredients (you will have to use your hands at this point). Turn the dough out onto a lightly-floured board and knead until smooth, about 5 minutes. Place in a greased bowl, cover and let rise until the dough is double. Punch down and let rise again until doubled. These two rising times will take about 2½ hours in all.

Turn dough out and shape it into 2 loaves. Place in greased loaf pans (9x5x3") and let rise again until doubled. Bake in preheated moderate oven (350°F.) for about 45 min. Cool. Before serving, sprinkle with confectioners' sugar. Makes 2 loaves.

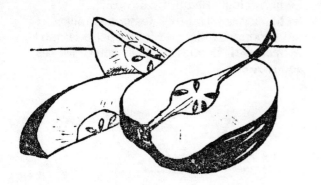

APPLESAUCE-DATE CAKE

2 Cups Unsifted All-purpose Flour
2 Tsp. Baking Soda
1 Tsp. Cinnamon
½ Tsp. Allspice
½ Tsp. Nutmeg
¼ Tsp. Cloves
¼ Tsp. Salt
2 Eggs
1 Cup Light Brown Sugar,
　firmly packed
½ Cup Butter or Margarine,
　softened
2 Cups Hot Applesauce
1 Cup Chopped Dates
¾ Cup Coarsely-chopped Walnuts
Cream Cheese Frosting

Grease and flour a 9x9x2'' baking pan.
Preheat oven to 350°F. In large bowl of
electric mixer, sift flour with baking soda,
cinnamon, allspice, nutmeg, cloves and
salt. Then add the eggs, brown sugar,
soft butter, and 1 cup hot applesauce.
Beat at low speed just until the ingredients
are combined. At medium speed, beat 2
minutes longer, occasionally scraping the
side of the bowl and guiding mixture into
the beater with a rubber scraper. Add remaining applesauce, dates and walnuts;
beat 1 minute. Pour batter into prepared
pan. Bake for 50 minutes, or until cake
tester inserted in center comes out clean.
Let cool in pan 10 minutes. Remove from
pan and let cool on wire rack. Frost top
of cooled cake with cream cheese frosting.
Cut into 9 squares. Makes 9 servings.

FRENCH BREAD

1 Envelope Active Dry Yeast
2½ Cups Very Warm Water (should
　feel comfortably warm when
　dropped on wrist)
7 Cups Sifted All-purpose Flour
2 Tbs. Sugar
1 Tbs. Salt
Corn Meal
Sesame Seeds

Sprinkle yeast into very warm water; stir
until yeast dissolves. Stir in 2 cups of the
flour, the sugar and salt and mix until
smooth; gradually beat in enough of the
remaining 5 cups of flour to make a stiff
dough. Turn out onto lightly-floured
board and knead for 5 minutes, or until
smooth and elastic. Add only enough
flour to keep dough from sticking.

Return dough to bowl; brush top with soft
shortening. Cover with a clean towel and
let rise in a warm place, free from drafts,
for 45 minutes, or until double in bulk.
Punch dough down; cover and let rise again
for 30 minutes, or until double in bulk.

While dough rises, make baking pans out of
heavy foil. Tear off 3 twenty-inch long
sheets of heavy foil. Fold each in quarters
lengthwise; grease and sprinkle lightly with
corn meal. Pinch ends together and seal,
pressing thumb inside to round slightly.
Turn each side up to form an edge.

Punch dough down; knead for 1 minute on
lightly-floured board. Divide into thirds &
roll out, one at a time, to a rope about 18
inches long. Place in prepared foil pan.
Make several evenly-spaced shallow cuts
diagonally in top of each loaf; brush with
water and sprinkle with sesame seeds.
Cover and let rise in a warm place, free
from drafts, for 30 minutes, or until double
in bulk. Place a pan of hot water on lower
shelf in oven. Slide loaves on shelf above.
Bake in 450°F. oven for 15 minutes, then
reduce heat to 350°F. and bake another
30 minutes, or until bread sounds hollow
when tapped. Remove from pans immediately and cool on wire racks. Makes 3
loaves.

CARROT CAKE

4 Eggs
1½ Cups Sugar
1½ Cups Vegetable Oil
3¼ Cups Whole Wheat Flour
2 Tsp. Baking Powder
2 Tsp. Baking Soda
½ Tsp. Salt
1 Tsp. Ground Cinnamon.
1 - 8 Oz. Can Juice-packed
    Crushed Pineapple, drained
2 Cups Finely-grated Carrots
    (about 1 lb.)
1 Cup Chopped Pecans
1 Cup Chopped Dates

Grease a 10" angel cake tube pan; line bottom of the pan with waxed paper. Beat eggs in a large mixing bowl. Gradually beat in the 1½ cups of sugar. Stir in oil. Combine whole wheat flour with the baking powder, baking soda, salt and cinnamon. Stir into egg mixture. Add drained pineapple and grated carrots; mix well. Stir in chopped pecans and dates. Turn mixture into the prepared pan. Bake at 350°F. for 1 hr. 15 min. Top should spring back when lightly pressed with fingertip. Cool cake in pan on wire rack for about 15 minutes. Remove cake from pan; peel off wax paper. Cool completely before slicing. Wrap tightly in foil or plastic wrap to store. Makes one 10" tube cake.

CHERRY-ALMOND BRAID

¾ Cup Milk
½ Cup Sugar (for dough)
1 Tsp. Salt
½ Cup Butter or Margarine
1 Envelope Active Dry Yeast
¼ Cup Very Warm Water
4 Eggs
5¼ Cups Sifted All-purpose Flour
1 - 8 Oz. Container Candied Red
    Cherries, chopped
1 - 8 Oz. Can Almond Paste
2 Tbs. Sugar (for filling)
1 Cup Sliced Blanched Almonds
½ Cup Confectioners' Sugar
2 Tbs. Water
¼ Tsp. Almond Extract

Combine milk, ½ cup sugar, salt and butter or margarine in a small saucepan. Heat slowly until butter or margarine melts; cool to lukewarm. Sprinkle yeast into very warm water (105°F to 115°F.). Stir until yeast dissolves, then stir in milk mixture and 2 eggs. Beat in 2 cups of flour until smooth; beat in 3 cups more flour to make a soft dough. Turn out onto lightly-floured board and knead until smooth and elastic, adding only enough of remaining ¼ cup of flour to keep dough from sticking. Place in a greased large bowl; turn to coat all over with shortening. Cover with a clean towel and let rise in a warm place, away from drafts, for 1½ to 2 hours, or until double in bulk. Punch dough down; knead a few times on lightly floured board; return to bowl and cover again. Let rise again for ½ hour, or until double in bulk. While the dough is rising, crumble almond paste in a small bowl; stir in 1 egg and 2 tablespoons remaining sugar until smooth.

Divide dough into 3 even pieces. Roll each piece into an 8x10" rectangle; spoon 1/3 cup filling in a narrow strip down middle of dough almost to ends. Sprinkle with 1/3 cup cherries. Cut dough on each side from outer edge just to filling in 1½"-wide strips (use scissors or knife). Fold strips, alternating from side to side, across filling at an angle; repeat with remaining 2 pieces of dough. Place on greased cooky sheets. Cover and let rise in a warm place, free from drafts, for 40 minutes, or until double in bulk. Beat remaining egg with 2 tablespoons water; brush on braids and sprinkle with sliced almonds. Bake in 350°F. oven for 25 minutes, or until golden. Remove from cookie sheets and cool slightly on wire racks. Combine the confectioners' sugar, almond extract and 2 tablespoons of water in a cup; blend until smooth and easy to pour from a spoon. Drizzle icing over braids. Garnish with additional red and green candied cherries, if you wish. Makes 3 braids.

BANANA DOUGHNUTS

5 Cups All-purpose Flour
3 Tsp. Baking Powder
1 Tsp. Soda
2 Tsp. Salt
1 Tsp. Nutmeg
¼ Cup Shortening
1 Cup Sugar
1½ Tsp. Vanilla
3 Eggs, well beaten
¾ Cup Mashed Bananas (about 2
    good-size bananas)
½ Cup Buttermilk
½ Cup Flour, for rolling
Deep Fat, for frying

Sift flour, measure and resift with baking powder, soda, salt and nutmeg. Cream the shortening, blend in sugar, add vanilla and eggs and beat until light and fluffy. Add combined bananas and buttermilk and stir until well mixed. Add flour mixture in 3 or 4 portions, stirring thoroughly after each addition. Chill dough before rolling. Remove one-fourth of dough from refrigerator at a time, knead it lightly 4 or 5 times and roll to 3/8" thickness. Cut with floured 2½" doughnut cutter. Fry in deep fat, heated to 375°F., until golden brown. Lift out and drain on absorbent paper. If desired, dough may be covered tightly and kept in the refrigerator for 1 or 2 days, to be fried as needed. Makes about 42 doughnuts.

FUDGE CAKE
(It's Fabulous)

3 Squares Unsweetened Chocolate
2¼ Cups Sifter Cake Flour
2 Tsp. Baking Soda
½ Tsp. Salt
½ Cup Butter or Margarine
2½ Cups Firmly-packed Brown Sugar
    (1 Lb.)
3 Eggs
2 Tsp. Vanilla
½ Cup Buttermilk
1 Cup Boiling Water

Melt chocolate in small saucepan over very low heat. Sift cake flour, baking soda and salt into a bowl. Cream butter or margarine in large bowl of electric mixer at medium speed. Gradually add sugar and beat until mixture is fluffy. Beat in eggs, one at a time. Beat until thick. Stir in vanilla and chocolate at low speed. Add sifted dry ingredients, a third at a time, alternately with buttermilk. Mix at low speed just until blended. Stir in boiling water.

Grease bottoms of three 9" layer cake pans and line with wax paper. Grease the wax paper. Pour batter into pans and bake in moderate oven (375°F) for 25 to 30 min., or until done. Cool in pans on wire racks for 5 minutes; loosen around edges with a knife and turn out onto racks. Remove wax paper and cool layers completely. Put layers together and frost with your favorite chocolate cream frosting.

LEMON-SAFFRON BREAD

1½ Cups All-purpose Flour
1½ Tsp. Baking Powder
¼ Tsp. Baking Soda
¼ Tsp. Salt
Pinch of Powdered Saffron
¼ Cup Hot Water
1 Tbs. Grated Lemon Peel
¼ Cup Lemon Juice
¼ Cup Shortening
½ Cup Sugar
1 Egg

Mix flour with baking powder, baking soda and salt. Dissolve saffron in hot water, then blend with lemon peel and lemon juice and set aside. Cream shortening; add sugar gradually, beating until thoroughly blended. Add egg and beat until light and fluffy.

Add dry ingredients in fourths and liquid in thirds, mixing just until blended after each addition. Turn into a well-greased and floured cooker bake pan or 2-pound coffee can. Cover bake pan with lid, or, if using coffee can, cover with 6 layers of paper toweling. Set in an electric cooker. Cover and cook on high 2 to 3 hours. Remove pan and let cool 10 minutes before removing bread. Makes 1 loaf.

PLANTATION PRUNE CAKE

1 Lb. Cooked Prunes
2½ Cups Sifted All-purpose Flour
1 Tsp. Baking Soda
1 Tsp. Salt
1 Tsp. Ground Allspice
1 Tsp. Ground Cinnamon
1 Tsp. Ground Nutmeg
1 Cup Finely-chopped Pecans
3 Eggs
1½ Cups Sugar
1 Cup Vegetable Oil
½ Cup Buttermilk
Vanilla Glaze (see recipe below)

Grease a 12-cup tube pan or 10-inch tube pan; flour lightly, tapping out any excess. Drain liquid from prunes into a cup. Pit the prunes, then cut each into 3 or 4 pieces; place in a 1-cup measure. Add enough prune liquid to make 1 cup.

Sift flour, soda, salt, allspice, cinnamon & nutmeg into a medium bowl; stir in pecans. Beat eggs well in a large bowl; slowly beat in sugar until mixture is light and fluffy. Beat in vegetable oil, then buttermilk. Stir in prunes. Beat in flour mixture, a third at a time, until well blended. Pour into prepared pan, spreading evenly. Bake in a moderate oven (350°F.) for 1 hour & 5 minutes, or until top springs back when lightly pressed with fingertip. Cool 10 min. in pan on a wire rack. Loosen cake around the edge and tube with a knife; turn out onto a rack and cool completely. Drizzle glaze slowly over cake, spooning any that drips onto plate back over cake.

Vanilla Glaze:

1 Cup Sugar
½ Tsp. Baking Soda
½ Cup Buttermilk
1 Tbs. Light Corn Syrup
½ Cup Butter or Margarine
1 Tsp. Vanilla

Combine all ingredients, except vanilla, in a medium saucepan. Heat slowly, stirring constantly, to boiling. Cook, stirring constantly, for 2 minutes. Remove from heat and stir in vanilla.

Note: This cake may be wrapped in wax paper or plastic wrap, then in heavy foil, and frozen for up to 8 weeks. The day before serving, remove cake from freezer and let stand, still wrapped, at room temperature to thaw. An hour before serving, unwrap cake and place on a deep plate, then cover with glaze.

BISMARCKS

1 Cup Milk, scalded
¾ Cup Sugar
1 Pkg, Active Dry Yeast
   (or 1 cake compressed yeast)
2 Tbs. Lukewarm Water
3½ Cups Sifted All-purpose Flour
2 Egg Yolks
1 Egg
1 Tsp. Salt
½ Tsp. Vanilla Extract
1/3 Cup Melted Butter
Thick Jam
Egg White
Fat for Frying

Cool milk to lukewarm; add 2 tablespoons of the sugar, the yeast dissolved in water and 2 cups of flour; beat well. Cover and let rise in a warm place until double in bulk, about 25 minutes. Beat egg yolks & egg until thick and lemon-colored. Beat in remaining sugar, salt, vanilla, yeast mixture, remaining flour and melted butter. The dough will be soft, but it can be kneaded in the bowl until smooth & satiny. Allow to rise in a warm place for 1 hour. Turn out on a lightly floured board and divide into 2 parts; cover and let rest for 10 minutes. Roll out to ½-inch thickness. Cut into 2½" rounds. On half of them place heaping teaspoons of jam. Brush edges with egg white. Top with remaining rounds, pressing edges firmly to seal. Arrange uncovered on board and allow to rise until very light, about 1 hour. Drop doughnuts into hot deep fat (375°F. on a frying thermometer). Turn as they rise to surface and show a little color. When nicely browned, lift from fat with tongs; do not prick. Drain on absorbent paper. Sprinkle with sugar. Makes about 3 dozen.

DESSERTS

AMBROSIA SQUARES

½ Cup Butter
2 Tbs. Brown Sugar
1 Cup Flour

Cream butter and brown sugar, mix in flour and pat into a greased 9x9x2" cake pan. Bake in a 350°F. oven for 15 minutes, only until light brown. Cool. Chill.

½ Cup Butter, melted
3 Cups Confectioners' Sugar
1 Small Egg, beaten

Combine ingredients and beat until smooth; spread over cooled shortbread in pan.

1 - 8 Oz. Can Crushed Pineapple

Drain pineapple well and pat fruit into the frosting layer.

1 Cup Cream
2 Tbs. Confectioners' Sugar
1 Tsp. Vanilla

Whip the cream; add sugar and vanilla and spread over pineapple. Put pan into freezer and keep frozen until ready to serve. Cut into squares and serve as dessert.

CHOCOLATE BAVARIAN

1 Tbs. Plain Gelatin
¾ Cup Cold Water
1 Square (1 Oz.) Unsweetened
   Chocolate
1½ Cups Whipping Cream or
   Evaporated Milk
½ Cup Sugar
½ Tsp. Vanilla

Soften the gelatin in ¼ cup of cold water. Melt the chocolate over boiling water; add ½ cup of the cream or evaporated milk, sugar and remaining ½ cup of water. Cook for about 5 minutes, stirring until smooth. Add the softened gelatin, stirring until dissolved. Add vanilla and cool until mixture

is thick and syrupy. Have rest of cream or evaporated milk thoroughly chilled and whip with rotary beater in chilled bowl until stiff. Whip chocolate mixture until smooth and fold in the whipped cream or evaporated milk lightly but thoroughly. Turn into mold or individual sherbets which have been rinsed with cold water and chill in refrigerator until set. Makes 5 servings.

LEMON CHEESECAKE

1 Cup Butter
2 Cups Sugar
1 Tbs. Baking Powder
3 Cups Sifted Cake Flour
¾ Cup Milk
6 Egg Whites, stiffly beaten
Cheesecake Filling (see recipe
   below)

Cream together the butter and sugar with a mixer, beating until light and fluffy. Sift the baking powder and flour together; add alternately with milk to creamed mixture. Fold in egg whites. Pour into 3 greased 8" round layer cake pans. Bake in 350°F. oven for 25 to 30 minutes, or until cake tests done. Cool on racks. Put layers together with filling and spread filling over the top. Sprinkle with coconut, if desired. White icing may be used to frost the sides of the cake.

Filling:
½ Cup Butter
1 Cup Sugar
6 Egg Yolks
Grated Peel and Juice of
   2 Lemons

Combine all ingredients in the top of a double boiler; cook over hot water, stirring constantly, until thick. Cool.

FRUIT AND NUT TORTE

2 Cups Walnut or Pecan Halves
1 Cup Brazil Nuts, halved; or
   ¾ Cup Whole, Blanched Almonds
1 Cup Whole Candied Red and
   Green Cherries, mixed
1 Cup Raisins or Sliced Dates
1½ Cups Sifted Flour
1 Tsp. Salt
4 Eggs
2 Egg Yolks
1¼ Cups Sugar
1 Tbs. Vanilla
2 Egg Whites
¼ Cup Sugar
¼ Cup Sifted Confectioners' Sugar
1 Tbs. Sugar, for topping
¼ Cup Brazil Nut Curls

Fit two lengths of brown paper into a 9"
square pan; allow a 1½" extension beyond
the pan edges. Grease lightly to settle the
papers into the pan.

Combine fruit and nuts in a large bowl;
toss with ½ cup flour. Sift remaining flour
with the salt. Beat eggs and egg yolks until thick and lemon colored. Gradually
beat in 1¼ cups sugar and the vanilla, beating until cream-colored. Fold in dry ingredients. Pour over the fruit-nut mixture;
fold until completely mixed. Turn into the
prepared pan. Bake in 375°F. oven for 50
to 60 minutes, or until cake tester comes
out clean when inserted in center of the
torte. If necessary, cover the torte with
foil toward the end of the baking time so
that it does not become too brown.

While torte is baking, prepare the topping.
Beat egg whites until peaks form. Gradually beat in ¼ cup sugar and the confectioners' sugar; continue beating until stiff
and glossy. Take the torte from the oven,
remove foil cover and spread topping evenly
over the crust. Be sure to cover the edges.
Sprinkle with remaining 1 tablespoon of
sugar and the Brazil nut curls. Return to
oven for 15 min., or until lightly browned.
Cool in pan 30 minutes. Lift from pan by
paper liner onto wire rack. Loosen the paper from the meringue edges. When cold,
cut paper off sides, but leave it on the bottom of the torte. Serve in slices or small
squares, plain or topped with whipped
cream. Makes 24 servings.

HAWAIIAN CREAM PIE

1 - 9" Pie Crust, baked and cooled
   (use your favorite recipe)
1 - 1 Lb. 5 Oz. Can Pineapple
   Tidbits
1 Envelope Unflavored Gelatin
¼ Cup Quartered Maraschino
   Cherries, drained
2 Cups Miniature Marshmallows
1 Cup Whipping Cream
½ Tsp. Vanilla

Drain syrup from pineapple tidbits into
a 2-cup measure; add water, if needed, to
make 1¼ cups liquid. Soften gelatin in ½
cup of the pineapple liquid in a small
saucepan; heat slowly, stirring constantly,
just until gelatin dissolves. Pour mixture
into a medium bowl. Stir in remaining ¾
cup syrup, pineapple tidbits, cherries and
marshmallows. Chill for 30 minutes, or
until as thick as unbeaten egg white.

Beat cream with vanilla until stiff; fold
into thickened gelatin mixture. Spoon
into cooled pastry shell. Garnish with
quarters of maraschino cherries arranged
in a pleasing pattern. Chill several hours,
or until firm. Makes one 9" pie.

APPLE CUSTARD PIE

Pastry for 1-Crust Pie
1 Pint Cooked Apples
1 Tbs. Butter
1 Cup Sugar
2 Eggs, well beaten
½ Cup Cream

Line pie plate with pastry. Stew quartered
apples in a very little water. When tender,
rub through a sieve. Add sugar, butter and
well-beaten eggs, then add cream. Mix well
until smooth.

Place filling in uncooked pastry-lined pie
plate. Bake at 450°F. for 10 minutes, then
reduce heat to 350°F. and continue baking
for 20 to 25 minutes. Serve cold.

DATE PUDDING

3 Tbs. Shortening
1 - 6½ Oz. Pkg. Pitted Dates, chopped
1 Cup Boiling Water
1 Egg
1 Cup Brown Sugar, packed
1 Tsp. Grated Lemon Peel
1½ Cups Sifted All-purpose Flour
1 Tsp. Salt
1 Tsp. Baking Soda
½ Cup Chopped Walnuts

Combine shortening and chopped dates in large bowl. Pour boiling water over and let cool slightly. Stir in egg, sugar and lemon peel. Sift flour, salt and soda together. Add to date mixture and mix well. Stir in nuts. Pour into a greased 1½-quart baking dish. Bake, uncovered, in a preheated 325°F. oven for 55 min., or until done. Serve hot with a hard sauce or sherry cream sauce. Makes 8 servings.

TRIPLE CHOCOLATE PIE

1 Baked 9" Chocolate Shell (see recipe below)
1 Envelope Unflavored Gelatin
¼ Cup Sugar, for filling
¼ Tsp. Salt
1 Tsp. Instant Coffee Powder
1 Cup Milk
3 Egg Yolks, beaten
3 Squares Unsweetened Chocolate
½ Tsp. Vanilla
3 Egg Whites
¼ Tsp. Cream of Tartar
¼ Cup Sugar, for meringue
2 Cups Whipping Cream
½ Square Semisweet Chocolate

Chocolate Shell:
1/3 Cup Shortening
1 Cup All Purpose Flour, sifted
¼ Tsp. Salt
½ Square Semisweet Chocolate, grated
2 Tbs. Water

Cut shortening into flour and salt in small bowl. Stir in grated semisweet chocolate; sprinkle with 2 tablespoons of water. Mix lightly, just until dough holds together. Roll out and line a 9" pie plate; flute the edge. Bake in 400°F. oven for about 12 minutes. Cool.

Mix gelatin, ¼ cup sugar, salt and instant coffee powder in a large heavy saucepan. Blend in milk and beaten egg yolks; add unsweetened chocolate. Heat slowly, stirring constantly, until chocolate is melted and mixture slightly thickened. Do not let it boil. Put mixture into a large bowl; add vanilla and stir until smooth and blended. Cool till mixture mounds.

Beat egg whites with cream of tartar until foamy in medium bowl; beat in ¼ cup of sugar, 1 tablespoon at a time, until meringue stands in stiff peaks. Beat 1 cup cream until stiff in second bowl, using same beater. Reserve the remaining 1 cup of cream for topping. Beat cooled chocolate mixture until smooth; fold in meringue, then fold in whipped cream. Pour into baked and cooled chocolate shell. Chill until firm enough to hold its shape when cut. Beat remaining 1 cup cream until stiff in small bowl. Mound on pie and grate semisweet chocolate over top. Makes one 9" pie.

CRACKER PIE

3 Egg Whites
¼ Tsp. Salt
¾ Cup Sugar
1 Cup Chopped Pecans
18 Plain Crackers (unsalted), crushed
1 Tsp. Vanilla Extract
½ Cup Heavy Cream
¼ Cup Pineapple Topping for Ice Cream

Beat egg whites with salt until almost stiff. Gradually add sugar and beat until stiff. Fold in nuts, cracker crumbs, and vanilla. Mix well and pour into well-buttered 9" pie pan. Bake in preheated 325°F. oven for about 35 minutes. Cool. Whip cream until stiff; fold in pineapple topping and spread on pie. Chill. Makes 6 to 8 servings.

PINEAPPLE PARTY TREATS

Filling:
¾ Cup Water
3 Tbs. Cornstarch
1 - 20 Oz. Can Crushed Pineapple,
  undrained
1 Egg Yolk
4 Egg Whites
1/8 Tsp. Yellow Food Coloring

Dough:
¾ Cup Warm Milk (105° to 115°F.)
1 Tbs. Sugar
1 Pkg. Active Dry Yeast
1¼ Cups Butter or Margarine
3 Cups All-purpose Flour
3 Egg Yolks, beaten

Frosting:
2 Cups Powdered Sugar
2 Tbs. Butter or Margarine,
  softened
2 to 3 Tbs. Lemon Juice

In a medium saucepan, combine water, cornstarch, pineapple and egg yolk. Cook over medium heat until thickened, stirring occasionally. Cool for 25 minutes. In a small bowl, beat egg whites until stiff peaks form; fold egg whites and food coloring into pineapple mixture. Set aside.

In small bowl, combine milk, sugar and yeast; let stand 5 minutes. Measure the flour and cut margarine into flour until the size of small peas. Add egg yolks and yeast mixture; blend well. Divide in half. On a lightly-floured surface, roll out half of dough into a 17x12" rectangle; place in ungreased 15x10" jelly-roll pan. Spread with pineapple filling. Roll out remaining half into a 15x10" rectangle; place over filling. Press edges to seal. Prick crust. Cover and let rise in a warm place (80° to 85°F.) for 40 minutes (will not be double in size).

Heat oven to 350°F. Bake 25 to 35 minutes or until light golden brown. Cool. In small bowl, combine all frosting ingredients. Spread over bars. Makes 15 servings.

SWEDISH CORNETS

2 Eggs
5/8 Cup Sugar
¼ Cup Sifted All-purpose Flour
¼ Tsp. Powdered Cinnamon
1 Cup Heavy Cream
1 Cup Raspberry or Strawberry Jam

Beat eggs with sugar until light. Stir in the flour and cinnamon. Blend smoothly together. Place tablespoon of batter on a greased baking sheet. Spread it into a 5" round. Repeat until all batter is used. Bake rounds 5 to 10 minutes, in a preheated 400°F. oven, until delicate brown. As soon as pan is removed from oven, loosen rounds, remove and shape each into a cone or cornucopia. Let cool. Fill with whipped cream or with whipped cream mixed with jam. Makes about 20 cornets.

KEY LIME PIE

1 Cup + 2 Tbs. Sugar
1/3 Cup Cornstarch
½ Tsp. Salt
¼ Cup Cold Water
1½ Cups Hot Water
6 Tbs. Fresh Lime Juice
3 Eggs, separated
3 Tbs. Butter or Margarine
1 Tbs. Grated Lime Rind
1 - 9" Pie Shell, baked
6 Tbs. Sugar
1/8 Tsp. Salt
Fresh Lime Slices, for garnish

Combine first 4 ingredients in a saucepan. Mix well. Add hot water and cook over low heat, stirring constantly, until very thick. Stir in fresh lime juice. Return to heat and cook until thickened. Beat egg yolks lightly. Beat in a small amount of hot mixture. Cook for about 2 minutes, stirring constantly. Add butter and lime rind. Cool. Pour into cold pastry shell.

Beat egg whites until stiff but not dry. Beat in remaining sugar and salt gradually, beating until blended. Spread over top of pie. Bake for 20 minutes in a preheated, slow oven (300°F.). Serve cold, garnished with fresh lime slices.

PRUNE WHIP

¾ Cup Prune Juice
½ Cup Sugar
1 Envelope Unflavored Gelatin
1 Cup Prune Pulp (use stewed
   prunes or baby-food prunes)
2 to 3 Tbs. Fresh Lemon Juice
¼ Tsp. Salt
2 Egg Whites, stiffly beaten

Heat ½ cup of prune juice combined with sugar. Soften gelatin in ¼ cup cold prune juice. Let stand for 5 minutes. Add hot prune juice mixture and stir until gelatin is dissolved. Add prune pulp, lemon juice to taste, and salt. Let cool over ice water or in the refrigerator until slightly thickened while you beat egg whites to stiff peaks. Fold whites gently but thoroughly into cooled prune mixture and spoon into a fancy mold or individual sherbet glasses. Chill until firm. This will take about 3 hours. Serve with whipped cream. Dust top with ground mace or nutmeg. Makes 4 servings.

GOLDEN RAISIN PIE

1 - 8" Pie Shell, baked and cooled
¼ Cup Sugar
1½ Tbs. Cornstarch
½ Tsp. Salt
½ Tsp. Ground Ginger
½ Tsp. Ground Cinnamon
1/8 Tsp. Ground Cloves
1/8 Tsp. Ground Nutmeg
½ Cup Light Corn Syrup
3 Egg Yolks, beaten
1 Cup Dairy Sour Cream
1 Cup Light Raisins
1 Tbs. Grated Orange Peel
Meringue (3 egg whites)

Mix sugar, cornstarch, salt and spices in top of double boiler. Stir in corn syrup, egg yolks, sour cream, raisins and orange peel. Cook over hot water, stirring, until smooth and thick, about 15 to 18 minutes. Pour into cooled pie shell. Top with meringue (use your favorite recipe), while filling is hot. Bake in moderate oven (350°F.) until brown, 12 to 15 minutes.

SHOOFLY PIE

¾ Cup Dark Molasses
¾ Cup Boiling Water
½ Tsp. Baking Soda
¼ Tsp. Salt
1½ Cups Sifted All-purpose Flour
¼ Cup Butter or Margarine
½ Cup Firmly-packed Brown Sugar
Pastry for 1-Crust 9" Pie

Mix first 4 ingredients. With hands, mix the next 3 ingredients. Pour about one third of molasses mixture into pie pan lined with pastry rolled 1/8" thick. Now sprinkle with one third of flour mixture. Continue alternating layers until all ingredients are used, ending with layer of flour. Bake in preheated oven (375°F.) for 35 minutes. Serve warm or cold. Makes 6 to 8 servings.

CHARLOTTE RUSSE

Ladyfingers
2 Tbs. Unflavored Gelatin
¼ Cup Cold Water
2 Cups Milk, scalded
½ Cup Sugar
¼ Tsp. Powdered Mace
4 Eggs
2 Tbs. Sherry
1/8 Tsp. Salt
1 Pint Heavy Cream

Line a 2-quart mold with ladyfingers. Soften gelatin in cold water about 5 minutes or longer. Stir into hot milk in saucepan. Continue to stir until gelatin is dissolved. Add sugar and mace. Beat egg yolks slightly and add. Place saucepan over low heat. Cook & stir until slightly thickened, then let cool. Add sherry. Whip egg whites with salt until they remain in stiff points when beater is removed. Fold custard into whites. Whip cream until stiff. Fold into mixture. Pour into prepared mold. Chill until firm. Unmold onto chilled platter. Makes 10 servings. Garnish servings with additional sherry-flavored whipped cream or leave plain. Some cooks prefer a light sprinkling of powdered nutmeg on top.

CANTALOUPE CREAM MOLD

1 - 3 Oz. Pkg. Orange-flavor
  Gelatin
1 Cup Boiling Water
1¾ Cups Orange Juice
¼ Tsp. Ground Ginger
1 Large, Ripe Cantaloupe
2 Envelopes Unflavored Gleatin
½ Cup Sugar
2 Tsp. Grated Orange Rind
1 - 2 Oz. Pkg. Whipped Topping Mix
Milk

Dissolve orange gelatin in boiling water in a medium-size bowl; stir in ¾ cup of orange juice and ginger. Cool and chill until as thick as unbeaten egg white. While orange gelatin mixture chills, halve and seed the cantaloupe. Shape 1 cup cantaloupe balls with a melon ball scoop or the ½ teaspoon from your measuring-spoon set. Save remaining cantaloupe.

Fold melon balls into chilled gelatin and pour into a 6-cup mold. Chill just until sticky-firm. Cut remaining cantaloupe into small pieces. Combine with remaining 1 cup orange juice in electric-blender container; cover. Whirl until very smooth. (If you do not have a blender, press the cantaloupe through a fine sieve or food mill; stir in orange juice.)

Combine unflavored gelatin and sugar in medium-size saucepan; stir in 1 cup of cantaloupe puree. Heat slowly, stirring constantly, just until gelatin dissolves. Remove from heat. Combine with remaining cantaloupe puree and orange rind in a large bowl. Chill about 30 minutes. Prepare whipped topping mix with milk, following label directions. Fold into cantaloupe puree mixture. Pour carefully over gelatin layer in mold. Chill about 4 hours, or until firm. Just before serving, loosen mold around edge with a knife; dip mold very quickly in and out of hot water. Wipe water off mold. Shake mold gently to loosen. Cover with a serving plate and turn upside down. Gently lift off mold. Garnish with fresh mint, if you wish. Makes 8 servings.

BLUEBERRY DESSERT

2 Cups Sifted All-purpose Flour
  (sift before measuring)
3 Tsp. Baking Powder
½ Tsp. Salt
½ Cup Soft Butter
½ Cup Granulated Sugar
2 Eggs
¾ Cup Milk
1 Cup Blueberries, washed and
  drained
2 Tbs. Light Brown Sugar
½ Tsp. Cinnamon

Sift flour, baking powder, and salt. In large bowl of electric mixer, combine butter, granulated sugar, eggs; beat at high speed until fluffy. At low speed, add dry ingredients alternately with milk. Fold in blueberries. Turn into prepared 8x8x2" pan (greased). Sprinkle with brown sugar and cinnamon and bake in preheated 375°F. oven for about 35 minutes. Serve warm. Makes 9 servings.

RICE MELBA

2/3 Cup Packaged Precooked Rice
2 Cups Milk
1/3 Cup Sugar
½ Tsp. Salt
1/8 Tsp. Powdered Nutmeg
1/8 Tsp. Powdered Cinnamon
½ Cup Heavy Cream
1 - No. 2½ Can Cling Peach Halves,
  drained
1/3 Cup Red Currant or Raspberry
  Jelly

Combine rice and milk in saucepan. Bring to a boil and boil gently, loosely covered, for 15 minutes, fluffing rice occasionally with fork. Remove rice from heat. Stir in sugar, salt, nutmeg and cinnamon. Let cool 5 minutes, then chill rice in freezing compartment of refrigerator 20 minutes, but do not let it freeze. Whip the cream. Fold chilled rice into cream. Heap into dessert dishes. Lay drained peach half on top, cut side down. Melt jelly over hot water. Pour a little jelly over peach. Makes 6 servings.

STRAWBERRY-PEACH PIE

Pastry for 2-Crust Pie
1½ Cups Frozen Strawberries
1½ Cups Frozen, Sliced Peaches
½ Cup Strawberry Juice
½ Cup Peach Juice
3 Tbs. Sugar
2½ Tbs. Quick-cooking Tapioca
1½ Tbs. Cornstarch
1 Tsp. Lemon Juice

Thaw the fruit until most of the ice has disappeared. Drain off the juices and measure, then stir into mixture of sugar, tapioca and cornstarch in saucepan. Heat rapidly until thickening is complete. Boiling is not necessary. Set aside to cool.

Add fruit and lemon juice to cooled, thickened juice. Pour filling into pastry-lined 9" pie pan. Cut vents in top crust; cover pie, seal and flute edge. Bake in 425°F. oven 30 to 35 minutes, or until nicely browned. Makes 1 - 9" pie.

DATE PECAN PIE

1 Unbaked 9" Pie Shell
1 Cup Dairy Sour Cream
3 Eggs, beaten
1 Cup Sugar
1 Tsp. Ground Cinnamon
¼ Tsp. Salt
¾ Cup Dates, cut into pieces
½ Cup Chopped Pecans
Whipped Cream, or Ice Cream

Combine sour cream, eggs, sugar, cinnamon and salt in a bowl; mix well. Add dates & pecans. Blend well and pour into pie shell. Bake in 375°F. oven for 30 minutes, or until filling is set and browned. Serve spread with whipped cream.

ROSE' CHIFFON PIE

2 - 4½ Oz. Cans Whole Blanched
   Almonds, ground (2 cups)
2 Tbs. Butter or Margarine, softened
3 Tbs. Sugar (for crust)
1 Envelope Unflavored Gelatin
¾ Cup Sugar (for filling)
4 Eggs, separated
½ Cup Rose' Wine
¼ Cup Water
¼ Tsp. Cream of Tartar
1 Cup Whipping Cream
5 Drops Red Food Coloring

Blend the almonds, butter or margarine & the 3 tablespoons of sugar in a small bowl. Press evenly over bottom and side of a very lightly-buttered 9" pie plate. Bake in 350°F. oven 10 minutes, or until lightly golden. Cool completely on wire rack.

Mix gelatin and ½ cup of the sugar in top of double boiler; beat in egg yolks until light and fluffy. Blend in wine and water; place over simmering water. Cook, stirring constantly, until gelatin dissolves and mixture coats a spoon. Pour into a large bowl. Set bowl in a pan of ice and water to speed setting. Chill at room temperature, stirring often, just until as thick as unbeaten egg white. While gelatin mixture is chilling, beat egg whites with cream of tartar until foamy and double in volume (use a medium bowl). Beat in remaining ¼ cup of sugar, 1 tablespoon at a time, beating constantly, until meringue stands in firm peaks. Beat cream until stiff in a second bowl. Fold meringue, then the whipped cream, into thickened gelatin mixture until no streaks of white remain. Fold in about 5 drops of food coloring to tint mixture pink. Chill again, if necessary, until thick enough to mound when spooned. Spoon into cooled crust. Chill at least 4 hours, or until firm. Just before serving, garnish with whipped cream. Makes one 9" pie.

CRANBERRY MOUSSE

1 - 3 Oz. Pkg. Soft Cream Cheese
¼ Cup Sugar
1/8 Tsp. Salt
1 Cup Heavy Cream, whipped
1 - 1 Lb. Can Whole-berry
   Cranberry Sauce (2 cups)

Beat the cream cheese until fluffy. Stir in sugar and salt and fold into cream. Add cranberry sauce and mix lightly. Pour into refrigerator tray and freeze until firm. Makes 6 servings.

PEARS SABAYON

1 Cup Granulated Sugar
4 Fresh Pears, pared, halved and
   cored

Sauce:

4 Egg Yolks
1 Cup Confectioners' Sugar
¼ Cup Sherry
¾ Cup Heavy Cream

In a 4-quart saucepan, combine granulated sugar and 3 cups of water; heat until sugar dissolves. Add pears; cover and simmer gently until tender--about 30 minutes. Remove from heat. Carefully place pears, with about 1 cup syrup, in a bowl and refrigerate for several hours.

To make sauce, combine egg yolks, confectioners' sugar and sherry in top of a double boiler and beat with rotary beater or wire whisk until light. Place over hot, not boiling, water and cook, stirring constantly, for 8 to 10 minutes. Water should not touch bottom of double boiler top.

Refrigerate sauce for several hours. Mixture thickens on standing. In a medium bowl, beat cream until soft peaks form when beater is raised. Carefully fold in chilled sauce. Drain the pears. Serve topped with sauce. Makes 8 servings.

REFRIGERATOR FRUIT PARFAIT

1 Angel Food Cake, cut into
   ½"-thick slices
2 Tbs. Sherry Wine
2 Tbs. Chopped Maraschino
   Cherries
2 Tbs. Salted, Slivered Almonds
1 Tbs. Plain Gelatin (1 envelope)
3 Tbs. Water
½ Cup Sugar
1/3 Cup Water
Pinch of Salt
1 Egg White
Few Drops of Almond Extract
½ Cup Whipping Cream
1 Cup Crushed, Canned Pineapple,
   drained

Line 2 refrigerator pans (4x8½") with half-inch slices of angel food cake. Sprinkle with sherry wine, cherries & nuts. Soften the gelatin in 3 tablespoons of water and dissolve over hot water. Cook sugar and water to soft ball stage (234°F.). Add salt to egg white and beat until fluffy, then slowly add the sugar syrup, beating constantly. Beat in dissolved gelatin. Fold in the flavoring, the stiffly-beaten cream and the pineapple. Spread mixture over cake and set in refrigerator to become firm. Makes 8 servings.

GINGER PUMPKIN PIE

1¾ Cups Canned Pumpkin
1 - 14 Oz. Can Sweetened Condensed Milk
2 Eggs
1 Tsp. Ground Cinnamon
1 Tsp. Ground Ginger
½ Tsp. Salt
¼ Tsp. Ground Nutmeg
1/8 Tsp. Ground Cloves
½ Cup Hot Water
Pastry for 1-Crust 9" Pie, unbaked

Put all ingredients, except pastry, into a bowl and beat until blended. Pour into pastry-lined pie pan and bake in preheated 375°F. oven for 45 to 50 minutes. Makes 6 to 8 servings.

CREAMY CHRISTMAS MOLD

2 Envelopes Unflavored Gelatin
½ Tsp. Salt
2/3 Cup Sugar
4 Eggs, separated
1½ Cups Milk
1 Cup Whipping Cream
½ Cup Bottled Nesselrode Dessert
   Sauce
2 Tbs. Chopped Green Maraschino
   Cherries
2 Tbs. Chopped Red Maraschino
   Cherries
1 Tsp. Vanilla

Mix gelatin, salt and 1/3 cup of sugar in
a cup (set remaining 1/3 cup sugar aside
to use later). Beat egg yolks with milk until blended in top of a small double boiler;
sprinkle in gelatin mixture. Cook, stirring
constantly, over hot (not boiling) water
for 15 minutes, or until gelatin dissolves
and mixture coats a metal spoon. Strain
into a medium bowl. Chill, stirring often,
for 50 minutes, or until as thick as unbeaten egg white.

Beat egg whites until foamy and double in
volume in large bowl; beat in remaining 1/3
cup sugar, 1 tablespoon at a time, until
meringue forms soft peaks. Beat ½ cup
of the cream until stiff in a small bowl
(reserve remaining cream for use later).
Place bowl of meringue in a deep pan
partly filled with ice and water to speed
setting. Fold in thickened gelatin mixture, then whipped cream, nesselrode
sauce, cherries and vanilla. Continue
folding, keeping bowl over ice, until no
streaks of white remain and the mixture
mounds on a spoon. Spoon into an 8-
cup mold. Chill several hours, or until
firm (overnight is best). When ready to
serve, run a sharp-tipped knife around
top of mold, then dip mold very quickly
in and out of a pan of hot water. Cover
mold with a serving plate; invert and
carefully lift off mold. Beat remaining
½ cup cream until stiff; spoon in puffs
on top of mold. If you wish, you can
spoon the whipped cream into a pastry
bag and, using a fancy tip, press out
desired decoration on top of mold.
Makes 8 to 10 servings.

STRAWBERRY-RHUBARB DESSERT

2 Cups Unsweetened Stewed
   Rhubarb, hot
1 Pkg. Strawberry-flavored Gelatin
¼ Lb. Marshmallows
Whipping Cream

Put gelatin into a bowl. Pour the hot
rhubarb over the gelatin and stir until the
gelatin is completely dissolved. Cool
slightly.

Cut the marshmallows into quarters (use
a scissors dipped into hot water) and add
to the mixture while it is still warm. Let
stand at room temperature for 15 min. to
allow marshmallows to soften slightly.
Pour into mold; place in refrigerator to
chill until set. Serve with plain or whipped
cream. Makes 6 to 8 servings.

BLACK BOTTOM LEMON PIE

1 Baked 9" Pie Shell
2 Squares Semisweet Chocolate
4 Eggs, separated
¼ Cup Lemon Juice
3 Tbs. Water
1 Tsp. Lemon Peel
1 Cup Sugar

Melt chocolate over hot water. Spread
evenly over bottom of cool pie shell.
In top of double boiler, beat egg yolks until thick and lemon-colored. Add lemon
juice and water, mixing well. Stir in lemon
peel and ½ cup sugar. Cook over hot, not
boiling, water, stirring constantly, until
thick, about 12 minutes. Remove from
hot water. Beat egg whites until frothy.
Add remaining ½ cup sugar gradually, beating constantly until stiff, glossy peaks form.
Fold half of this mixture into egg yolk mixture. Pour over chocolate in pie shell.

Spoon the remaining egg white mixture into
a pastry tube and make a lattice design on
top of filling. Bake in 325°F. oven for 10
to 15 minutes, or until lightly browned.
Cool. Makes one 9" pie.

RAISIN ICE CREAM

1 Cup Seedless Raisins
1/3 Cup Sugar
1 Tbs. Cornstarch
½ Tsp. Powdered Cinnamon
¼ Tsp. Powdered Cloves
¼ Tsp. Powdered Nutmeg
1/8 Tsp. Salt
1 Cup Milk
2 Eggs, beaten
½ Tsp. Vanilla
1 - 6 Oz. Can Evaporated Milk,
    chilled and whipped (2/3 cup)
¼ Cup Chopped California Walnuts

Mix raisins, sugar, cornstarch, spices and
salt together in saucepan. Stir in 1 cup of
milk. Cook, over moderate heat, stirring
constantly until mixture thickens. Add to
eggs gradually, beating well. Add vanilla.
Pour into freezer tray and freeze until it
is mushy. Turn out into chilled bowl and
beat thoroughly. Fold in whipped evaporated milk and nuts. Return to freezer
tray and freeze for 3 hours, or until firm.
Makes 6 servings.

BROWNIE PUDDING

1 Cup Sifted All-purpose Flour
¾ Cup Granulated Sugar
2 Tbs. Cocoa
2 Tsp. Baking Powder
½ Tsp. Salt
½ Cup Milk
2 Tbs. Salad Oil or Melted Shortening
1 Tsp. Vanilla
¾ to 1 Cup Chopped Walnuts
¾ Cup Brown Sugar
¼ Cup Cocoa
1¾ Cups Hot Water

Sift together first 5 ingredients. Add milk,
salad oil and vanilla; mix until smooth. Stir
in nuts. Pour into greased 8x8x2" pan.
Mix together brown sugar and ¼ cup cocoa;
sprinkle over batter. Pour hot water over
entire batter. Bake in moderate oven, 350°
F., for 45 minutes. Serve warm. Makes 6
to 8 servings.

ENGLISH TRIFLE

Custard:

1 Cup Sugar
1 Tbs. Cornstarch
½ Tsp. Salt
4 Cups Milk
8 Egg Yolks
2 Tsp. Vanilla Extract
1 Tbs. Cream Sherry

2 - 8" Spongecake Layers
¾ Cup Cream Sherry
6 Tbs. Raspberry Preserves
6 Tbs. Toasted Slivered Almonds
½ Cup Heavy Cream, whipped
Candied Green and Red Cherries

In a heavy, medium saucepan, combine sugar,
cornstarch and salt. Gradually add milk and
stir until smooth. Cook over medium heat,
stirring constantly, until mixture is thickened
and comes to a boil. Boil for 1 minute .
Remove from heat.

In a medium bowl, slightly beat egg yolks.
Gradually add a little hot mixture, beating
well. Stir into rest of hot mixture and cook
over medium heat, stirring constantly, just
until mixture boils. Remove from heat and
stir in vanilla and 1 tbs. sherry. Strain the
custard immediately into a bowl. Refrigerate until well chilled--several hours or overnight.

Split spongecake layers in half crosswise, to
make 4 layers in all. Sprinkle each layer
with sherry. Spread each of three layers
with 2 tablespoons preserves, then sprinkle
each with 2 tablespoons almonds. In an at-
tractive deep serving bowl, stack prepared
layers, jam side up, spreading each with approximately 1 cup custard. Top with plain
layer, then with remaining custard. Decorate with the whipped cream and candied
cherries. Refrigerate until serving time.
Makes 8 to 10 servings.

POPOVERS

1 Cup Sifted All-purpose Flour
½ Tsp. Salt
1 Cup Milk
2 Eggs

Heat oven to 425°F. Beat ingredients together with rotary beater just until smooth. Overbeating will reduce the volume. Pour batter into well-greased deep muffin cups (¾ full) or oven-proof glass cups (½ full). Bake until golden brown, 40 to 45 minutes. Be sure to bake the popovers long enough as they will collapse otherwise. Serve at once. Makes 5 to 9 popovers.

CREPES SUZETTE

Crepes:
1 Cup Unsifted All-purpose Flour
¼ Cup Butter or Margarine, melted
    and cooled, or ¼ Cup Salad Oil
2 Eggs
2 Egg Yolks
1½ Cups Milk

In medium bowl, combine flour, melted butter, eggs, egg yolks and ½ cup milk; beat with a rotary beater until smooth. Beat in the remaining milk until mixture is well blended. Refrigerate, covered, at least 30 minutes.

Orange Butter:
¾ Cup Sweet Butter
½ Cup Sugar
1/3 Cup Grand Marnier
¼ Cup Grated Orange Peel

In small bowl, with electric mixer, cream the sweet butter with sugar until light & fluffy. Add Grand Marnier and orange peel; beat until well blended. Set aside.

Orange Sauce:
½ Cup Sweet Butter
¾ Cup Sugar
2 Tbs. Shredded Orange Peel
2/3 Cup Orange Juice
2 Oranges, peeled and sectioned
½ Cup Grand Marnier

In large skillet, melt sweet butter. Stir in sugar, orange peel and orange juice; cook over low heat, stirring occasionally, until peel is translucent--about 20 minutes. Add orange sections and ½ cup Grand Marnier. Keep warm.

To assemble: Cook crepes. Slowly heat an 8" skillet until a drop of water sizzles and rolls off. For each crepe, brush the skillet lightly with butter. Pour in about 2 tablespoons of batter and rotate pan quickly to spread batter completely over bottom of skillet. Cook until lightly browned; turn and brown other side. Turn out onto a wire rack. Spread each crepe with Orange Butter, dividing evenly. Fold each in half, then in half again. When all are folded, place in Orange Sauce in skillet or chafing dish; cook over low heat until heated through. To serve, gently heat 3 tablespoons of Grand Marnier in a small saucepan just until the vapor rises. Ignite with a match and pour over crepes. Serve flaming. Makes 6 to 8 servings.

APPLE SQUARES

1 Cup Sifted All-purpose Flour
2½ Tsp. Baking Powder
1/8 Tsp. Salt
2 Tbs. Butter or Margarine, melted
1 Cup Granulated Sugar
½ Cup Brown Sugar, firmly packed
2 Eggs
1 Tsp. Vanilla
1 - 8 Oz. Pkg. Pitted Dates, chopped
½ Cup Chopped Pecans
6 Medium Apples, pared, quartered,
    cored and sliced thin (6 cups)

Sift flour, baking powder and salt into a bowl. Blend butter or margarine with granulated and brown sugars in a large bowl; beat in eggs, one at a time, and vanilla. Fold in flour mixture (dough will be stiff). Stir in dates, pecans and apples. Spoon into a greased 9x9x2" pan. Bake in 400°F. oven for 1 hour, or until cake tests done. Cool on wire rack. Cut into squares. Serve warm with vanilla ice cream. Makes 12 servings.

BLUEBERRY COBBLER

2 Cups Blueberries
1/3 Cup Sugar
1/8 Tsp. Powdered Cinnamon
1 Cup Sifted Cake Flour
1 Tsp. Baking Powder
1 Tsp. Salt
1 Egg
2/3 Cup Sugar
¼ Cup Shortening
½ Cup Milk
½ Tsp. Vanilla

Preheat oven to 350°F. Grease an 8″ square baking dish. Wash and drain the berries. Look over for discards. Combine berries with 1/3 cup sugar and cinnamon. Spread evenly in prepared dish.

Sift flour, baking powder and salt together into a mixing bowl. Combine remaining ingredients in glass container of blender. Cover and blend thoroughly about 1 min. Pour over sifted flour mixture. Stir lightly, just until smooth. Spread this batter over berries in baking dish. Bake about 35 minutes, or until cobbler is done. Serve warm with top milk, cream, or ice cream. Makes 6 servings.

The following substitutions may be made:
Cherry Cobbler--substitute 2 cups drained canned or quick-frozen sweet cherries for blueberries;
Peach Cobbler--substitute 2 cups sliced, fresh, canned, or defrosted quick-frozen peaches for blueberries;
Plum Cobbler--substitute 2 cups halved ripe or canned sweet plums for blueberries. Add more sugar if plums are tart.
Strawberry Cobbler--substitute 2 cups defrosted quick-frozen sliced strawberries for blueberries.

TWO-CRUST PINEAPPLE PIE

1 - 1 Lb. 4½ Oz. Can Crushed Pineapple (about 2½ cups)
¼ Cup Sugar
2 Tbs. Cornstarch
¼ Tsp. Salt
1 Tbs. Butter
1 Tbs. Fresh Lemon Juice
Pastry for 2-Crust 8″ Pie, unbaked

Put pineapple in saucepan. Mix the next three ingredients and stir into pineapple. Bring to a boil and cook, stirring, for 2 minutes, or until thick and clear. Remove from heat and stir in butter and lemon juice. Line pie pan with pastry, pour in filling, and add top crust. You may use lattice strips if preferred. Bake in a preheated oven (425°F.) for 25 to 30 min. Makes 6 servings.

WALNUT PIE

1 - 9″ Pie Shell, unbaked
½ Cup Brown Sugar, packed
½ Cup Butter or Margarine, softened
¾ Cup Granulated Sugar
3 Eggs
¼ Tsp. Salt
¼ Cup Light Corn Syrup
½ Cup Light Cream
1 Cup Coarsely-chopped California Walnuts
½ Tsp. Vanilla
¼ Cup Walnut Halves

Prepare pastry and line the pie plate. Start oven at 350°F. Combine brown sugar and butter or margarine in upper part of double boiler. Beat until smooth. Add granulated sugar and mix thoroughly. Add eggs, one at a time, beating after each addition. Add salt, syrup and cream. Mix well. Cook over boiling water, stirring, for 5 minutes. Remove from heat. Stir in chopped walnuts and vanilla. Pour into prepared pie shell. Bake for 1 hour. Scatter walnut halves on top of pie and bake 5 minutes longer. Let cool. Makes 6 servings. Pecans may be used in place of the walnuts, if preferred.

INDIAN PUDDING

½ Cup Yellow Cornmeal
4 Cups Hot Milk
½ Cup Maple Syrup
¼ Cup Light Molasses
2 Eggs, slightly beaten
2 Tbs. Butter or Margarine, melted
1/3 Cup Brown Sugar, packed
1 Tsp. Salt
¼ Tsp. Cinnamon
¾ Tsp. Ginger
½ Cup Cold Milk

In a double boiler, slowly stir cornmeal into hot milk. Cook over boiling water, stirring occasionally, for 20 minutes. Preheat oven to 325°F. Lightly grease a 2-quart baking dish (9" round). In small bowl, combine rest of ingredients, except for the cold milk. Stir into cornmeal mixture and mix well. Turn into prepared dish and pour cold milk on top, without stirring. Bake, uncovered, 50 minutes, or until just set. Do not overbake. Let stand 15 minutes before serving. Serve warm, with vanilla ice cream or light cream. Makes 8 servings.

SWEDISH ORANGE CREPES

Crepes:
¾ Cup Sifted All-purpose Flour
2 Tbs. Confectioners' Sugar
1 Tsp. Baking Powder
½ Tsp. Salt
2 Eggs
2/3 Cup Milk
1/3 Cup Water
½ Tsp. Brandy Extract

Filling:
3 Egg Yolks
¼ Cup Sugar
1 Tbs. Grated Orange Rind
½ Cup Orange Juice
4 Tbs. Butter or Margarine

To make filling, beat egg yolks with sugar until fluffy in top of small double boiler; stir in orange rind and juice. Cook over simmering water, stirring constantly, until thick. Stir in butter or margarine until melted; cool.

Make the pancakes. Measure flour, confectioners' sugar, baking powder, and salt into sifter. Beat eggs until frothy in a medium-size bowl; sift dry ingredients into this and blend just until smooth. Stir in milk, water and brandy extract to make a thin batter. Heat a large heavy frying pan, or Swedish pancake pan, over low heat. Test temperature by sprinkling on a few drops of water; when drops bounce about, the temperature is right. Lightly grease pan with butter or margarine.

Spoon batter, 2 tablespoons for each 3" pancake, into pan. Bake until top appears dry and underside is golden; turn and lightly brown on other side. Repeat, lightly greasing pan before each baking, to make 48 thin pancakes. Spoon about ½ teaspoon filling into center of each pancake as it is baked; roll up and place, seam-side down, in broilerproof serving dish. Just before serving, sprinkle rolls with additional confectioners' sugar and slide into broiler, as far from heat as possible; broil 3 to 5 minutes, or until sugar is melted and pancakes are hot. The pancakes may be made and filled ahead, chilled, then reheated in a 350° F. oven for 10 minutes before finishing them for serving. Makes 12 servings.

GUAVA-PECAN PIE

1 Cup Guava Jelly
2 Tbs. Butter
½ Cup Water
2 Tbs. Fresh Lemon Juice
3 Eggs, separated
Pinch of Salt
Pastry for 1-Crust 9" Pie, unbaked
1 Cup Pecans

Melt jelly and butter in water; allow to cool to lukewarm. Add lemon juice; beat in egg yolks, one at a time. Fold in stiffly-beaten salted whites. Turn into pastry-lined pie pan. Sprinkle the pecans over pie filling. Bake in a preheated 300°F. oven for 50 minutes. Makes 6 to 8 servings.

RICH DESSERT CAKE
(Italian)

1 - 9" or 10" Spongecake, or
   2 Sponge Layers
1½ Lbs. Ricotta Cheese
1/3 Cup Sugar
½ Cup Light Cream
1 Tsp. Vanilla Extract
¼ Tsp. Almond Extract
1 Oz. (1 Square) Semisweet Chocolate,
   chopped (or ¼ cup semisweet chocolate pieces)
¼ Cup Chopped Toasted Almonds
2/3 Cup Finely-diced Mixed Candied
   Fruit
¼ Cup Rum
Frosting (see recipe below)
Candied Cherries

If a whole cake is used, cut it into two
layers; chill. Combine ricotta cheese,
sugar, light cream, flavorings; mix well.
Rub through a sieve or whip until mixture is smooth. Add chocolate, almonds,
and fruit. Chill. Place 1 cake layer on
a serving plate and spread with filling.
Top with remaining layer. Sprinkle with
rum. Chill until shortly before serving
time, then frost top. Reserve some of
the frosting to tint pink and use for
decorative swirls on cake. Decorate with
cherries.

Frosting:

1 Egg White
2 Cups Confectioners' Sugar
1 Tsp. Almond Extract
1 Tbs. Fresh Lemon Juice

Mix all ingredients until smooth. If necessary, add a little water, a half teaspoon
at a time, to achieve spreading consistency.

BREAD PUDDING

3 Cups Toasted Bread Cubes
4 Eggs
4 Cups Milk, scalded
1 Cup Sugar
¼ Tsp. Salt
1 Tsp. Vanilla Extract
1/3 Cup Melted Butter or Margarine
¾ Cup Raspberry Jam

Place bread cubes in a 2-quart casserole.
Beat 2 eggs with 2 egg yolks, reserving 2
egg whites for the meringue. Gradually
beat scalded milk into eggs. Beat in ½
cup sugar, salt, vanilla and butter. Pour
milk mixture over bread cubes. Bake in
a preheated 350°F. oven for 25 minutes.

Spread raspberry jam evenly over top of
pudding. Beat egg whites until stiff but
not dry. Beat in sugar, 1 tablespoon at
a time, until meringue is stiff and glossy.
Pile meringue over jam, making sure to
spread meringue to edge of dish. Bake
for another 15 minutes. Makes 8
servings.

MINCE SQUARES

3 Cups Biscuit Mix
½ Cup Firmly-packed Brown Sugar
¼ Cup Granulated Sugar
2 Eggs
1 Cup Prepared Mincemeat
1 Small Can Evaporated Milk (2/3 cup)
4 Tbs. Butter or Margarine, melted
1 Cup Cream, for whipping
2 Tbs. Confectioners' Sugar

Combine biscuit mix and brown and granulated sugars in a large bowl. Beat eggs
slightly in a small bowl; stir in mincemeat,
evaporated milk, and melted butter or margarine. Pour all at once into biscuit mixture. Stir just until evenly moist. Spread
in a greased 9x9x2" baking pan. Bake in
350°F. oven for 35 minutes, or until a
wooden pick inserted in center comes out
clean. Cool slightly in pan on a wire rack.
Beat cream with confectioners' sugar until
stiff (use medium-size bowl). Cut loaf
into squares; place on serving plates and
spoon whipped cream on top. Serve warm.
Makes 8 to 12 servings.

LIME-MARSHMALLOW DESSERT SQUARES

Base:
¾ Cup Butter
1½ Cups Flour
½ Cup Brown Sugar

Rub butter, flour and sugar together; press into a 9" square pan. Bake in 350°F. oven for 15 minutes, or until lightly browned.

Topping:
2 - 3 Oz. Pkgs. Lime-flavored
  Gelatin
1 Tsp. Salt
1 Cup Cold Water
2 Egg Whites

Place gelatin in cold water; bring to a rolling boil for 1 minute. Beat egg whites and salt until foamy. Add the gelatin mixture and beat until soft mounds form. This will take quite a while. Spread mixture quickly over the base. If desired, sprinkle with coconut and decorate with cherries. Place in refrigerator and chill until set. Makes 9 servings.

NESSELRODE PUDDING

8 Egg Yolks
½ Cup Sugar
¼ Tsp. Salt
3½ Cups Milk or Light Cream
2 Tsp. Vanilla Extract
1 Cup Sweetened Chestnut Puree
½ Cup Diced Candied Orange Peel
½ Cup Whole Candied Cherries
½ Cup Dried Currants
½ Cup Raisins
½ Cup Malaga Wine
2 Cups Heavy Cream, whipped
1/3 Cup Maraschino Liqueur
Glaceed Chestnuts

Beat egg yolks and stir in the sugar and salt. Scald milk and stir hot milk gradu-ally into egg yolks. Cook in top part of double boiler over hot water. Cook, stirring, until mixture thickens and coats a spoon. Add vanilla. Cool and then chill. Gradually beat custard into chestnut puree. Add orange peel, cherries, currants and raisins to wine. Let stand until fruit is well soaked. Drain fruit & stir into custard. Whip cream and gradually beat in liqueur. Fold whipped cream into custard. Pour mixture into a 3-quart mold. Cover with foil; freeze until half frozen. Remove cover and stir to distribute fruit. Cover again and freeze until firm. Unmold by dipping mold for a few seconds into lukewarm water. Surround with glacéed chestnuts. Makes 10 to 12 servings.

LEMON AMBROSIA PIE

½ Tsp. Salt
1½ Cups Sugar
6 Tbs. Cornstarch
1½ Cups Boiling Water
2 Eggs, separated
2 Tbs. Butter or Margarine
1 Tsp. Grated Lemon Rind
1/3 Cup Fresh Lemon Juice
1 Tsp. Vanilla Extract
1 Envelope Unflavored Gelatin
¼ Cup Cold Water
1 Cup Light Cream
1 Baked and Cooled 9" Pie Shell
½ Cup Flaked Coconut, toasted
  and cooled

In top part of double boiler, mix salt, sugar and cornstarch. Gradually stir in boiling water. Cook over direct heat, stirring, until smooth and thickened. Put over boiling water and cook, covered, for 10 minutes. Stir small amount into beaten egg yolks, then combine the two mixtures in double boiler and cook, stirring, for 2 minutes. Add butter, rind, juice and vanilla. Take out 1 cup of filling and set aside. Soften gelatin in cold water and stir into remaining filling. When dissolved, stir in cream. Chill until thickened; fold in stiffly beaten egg whites. Pour into cooled pie shell; chill until firm. Spread reserved filling on top of pie; top with coconut. Chill. Makes 6 to 8 servings.

CHOCOLATE UPSIDE-DOWN DESSERT

1¼ Cups Cake Flour
¾ Cup Sugar
2 Tsp. Baking Powder (Double-Action)
¼ Tsp. Salt
1 Square (1 Oz.) Unsweetened
   Chocolate
2 Tbs. Butter
½ Cup Milk
1 Tsp. Vanilla
½ Cup Coarsely Chopped Nuts

Sift the flour, measure and resift three times with ¾ cup sugar, baking powder and salt. Melt chocolate and butter over hot water, add milk and vanilla. Add all at once to the dry ingredients and stir until thoroughly mixed. Add nuts and blend just enough to distribute them evenly through the dough. Turn into a well-greased, 8" round glass cake pan, ¾" deep.

Topping:

2 Tbs. Cocoa
½ Cup Brown Sugar, firmly packed
½ Cup Granulated Sugar
1 Cup Boiling Water
Whipping Cream

Combine cocoa, brown sugar and granulated sugar thoroughly and sprinkle over the batter. Pour the boiling water over the top and bake at once in a moderate oven (350°F.) for 45 to 50 minutes. When done, you will have a rich cake with a creamy chocolate sauce underneath. Spoon into serving dishes and serve warm with whipped cream or vanilla ice cream. Makes 10 servings.

PERSIMMON PUDDING

½ Cup Butter or Margarine
1 Cup Firmly-packed Brown Sugar
3 Eggs
1½ Cups Sifted All-purpose Flour
2 Tsp. Baking Powder
½ Cup Milk
1½ Cups Persimmon Pulp
½ Tsp. Ground Cinnamon
¼ Tsp. Ground Cloves

Cream the butter or margarine until light and fluffy. Gradually beat in the brown

sugar. Add the eggs, one at a time, beating well after each addition. Sift flour with baking powder. Add flour alternately with milk, beginning and ending with flour. Fold in persimmon pulp and spices. Pour mixture into a greased 1½-quart pudding mold. Steam for 1½ hours. Makes 6 to 8 servings.

JELLIED PEACH MELBA

1 - 3 Oz. Pkg. Raspberry Gelatin
1 Cup Hot Water
1 - 12 Oz. Pkg. Frozen Raspberries
6 Fresh or Canned Peach Halves
1 Pint Vanilla Ice Cream

Dissolve gelatin in hot water. Add the raspberries and stir gently until thawed. Chill until slightly thickened. Put a peach half, rounded side up, in bottom of each of 6 individual molds. Pour the gelatin over peach halves and chill until firm. Unmold & top each with a scoop of ice cream. Makes 6 servings.

BANANA FRITTERS

4 Medium Firm Bananas
Juice of ½ Lemon
2 Tbs. Confectioners' Sugar
½ Cup Biscuit Mix
1 Tbs. Sugar
1 Egg
¼ Cup Milk
Fat for Deep Frying

Cut each banana into 3 chunks and sprinkle with lemon juice and confectioners' sugar. Let stand for 20 minutes. Mix biscuit mix, sugar, egg and milk. Dip banana chunks in the batter and fry in deep fat (375°F.) on frying thermometer) in electric cooker-fryer or deep skillet until brown. Serve as dessert, with maple syrup, if desired. Makes 4 servings.

CARROT DESSERT
(A Favorite of India)

1 - 14 Oz. Can Sweetened
   Condensed Milk
Water
2 Cups Grated Carrot
1 Cup Cooking Oil, Butter or
   Margarine
2 Tbs. Chopped Blanched Almonds
2 Tbs. Chopped Raisins
¼ Tsp. Ground Saffron
1 Tbs. Fresh Lime Juice, heated

Add 1 can of water to condensed milk in saucepan and bring to boil. Add carrots and cook for about 45 minutes over low heat, stirring occasionally. Add oil gradually. Cook until fat begins to separate. Add almonds and raisins, and the saffron dissolved in the hot lime juice. May be eaten hot or cold. Makes 6 servings.

CHOCOLATE PASTRY

1½ Cups Sifted All-purpose Flour
½ Tsp. Salt
2 Tbs. Cocoa
½ Cup Shortening
3 Tbs. Water

Mix dry ingredients thoroughly. Cut in the shortening until pieces are the size of peas. Gradually add water, mixing until pastry cleans the sides of the bowl. With hands, press dough together into a firm ball. Smooth the edges. Put pastry between two long strips of wax paper, crossed in the center to form a 12" square. Wipe table with a damp cloth to keep paper from slipping. Roll pastry in a circle to edges of square. Peel off top paper and put crust in pan, paper-side up. Peel off paper and fit pastry loosely into pan. Trim pastry ½" from edge of pan; fold under, even with pan. Flute edges. With a fork, prick shell on bottom and sides. Bake in a preheated 450°F. oven for 10 to 12 minutes. Cool and fill as desired. Makes one 8" or 9" pie shell.

IMPERIAL RICE PUDDING

1 Envelope Unflavored Gelatin
¼ Cup Water
4 Egg Yolks
6 Tbs. Sugar
3 Cups Milk
2 Tsp. Vanilla
1 Cup Uncooked Regular Rice
1 Tbs. Grated Orange Rind
1/8 Tsp. Salt
1 - 8 Oz. Jar Candied Red Cherries
2 Tbs. Orange Juice
1 Cup Whipping Cream
¼ Cup Toasted Slivered Almonds

Soften gelatin in water in a cup; set aside. Beat egg yolks slightly in top of a large double boiler; beat in sugar and 1½ cups of milk. Cook, stirring constantly, over simmering water for 15 minutes, or until custard thickens and coats a metal spoon. Stir in softened gelatin until dissolved.

Pour into a large bowl; stir in 1 teaspoon of vanilla. Set aside. Combine rice with water to cover in top of same double boiler. Heat to boiling over direct heat. Drain, then return rice to pan. Stir in remaining 1½ cups milk and 1 teaspoon of vanilla, orange rind and salt. Cook, stirring often, over simmering water for 40 minutes, or until rice is tender and liquid is absorbed. Stir into custard mixture. Let stand at room temperature until cool. Save 8 whole cherries for garnish; chop remaining and stir with orange juice into rice mixture. Beat cream until stiff in a small bowl; fold into rice mixture. Spoon into a buttered 8-cup mold. Chill at least 4 hours, or overnight. Unmold by loosening around edge with a knife, shaking mold gently to loosen at bottom. Invert onto serving plate and lift mold off carefully. Stuff the reserved cherries with the slivered almonds; arrange around base of pudding. Pile remaining almonds on top. Makes 8 to 10 servings.

FROZEN COOKIE DESSERT

2 Dozen Chocolate Wafers
1 Cup Whipping Cream, whipped
1 Tbs. Sugar
1 Tsp. Rum or Vanilla Flavoring
1 - No. 2½ Can Fruit Cocktail,
    drained (about 3½ cups)
1 Ripe Banana, sliced
½ Cup Miniature Marshmallows
¼ Cup Chopped Walnuts

Line the bottom and sides of an 8x8x2"
pan with the chocolate wafers. Combine
the whipped cream with the sugar and rum
flavoring. Fold in drained fruit cocktail,
banana slices, marshmallows, and walnuts.
Pile into cooky-lined pan. Freeze until
firm. Remove from freezer ½ hour before
serving. Cut into squares. Makes 9 servings.

SWEDISH APPLE PUDDING
with MERINGUE

6 Cooking Apples
1 Cup Light Brown Sugar, packed
¼ Tsp. Ground Cloves
½ Tsp. Ground Cinnamon
¼ Tsp. Powdered Nutmeg
1 Tbs. Melted Butter or Margarine
¼ Cup Boiling Water
3 Egg Whites
1/8 Tsp. Salt
½ Cup Sugar
1 Tbs. Grated Lemon Peel
1/3 Cup Slivered, Blanched Almonds

Wash, pare and core apples; slice thin. Pour
into a buttered, shallow 2-quart baking dish.
Combine brown sugar, spices, and melted
butter or margarine. Sprinkle over apples.
Add boiling water. Bake about 20 minutes
in a preheated 350°F. oven, or until apples
are tender. Let cool slightly.

Beat egg whites until foamy. Add salt and
sugar, 2 tablespoons at a time. Continue to
beat meringue until it is satiny and stands in
peaks. Fold in lemon peel. Spread over apples. Sprinkle with almonds. Return to the
oven and bake 15 minutes longer, or until
meringue is golden brown. Serve warm or
cold. Makes 6 servings.

REFRIGERATOR CAKE
(Strawberry-Pineapple)

1 Cup Finely-crushed Corn-flake Crumbs
¼ Cup Soft Butter or Margarine
1¼ Cups Sugar
½ Tsp. Ground Cinnamon
3 Envelopes Unflavored Gelatin
3 Eggs, separated
¾ Tsp. Salt
1½ Cups Milk
1½ Lbs. Creamed Cottage Cheese
    (3 Cups)
Grated Rind and Juice of 1½ Lemons
1½ Cups Heavy Cream
Sweetened Halved Strawberries and
    Pineapple Tidbits

Have cheese and eggs at room temperature.
Combine crumbs, butter, ¼ cup sugar and
cinnamon; mix well. Press firmly on bottom
of a 9" springform or loose-bottomed pan;
chill.

In the top part of a double-boiler combine
1 cup sugar and gelatin. Add egg yolks,
salt and milk; beat with rotary beater until
blended. Cook over simmering water, stirring, until slightly thickened. Cool.

Force the cottage cheese through a food
mill or sieve. Beat into first mixture with
lemon juice and lemon rind. Whip cream
until stiff and fold with stiffly beaten egg
whites into mixture. Pour into a prepared
pan and chill until firm. Remove sides
of the pan and put the cake on a serving
plate. Decorate with strawberry halves
and pineapple.

SOUR-CREAM WALNUT CHEESECAKE

1 Cup Zwieback Crumbs
2 Tbs. Sugar
¼ Cup Walnuts, finely chopped
2 Tbs. Butter or Margarine, melted
2 - 8 Oz. Pkgs. Cream Cheese,
    softened
½ Cup Sugar
1½ Tsp. Vanilla
3 Eggs, well beaten
1 Cup Dairy Sour Cream
1 Tbs. Sugar

Combine zwieback crumbs, 2 tablespoons of sugar and 2 tablespoons of the walnuts; blend in butter or margarine. Press mixture evenly on bottom and sides of an 8" spring-form pan. Chill. Beat cream cheese with electric mixer at medium speed in a large bowl until fluffy. Gradually beat in sugar and 1 tsp. of the vanilla. Beat in eggs, one third at a time. Turn into prepared pan. Bake in moderate oven (350°F.) for 40 minutes, or until center is firm. Remove from oven. Cool on a wire rack for 5 min., away from drafts. Combine sour cream, remaining sugar and vanilla. Spread over top of cake; sprinkle with remaining walnuts. Return to oven for 5 minutes, or until the topping is set. Remove from oven and cool in the pan, on a wire rack and away from drafts. Remove side of pan. Refrigerate several hours before serving. Makes one 8" cheesecake.

STRAWBERRY PIE

½ Cup Chopped Pecans
    (more, if desired)
2 - 9" Unbaked Pie Shells
1 - 8 Oz. Pkg. Cream Cheese
1 Cup Sugar
1 Tsp. Vanilla Extract
1 Pint Whipping Cream, whipped
Fresh or Frozen Strawberries

Press the pecans into the pie shells and bake at 350°F. until browned. Combine cream cheese, sugar and vanilla; beat until fluffy. Fold whipped cream into cheese mixture & pour into the pie shells. Top with whole strawberries; chill thoroughly. Makes two pies.

MANGO CREAM

2 Mangoes
1 Orange
½ Cup Sifted Confectioners' Sugar
1 Cup Heavy Cream, whipped
1/3 Cup Coarsely-chopped Toasted
    Pecans

Peel the mangoes and cut the flesh away from the stones. Peel and section the orange. Combine the mangoes, orange sections and sugar. Using a potato masher, mash the fruits or blend in an electric blender. Fold in the whipped cream and pecans and spoon into sherbet glasses; refrigerate until well chilled. If desired, garnish with more whipped cream and pecan halves. Makes 6 servings.

CAKE AND WINE PUDDING
(Oriental-Style)

1 Purchased Spongecake, broken
    into pieces
Macaroons
1 Tsp. Cornstarch
1 Tbs. Sugar
2 Cups Wine
3 Eggs, separated
¼ Cup Sugar
½ Cup Slivered, Toasted Almonds

Put pieces of sponge cake and a few macaroons into a large baking dish until the dish is half full. Mix the cornstarch and sugar together in the top of a double boiler and slowly add ½ cup of the wine, stirring to blend. Heat the remaining wine. Add the hot wine gradually to the cornstarch mixture, stirring constantly. Continue to stir, bring to a boil and cook about three minutes. Stir a small amount of hot mixture into the beaten egg yolks. Blend in remaining wine mixture. Cook over simmering water for 3 to 5 minutes, stirring slowly. Pour over the cake and set aside to cool. When cool, beat the egg whites until frothy. Add the sugar gradually, beating well after each addition. Cover the pudding with meringue and sprinkle with nuts. Bake at 325°F. about 10 minutes, or until meringue is lightly browned. Serve cold. Makes about 8 servings.

ORANGE AMBROSIA DESSERT

1 Cup Hot Water
1 - 3 Oz. Pkg. Lemon-flavored
  Gelatin
¼ Cup Sugar
Dash of Salt
1 Tbs. Grated Orange Rind
¼ Cup Fresh Orange Juice
1 Cup Heavy Cream
½ Cup Shredded Coconut,
  cut with scissors
½ Cup Drained Orange Pieces
4 Ladyfingers, split

Add water to gelatin and stir until dissolved. Stir in sugar, salt, rind and the juice. Chill until mixture begins to set. Whip the cream with an electric mixer and fold into gelatin mixture with the coconut and orange pieces. Line a 1-quart mold with ladyfingers. Pour in mixture and chill until firm. Unmold. Makes 6 servings.

VERMONT APPLE PIE

Pastry for 1 - 9" Two-crust Pie
6 to 8 Large, Tart Apples
1 Cup Maple Sugar, packed
2 Tsp. Flour
¼ Tsp. Powdered Nutmeg
½ Tsp. Powdered Cinnamon
2 Tbs. Butter or Margarine
1 Egg Yolk, beaten

Prepare pastry and line pie plate. Pare, core and slice apples. Combine sugar, flour and spices. Rub a little flour mixture into pastry-lined pan. Arrange sliced apples in pan and sprinkle with remaining sugar mixture. Dot with butter. Preheat oven to 425°F. Roll out remaining pastry for top crust. Cut a small circle out of center. Place top crust over apples, trim pastry and seal edges of pie. Using a cardboard pattern, cut an apple from the small pastry circle. Place the pastry apple in hole in center of top crust. Brush pastry with beaten egg. Bake 40 to 45 minutes, or until pastry is browned. Makes 6 servings.

LEMON-RICE CROQUETTES

½ Cup Boiling Water
½ Cup Uncooked Rice
1 Tsp. Salt
1 Cup Milk
1 Egg
1 Tbs. Sugar
Grated Rind of 1 Lemon
1 Tbs. Butter
1 Egg
2 Tbs. Water
Fine, Dry Bread Crumbs
Fat, for deep frying
Custard Sauce (see recipe below)

In a saucepan, mix the first 3 ingredients. Cover and cook slowly until water is absorbed--about 10 min. Add milk and stir lightly with a fork; cover and cook until rice is tender. Stir in egg, sugar, lemon rind and butter. Refrigerate until cool. Shape into 8 croquettes, dip into egg mixed with water, then into crumbs. Fry in deep fat (375°F. on frying thermometer) until golden, about 5 minutes. Serve warm, topped with custard sauce. Makes 4 servings.

Custard Sauce:

1 Cup Milk
Dash of Salt
1 Egg (or 2 egg yolks)
2 Tbs. Sugar
¼ Tsp. Vanilla Extract (or a
  little grated lemon rind)

In top part of a small double boiler, beat together milk, salt, egg and 2 tablespoons of sugar. Put over simmering water and cook, stirring, until mixture thickens slightly and coats a metal spoon. Remove from hot water and pour into small bowl. Add ¼ teaspoon vanilla extract, or a little grated lemon rind. Cool and chill. Makes 1 cup of sauce.

AUSTRIAN LINZERTORTE

¾ Cup Butter or Margarine
¾ Cup Granulated Sugar
2 Eggs
¼ Tsp. Salt
2 Tsp. Grated Lemon Peel
¼ Tsp. Cinnamon
1/8 Tsp. Ground Cloves
1½ Cups Almonds, finely ground
2 Cups Sifted All-purpose Flour
Raspberry Jam
1 Egg, beaten

A day ahead of time you are going to serve the linzertorte, prepare the following. In a large bowl, with mixer at medium speed, beat butter with the sugar until creamy, gradually beat in eggs, salt, lemon peel, cinnamon, and cloves. Fold in almonds and flour until well blended. Wrap in waxed paper and refrigerate several hours, or overnight. Use about three-fourths of this dough to press on bottom of a 9" layer-cake pan, building a rim around edge, slightly higher than center. Over center of dough, spread ½ cup raspberry jam. Start heating oven to 350°F. On a floured board, roll out rest of dough about ¼" thick. With a pastry wheel, cut out 6 strips, ¾" wide. Place them, lattice-fashion, over raspberry jam. Cut rest of dough into 1" strips and lay around top edge of the torte; or cut out small shapes with cookie cutter and place them around the edge, slightly overlapping. Brush dough with beaten egg. Bake 40 to 45 minutes, or until golden. Cool on a wire rack. Makes 8 to 12 servings.

HOLIDAY FRUIT PUDDING
(A Favorite of Italy)

2 Envelopes Unflavored Gelatin
2 Tbs. Sugar
6 Oranges
Orange Juice
½ Cup Lemon Juice
2 Cups Sugar
1 Cup Seedless Green Grapes, halved
½ Cup Chopped Walnuts
½ Cup Light Raisins
12 Pitted Dates, cut in small pieces
12 Maraschino Cherries, quartered
Whipped Cream

In small saucepan, combine gelatin and 2 tablespoons of sugar; add 1 cup water. Stir, over low heat, until gelatin is dissolved. Set aside.

Peel the oranges and cut into sections, holding over a bowl to catch juice. Measure the juice and add enough more orange juice to measure 2 cups. Pour orange juice into a large bowl. Add lemon juice, 2 cups sugar, and the gelatin mixture; stir until sugar is dissolved. Refrigerate, stirring occasionally, until consistency of unbeaten egg white. Fold in orange sections, grapes, walnuts, raisins, dates and cherries. Turn into a 12-cup serving bowl and refrigerate for at least 12 hours. Serve right from bowl and garnish with whipped cream. Makes 12 to 16 servings.

FROZEN LIME SQUARES

1 - 3 Oz. Can Flaked Coconut
½ Cup Vanilla Wafer Crumbs
2 Tbs. Melted Butter
2 Tbs. Sugar
2 - 3 Oz. Pkgs. Lime Flavor Gelatin
2 Cups Boiling Water
1 - 6 Oz. Can Frozen Limeade Concentrate
Green Food Color (a few drops)
1 Quart + 1 Pint Vanilla Ice Cream, softened
1/8 Tsp. Salt
Pecans (optional)

Carefully toast ½ cup coconut in 375°F. oven for about 5 minutes, until lightly browned. Set aside. Combine remaining coconut, crumbs, butter and sugar. Lightly press into an 11x7x1½" pan and bake in a moderate oven, 375°F., for 6 to 7 min. Cool.

Dissolve the gelatin in boiling water. Add limeade concentrate, food color, ice cream and salt; stir until dissolved. Pour into the crust. Top with reserved toasted coconut and garnish with pecans if desired. Freeze until firm. Cover tightly and return to the freezer. Thaw for several hours in the refrigerator before serving. Makes 6 to 8 servings.

GINGER FRUIT FREEZE

1 - 3 Oz. Pkg. Cream Cheese
3 Tbs. Mayonnaise
1 Tbs. Lemon Juice
¼ Tsp. Salt
½ Cup Chopped Preserved
　　Kumquats
½ Cup Dates, cut up
¼ Cup Quartered Maraschino Cherries
1 - 9 Oz. Can Crushed Pineapple,
　　drained
2 Tbs. Finely-chopped Candied
　　Ginger
1 Cup Whipping Cream, whipped
¼ Cup Toasted Slivered Almonds

Soften cream cheese; blend in next three ingredients. Stir in fruits and ginger; fold in whipped cream. Pour into 1-quart refrigerator tray. Sprinkle with nuts. Freeze until firm. Makes 6 to 8 servings.

PUMPKIN PUDDING

1½ Cups Sifted All-purpose Flour
1 Envelope Instant Mashed-Potato
　　Powder (½ cup)
1 Tsp. Baking Soda
1 Tsp. Salt
1½ Tsp. Pumpkin-pie Spice
4 Tbs. Butter or Margarine
¾ Cup Brown Sugar, firmly packed
2 Eggs
1 Tsp. Vanilla
1 Tsp. Grated Orange Rind
¾ Cup Orange Juice
1 Cup Pumpkin
½ Cup Chopped Walnuts

Measure flour, instant mashed-potato powder, soda, salt and pumpkin pie spice into a sifter. Cream butter or margarine with brown sugar until fluffy in a large bowl; beat in eggs, then vanilla and orange rind. Sift in dry ingredients, adding alternately with orange juice, beating well after each addition; fold in pumpkin and walnuts. Pour into a well-greased 8-cup tube mold; cover with foil, transparent wrap, or double thickness of wax paper; fasten with string to hold tightly. Place on a rack or trivet in a kettle or steamer; pour in boiling water to half the depth of pudding in mold;

cover tightly. Steam for 2 hours, or until a long thin skewer inserted near center comes out clean (keep water boiling gently during entire time, adding more boiling water, if needed). Cool mold 5 minutes; loosen pudding around edge with a knife. Unmold onto a serving plate; cool slightly. Spoon about ¼ cup hot Butterscotch Sauce over pudding; top with several coconut ice-cream balls, if you wish. Cut in wedges and serve with remaining sauce and additional ice-cream balls. Makes 8 servings.

Butterscotch Sauce:
1¼ Cups Light Brown Sugar,
　　firmly packed
¼ Cup Whipping Cream
2 Tbs. Light Corn Syrup
4 Tbs. Butter or Margarine
1 Tsp. Vanilla

Combine brown sugar, whipping cream, corn syrup and butter or margarine in a small saucepan. Heat to boiling, then cook for 1 minute. Remove from heat and stir in the vanilla. Serve hot. Makes 1¼ cups of sauce.

COFFEE CUSTARD PUDDING
WITH CARAMEL GLAZE

Caramel Glaze: Caramelize ¾ cup sugar in a heavy saucepan and pour into a 1½-quart casserole, turning to glaze completely.

Coffee Custard:

6 Eggs
5 Tbs. Sugar
¼ Tsp. Salt
1 Cup Strong Coffee
1 Cup Light Cream
3 Tbs. Sherry

Beat eggs slightly; add remaining ingredients and mix well. Pour into caramel-glazed casserole. Set casserole in pan of hot water. Bake in preheated 350°F. oven for 40 to 45 minutes, or until a silver knife inserted in custard comes out clean. Cool completely. Makes 6 servings.

RASPBERRY PIE

2 Eggs, separated
½ Cup Sugar
1/8 Tsp. Salt
1¼ Cups Milk
1 Envelope Unflavored Gelatin
1 Tbs. Lemon Juice
½ Tsp. Vanilla
1 Cup Whipping Cream
2 Cups Fresh Red Raspberries,
   washed and patted dry
1 - 9" Pie Crust, baked

Beat the egg yolks slightly in the top of
a double boiler; stir in ¼ cup of sugar, salt
and milk; sprinkle gelatin over top to
soften. Cook gelatin mixture, stirring constantly, over simmering water, for 15 min.,
or until gelatin dissolves completely and
mixture thickens slightly and coats a metal
spoon. Strain into a large bowl; stir in
lemon juice and vanilla. Set bowl in a pan
of ice and water to speed setting. Chill,
stirring often, at room temperature just
until as thick as unbeaten egg white.

While gelatin mixture chills, beat egg whites
until foamy-white and double in volume in
a small bowl; sprinkle in remaining ¼ cup
of sugar, 1 tablespoon at a time, beating all
the time until sugar dissolves and meringue
stands in firm peaks. Beat cream until stiff
in a bowl. Fold meringue, then whipped
cream, into thickened gelatin mixture.
Gently fold in raspberries. Spoon into a
cooled pastry shell. Chill for several
hours, or until firm. Makes one 9" pie.

PECAN TARTS

Pastry for 12 - 4" Tarts, unbaked
2 Cups Chopped Pecans
2 Cups Sugar
2 Cups Light Corn Syrup
4 Eggs, beaten
2 Tsp. Vanilla Extract

Line tart pans with pastry. Combine all
other ingredients and mix well. Spoon
into the tart pans. Bake in a preheated
oven (300°F.) for 55 to 60 minutes.
Serve cold, garnished with whipped cream.
Makes 12.

ROLLED-OATS PIE CRUST

1 Cup Rolled Oats
1/3 Cup Sifted All-purpose Flour
1/3 Cup Brown Sugar, packed
½ Tsp. Salt
1/3 Cup Melted Shortening

Combine oats, flour, sugar & salt in mixing
bowl. Add the shortening and mix in until crumbly. Pack mixture firmly in bottom
and sides of a 9" pie plate. Set an 8" pie
plate on top of mixture and press evenly.
Bake in preheated 375°F. oven for about
15 minutes. Let stand 5 minutes. Remove
smaller pan. Let crust cool in its plate.
Fill with pie mixture. Makes 1 - 9" crust.

NUT PIE

1 Cup Brown Sugar, firmly packed
1/3 Cup Flour
2 Cups Milk, scalded
2 Tbs. Butter
¼ Tsp. Salt
2 Eggs, separated
½ Tsp. Vanilla
½ Cup Nutmeats (pecans, hickory
   nuts, walnuts, etc.)
Baked 8" Pie Shell
¼ Cup Granulated Sugar

Blend brown sugar and flour thoroughly in
a saucepan; add 1 cup of scalded milk; stir
until smooth. Add remaining hot milk, butter and salt. Heat to boiling; reduce heat &
cook slowly over direct heat 5 minutes
longer, stirring constantly. Remove from
heat and slowly stir part of hot mixture into
the well-beaten egg yolks. Return to pan &
cook 2 minutes longer, stirring constantly.
Remove from heat; add vanilla and stir well.
Add nuts and stir enough to distribute.
Turn into the cooled baked pie shell. Cool.
Beat egg whites until stiff, then add granulated sugar gradually, a tablespoon at a time,
and beat until thick and smooth. Pile this
lightly and quickly over surface of pie filling
so it touches the sides of the crust all around.
Bake in a moderate oven (350°F.) for 12 to
15 minutes, or until meringue is nicely
browned. Cool on cake rack before cutting.
Makes 5 to 6 servings.

BLUEBERRY SQUARES

1/3 Cup Shortening
1 Cup White Sugar
1 Tsp. Vanilla
1 Egg, unbeaten
2 Cups Sifted Cake Flour
2½ Tsp. Baking Powder
¼ Tsp. Salt
2/3 Cup Milk
1½ Cups Fresh Blueberries
1 Tsp. Grated Lemon Rind

Cream together shortening and ¾ cup of sugar. Add vanilla and egg. Beat until fluffy. Add sifted dry ingredients alternately with milk. Pour half of batter into a 9x9" greased pan. Cover with mixture of blueberries, remaining ¼ cup of sugar and the lemon rind. Pour remaining batter over berries. Bake in moderate oven for 40 to 45 minutes. Dust with confectioners' sugar. Serve with cream.

CRANBERRY CRUNCH

2 Cups Cranberries
½ Cup Raisins
1 Cup Granulated Sugar
1 Tbs. Cornstarch
1/8 Tsp. Salt
1 Cup Oats (uncooked)
1 Cup Brown Sugar
½ Cup All-purpose Flour
1 Tsp. Vanilla
1/3 Cup Butter

Combine cranberries, raisins, granulated sugar, cornstarch and salt in a saucepan; bring to a boil and cook for 5 minutes, stirring constantly. Remove from heat & cool.

Blend oats, brown sugar, flour, vanilla & butter together. Press crumb mixture into an 8x8x2" pan (reserve a few crumbs to sprinkle on top). Add cranberry mixture. Sprinkle reserved crumbs on top and bake in 350°F. oven for 35 minutes, or until golden brown. Cut into large squares. Serve with whipped cream. Makes 8 servings.

SWISS STRAWBERRY RICE

1 Cup Uncooked Rice
3 Cups Milk
½ Cup Sugar
½ Tsp. Salt
2 Eggs, beaten
½ Cup Heavy Cream
1 Tsp. Almond Extract
1 - 10 Oz. Pkg. Frozen,
    Sliced Strawberries

Cook rice in top of double boiler, in milk, until tender. Stir occasionally. Cook for about 1 hour. Add sugar and salt. Add a little of the hot mixture gradually to the beaten eggs; stir eggs into remaining hot mixture. Blend well and cook for 1 minute more; cool. Whip the cream; add almond extract and fold into rice. Chill. Serve with partly thawed strawberries, or use fresh berries when in season. Makes 6 servings.

DEEP-FRIED CHERRIES

1 Cup Sifted All-purpose Flour
¼ Cup Sugar
½ Tsp. Ground Cinnamon
1/3 Cup Milk
½ Cup Dry White Wine
3 Eggs, lightly beaten
1 Lb. Ripe, Firm Sweet Cherries,
    with stems
Shortening for deep frying
Confectioners' Sugar

Combine flour, sugar and cinnamon. Stir in milk and wine to make a smooth paste. Beat in the eggs. Let batter rest for 30 minutes. Make a cluster of four or five cherries and tie with thread. Dip each cluster into the batter, making sure the cherries are well coated. Carefully lower the clusters into hot, deep fat (370°F. on frying thermometer). When browned, remove with a slotted spoon. Cook only a few clusters at one time. Drain on absorbent paper and sprinkle with confectioners' sugar. Serve at once. Serve 1 or 2 clusters for each individual helping.

STRAWBERRY SHORTCAKE

3 Pints Strawberries
¾ Cup Sugar
4 Cups Biscuit Mix
1-1/3 Cups Milk
2 Tbs. Grated Orange Rind
2 Cups Whipping Cream
1 Tbs. Vanilla

Wash strawberries; hull and slice into a medium bowl. Sprinkle with ¼ cup of sugar and toss lightly to mix. Let stand while making the shortcake.

Prepare biscuit mix with milk, following the directions on the label for rolled biscuits. Roll out half to a 16x12 rectangle (use a lightly floured board or pastry cloth). Mix remaining ½ cup sugar and orange rind in a cup; sprinkle half of mixture over dough. Roll up, jelly-roll fashion. Cut into 16 one-inch-thick slices. Place, cut side down, in a greased baking pan, 8x8x2", making 4 rows of 4 biscuits each. Repeat with remaining half of dough and sugar mixture and place in a second 8x8x2" baking pan. Bake in 425°F. oven for 25 minutes, or until golden. Combine cream and vanilla in a medium bowl; beat until stiff. Remove biscuits from pans by turning upside down on a wire rack so as not to break layers. Place one layer on a flat serving plate; top with half of the berries. Put remaining shortcake layer and remaining berries over first layer. Spoon part of the whipped cream on top and serve remaining whipped cream separately. To serve the shortcake, break apart with two forks. Makes 8 to 10 servings.

APPLE CRISP

4 Cups Pared, Cored Cooking Apples
1 Tbs. Lemon Juice
1/3 Cup Sifted All-purpose Flour
1 Cup Oatmeal, uncooked
½ Cup Brown Sugar, packed
½ Tsp. Salt
1 Tsp. Powdered Cinnamon
1/3 Cup Melted Butter or
   Margarine

Preheat oven to 375°F. Grease a shallow 1½-quart baking dish. Pour apples into the prepared dish. Sprinkle with lemon juice. If tart apples are used, add a light sprinkling of brown sugar. Combine dry ingredients and add melted butter or margarine. Mix until coarse crumbs are formed. Sprinkle crumb mixture over apples. Bake 30 min., or until apples are done. Serve warm or cold, with top milk or light cream. Makes 6 servings.

PINEAPPLE SPONGE ROLL

¼ Cup Butter or Margarine
¾ Cup Light Brown Sugar,
   firmly packed
1 Can Crushed Pineapple (about
   14 oz.), well drained
1 Cup Sifted Cake Flour
1 Tsp. Baking Powder
¼ Tsp. Salt
3 Eggs
1 Cup Granulated Sugar
¼ Cup Water
1 Tsp. Vanilla
Confectioners' Sugar
Whipped Cream

Melt the butter or margarine in a small saucepan. Stir in brown sugar and pineapple. Spread evenly in a 15x10x1" jelly-roll pan.

Sift flour, baking powder and salt together. Beat eggs in a medium bowl until frothy; slowly beat in granulated sugar until mixture is thick and fluffy. Stir in water and vanilla. Fold in flour mixture until there are no streaks of white remaining. Spread over pineapple mixture in pan. Bake in a 375°F. oven for 12 minutes, or until center of the cake springs back when lightly pressed with fingertip. Cool cake in pan on a wire rack for several minutes, then loosen around edges with a knife; invert onto a towel sprinkled with confectioners' sugar. Starting at one end, roll up, jelly-roll fashion. Cool and cut into slices. Serve warm or cold with whipped cream. Makes one 10" jelly-roll.

FRIED APPLE PIES

2 Cups Sifted All-purpose Flour
½ Tsp. Salt
1 Tsp. Baking Powder
3 Tbs. Butter or Margarine
1 Egg, beaten
½ Cup Milk
2 Cups Dried Apples, cooked
½ Tsp. Ground Cinnamon
½ Tsp. Ground Nutmeg
1 Tbs. Sugar
Fat, for deep frying

Sift together flour, salt and baking powder. Cut in the butter. Add egg and milk and mix to a soft dough. Roll out thin & cut into 5" circles. In the center of each, put ½ cup dried apples sprinkled with spices & sugar. Fold over. Wet edges with milk & seal with a fork. Fry in hot fat (370°F. on frying thermometer) until golden brown. Drain. Serve warm with cream, if desired. Makes 4 pies.

FRESH PEACH KUCHEN

Boiling Water
2 Lbs. Ripe Peaches (about 6) peeled
  and sliced
2 Tbs. Lemon Juice

Kuchen Batter:

1½ Cups Sifted All-purpose Flour
½ Cup Sugar
2 Tsp. Baking Powder
½ Tsp. Salt
2 Eggs
2 Tbs. Milk
1½ Tbs. Grated Lemon Peel
¼ Cup Butter or Margarine, melted

Topping:

¼ Cup Sugar
½ Tsp. Ground Cinnamon
1 Egg Yolk
3 Tbs. Heavy Cream

Pour enough boiling water over peaches in a large bowl to cover. Let stand one minute to loosen skins, then drain and plunge into cold water for a few seconds to prevent softening of fruit. With paring knife, pare peaches; place in a large bowl. Sprinkle peaches with lemon juice to prevent darkening. Slice into the bowl and toss with lemon juice; set aside.

Sift flour with sugar, baking powder, and salt. In large mixing bowl, using fork, beat eggs with milk and lemon peel. Add flour mixture and melted butter, mixing with fork until smooth--about 1 minute. Do not overmix. Butter a 9" springform pan, or a 9" round layer-cake pan. Turn batter into pan and spread evenly over bottom. At this point, kuchen may be refrigerated several hours, or until about ½ hour before baking.

Combine sugar and cinnamon and mix well. Drain peach slices; arrange on batter, around edge of pan. Fill in center with 5 peach slices. Sprinkle evenly with sugar-cinnamon mixture. Bake in preheated 400°F. oven for 25 minutes. Remove from oven.

With a fork, beat egg yolk with cream. Pour over peaches. Bake 10 minutes longer. Cool 10 minutes on wire rack. To serve, cut into wedges and serve warm with sweetened whipped cream or soft vanilla ice cream. Makes 8 to 10 servings.

CRANBERRY CREAM PIE

1 - 3 Oz. Pkg. Raspberry Gelatin
1¼ Cups Boiling Water
1 - 1 Lb. Can Whole Cranberry
  Sauce
1 Cup Dairy Sour Cream
1 - 9" Baked Pastry Shell
1¼ Cups Miniature Marshmallows
½ Cup Whipping Cream, whipped
1 Tbs. Sugar

Dissolve gelatin in boiling water; add the cranberry sauce. Chill until slightly thickened. Beat in sour cream with rotary beater until blended. Chill until partially set. Spoon into pastry shell. Sprinkle marshmallows on top. Fold sugar into whipped cream; spread over pie. Chill until firm.

HOT ORANGE PUDDING

½ Cup Pearl Tapioca
1 Large Orange
2½ Cups Cold Water
¼ Cup Sugar

In a small bowl, cover tapioca with ½ cup of cold water and let it soak for at least 4 hours. With a small knife, peel the orange and remove the white membrane clinging to each section. Break the orange sections into small pieces.

In a 2-quart saucepan combine 2 cups of cold water with the sugar. Bring to a boil over high heat, stirring until the sugar dissolves. Drain the tapioca and pour it into the pan slowly, stirring constantly. Cook over moderate heat, stirring, for 2 minutes, until the pudding thickens. Stir in the orange and bring to a boil again. Serve at once. Makes 4 to 6 servings.

BAKED PINEAPPLE

1 Large Pineapple
1 Large, Ripe Peach
½ Cup Blanched Almonds
4 Oz. Light Rum
¼ Cup Sugar
Butter
1 Oz. Brandy

Cut off and retain the top of the pineapple. Scoop out the flesh, taking care not to puncture the skin. Discard any tough or pithy flesh and cut the rest into ½" cubes. Shred the almonds and mix with the pineapple and peach, pour the rum over the mixed fruit & almonds, sprinkle with sugar and toss lightly. Put the fruit back into the pineapple shell in layers, dotting each layer with butter. Replace the top of the pineapple and bake in a moderate oven (350°F.) until the fruit is tender--about 20 to 30 minutes. Place on a platter, pour 1 oz. warm brandy over the pineapple and set it alight.

COMPANY SQUASH PIE

1 Cup Strained, Cooked Hubbard
  Squash
1 Cup Heavy Cream
1 Cup Sugar
3 Eggs, slightly beaten
2 Tbs. Brandy
1 Tsp. Ground Cinnamon
1 Tsp. Ground Nutmeg
½ Tsp. Ground Ginger
½ Tsp. Salt
1 Unbaked 9" Pie Shell

Mix all filling ingredients, pour into pie shell and bake in preheated 375°F. oven for about 45 minutes, or until firm. Cool before serving. Makes 6 servings.

STREUSEL PECAN SQUARES

Crust:
3 Cups All-purpose Flour
¾ Cup Brown Sugar, firmly packed
1½ Cups Butter or Margarine, chilled

Measure flour into a large bowl and combine with brown sugar and butter or margarine. Blend until crumbly. Reserve 2 cups of the crumbs for filling and topping. Press remaining crumbs into bottom and ¾" up sides of an ungreased 15x10" jelly roll pan. Bake at 400°F. for 10 minutes.

Filling:
¾ Cup Brown Sugar, firmly packed
1½ Cups Corn Syrup or Maple-flavored
  Syrup
1 Cup Milk
1/3 Cup Butter or Margarine, melted
1 Tsp. Vanilla Extract
4 Eggs
1½ Cups Chopped Pecans

In a large bowl, combine ¼ cup reserved crumbs and all filling ingredients except pecans; mix well. Stir in the pecans. Pour over the prebaked crust and bake an additional 10 minutes. Reduce oven temperature to 350°F. Sprinkle remaining 1¾ cups reserved crumbs over filling; bake at 350°F. for 20 to 25 minutes, or until filling is set and crumbs are golden brown. If desired, serve with whipped cream or ice cream. Makes 15 servings.

CHOCOLATE CHIFFON PIE

Crust:

1½ Cups Graham-cracker or
  Zwieback Crumbs
1/3 Cup Unblanched Almonds
6 Tbs. Sugar
¼ Cup Light Cream
½ Cup Melted Butter or Margarine
½ Tsp. Ground Cinnamon

Filling:

1 Envelope Unflavored Gelatin
¼ Cup Cold Water
2 Tbs. Hot Water
4 Eggs, separated
1 Cup Commercial Chocolate Sauce
1/8 Tsp. Salt
1 Tsp. Vanilla Extract
½ Cup Sugar
Whipped Cream
Shaved Semisweet Chocolate

Blend crumbs at low speed until very fine. Add almonds and blend fine at low speed. Remove from blender and mix thoroughly with remaining crust ingredients. Pat firmly into lightly buttered 10-inch pie pan. Prick bottom several times with fork tines. Bake in preheated moderate oven (375°F.) for 12 to 15 minutes. Cool.

To make filling, soften gelatin in cold water. Add hot water and stir until dissolved. Put egg yolks in blender, add gelatin, cover and blend at low speed until thoroughly mixed. Add chocolate sauce, salt, and vanilla. Blend at high speed for 4 or 5 seconds, or until thoroughly blended. Chill until consistency of raw egg white. With rotary beater, beat egg whites until foamy. Gradually add sugar and beat until very stiff. Fold into chocolate mixture. Pour into shell and chill. Decorate with whipped cream and shaved chocolate.

CHERRY BAVARIAN PIE

1 Cup Undiluted Evaporated Milk
2 Cups (1 - 1 Lb. Can) Pitted Red
  Sour Cherries
¾ Cup Sugar
1 Envelope Unflavored Gelatin
3 Tbs. Fresh Lemon Juice
Red Food Coloring
1 - 9" Baked and Cooled Pie Shell

Chill the evaporated milk in freezer tray until ice crystals form around the edge. Drain cherries, reserving liquid. In saucepan mix sugar and gelatin; gradually add liquid and heat, stirring constantly until sugar and gelatin are dissolved. Remove from heat and add lemon juice and cherries. Chill until thickened but not firm. Add a few drops of red food coloring. Whip milk until stiff and fold into first mixture. Pile into cool shell and chill until firm. Makes 6 to 8 servings.

BUTTERSCOTCH PIE

1 Cup Brown Sugar, firmly packed
3 Tbs. Flour
4½ Tsp. Cornstarch
½ Tsp. Salt
1½ Cups Scalded Milk
3 Eggs, separated
3 Tbs. Butter
¾ Tsp. Vanilla
Baked 8" Pie Shell
½ Cup Whipping Cream

In the top of a double boiler mix the sugar, flour, cornstarch and salt thoroughly. Add ¾ cup of the hot milk and stir over direct heat until smooth. Add the remaining milk, then place over boiling water and cook, stirring frequently, for 15 minutes. Beat egg yolks thoroughly; stir in a little of the hot mixture, and pour back into double boiler. Cook for 3 minutes longer, stirring constantly. Remove from heat, add butter and vanilla, and stir until mixed. Beat egg whites until stiff and fold into the hot mixture. Pour immediately into cooled pie shell. Spread lightly with whipped cream just before serving. Makes 5 to 6 servings.

CHOCOLATE-WALNUT TORTE

6 Eggs, separated
¾ Cup Sugar
¼ Cup Water
1 Tsp. Vanilla
1 Cup Broken Walnuts, ground
1/3 Cup Packaged Bread Crumbs
½ Tsp. Salt
Chocolate Sour Cream Frosting
   (recipe below)
Chocolate Rum Glaze (recipe
   below)
Whole Walnuts

Line three 8x1½" layer-cake pans with a double thickness of waxed paper (do not grease). Beat egg whites in a large bowl at high speed with an electric mixer, until foamy white and double in volume. Gradually beat in ¼ cup of the sugar, until meringue stands in soft peaks. Beat egg yolks in a small bowl at high speed with an electric mixer until thick and lemon-colored. Gradually beat in remaining sugar until mixture is very light and fluffy and falls in ribbons from beaters when the beaters are lifted (about 5 minutes). Lower speed and beat in the water and vanilla.

Fold walnuts, bread crumbs, and salt into egg-yolk mixture; blend completely. Fold egg yolk mixture into meringue until no streaks of yellow or white remain. Pour into pans, dividing equally. Bake in a 350°F. oven for 15 minutes, or until centers spring back when lightly pressed with fingertip. Invert pans over wire rack; let cool 20 minutes. Loosen cakes around edges with a knife; carefully loosen cakes from bottom with small spatula, being careful not to tear cakes (they are very delicate). Turn out of pans and peel off wax paper.

Prepare Chocolate Sour Cream Frosting. Reserve 1 cup and put layers together with part of remaining frosting. Spread the Chocolate Rum Glaze on top and side of cake. Pipe reserved frosting decoratively on top and side of cake. Decorate with whole walnuts.

Chocolate Sour Cream Frosting:
¾ Cup Butter or Margarine
4 Squares Semisweet Chocolate,
   melted
1 - 1 Lb. Pkg. Confectioners' Sugar
4 Tbs. Dairy Sour Cream
1½ Tsp. Vanilla

Combine butter or margarine and chocolate in a small bowl. Beat until thoroughly blended. Add sugar alternately with sour cream and vanilla, beating until mixture is spreadable. Makes enough to fill and frost one 8-inch cake.

Chocolate Rum Glaze:
1 Square Semisweet Chocolate
1 Tbs. Butter, or Margarine
1 Tbs. Confectioners' Sugar
1 Tbs. Rum or Brandy

Combine all ingredients in a small bowl; set bowl in a small saucepan partly filled with water. Heat, stirring often, until chocolate is melted. Cool slightly. If glaze separates, add a few drops of cold water or milk, then stir until it is smooth.

NO-BAKE APPLE PIE

1 - 3 Oz. Pkg. Lemon-flavored
   Gelatin
1¾ Cups Boiling Water
1 Can Apple Pie Filling (about 2½ cups)
½ Tsp. Cinnamon
¼ Tsp. Nutmeg
½ Tsp. Grated Lemon Peel
1 - 9" Graham-cracker Crumb Crust
1 Tbs. Sugar
½ Cup Shredded Sharp American Cheese
½ Cup Whipping Cream, whipped

Dissolve gelatin in boiling water; chill until partially set. Combine pie filling, spices & lemon peel. Reserve ¼ cup of the gelatin; stir remainder of gelatin into the apple mixture and pour into the crust. For the "meringue", fold the reserved gelatin, sugar and cheese into the whipped cream. Spread over the pie and chill until firm. Makes 1 nine-inch pie.

CARAMEL FLUFF PIE

½ Lb. Vanilla Caramels
   (about 28)
1 Cup Milk
Dash of Salt
1 Envelope (1 Tbs.) Unflavored
   Gelatin
¼ Cup Cold Water
1 Cup Whipping Cream, whipped
½ Cup Chopped Pecans
1 Tsp. Vanilla
1 - 9" Gingersnap Crust

Melt caramels in milk in top of double
boiler over boiling water, stirring occasionally. Add salt. Soften gelatin in
cold water; add to caramels and stir to
dissolve. Chill until mixture is partially
set. Fold in the whipped cream, nuts
and vanilla. Fill the crust. Chill for 2
or 3 hours, or until firm.

CINNAMON FLUFF

Topping:
½ Cup Sugar
1 Tbs. Butter or Margarine
1 Tbs. Powdered Cinnamon

Fluff:
½ Cup Butter or Margarine
2/3 Cup Sugar
2 Eggs, well beaten
1½ Cups Sifted All-purpose Flour
1 Tsp. Baking Soda
1 Tsp. Baking Powder
1 Tbs. Powdered Cinnamon
1 Cup Sour Milk

Mix topping ingredients together until they
are smooth. Preheat oven to 350°F. Butter a 1½-quart baking dish. Prepare the
fluff. Cream butter or margarine and sugar
together; stir in eggs. Sift flour with remaining dry ingredients. Add alternately with
sour milk to creamed mixture. Beat one
minute. Pour batter into prepared baking
dish. Spread with topping. Bake for 1
hour, or until tester comes out clean.
Serve warm, with cream or any preferred
fresh fruit sauce. Makes 6 servings.

APPLE DUMPLINGS

1 Cup Sifted All-purpose Flour
1 - 3 Oz. Pkg. Cream Cheese
½ Cup Butter or Margarine
1/8 Tsp. Salt
4 Apples, peeled and cored
½ Cup Sugar
1 Tsp. Ground Cinnamon
2 Tbs. Butter
Cinnamon Syrup

Sift the flour and blend in the cream
cheese, butter and salt. Chill. Roll in
a rectangle about 9x14" on a lightly
floured board. Cover with coarsely-
grated apples and sprinkle with a mixture of sugar and cinnamon. Dot with
butter. Roll as for jelly roll. Cut into
1½" slices. Place, cut-side up, 1" apart,
in a buttered shallow baking dish (8x14")
or unbuttered individual custard cups.
Cover with Cinnamon Syrup. Bake in
a preheated 400°F. oven for 10 minutes.
Reduce the temperature to 325°F. and
bake for 45 minutes longer. Makes 8
to 9 dumplings.

Cinnamon Syrup:

1/3 Cup Firmly-packed Dark Brown
   Sugar
2 Tbs. All-purpose Flour
1 Cup Water
1 Tbs. Butter
¼ Cup Brandy
¼ Tsp. Ground Allspice
1 Tsp. Ground Cinnamon
½ Tsp. Ground Nutmeg

Combine all of the ingredients and cook
until thickened and clear. Pour over
dumplings.

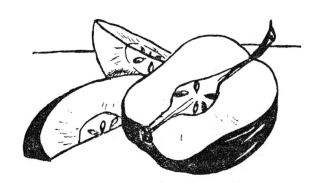

CHANTILLY CHERRY PIE

1 Cup Unsifted All-purpose Flour
Dash of Salt
1 Tbs. Sugar
½ Cup Butter or Margarine, softened
1 Egg Yolk
Dairy Sour Cream
1 Can Cherry Pie Filling
Sweetened Whipped Cream, flavored
   with almond extract
Grated Orange Rind

Sift dry ingredients into bowl and cut in
butter. Add egg yolk and enough sour
cream to make a smooth pastry dough.
Wrap in wax paper and chill overnight.
Roll to 1/8" thickness and fit into an
8" pie pan. Trim edges and flute. Prick
well with a fork. Bake in preheated oven
(450°F.) for about 10 minutes. Cool &
fill with pie filling. Top with whipped
cream and sprinkle with orange rind.
Chill until ready to serve. Makes 6
servings.

BLACK BOTTOM PIE

2 Cups Milk
1/3 Cup Cornstarch
1 Cup Sugar
¼ Tsp. Salt
3 Eggs, separated
1 Tbs. Butter
1 Tsp. Vanilla
1 Square Unsweetened Chocolate
   (1 oz.), cut up fine
1/3 Cup Sugar
Baked 8" Pie Shell

Scald 1½ cups of the milk in top of a
double boiler. Mix together cornstarch,
sugar, and salt and blend with remaining
cold milk to form a smooth paste. Add
cornstarch mixture gradually to scalded
milk and cook over boiling water with
frequent stirring until smooth and thick,
about 10 min.

Remove from heat and slowly stir a small
amount of the hot mixture into well-beaten
egg yolks. Return to the double boiler and
cook 2 min. longer, stirring constantly. Add
butter and vanilla. Pour one half of filling
into a bowl. Keep warm over hot water.

Add chocolate to the remaining half of the
filling in top of double boiler. Place over
hot water and stir until well blended, about
3 minutes. Immediately pour chocolate
cream into cooled pie shell. Let cool thoroughly, then pour remainder of filling on
top.

Beat egg whites until stiff and gradually add
the 1/3 cup sugar, 1 tbs. at a time, and beat
until smooth and thick. Pile the meringue
lightly over the pie and bake in a moderate
oven (350°F.) for 12 to 15 minutes, or until nicely browned. Cool to serve. Makes
5 to 6 servings.

PLUM PUDDING

1 Lb. Currants
1 Lb. Sultana Raisins
1 Lb. Seeded Raisins
½ Lb. Figs
1 Cup Finely-chopped Suet
½ Lb. Split Blanched Almonds
1½ Cups Brown Sugar
½ Lb. Mixed Candied Peel
   and Citron, cut up
2 Cups All-purpose Flour
½ Tsp. Salt
1/8 Tsp. Baking Soda
½ Tsp. Baking Powder
4 Tsp. Cinnamon
2½ Tsp. Allspice
1½ Tsp. Nutmeg
8 Eggs
½ Cup Fruit Juice

Wash currants and dry well. Combine the
currants with the raisins, figs, suet and almonds and mix well. Add brown sugar,
peel and citron. Sift flour several times
with the remaining dry ingredients and combine with the fruit mixture. Beat the eggs
until very light; combine with fruit juice.
Add to mixture of fruit and dry ingredients
and mix thoroughly. Turn into well-greased
molds, two-thirds full. Cover and cook in
steamer over boiling water, tightly covered
for 4 hours. Serve warm. May be reheated
in the steamer, over boiling water, for 1 hr.
before serving.

RUM-RAISIN ICE CREAM

2 Egg Yolks
½ Cup Sugar
Dash of Salt
1 Cup Light Cream
1 Cup Heavy Cream
1½ Tsp. Vanilla Extract
½ Cup Seeded Raisins, slivered or
    ground
2 to 3 Tbs. Rum

Soak the raisins in the rum for several
hours. Beat egg yolks until light; add
sugar, then salt and light cream. Blend
well. Fold in whipped heavy cream and
the vanilla. Partially freeze. Stir once,
and when it is of frappe' consistency,
add the raisins. Continue freezing.
Makes 6 servings.

PEACH-CRANBERRY PIE

¾ Cup Sugar
2 Tbs. All-purpose Flour
1 Tsp. Grated Lemon Peel
¼ Tsp. Ground Cinnamon
2 - 1 Lb. Cans Sliced Cling
    Peaches, drained
2 Cups Fresh Cranberries, washed
    and stemmed
1 Pkg. Pie Crust Mix
1 Egg, well beaten
½ Cup Confectioners' Sugar
2 Tsp. Water

Mix sugar, flour, lemon peel and cinnamon
in a medium bowl; add peaches and cranberries. Toss lightly to coat fruit. Prepare
the pie crust mix, following label directions,
or use your favorite double-crust recipe.
Line bottom of a 9" pie plate and spoon in
the peach-cranberry mixture. Roll out remaining pastry, cut several slits near center
to let steam escape; cover pie. Trim overhang, turn edges under and flute to make
a stand-up edge. Mix egg with 1 tablespoon of water in a small bowl; brush over
the pastry for a rich glaze when baked.
Bake in a 400°F. oven for 45 minutes, or
until top is golden brown and juices are
bubbling up. Cool on a wire rack. While
pie is still warm, mix the confectioners'
sugar with water until smooth; drizzle
over the pie. Makes one 9" pie.

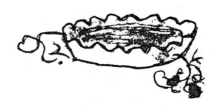

HONEY-NUT APPLE PIE

3 Tbs. All-purpose Flour
¼ Tsp. Salt
1 Tsp. Ground Cinnamon
½ Tsp. Ground Nutmeg
½ Cup Dairy Sour Cream
¾ Cup Honey
½ Cup Chopped Pecans
6 Medium Tart Apples
Pastry for 2-Crust 9" Pie, unbaked

Mix flour, salt, cinnamon and nutmeg; add
sour cream, honey and pecans. Peel and
slice apples and stir into first mixture. Line
pie pan with half of pastry; add filling and
adjust top crust. Bake in preheated hot
oven (425°F.) for 30 minutes. Reduce heat
to 350°F. and bake about 15 min. longer.
Makes 6 to 8 servings.

FRENCH PEAR PIE

1 - 9" Unbaked Pie Shell
5 Large Bartlett Pears
3 Tbs. Frozen Orange Juice
    Concentrate
½ Tsp. Grated Lemon Peel
¾ Cup Flour
½ Cup Sugar
1/8 Tsp. Salt
1 Tsp. Ground Cinnamon
½ Tsp. Ground Ginger
1/3 Cup Butter or Margarine

Peel, core and slice pears thinly. Toss lightly
with orange juice concentrate and lemon peel.
Arrange in the pie shell. Mix together the remaining ingredients until crumbly. Sprinkle
over the pears, being careful to cover all of
the fruit. Bake in 400°F. oven for 40 min.,
or until pears are tender. Makes 1 nine-
inch pie.

LEMON RICE PUDDING

¾ Cup Quick Cooking Rice
2½ Cups Milk
1 Egg, slightly beaten
1/3 Cup Sugar
½ Tsp. Salt
1 Tbs. Lemon Juice
1 Tsp. Lemon Rind
1 Tbs. Butter

Combine rice and milk in a saucepan and bring to a full, rolling boil. Remove from the heat; cover and let stand for 10 min. Combine the slightly-beaten egg, sugar, lemon juice and lemon rind. Add a small amount of the hot mixture. Stir well and return to saucepan. Add butter. Cook gently over hot water for about 4 minutes. Stir constantly. Serve warm with cream. Makes 6 servings.

MINCEMEAT CHIFFON PIE

22 Gingersnaps, rolled into
   fine crumbs
¼ Cup Sugar
3 Tbs. Butter or Margarine

Blend crumbs, sugar and butter or margarine smoothly together. Pour mixture into a 9" pie plate. Spread in bottom & press firmly into an even layer on the sides. Use an 8" pie plate pressed into the larger pie plate to get smooth, firm crust. Smooth edge of crust all around.

Filling:
1 - 9 Oz. Box Condensed Mincemeat
2 Envelopes Unflavored Gelatin
½ Cup Cold Water
½ Cup Heavy Cream, whipped
3 Egg Whites
6 Tbs. Sugar
Extra Cream and Crumbs

Prepare mincemeat according to package directions. Soak gelatin in water in a cup for about 5 minutes. Set cup in hot water and heat until gelatin dissolves. Blend into mincemeat. Chill until partially set. Fold in whipped cream. Beat egg whites until they stand in soft peaks. Add sugar gradually, beating until mixture stands in stiff points when beater is removed. Fold the mincemeat into meringue. Spoon into pie shell. Chill in refrigerator. Serve, garnished with additional whipped cream, and sprinkle with a few gingersnap crumbs. Makes 6 servings. This pie should be prepared the day before it is to be served.

CHOCOLATE CHEESE PIE

1 - 9" Chocolate Graham Crust
   (see recipe below)
1 - 6 Oz. Pkg. Semisweet Chocolate
   Pieces
1 - 8 Oz. Pkg. Cream Cheese,
   softened
¾ Cup Light Brown Sugar, firmly
   packed
1/8 Tsp. Salt
1 Tsp. Vanilla
2 Eggs, separated
1 Cup Heavy Cream, whipped

Melt chocolate over hot, not boiling, water. Cool about 10 minutes. Blend cream cheese, ½ cup sugar, salt and vanilla. Beat in egg yolks, one at a time. Beat in cooled chocolate. Blend well. Beat egg whites until stiff but not dry. Gradually beat in ¼ cup sugar; beat until stiff and glossy. Fold the chocolate mixture into beaten whites. Fold in the whipped cream. Pour into chilled crust, reserving one-fourth of the mixture for decorating. Chill until filling sets slightly. With tapered spoon, drop reserved mixture in mounds over top of pie; chill overnight.

Chocolate Graham Crust:
1½ Cups Graham Cracker Crumbs
¼ Cup Brown Sugar, firmly packed
1/8 Tsp. Ground Nutmeg
1/3 Cup Melted Butter or Margarine
1 Square Unsweetened Chocolate, melted

Mix all ingredients together until thoroughly blended. Press into a 9" pie pan; chill until firm.

CHERRY DESSERT

1 Cup Prepared Biscuit Mix
2 Tsp. Butter or Margarine
¼ Cup Light Cream
Melted Butter
1 Cup Red Sour Cherries (canned,
   pitted variety) drained
2 Tbs. Diced, Candied Lemon Peel
Cherry Sauce (see recipe below)

Blend together biscuit mix and butter; add
the cream and stir well. Turn out onto a
lightly-floured board; knead for 30 seconds.
Roll out into a rectangle ¼" thick. Brush
with melted butter. Top with cherries and
lemon peel. Roll up as for a jelly roll.
Place on a buttered baking sheet; brush
with melted butter.

Bake in a preheated hot oven (425°F.) for
20 minutes. Slice and serve hot with
Cherry Sauce. Makes 6 servings.

Cherry Sauce:

¾ Cup Cherry Juice
½ Cup Sugar
1/8 Tsp. Salt
1½ Tsp. Potato Flour or Cornstarch
¼ Cup Drained, Canned Pitted Red Sour
   Cherries
1 Tbs. Butter or Margarine
1 Tbs. Fresh Lemon Juice

Combine sugar, salt, and potato flour. Stir
in cherry juice. Cook over low heat for 5
minutes, stirring constantly. Add cherries,
butter, and lemon juice. Serve hot. Makes
1 cup sauce.

WALNUT PUDDING

½ Cup Walnuts
1½ Cups Flour
½ Cup Sugar
Pinch of Salt
½ Cup Raisins
1½ Tsp. Baking Powder
¾ Cup Sweet Milk
2 Tbs. Melted Butter

Sift dry ingredients. Mix in raisins and
nuts. Add milk and melted butter.
Steam for 2 hours. Serve with hard
sauce.

LEMON CHIFFON PIE

1 - 9" Pastry Shell, baked and
   cooled
1 Envelope Unflavored Gelatin
1 Cup Sugar
¼ Cup Water
4 Eggs, separated
½ Tsp. Salt
½ Cup Lemon Juice
1 Tsp. Grated Lemon Peel
1 Square Semisweet Chocolate
1 Tsp. Vegetable Shortening
1 Cup Whipping Cream

Soften gelatin with ½ cup of sugar in ¼
cup water in top of double boiler. Set
remaining sugar aside. Beat egg yolks
slightly in a small bowl; stir into gelatin
mixture with salt and lemon juice. Cook,
stirring constantly, over simmering water
for 5 minutes, or until mixture thickens
slightly and coats a metal spoon. Strain
into a large bowl; stir in lemon peel.

Set bowl in a deep pan partly filled with
ice and water to speed setting. Chill, stirring often, 5 minutes, or just until the
consistency of unbeaten egg white. While
gelatin mixture chills, melt semisweet
chocolate with vegetable shortening in a
cup over simmering water. Beat egg whites
until foamy and double in volume in a
medium bowl; sprinkle in remaining ½ cup
of sugar, a tablespoon at a time, beating
all the time until sugar completely dissolves
and meringue stands in firm peaks. Beat
cream until stiff in a second bowl. Fold
meringue, then whipped cream, into the
thickened gelatin mixture until no streaks
of white remain. Remove from pan of
ice and water. Spoon about one-third of
the gelatin mixture into cooled pastry
shell; drizzle with part of the chocolate
mixture. Repeat with remaining gelatin
mixture and chocolate to make two more
layers of each. Chill pie several hours, or
until firm. Makes one 9" pie.

CREAMY BANANA NUT PIE

2 Cups Water
¼ Cup Fresh Lemon Juice
4 Medium Bananas, sliced (about
   3½ cups)
½ Cup Sifted Confectioners' Sugar
¼ Tsp. Salt
1 Tsp. Ground Ginger
1 Envelope Unflavored Gelatin
¼ Cup Water
1 Cup Heavy Cream, whipped
1 Cup Chopped Pecans
1 Deep 9" Pie Shell, baked

Combine water and lemon juice. Add the sliced bananas; cover and refrigerate for 1 hour. Mix next 3 ingredients. Soften the gelatin in cold water; dissolve over hot water. Drain bananas and beat until almost smooth. Stir in sugar mixture and gelatin. Fold in whipped cream and ¾ cup nuts. Pour into baked shell and sprinkle with remaining nuts. Chill until set. Makes 6 to 8 servings.

RHUBARB PIE

3 Tbs. All-purpose Flour
1 to 1¼ Cups Sugar
¼ Tsp. Salt
4 Cups Diced Rhubarb
Grated Rind of 1 Orange
¼ Cup Fresh Orange Juice
Pastry for 9" Pie, with strips,
   unbaked
2 Tbs. Butter or Margarine

Mix flour, sugar, salt and rhubarb. Add orange rind and juice. Turn into pastry-lined pie pan. Dot with butter. Cover with strips of pastry, lattice fashion. Bake in a preheated hot oven (450°F.) for 20 minutes. Reduce heat to moderate (350°F.) and bake for about 20 minutes longer. Makes 6 to 8 servings.

STRAWBERRY TORTE

6 Egg Whites
½ Tsp. Cream of Tartar
¼ Tsp. Salt
1½ Cups Sugar
1 Tsp. Vanilla
¼ Cup Slivered Blanched Almonds
2 Cups Strawberries, washed and
   hulled or 1 - 10 Oz. Pkg. Frozen
   Sliced Strawberries, thawed and
   drained
1 Cup Whipping Cream
Red Food Coloring

Preheat oven to 400°F. Beat egg whites, cream of tartar and salt until foamy and double in volume (use large bowl). Beat in sugar, 1 tablespoon at a time, beating well after each addition. Beat until meringue stands in firm peaks (sugar should be completely dissolved before adding more--beating will take about 30 minutes). Fold in vanilla. Spoon the meringue into a buttered 8" springform pan; make a slight hollow in middle with a spoon and sprinkle slivered almonds over. Place in preheated oven; close oven door and turn heat off immediately. Leave torte to slow-bake, without peeking even once, overnight or at least 12 hours. Remove torte from oven, loosen around edge with a knife. Release the spring and carefully lift off side of pan. Carefully slide torte off pan onto a serving plate.

About 1 hour before serving, hull & slice enough strawberries to make 1 cup; spoon over meringue. If using frozen berries, drain (saving a few berries for garnish). Beat cream until stiff; blend in a few drops of red food coloring to tint a delicate pink. Spoon over strawberries; top with a halved berry; chill. Garnish torte with remaining whole or sliced berries; slice in wedges with a sharp knife to serve. Makes one 8-inch torte.

LEMON SLUMP

Grated Rind and Juice of 2 Lemons
2 Cups Sugar
2 Cups Water
2 Cups Sifted All-purpose Flour
1 Tsp. Cream of Tartar
1 Tsp. Baking Soda
¼ Tsp. Salt
1 Cup Milk (approximate)

Mix lemon rind and juice with sugar and water. Bring to a boil, lower heat and simmer. Sift flour with cream of tartar, baking soda, and salt. Stir in enough milk to make a dough that will drop from the end of a spoon. Drop dough by table-spoons into simmering sauce. Simmer for 10 minutes, then cover and simmer for 10 minutes longer. Serve dumplings plain, with sauce, or with whipped cream. Makes 6 to 8 servings.

APPLE-PUMPKIN PIE

1 - 1 Lb. 9 Oz. Can Apple Pie
   Filling
1 Unbaked 10" Pie Shell
1 Tbs. Cornstarch
½ Tsp. Cinnamon
½ Tsp. Nutmeg
½ Tsp. Ginger
¼ Tsp. Powdered Cloves
½ Tsp. Salt
1 Cup Sugar
1 - 1 Lb. Can Pumpkin
2 Tbs. Molasses
1½ Tbs. Melted Butter or Margarine
1¼ Cups Milk
2 Eggs, slightly beaten

Pour apple pie filling into unbaked pie shell. Combine cornstarch, spices, salt and sugar. Add pumpkin, molasses, melted butter or margarine and blend well. Combine milk & eggs and stir into pumpkin mixture. Pour over apple filling. Bake at 425°F. for 40 minutes, or until knife inserted in pumpkin mixture near rim comes out clean. Chill, then garnish with whipped cream.

BREAD PUDDING with RUM SAUCE

Pudding:
3 Cups Milk
10 Cups Bread Cubes
1-2/3 Cups Raisins
½ Cup Pecans, minced
½ Stick Butter, melted
4 Eggs
1 Cup Sugar
¼ Tsp. Vanilla
¼ Tsp. Allspice
¼ Tsp. Nutmeg
1¼ Tsp. Cinnamon
¼ Tsp. Salt

In a 4-quart pot, scald milk and let cool for several minutes. Add the bread, raisins, pe-cans and butter and blend well. In a sepa-rate bowl, beat the eggs and combine them with the remaining ingredients, blending un-til they are mixed well. Add egg mixture to the bread mixture. Heat oven to 350°F. Grease well an 8x8" square cake pan. Pour pudding mixture into pan and cook for ap-proximately 1½ hours. To test for doneness, insert a straw in the center of the pan to see if it comes out clean; if not, bake a few min-utes longer. The top should be a moderate brown color when done. Serve pudding with hot rum sauce.

Sauce:
¾ Cup Sugar
½ Cup Water
¾ Stick Sweet Butter
   (6 tablespoons)
¾ Cup Dark Rum

Cook the sugar, water and butter for 5 min. Gradually add the rum and cook 2 minutes longer. Serve hot over the pudding.

COOKIES

MARDI GRAS BARS

1¼ Cups All-purpose Flour
¼ Tsp. Salt
2/3 Cup Brown Sugar, lightly packed
½ Cup Butter
2 Egg Yolks
½ Tsp. Vanilla

Blend flour and salt together. Cream together remaining ingredients; blend in dry ingredients and press into bottom of a greased 9" square cake pan. Bake at 350° F. for 15 minutes.

Topping:
2 Egg Whites
2 Tbs. All-purpose Flour
½ Cup Chocolate Sundae Topping
½ Cup Coconut
½ Cup Chopped Maraschino Cherries
½ Cup Chopped Nuts

Beat egg whites until they form stiff peaks. Blend in flour and chocolate sauce. Stir in coconut, cherries and nuts. Spread over baked crust. Return to oven and bake for an additional 18 to 20 minutes. Cool and cut into bars. Makes 24 bars.

SALTED PEANUT CHEWS

Crust:
1½ Cups All-purpose Flour
2/3 Cup Brown Sugar, firmly
    packed
½ Tsp. Baking Powder
½ Tsp. Salt
¼ Tsp. Soda
½ Cup Margarine or Butter,
    softened
1 Tsp. Vanilla
2 Egg Yolks
3 Cups Miniature Marshmallows

Topping:
2/3 Cup Corn Syrup
¼ Cup Margarine or Butter
2 Tsp. Vanilla
1 - 12 Oz. Pkg. Peanut Butter
    Chips (2 cups)
2 Cups Crisp Rice Cereal
2 Cups Salted Peanuts

Lightly spoon flour into measuring cup; level off. In large bowl, combine all of the crust ingredients, except marshmallows, until crumb mixture forms. Press into bottom of ungreased 13x9" pan. Bake at 350°F. for 12 to 15 minutes, or until light golden brown. Immediately sprinkle with marshmallows and bake 1 to 2 minutes longer, or until marshmallows just begin to puff. Cool while preparing topping.

In a large saucepan, heat corn syrup, ¼ cup margarine, 2 tsp. vanilla and peanut butter chips just until chips are melted and mixture is smooth, stirring constantly. Remove from heat and stir in cereal and nuts. Immediately spoon warm topping over marshmallows and spread to cover. Chill and cut into bars. Makes 36 bars.

BOOSTER BARS

¼ Cup Sifted All-purpose Flour
¾ Tsp. Baking Powder
1½ Tsp. Salt
1 Cup Quick or Old-fashioned
    Oats, uncooked
4 Cups Instant Nonfat Dry Milk
¾ Cup Light Brown Sugar,
    firmly packed
½ Cup Raisins
½ Cup Semi-sweet Chocolate Pieces
½ Cup Butter or Margarine, melted
1 Egg, beaten
½ Cup Water

Preheat oven to 350°F. Grease a baking pan, 11x7x2". Sift together flour, baking powder and salt. Combine in a large bowl with the oats, nonfat dry milk, brown sugar, raisins and chocolate pieces. Allow melted butter to cool, then add egg and water. Stir this into the oat mixture, blending well. Spread batter evenly over bottom of greased baking pan. Bake about 25 to 30 minutes until golden. Cool in pan about 10 minutes. Cut into bars. Makes 12 bars.

COUNTRY-STYLE BANANA COOKIES

1 Cup Mashed Banana (2 or 3 medium)
2 Eggs
1 Cup Soft Butter or Shortening
1 Cup Sugar
2 Cups Flour
1½ Tsp. Salt
1 Tsp. Baking Powder
1 Tsp. Soda
1 Tsp. Cinnamon
¼ Tsp. Nutmeg
2 Cups Rolled Oats
1 Pkg. Chocolate Chips (6 oz.)

Beat eggs into mashed banana. Add butter or shortening and beat well. Sift dry ingredients together and stir into the creamed mixture. Stir in rolled oats and chocolate chips. Drop by teaspoonfuls onto greased baking sheets. Bake about 8 minutes in a 350°F. oven. Makes approximately 5 dozen.

SWEDISH OATMEAL COOKIES

¾ Cup All-purpose Flour
½ Cup Sugar
½ Cup Brown Sugar, firmly packed
½ Tsp. Salt
½ Tsp. Soda
½ Cup Shortening or Margarine
½ Tsp. Vanilla
1 Egg
1½ Cups Rolled Oats

Topping:
1/3 Cup Sugar
¼ Cup Butter or Margarine
1 Tbs. Corn Syrup
1/3 Cup Chopped Almonds
1/8 Tsp. Almond Extract

In a large bowl, combine flour, sugar, brown sugar, salt, soda, shortening, vanilla and egg. Beat 1 minute at medium speed. Stir in the rolled oats.

In a small saucepan, combine 1/3 cup sugar, ¼ cup margarine and 1 tbs. corn syrup; bring to a boil. Remove from heat and stir in the almonds and almond extract. Set aside. Drop cookie dough by rounded teaspoonfuls, 2″ apart, onto ungreased cookie sheets. Bake at 350°F. (preheated oven) for 8 minutes. Spoon a scant ½ tsp. of topping onto center of each cookie, pressing lightly. Return to oven and bake 6 to 8 minutes longer, or until golden brown. Cool the cookies slightly before removing from cookie sheets. Makes 34 cookies.

RAW APPLE COOKIES

1-1/3 Cups Brown Sugar, firmly packed
½ Cup Shortening
¼ Cup Milk or Apple Juice
1 Egg
2 Cups All-purpose Flour
1 Tsp. Soda
1 Tsp. Cinnamon
½ Tsp. Salt
½ Tsp. Cloves
½ Tsp. Nutmeg
1 Cup Peeled, Finely-chopped Apple (1 medium apple)
1 Cup Chopped Dates
1 Cup Chopped Nuts

Combine brown sugar, shortening, milk & egg in a large bowl. Beat until well blended. Measure flour and combine with remaining cookie ingredients; stir until well blended. Combine with shortening mixture and blend well. Drop by rounded teaspoonfuls, 2″ apart, on ungreased cookie sheets. Bake at 375°F. for 10 to 15 minutes, or until light golden brown. Cool.

Icing:
2 Tbs. Margarine or Butter, softened
2 Cups Confectioners' Sugar
Dash of Salt
½ Tsp. Vanilla
2 to 3 Tbs. Lemon Juice

Combine all icing ingredients in a small bowl; beat until light and fluffy. Frost the cooled cookies. Makes 48 to 60 cookies.

BILLY GOAT COOKIES

½ Cup Butter or Margarine
1 Cup Granulated Sugar (or use
    half granulated and half brown
    sugar)
2 Eggs
½ Cup Sour Cream
½ Tsp. Baking Soda
2 Tsp. Baking Powder
1 Tsp. Allspice or 1 Tsp.
    Almond Extract
1 Cup Chopped Walnuts
2 Cups Flour
1 Lb. Pitted Dates, chopped

Cream butter and sugar; add eggs and beat
well. Blend in sour cream. Sift dry ingredients together and add to the creamed mixture. Stir in nuts and dates and mix well.
Drop by teaspoonfuls onto greased cookie
sheets. Bake in 350°F. oven for 10 to 13
minutes, until browned. Drizzle confectioners' icing over the tops of cooled cookies,
if desired. Makes about 5 dozen.

LEMON YOGURT COOKIES

1½ Cups Sugar
1 Cup Shortening
1 Tbs. Grated Lemon Peel
2 Eggs
1 Cup Lemon Yogurt, or
    dairy sour cream
1 Tsp. Lemon Extract
3½ Cups All-purpose Flour
2 Tsp. Baking Powder
½ Tsp. Soda
½ Tsp. Salt
Sugar

Grease cookie sheets. In large bowl, cream
sugar, shortening and lemon peel until light
and fluffy. Add eggs; beat well. Add yogurt and lemon extract; mix well. Lightly
spoon flour into measuring cup; level off.
Stir flour, baking powder, soda and salt together and add to creamed mixture; blend
well. Drop by rounded teaspoonfuls 2"
apart on prepared cookie sheets; sprinkle
with sugar. Bake at 350°F. for 10 to 12
minutes, or until light golden brown around
the edges. Makes 72 cookies.

OLD-TIME RAISIN COOKIES

1½ Cups Brown Sugar, packed
¾ Cup Butter
3 Eggs
2½ Cups Flour
2 Tbs. Molasses
1 Tsp. Baking Soda
1 Cup Raisins
1 Cup Nutmeats

Cream the butter and sugar; add eggs and
mix well. To the molasses, add the soda
and combine with the first mixture. Add
the sifted flour; stir in raisins and nuts.
Drop from teaspoon onto a greased cookie
sheet. Bake 12 minutes at 350°F.

DATE-FILLED COOKIES

1 Cup Soft Shortening
2 Cups Brown Sugar, packed
2 Eggs
½ Cup Water or Buttermilk
1 Tsp. Vanilla
3½ Cups Sifted All-purpose Flour
½ Tsp. Salt
1 Tsp. Soda
1/8 Tsp. Cinnamon
Date Filling (recipe follows)

Preheat oven to 400°F. Mix shortening,
brown sugar and eggs thoroughly. Stir in
the water and vanilla. Sift together flour,
salt, soda and cinnamon and stir into the
shortening mixture. Drop with teaspoon
on ungreased baking sheet. Place ½ tsp.
Date Filling on dough; cover with another
½ tsp. dough. Bake until lightly browned,
10 to 12 minutes. Makes 5 to 6 dozen
cookies.

Date Filling:
2 Cups Dates, finely cut up
¾ Cup Sugar
¾ Cup Water
½ Cup Chopped Nuts, if
    desired

Cook dates, sugar and water together slowly,
stirring constantly, until thickened. Add the
nuts; cool.

JEWEL COOKIES

1½ Cups Sifted All-purpose Flour
1½ Tsp. Baking Powder
½ Tsp. Salt
4 Tbs. Butter or Margarine
¾ Cup Sugar
1 Egg, separated
¼ Tsp. Vanilla or Brandy Flavoring
2 Tbs. Milk
¼ Cup Mint Jelly
¼ Cup Peach Jelly
¼ Cup Red-Currant Jelly
Silver Candies

Measure flour, baking powder and salt into sifter. Cream butter or margarine and ½ cup sugar until fluffy in medium bowl; beat in egg yolk and vanilla or brandy flavoring. (Save remaining ¼ cup sugar and egg white for topping in last part of recipe.)

Sift in dry ingredients, a third at a time, adding alternately with milk; stir just until well blended. Chill for several hours, or until firm enough to roll easily. Roll out, a quarter at a time, to 1/8" thickness on a lightly-floured pastry cloth or board. Cut into ovals or rounds with a floured 2" cutter, then cut a small oval or circle in middle of half the cookies and lift out with tip of knife (save cut out part to re-roll and cut out along with trimmings).

Place whole ovals or rounds on greased cookie sheets; spoon about ½ teaspoonful of mint, peach, or red-currant jelly in middle of each. Top, sandwich style, with a cutout oval or round; press edges together lightly with a fork or thumb to seal. Re-roll trimmings; cut out more cookies, & fill. Beat egg white slightly in a cup; brush over cookies. Sprinkle lightly with sugar; decorate with silver candies. Bake in 400°F. oven for 8 minutes, or until golden. Cool on cookie sheets for about 5 minutes, then remove carefully. Cool on wire racks. Stack not more than two layers high, with wax paper or transparent wrap between, on tray or in open pan.

MAPLE-PEANUT COOKIES

1¾ Cups All-purpose Flour
½ Cup Brown Sugar, firmly packed
½ Tsp. Salt
½ Tsp. Soda
¼ Tsp. Baking Powder
½ Cup Shortening or Margarine
½ Cup Peanut Butter
1/3 Cup Maple Syrup
1 Egg

Heat oven to 350°F. Measure flour and combine with remaining ingredients in a large bowl; mix well. Shape into 1-inch balls. Place the balls 2" apart on an un-greased cookie sheet. Press with a fork dipped into sugar; make a criss-cross design. Bake for 12 to 15 minutes, or until light golden brown. Cool about 1 minute and then remove from cookie sheets. Makes about 44 cookies.

ALMOND MACAROONS

2 Egg Whites
1½ Cups Blanched Almonds,
   ground
1 Cup Sifted Confectioners' Sugar
¼ Tsp. Salt
1 Tsp. Almond Extract
½ Tsp. Vanilla Extract
Blanched Almonds

In large bowl of electric mixer, let egg whites warm to room temperature--about 1 hour. Preheat oven to 300°F. Lightly grease cookie sheets. In medium bowl, combine the ground almonds with the sugar, mixing well. Beat egg whites with salt until stiff peaks form when beaters are slowly raised. Using a wooden spoon, stir almond mixture into the beaten egg whites, along with the almond and vanilla extracts, just until well combined. Drop by slightly rounded teaspoonfuls, 2 inches apart, onto prepared cookie sheets. Top each with a blanched almond. Bake for 20 minutes, or until a light brown color. With spatula, remove to wire rack to cool completely. Store, covered, over-night. Makes 2½ to 3 dozen.

ACORN COOKIES

1 Cup Butter or Margarine
¾ Cup Brown Sugar, firmly packed
2½ Cups All-purpose Flour
½ Tsp. Baking Powder
1 Tsp. Vanilla
2 Egg
24 Vanilla Caramels
2 Tbs. Water
½ Cup Finely-chopped Pecans

In a medium saucepan, heat margarine and brown sugar until margarine melts; stir until smooth. Measure flour into a large bowl and add baking powder, vanilla, egg and brown sugar mixture. Blend well. Shape into 1" balls. Place, 2 inches apart, on an ungreased cookie sheet; pinch one end of the cookies. Bake at 350°F. for 12 to 15 minutes, or until light golden brown. Cool. In top of double boiler, melt caramels and stir in water. Dip flat end of cookie into caramel mixture, then into chopped pecans. Place on waxed paper, with flat side down. Makes 60 cookies.

CHERRY COCONUT SQUARES

1¼ Cups Unsifted All-purpose Flour
½ Cup Soft Butter or Margarine
3 Tbs. Confectioners' Sugar
2 Eggs, beaten
½ Cup Granulated Sugar
½ Tsp. Baking Powder
¼ Tsp. Salt
1 Tsp. Vanilla Extract
¾ Cup Chopped Nuts
½ Cup Flaked Coconut
½ Cup Diced, Well-drained Maraschino
    Cherries

With hands, mix 1 cup flour, butter and confectioners' sugar until well blended. Spread in a greased 8" square pan. Bake in moderate oven (350°F.), preheated, for about 20 minutes. Mix ¼ cup flour and remaining ingredients. Spread carefully over baked mixture. Bake for about 25 minutes. Cool and cut into squares. Makes 16.

DATE PINWHEELS

1 Lb. Pitted Dates
1 Cup White Sugar
1 Cup Water
1 Cup Shortening
2 Cups Brown Sugar, packed
3 Eggs, beaten
1 Tsp. Vanilla
½ Tsp. Salt
½ Tsp. Soda
4 Cups Flour

Cook dates, sugar and water for 10 minutes and cool. Cream shortening and brown sugar; add eggs and vanilla and beat till light and fluffy. Add sifted dry ingredients. Chill dough about 2 hours. Divide in half and roll each part into a rectangle. Spread date filling over dough and roll up like a jelly-roll. Chill overnight. Slice and bake in a 375°F. oven for about 10 minutes.

CRUMB RAISIN BARS

Filling:
2½ Cups Raisins
1 Cup Water
1 Cup Applesauce
1 Tsp. Lemon Juice
¼ Tsp. Ground Cinnamon
Nuts, if desired

Bar:
2 Cups Rolled Oats
1 Cup All-purpose Flour
½ Cup Sugar
½ Cup Coconut
¾ Cup Margarine or Butter

Preheat oven to 350°F. In a medium saucepan, heat raisins and water to boiling; simmer 15 minutes. Drain well and stir in the applesauce, lemon juice and cinnamon. Lightly spoon flour into measuring cup; level off. Combine flour with oats, sugar and coconut in a medium bowl. Cut in margarine until crumbly. Measure 2½ cups of crumbs and press into bottom of an ungreased 13x9" pan. Spread raisin mixture over the crumbs. Sprinkle with nuts, if desired. Sprinkle the remaining crumbs on top of raisin mixture; press lightly. Bake at 350°F. for 30 to 40 minutes, or until light golden brown. Cool completely; cut into bars. Makes 36 bars.

DEEP-FRIED WONTON with DATE FILLING

1 Lb. Ready-made Egg-roll Wrappers,
   cut into quarters
4 - 8 Oz. Pkgs. Pitted Dates
2 Cups Finely-chopped Walnuts
3 Tbs. Grated Fresh Orange Rind
3 to 5 Tbs. Orange Juice, or
   cold water, if needed
3 Cups Peanut Oil, or vegetable oil
   (not flavored)
Confectioners' Sugar

Prepare the filling ahead of time. With a cleaver or sharp knife, chop the pitted dates fine, adding a teaspoon or so of orange juice if they are too sticky to cut. Combine the dates, walnuts and grated rind in a small bowl. Knead the mixture with your fingers until it can be gathered into a ball. If the mixture is dry, moisten it with orange juice or water. Roll filling, a tablespoon at a time, between the palms of your hands to form cylinders 1" long and about 1/3" in diameter.

To assemble the wontons, place a cylinder of filling diagonally across each wrapper, just below the center. With a finger dipped in water, moisten the lower point of the wrapper. Fold the point over the filling & tuck it underneath. Roll up the resulting tube until all the dough surrounds the filling. Stick a finger into each end of the tube and give it a twist to seal the ends.

Pour the oil into a 12" wok or deep fryer and heat the oil until it reads 375° on a deep-frying thermometer. Deep-fry the wontons, 8 or 10 at a time, turning them occasionally, for 2 to 3 minutes, or until they are golden brown and crisp. As they are finished cooking, transfer them to paper towels to drain and cool. Just before serving, sprinkle the wontons with confectioners' sugar. Makes about 4 dozen.

MACADAMIA-PINEAPPLE COOKIES

1 Cup Shortening
1½ Cups Sugar
1 Egg
1 - 8½ Oz. Can Crushed Pineapple,
   with syrup
3½ Cups All-purpose Flour
1 Tsp. Soda
½ Tsp. Salt
¼ Tsp. Nutmeg
½ Cup Chopped Macadamia Nuts

Mix shortening, sugar and egg together well. Stir in pineapple, with the syrup, and the remaining ingredients. Drop by teaspoonfuls about 2 inches apart on an ungreased baking sheet. Bake 8 to 10 minutes, in a preheated 400°F. oven, or until golden brown. Makes 5 dozen cookies.

RAISIN-NUT PINWHEELS

1 Cup Butter or Margarine,
   softened
½ Cup Sugar
1 Egg
2 Cups Sifted All-purpose Flour
1 Tsp. Baking Powder
1 Cup Dairy Sour Cream
Raisin-Nut Filling (see
   recipe below)

Cream butter and sugar until light. Beat in egg. Add the sifted dry ingredients alternately with sour cream, beating until smooth. Chill overnight. Roll one fourth of dough at a time on well-floured board or pastry cloth to form a rectangle 10x6". Dough will be soft. Keep in refrigerator until ready to use. Spread with one fourth of Raisin-Nut Filling and roll up from 10" side. Cut into 12 pieces and put 3 inches apart on greased cookie sheet. Bake in preheated moderate oven (350°F.) for about 15 minutes. Repeat until all ingredients are used. Makes 4 dozen cookies.

Raisin-Nut Filling: Mix 1 cup chopped nuts, ¼ cup raisins, ¾ cup orange marmalade, ¼ cup sugar, and 1 teaspoon ground cinnamon.

ORANGE-SLICE COOKIES

2 Cups Firmly-packed Brown Sugar
1 Cup Shortening
3 Eggs
3 Cups Flour
1 Tsp. Soda
1 Tsp. Cream of Tartar
2 Cups Finely-cut Candy Orange
   Slices (about 16 slices)
1 Cup Chopped Walnuts
1 Tsp. Vanilla

Cream the shortening and sugar; add eggs
and beat well. Sift dry ingredients together. Blend into sugar mixture. Add
orange slices, nuts and vanilla; blend well.
Drop by teaspoonfuls onto cookie sheets.
Bake 12 to 15 minutes in 350°F. oven.
Makes about 7 dozen cookies.

ORANGE OATMEAL COOKIES

2 Cups All-purpose Flour
1 Tsp. Baking Soda
¾ Tsp. Salt
½ Tsp. Ground Cinnamon
1/8 Tsp. Allspice
1 Cup Shortening
½ Cup Granulated Sugar
½ Cup Light Brown Sugar,
   firmly packed
2 Eggs
2 Cups Quick Cooking Rolled Oats
1/3 Cup Orange Juice
1 Cup Seedless Raisins, washed
   and dried
½ Cup Coarsely Cut Nuts
2 Tsp. Grated Orange Rind

Sift flour, measure and resift 3 times with
soda, salt and spices. Cream shortening until smooth and soft. Add both sugars
gradually and beat until thoroughly blended.
Add eggs one at a time and beat until very
light. Stir in the oats; add flour mixture &
orange juice alternately in 2 or 3 portions
and beat well after each addition. Stir in
the raisins, nuts and rind. Drop by teaspoonfuls onto greased baking sheets and bake in
a 350°F. oven for 10 to 12 minutes. Makes
8 dozen small cookies.

LEMON/COCONUT SQUARES

Cookie Dough:
1½ Cups Sifted Flour
½ Cup Brown Sugar, firmly packed
½ Cup Butter or Margarine

Filling:
2 Eggs, beaten
1 Cup Brown Sugar, firmly packed
1½ Cups Flaked or Shredded Coconut
1 Cup Chopped Nuts
2 Tbs. Flour
½ Tsp. Baking Powder
¼ Tsp. Salt
½ Tsp. Vanilla

Frosting:
1 Cup Confectioners' Sugar
1 Tbs. Melted Butter or Margarine
Juice of 1 Lemon

Mix together cookie-dough ingredients; pat
down well in a buttered 13x9x2" pan. Bake
in a very slow oven, 275°F., for 10 minutes.

To make the filling, combine eggs, sugar,
coconut, nuts, flour, baking powder, salt
and vanilla. Spread on top of baked mixture. Bake in a 350°F. oven for 20 min.

While still warm, spread with frosting that
is made by combining confectioners' sugar,
melted butter and lemon juice. Cool the
bars slightly, then cut into 2" squares.
Complete cooling on racks. Makes about
24 squares.

BUTTER COOKIES

1-1/3 Cups Sugar
1 Cup Butter
3 Eggs
1 Tsp. Vanilla
3 Cups Flour
1 Tsp. Soda
2 Tsp. Cream of Tartar
1 Tsp. Salt

Cream together the butter and shortening.
Add eggs and vanilla and beat well. Stir
in the sifted dry ingredients to make a
soft dough. Roll out on a well-floured
board. Cut into desired shapes and bake
in 350°F. oven until delicately browned.

SNAPPY TURTLES

½ Cup Brown Sugar, firmly packed
½ Cup Margarine or Butter,
  softened
¼ Tsp. Vanilla
1/8 Tsp. Maple Flavoring (optional)
2 Eggs (reserve 1 white)
1½ Cups All-purpose Flour
¼ Tsp. Salt
¼ Tsp. Soda
½ to 2 Cups Split Pecan Halves

Icing:
1/3 Cup Semi-sweet Chocolate
  Chips
3 Tbs. Milk
1 Tbs. Margarine or Butter
1 Cup Powdered Sugar

In a medium bowl, blend brown sugar and ½ cup margarine. Add vanilla, maple flavoring, egg and egg yolk; beat well. Measure flour and combine with salt and soda; stir into egg mixture by hand, blending thoroughly. Dough will be soft; chill for easier handling.

Heat oven to 350°F. Grease cookie sheets. Arrange pecan pieces in groups of 3 or 5 on prepared cookie sheets to resemble head & legs of turtle. Beat reserved egg white. Shape rounded teaspoonfuls of dough into balls; dip bottoms into white of egg and press lightly onto nuts. Tips of nuts should show after baking. Bake at 350°F. for 10 to 12 minutes, or until golden brown around edges. Do not overbake.

In small saucepan, melt chocolate chips, milk and 1 tablespoon of margarine over low heat, stir until smooth. Remove from heat and stir in powdered sugar. If too thin, add powdered sugar until of desired consistency. Generously frost cooled cookies. Makes 36 to 48 cookies.

COCONUT CRISPS

6 Cups Rice Cereal, toasted
  lightly in oven
1 Cup Chopped Walnuts
¾ Cup Butter or Margarine
1¼ Cups Sugar
2 Tbs. Milk
¼ Tsp. Salt
1 Cup Chopped Dates
1 Tbs. Vanilla
2 Tbs. Lemon Juice
1 - 3½ Oz. Can Flaked Coconut

Combine the cereal and the walnuts in a greased 13x9x2" pan. Combine butter, sugar, milk, salt and dates. Cook to the soft ball stage (240°F. on candy thermometer); stir occasionally. Remove from heat; add vanilla and lemon juice. Pour hot syrup over the cereal mixture and stir lightly to coat cereal. Spread mixture evenly in the pan. Sprinkle coconut over the top and press firmly. Let set 4 hours, or longer. When firm, cut into bars. Makes 30.

CHILDREN'S FAVORITE COOKIES

2¼ Cups All-purpose Flour
½ Cup Sugar
½ Cup Brown Sugar, firmly packed
½ Tsp. Soda
½ Tsp. Salt
½ Tsp. Cinnamon
¼ Tsp. Nutmeg
1 Cup Shortening
½ Cup Peanut Butter
¼ Cup Applesauce
½ Tsp. Vanilla
1 Egg
1 Cup Rolled Oats
3 Tbs. Grape Jelly

In a large bowl, combine all ingredients except for 1 cup of flour, the oats and the jelly. Mix well. Stir in reserved 1 cup of flour and the oats. Shape dough into 1" balls; place 2" apart on ungreased cookie sheets. Flatten in a crisscross pattern with a fork dipped in sugar. Place 1/8 tsp. of jelly on center of each cookie. Bake in preheated 350°F. oven for 12 to 14 minutes, or until golden brown. Makes 60 cookies.

MINCEMEAT/CHEESE COOKIES

1 Cup Butter or Margarine
2 Cups Grated Cheddar Cheese
 (½ lb.)
2 Cups Sifted Flour
1 - 9 Oz. Pkg. Prepared Mincemeat
½ Cup Water

Cream butter until light; add cheese (at
room temperature) and cream until well
blended. Stir in flour; mix well and chill.
Cook mincemeat and water until slightly
thickened; set aside to cool. Roll dough
1/8" thick on lightly-floured surface; cut
into 2" circles. Put half of circles about
1" apart on lightly-greased baking sheet.
Place 1 tsp. cooled mincemeat mixture in
center of each cookie on baking sheet.
Top each with another circle of dough;
press edges with fork to seal. Prick the
cookies on top in several places with the
tines of a kitchen fork. Bake in moderate oven, 350°F., for 15 minutes, or
until lightly browned. Remove cookies
to racks to cool. Makes 3½ dozen.

COCONUT COOKIE SNOWBALLS

1 Cup Soft Butter or Margarine
2 Cups Granulated Sugar
2 Eggs
1 Tsp. Vanilla Extract
5 Cups Sifted All-purpose Flour
1 Tsp. Baking Soda
2 Tsp. Baking Powder
½ Tsp. Salt
¾ Cup Dairy Sour Cream
1 Cup Flaked Coconut
Colored Sugar

Cream butter and granulated sugar until
light. Add eggs and vanilla and beat well.
Add sifted dry ingredients, sour cream &
coconut; mix well. Chill for several hours.
Shape into 1" balls and sprinkle with the
colored sugar. Put on ungreased cookie
sheets and bake in preheated 375°F.
oven for about 10 minutes. Makes about
6 dozen.

RIBBON AND CHECKERBOARD COOKIES

1 - 1 Oz. Square Unsweetened
 Chocolate, melted
2½ Cups All-purpose Flour
¾ Tsp. Baking Powder (Double-Action)
½ Tsp. Salt
2/3 Cup Butter (or half butter
 and half shortening)
1 Cup Sugar
2 Eggs, well beaten
1 Tsp. Vanilla

Put chocolate into a custard cup and set in
hot, not boiling, water to melt. Sift flour,
measure and resift with baking powder and
salt. Cream butter, blend in sugar thoroughly. Add eggs and beat until smooth &
fluffy. Stir in vanilla. Add flour mixture
in 4 portions and stir until smooth. Divide
dough into two portions and mix the cooled
melted chocolate into one portion, kneading
with hands or back of a spoon until well
blended. Line a small loaf pan or refrigerator tray with wax paper, then pack half
the chocolate dough into tray, pressing
down with pancake turner to obtain a uniform layer. Cover with half of the plain
dough, then add another layer of chocolate
and another layer of plain. Keep layers
uniform in thickness and smooth. Cover
with wax paper and chill overnight.

Turn layered loaf out onto wax paper on a
cutting board; slice with a very sharp knife.
To make checkerboard cookies, cut these
slices ¼" thick, and lay four together so
that, as viewed from the end, each chocolate
strip lies above a white strip of dough. If
the dough softens from handling, wrap these
smaller loaves in wax paper and again chill.
Slice thinly and uniformly; place on a
greased baking sheet. Bake in 375°F. oven
for 8 to 10 minutes, or until lightly browned.
Use spatula to lift cookies to racks to cool.
Makes about 60 cookies, depending on size.

SWEET POTATO COOKIES

¼ Cup Milk
2 Cups Sifted Flour
½ Tsp. Baking Soda
1 Tsp. Baking Powder
½ Tsp. Salt
½ Cup Butter
¼ Cup Sugar
1 Egg
1 Tsp. Grated Lemon Rind
½ Cup Honey
1 Cup Grated, Raw Sweet Potato

Combine sugar and butter in a bowl and beat until fluffy. Blend in egg, honey, sweet potato and lemon rind. Sift together flour, baking soda, baking powder and salt. Blend in butter mixture & milk. Drop from a teaspoon 2 inches apart on greased cookie sheets. Prick holes in the cookies with a toothpick. Bake at 350°F. for 15 to 20 minutes, until brown. Place cookie sheets on a rack and let stand for 5 minutes. Remove cookies carefully and cool on rack. Makes 3 dozen.

CREAM CHEESE COOKIES

¾ Cup Butter
1 - 3 Oz. Pkg. Cream Cheese
1 Cup Sifted Confectioners' Sugar
1 Tbs. Lemon Juice
1 Tsp. Vanilla
2 Tsp. Grated Lemon Peel
2 Cups Sifted Cake Flour
1 Cup Chopped Pecans
Sifted Confectioners' Sugar

Cream butter and cream cheese until light and fluffy. Gradually add 1 cup confectioners' sugar, beating thoroughly. Stir in the lemon juice, vanilla and lemon peel. Add flour and mix well; stir in nuts.

Drop by scant teaspoonfuls about 2" apart on ungreased cookie sheet. Bake in slow oven (300°F.) for about 25 minutes. The cookies should be set but not brown. While the cookies are still hot, roll in sifted confectioners' sugar. Cool on racks. Makes 4 dozen.

GINGERSNAPS

1 Cup Granulated Sugar
½ Cup Butter or Margarine
1 Egg, beaten
¼ Cup Molasses
2 Cups All-purpose Flour
Pinch of Salt
1 Tsp. Soda
1 Tsp. Ginger
1 Tsp. Cinnamon
½ Tsp. Cloves
1 Tbs. Vinegar

Cream the butter and sugar; add the egg and molasses and beat well. Sift dry ingredients together and add to the creamed mixture; add vinegar and blend well. Roll in small balls and place on ungreased cookie sheet. Bake at 375°F. for 12 to 15 minutes.

GINGER OATMEAL COOKIES

¾ Cup Butter or Margarine
1 Cup Sugar
1 Egg
¼ Cup Light Molasses
1½ Cups All-purpose Flour, unsifted
2 Tsp. Soda
½ Tsp. Salt
1 Tsp. Ground Cinnamon
¾ Tsp. Ground Cloves
¾ Tsp. Ground Ginger
2 Cups Regular or Quick-cooking Rolled Oats

In a bowl, cream together the butter and sugar; beat in the egg and molasses until smooth. Stir together the flour, soda, salt, cinnamon, cloves and ginger. Stir into the butter mixture until blended. Stir in the rolled oats. Drop by level tablespoonfuls on lightly greased cooky sheets, placing dough about 3 inches apart. Bake in a 350° F. oven for about 8 minutes, or until the cookies are browned. Cool for about 1 minute on the pan, then remove and cool completely on wire racks. Makes about 4 dozen.

RASPBERRY DELIGHTS

1¼ Cups Sifted All-purpose Flour
½ Tsp. Salt
1½ Cups Sugar (approximately)
1 Tsp. Baking Powder
½ Cup Butter
1 Egg Yolk
2 Tbs. Brandy or Milk
¾ Cup Thick Raspberry Jam
2 Eggs
2 Tsp. Vanilla Extract
6 Tbs. Melted Butter
2½ Cups Flaked Coconut

Sift flour with salt, 1 teaspoon sugar, and baking powder. Blend in the butter. Add egg yolk and brandy and mix. Pat into a buttered pan (11x7x2"). Spread with the raspberry jam. Beat eggs until thick and lemon colored; beat in 1½ cups sugar, vanilla and melted butter. Add coconut. Spoon over jam. Bake in preheated oven (350°F) for 35 minutes. Cool and cut into 1-inch squares. Makes 77.

SPICY OATMEAL SQUARES

1¾ Cups Sifted All-purpose Flour
1½ Tsp. Baking Soda
¾ Tsp. Ground Cinnamon
¼ Tsp. Ground Cloves
¼ Tsp. Ground Nutmeg
½ Cup Butter or Margarine
1 Cup Light Brown Sugar, firmly
   packed
2 Eggs
1 Tsp. Vanilla
1 Cup Applesauce
1½ Cups Quick-cooking Rolled Oats
1 - 8 Oz. Pkg. Pitted Dates,
   finely chopped
½ Cup Chopped Walnuts
Citrus Glaze (see recipe below)

Sift flour, soda, cinnamon, cloves and nutmeg into a bowl. In a large bowl, cream butter or margarine with brown sugar until fluffy. Beat in eggs, one at a time, and vanilla. Stir in flour mixture, half at a time, alternately with applesauce. Stir just until blended. Stir in rolled oats, dates and walnuts. Spoon into a greased pan, 13x9x2". Level top of dough with back of spoon.

Bake in 375°F. oven for 35 minutes, or until it tests done. Cool completely on a wire rack, in the pan. Drizzle citrus glaze over top; let stand until firm. Cut into serving-size squares. Makes 24 squares.

Citrus Glaze: Blend ½ cup confectioners' sugar with 2 teaspoons of water and 2 teaspoons of lemon juice until smooth.

WALNUT FROSTIES

1 Cup Sifted All-purpose Flour
2 Tbs. Confectioners' Sugar
½ Cup Butter or Margarine

Combine flour and sugar in medium-size bowl. Cream in butter or margarine until well-blended. Pat firmly and evenly into the bottom of an ungreased 9" square baking pan. Bake in moderate oven (350° F.) for 10 minutes; remove and let cool on wire rack for 5 minutes. Leave oven on.

2 Eggs
1 Cup Firmly-packed Brown Sugar
2 Tbs. All-purpose Flour
½ Tsp. Baking Powder
1/8 Tsp. Salt
1 Cup Coarsely-chopped Walnuts
½ Cup Flaked Coconut
Orange Butter Cream (see
   recipe below)

Beat eggs slightly in a medium bowl; stir in brown sugar until well blended, then add the flour, baking powder and salt. Fold in walnuts and coconut; pour over crust. Bake 25 minutes longer, or until top is firm. Cool completely in pan. Frost with orange butter cream. Cut into 36 tiny squares (these are very rich). Top each with a walnut half, if you wish.

Orange Butter Cream:
2 Tbs. Melted Butter or Margarine
1½ Tsp. Orange Juice
1¼ Cups Sifted Confectioners' Sugar
1½ Tsp. Grated Orange Rind

Combine first three ingredients in a small bowl and beat until smooth and creamy. Stir in grated orange rind. Makes about ½ cup.

PEANUT-BUTTER BARS

1 Cup Crunchy Peanut Butter
2/3 Cup Butter or Margarine,
    softened
1 Tsp. Vanilla
2 Cups Light Brown Sugar, firmly
    packed
3 Eggs
1 Cup Sifted All-purpose Flour
½ Tsp. Salt
¾ Cup Sifted Confectioners' Sugar
2 Tsp. Water
¼ Cup Semisweet Chocolate Pieces
1 Tsp. Vegetable Shortening

Combine peanut butter, butter or margarine
and vanilla in a large bowl; beat with electric
beater until well-blended; beat in sugar until
light and fluffy. Beat in eggs, one at a time.
Stir in flour and salt just until well-blended.
Spread batter in a greased 13x9x2" baking
pan. Bake in moderate oven (350°F.) for
35 minutes, or until center springs back when
lightly touched with fingertip. Remove pan
from oven to wire rack and cool slightly.
Combine confectioners' sugar with water in
a small bowl and stir until smooth. Drizzle
from a spoon over still-warm cookies in pan.

Melt chocolate with shortening over simmering water in top of double boiler. Drizzle
over the white glaze for a black and white
pattern. When cool, cut into 36 rectangles.
using a sharp knife. Carefully lift out of pan
with spatula.

SAND TARTS

½ Cup Shortening
1 Cup Sugar
1 Egg
1¾ Cups Flour
2 Tsp. Baking Powder
¼ Tsp. Cinnamon
Nuts or Raisins

Cream shortening; add sugar slowly, then
the unbeaten egg. Sift in the flour and
baking powder, and add more flour if necessary to make a stiff dough. Roll out
very thin. Cut with a doughnut cutter.
Sprinkle with sugar and cinnamon, and,
if desired, decorate with nuts and fruit.
Bake in a 350°F. oven for 10 to 12 min.

NO-BAKE APRICOT
CHOCOLATE COOKIES

1 - 6 Oz. Can Undiluted
    Evaporated Milk
4 Squares Semi-sweet Chocolate
½ Tsp. Vanilla
2½ Cups Crushed Vanilla Wafers
½ Cup Sifted Confectioners' Sugar
½ Cup Chopped Dried Apricots
Chopped Pecans

Combine evaporated milk and semi-sweet
chocolate in a saucepan; cook, stirring
constantly, until smooth. Remove from
heat and stir in the vanilla. Blend in the
crushed vanilla wafers, sugar and dried apricots. Allow to cool until firm enough to
shape (about 1 hr. at room temperature).
Form into 1" balls and roll in chopped
pecans. Makes 4 dozen cookies.

For Raisin Smoothies, follow above recipe
but substitute ½ cup chopped raisins and
¼ cup chopped pecans for the chopped
dried apricots.

RAISIN GRIDDLE COOKIES

3½ Cups Sifted Flour
1 Cup Sugar
1½ Tsp. Baking Powder
1 Tsp. Salt
½ Tsp. Baking Soda
1 Tsp. Ground Nutmeg
1 Cup Shortening
1 Egg
½ Cup Milk
1¼ Cups Raisins

Sift dry ingredients together into a bowl.
Cut in shortening until mixture is like
cornmeal. Beat egg; add milk and blend.
Add egg mixture and raisins to the flour
mixture. Stir until all the ingredients are
moistened and dough holds together. Roll
on lightly-floured board to ¼" thickness.
Cut with a 2" round cutter. Heat griddle
until a few drops of water dance on it
(do not overheat). Oil griddle lightly and
place cookies on it. As the bottoms of
the cookies brown, the tops become puffy.
Turn and brown on other side. Serve warm.
Makes about 4 dozen.

SPICY CHOCOLATE STICKS

4 Eggs
2 Cups Brown Sugar, firmly packed
1 Tsp. Ground Cinnamon
¼ Tsp. Ground Allspice
¼ Tsp. Ground Cloves
1 - 4 Oz. Pkg. Sweet Cooking Chocolate,
  grated fine
1 Tsp. Grated Lemon Rind
3 Cups Sifted All-purpose Flour
1 Tsp. Baking Powder
1 Cup Chopped Blanched Almonds
¼ Cup Finely-chopped Candied Orange
  or Lemon Peel

Beat eggs and sugar until light. Stir in the
spices, chocolate and lemon rind. Sift the
flour and baking powder over almonds and
candied peel and coat fruit thoroughly.
Stir into egg mixture. If dough is too soft
to roll out, add a little more flour, 1 tablespoon at a time. Roll out dough on lightly
floured board to ¼" thickness. Cut into
sticks 1x3". Bake on greased cookie sheet
in preheated 350°F. oven for 10 to 12
minutes. Makes about 4½ dozen.

APPLE OATMEAL COOKIES

½ Cup Butter or Margarine, softened
2/3 Cup Sugar
2 Eggs
1 Cup Sifted All-purpose Flour
1 Tsp. Baking Powder
1 Tsp. Ground Cinnamon
½ Tsp. Ground Nutmeg
½ Tsp. Salt
1 Cup Quick-cooking Rolled Oats
1 Cup Chopped Well-drained Canned
  Apples
1 Cup Coarsely-chopped Walnuts

Cream butter and sugar until light. Add
eggs, one at a time, beating well after
each addition. Sift flour, baking powder,
spices and salt, and add to egg mixture.
Stir in oats and apples and beat well.
Fold in nuts. Drop by teaspoon onto a
greased cookie sheet. Bake in preheated
oven (350°F.) for about 15 minutes.
Makes about 3½ dozen cookies.

POTATO CHIP COOKIES

1 Cup Butter or Margarine
½ Cup Sugar
1 Tsp. Vanilla
2 Cups Sifted Flour
½ Cup Crushed Potato Chips
½ Cup Chopped Pecans

Beat butter, sugar and vanilla until light
and fluffy. Add flour, potato chips and
nuts; mix well. Drop by scant teaspoonfuls 2" apart onto an ungreased cookie
sheet. Flatten by pressing with bottom
of a glass, greased and dipped in sugar,
as needed. Bake in 350°F. oven for 10
to 11 minutes. Remove to racks to cool.
Makes about 5 dozen cookies.

GRAHAM CRACKERS

2 Cups Whole Wheat Flour
1 Cup All-purpose Flour
1 Tsp. Baking Powder
½ Tsp. Baking Soda
½ Cup Shortening
¾ Cup Packed Brown Sugar
1/3 Cup Honey
1 Tsp. Vanilla
½ Cup Milk
3 Tbs. Granulated Sugar
1 Tsp. Ground Cinnamon

Stir together whole wheat flour, all-purpose
flour, baking powder, baking soda, and ¼
tsp. salt. Cream together shortening and
brown sugar until light. Beat in honey &
vanilla until fluffy. Add flour mixture alternately with milk to creamed mixture,
beating well after each addition. Chill
dough several hours or overnight. Divide
chilled mixture into quarters. On a well-
floured surface roll each quarter to a 15x5"
rectangle. Cut rectangle crosswise into 6
small rectangles measuring 5x2½". Place
on ungreased baking sheet. Mark a line
across center of each small rectangle with
tines of fork and score a pattern of holes
on squares with fork tines. Combine the
granulated sugar and ground cinnamon;
sprinkle over crackers. Bake at 350°F for
13 to 15 minutes. Remove from baking
sheet immediately. Makes 24 crackers.

SCANDINAVIAN VANILLA COOKIES

1 Cup Butter
½ Cup Confectioners' Sugar
1 Egg Yolk
2½ Cups Flour
2 Tsp. Vanilla Extract
Confectioners' Sugar

Blend butter and sugar together until fluffy. Add egg yolk and flour. Add vanilla and mix thoroughly. Using a teaspoon, drop cookies onto greased cookie sheets. Bake at 350°F. for 8 minutes. Do not let the cookies brown. Remove sheets to a rack & let stand for a couple of minutes. Remove cookies carefully with spatula. When cold, sprinkle tops of cookies with confectioners' sugar. Makes 4 dozen.

CARAMEL APPLE COOKIES

½ Cup Shortening
1-1/3 Cups Brown Sugar, firmly
  packed
1 Egg
2½ Cups Sifted All-purpose Flour
1 Tsp. Baking Soda
½ Tsp. Salt
1 Tsp. Ground Cinnamon
1 Tsp. Ground Cloves
½ Tsp. Ground Nutmeg
1 Cup Grated Peeled Apples
1 Cup Light Raisins
½ Cup Apple Juice
1 Cup Chopped Walnuts
Caramel Icing

Cream shortening, sugar and egg until light and fluffy. Sift together dry ingredients & add to creamed mixture. When well blended, stir in remaining ingredients, except icing. Drop by level tablespoonfuls 3" apart onto greased baking sheet. Bake in 350°F. oven for 12 minutes, or until lightly browned. Remove cookies and cool on racks. When cool, spread with Caramel Icing. Makes about 4 dozen cookies.

Caramel Icing:
¼ Cup Butter
¼ Cup Brown Sugar, firmly packed
1½ Cups Sifted Confectioners'
  Sugar
¼ Tsp. Salt
2½ Tbs. Dairy Half-and-Half or
  Light Cream

Combine butter and brown sugar in saucepan; cook until sugar dissolves, about 3 minutes. Add 1½ cups sifted confectioners' sugar, the salt and half-and-half; beat until smooth. (If frosting becomes too thick when spreading on cookies, thin it by adding a little more cream.)

SWEDISH JELLY COOKIES

½ Cup Butter, at room temperature
1/3 Cup Sugar
1 Egg, separated
1¼ Cups Sifted All-purpose Flour
¼ Tsp. Salt
¼ Cup Finely-chopped Blanched
  Almonds
¼ Cup Sugar
Currant Jelly

Cream butter and gradually add the sugar. Beat in egg yolk, flour and salt. Blend thoroughly. On floured surface, roll out to about ¼" thickness. The dough must be rolled thin. Divide dough. Cut one portion of the dough with a 2-1/3" round cookie cutter. Cut the other portion of dough with a round or scalloped 2" cookie cutter. Remove center of the 2" cookies with a thimble. Beat egg white slightly. Combine almonds and sugar. Brush each 2" cookie (those with the hole) with egg white and sprinkle with almond-sugar mixture. Place on buttered and floured cookie sheets almond side up. Bake all cookies in preheated 375° F. oven for 6 to 8 minutes. Do not let the cookies brown. Cool cookies on racks. Place about ½ teaspoon currant jelly on bigger cookie and top with a smaller cookie, almond side up. The jelly should appear in the hole in the center of the top cookie. Makes about 12 cookies.

BUTTERMILK BROWNIES

½ Cup Margarine
¼ Cup Cocoa
½ Cup Shortening
2 Cups Flour
2 Cups Granulated Sugar
¼ Tsp. Salt
½ Cup Buttermilk
2 Eggs, beaten
1 Tsp. Soda
1 Tsp. Vanilla Extract

Combine margarine, 1 cup water, cocoa and shortening in a saucepan. Heat, stirring constantly, until margarine and shortening are melted. Combine remaining ingredients. Pour hot mixture over the flour mixture & mix well. Pour into a greased and floured 13x18" cookie sheet. Bake in preheated 350°F. oven for 20 minutes. Makes 48 servings.

CALIFORNIA FIG COOKIES

1 Cup Chopped Golden or
  Black Figs (½ lb.)
1/3 Cup Water
1 Cup Butter or Margarine
½ Cup Sugar
½ Cup Brown Sugar, firmly
  packed
1 Egg
1 Tsp. Vanilla
2 Cups Sifted Flour
2 Tsp. Baking Powder
½ Tsp. Salt
Walnut or Pecan Halves

Cook figs with water, stirring frequently, until thickened, about 5 minutes. Set aside to cool.

Beat butter with both sugars until light and fluffy. Beat in egg and vanilla to blend well. Sift together flour, baking powder and salt. Mix into creamed mixture. Stir in cooled figs. Drop by teaspoonfuls about 2" apart onto lightly-greased cookie sheets. Press a walnut half on top of each cookie. Bake in moderate oven, 375°F., for 10 to 12 min., until lightly browned. Remove cookies to a rack to cool. Makes 4 dozen.

CHOCOLATE MERINGUES

3 Egg Whites
½ Tsp. Salt
1/8 Tsp. Cream of Tartar
1 Cup Sugar
1 Cup Very finely-chopped Blanched
  Almonds
4 Oz. Unsweetened Chocolate, (4
  squares), grated
1 Can Milk Chocolate Creamy-type
  Frosting
Candied Cherries (green), slivered

Beat egg whites with salt and cream of tartar until foamy-white and double in volume. Use a large bowl. Sprinkle in sugar, 1 tbs. at a time, beating all the time, until sugar completely dissolves and meringue stands in firm peaks. Gently fold in almonds and chocolate. Drop by teaspoonfuls, one inch apart, on lightly greased large cookie sheets. Bake in a very slow oven (275°F.) for 25 minutes, or until firmly set. Remove carefully from cookie sheets to wire racks, cool completely. Decorate each meringue with a swirl of frosting and a sliver of green cherry. Makes 6 dozen.

SESAME SEED COOKIES

4 Cups Sifted All-purpose Flour
2 Tsp. Baking Powder
½ Tsp. Salt
1 Cup Butter, at room temperature
1¾ Cups Granulated Sugar
2 Eggs
3 Tbs. Toasted Sesame Seeds
¼ Cup Water

Sift together the flour, baking powder and salt. Cream the butter and sugar together; beat in the eggs and stir in the sesame seeds. Add the flour mixture alternately with the water. Chill dough 3 to 4 hours. Drop the dough from a teaspoon onto ungreased cookie sheets. Flatten to 1/16" thickness with a glass covered with a damp cloth. Bake until the cookies are lightly browned around the edges, about 10 minutes. Bake in a preheated 375°F. oven. Makes 6 dozen cookies.

BROWNIES WITH CANDY TOPPING

2 Cups Sugar
2 Eggs
4 Squares Unsweetened Chocolate
½ Cup Butter or Margarine
½ Cup Flour
2 Tsp. Vanilla
½ Cup Chopped Walnuts
1 Egg, beaten
2 Tbs. Light Cream
2 Tbs. Butter or Margarine

Combine 1 cup sugar and 2 eggs; beat well. Melt 2 squares of chocolate with ½ cup butter; add to egg mixture. Blend in flour, 1 teaspoon of vanilla and the nuts. Spread in a greased 8" square pan. Bake in 350°F. oven for 25 to 35 minutes; cool on a rack.

Combine remaining 1 cup of sugar, the beaten egg, cream, 2 squares of chocolate, 2 tbs. butter or margarine and 1 tsp. vanilla. Bring to a boil, stirring constantly. Remove from heat and stir until of spreading consistency. Spread over cooled brownies. Cut into 2" squares. Makes 16.

APPLESAUCE-FUDGE SQUARES

2 Squares Unsweetened Chocolate
½ Cup Butter
½ Cup Sweetened Applesauce
2 Eggs, beaten
1 Cup Brown Sugar, firmly packed
1 Tsp. Vanilla
1 Cup Sifted Flour
½ Tsp. Baking Powder
¼ Tsp. Baking Soda
¼ Tsp. Salt
½ Cup Chopped Walnuts

Melt chocolate and butter together over low heat. Mix applesauce, eggs, sugar & vanilla together. Sift the dry ingredients into applesauce mixture; stir until blended. Add the chocolate and mix well. Pour into a greased 9" square pan. Sprinkle with walnuts. Bake in 350°F. oven for 30 minutes. Cut into 2¼" squares; cool in pan on rack. Makes 16.

BREAKFAST BARS

½ Cup Butter or Margarine
3 Cups Miniature Marshmallows
½ Cup Peanut Butter
½ Cup Nonfat Dry Milk
¼ Cup Orange-flavored Instant
   Breakfast Drink
1 Cup Raisins
4 Cups O-shaped Puffed Oat Cereal

In large saucepan, melt butter and marshmallows over low heat, stirring constantly. Stir in peanut butter until melted. Mix in milk and breakfast drink. Remove from heat; fold in raisins and cereal, stirring until evenly coated. With buttered hands, pat evenly into buttered 9x9x2" baking pan. Cool and cut into bars, about 3x1". Makes 24 bars.

MOLASSES HERMITS

¾ Cup Soft Butter or Margarine
1½ Cups Light Brown Sugar, packed
½ Cup Molasses
3 Eggs
4 Cups Sifted Cake Flour
1 Tsp. Salt
1 Tsp. Cinnamon
1 Tsp. Ground Nutmeg
½ Tsp. Cloves
½ Tsp. Allspice
½ Tsp. Mace
¼ Cup Strong Coffee
1 Cup Chopped Nuts
1 Cup Raisins
1 Cup Currants
Confectioners' Sugar

Cream butter and sugar until light. Beat in molasses. Add eggs, one at a time, beating thoroughly after each addition. Sift flour, salt and spices and add to first mixture alternately with coffee, beating until smooth. Fold in nuts & fruit; pour into a 15x10x1" pan which has been lined with wax paper. Bake in preheated 350°F. oven for about 20 minutes. Turn out on rack and peel off paper. Slip onto cutting board and cut into 35 bars about 3" x 1½". Sprinkle with confectioners' sugar.

DATE-MARMALADE SQUARES

2 Cups All-purpose Flour
½ Tsp. Salt
½ Cup Soft Butter
¾ Cup Granulated Sugar
1 Egg
¼ Cup Milk
½ Cup Orange Marmalade
¼ Cup Milk
2 Eggs, beaten
½ Cup Granulated Sugar
1½ Cups Chopped Dates
1½ Cups Raisins
1 Cup Chopped Nuts

Grease two 8" square cake pans. Blend together the flour and salt. Cream butter and granulated sugar together; beat in the egg and milk. Blend in dry ingredients. Press dough into prepared pans. Bake in preheated 350°F. oven for 15 minutes.

Mix together the marmalade, ¼ cup milk and beaten eggs. Combine and stir in the granulated sugar, dates, raisins and nuts. Spread over baked pastry, about 2 cups of mixture on each. Return to oven and continue baking for 25 minutes, or until set. Decorate with bits of red and green glace' cherries and nuts. Makes 48 squares.

CHINESE ALMOND COOKIES

1 Cup Shortening
1 Cup Sugar
1 Egg
1 Tsp. Almond Extract
2½ Cups Flour
1 Tsp. Baking Powder
½ Tsp. Salt
1 Tbs. Water
Whole Blanched Almonds

Cream shortening; gradually add sugar & beat until light and fluffy. Beat in egg and almond extract. Gradually add sifted dry ingredients and water. Chill the dough for about 2 hours. Form into balls 1" in diameter. Place on baking sheet and press down to ¼" thickness. Press almond in center of each. Bake at 350°F. for 12 to 15 minutes.

PEANUT CHEWS

9 Cups Corn Flakes
1½ Cups Sugar
¼ Tsp. Salt
¾ Cup Light Corn Syrup
¼ Cup Butter or Margarine
¾ Cup Water
2 Tsp. Vanilla
½ Cup Crunchy Peanut Butter

Put the corn flakes in a large bowl. Combine the sugar, salt, syrup, butter and water. Bring to a boil; reduce heat and cook to hard ball stage (250°F. on candy thermometer). Be careful not to overcook.

Remove from heat and stir in vanilla and peanut butter. Pour over corn flakes. Toss with fork to completely cover corn flakes with syrup. Work quickly. Drop mixture into clusters on wax paper. Makes about 40 clusters, 2½" in diameter.

CRINKLY LEMON WAFERS

¾ Cup Butter or Margarine
1¼ Cups Sugar
1 Egg
½ Tsp. Vanilla
½ Tsp. Lemon Extract
¼ Cup Milk
2 Cups Sifted All-purpose Flour
1 Tsp. Baking Powder
½ Tsp. Salt
¼ Tsp. Baking Soda
1 Tbs. Grated Lemon Peel

Cream butter or margarine with ¾ cup sugar until light (reserve ½ cup sugar for use later). Beat in egg, vanilla, lemon extract and milk. Sift in flour, baking powder, salt and baking soda, a little at a time, blending after each addition; chill dough several hours, or until firm. Form into marble-size balls (about 1 teaspoonful for each) by rolling lightly between palms of hands. Coat balls by rolling in a mixture of reserved ½ cup sugar & lemon peel. Place 2" apart on ungreased cookie sheets. Bake in moderate oven (350°F.) for 8 to 10 minutes, or until the tops are crackled and edges are lightly browned. Cool completely on wire racks. Makes about 5 dozen.

PINEAPPLE-OATMEAL COOKIES

½ Cup Soft Butter or Margarine
½ Cup Granulated Sugar
½ Cup Firmly-packed Brown Sugar
1 Egg
1 - 9 Oz. Can Crushed Pineapple
    (1 cup)
1½ Cups Rolled Oats
1 Cup Sifted All-purpose Flour
½ Tsp. Baking Soda
½ Tsp. Salt
½ Tsp. Ground Cinnamon
Dash of Ground Nutmeg
½ Cup Chopped Walnuts

Cream the butter. Add sugars and beat
until light. Add the egg and beat well.
Add pineapple, oats, sifted dry ingredients
and nuts; mix well. Drop by teaspoonfuls
onto an ungreased cookie sheet. Bake in
preheated oven (375°F.) for about 15
minutes. Makes about 4 dozen cookies.

CHERRY-CHIP SQUARES

½ Cup Brown Sugar
½ Cup Granulated Sugar
½ Cup Butter
2 Unbeaten Eggs
1 Tsp. Vanilla
2 Cups All-purpose Flour
1½ Tsp. Baking Powder
½ Tsp. Salt
¾ Cup Milk
½ Cup Drained Cherries
1 Cup Chocolate Chips
1 Cup Chopped Nuts

Cream white and brown sugars with butter;
add eggs and vanilla. Sift dry ingredients &
add alternately with milk. Mix well. Add
cherries and chocolate chips and nuts. Bake
in greased and floured 9x9x2" pan at 350°
F. for 45 minutes, or until toothpick comes
out clean. While still hot, ice with the
following:

¼ Cup Melted Margarine
2 Cups Confectioners' Sugar
1 Tsp. Vanilla
2 Tbs. Milk

Combine all ingredients and mix well;
spread over cookies.

PEPPERMINT CREAM BROWNIES

2/3 Cup All-purpose Flour
¼ Tsp. Baking Powder
1/8 Tsp. Salt
1/3 Cup Butter
¾ Cup Sugar
½ Tsp. Vanilla
2 Eggs, well beaten
2 Squares (2 Oz.) Unsweetened
    Chocolate, melted
1 Tbs. Milk
½ Cup Chopped Walnuts
½ Cup Chopped Raisins

Sift flour, measure and resift with baking
powder and salt. Cream butter. Add the
sugar gradually and blend thoroughly. Add
vanilla and eggs and mix thoroughly. Stir
in chocolate. Mix in the sifted dry ingredients and milk. Add nuts and raisins. Spread
into two 8" square pans lined with waxed
paper. Bake in moderate oven (350°F.)
for 20 minutes. Cool. Put layers together,
bottom sides facing, with Peppermint Butter Cream.

Peppermint Butter Cream:

1 Tbs. Butter
1 Cup Unsifted Confectioners'
    Sugar, firmly packed
2 Tbs. Hot Milk
1/8 Tsp. Peppermint Extract, or
    2 drops oil of peppermint

Cream butter and mix thoroughly with
sugar. Add milk and flavoring. Blend
until smooth and thick. Spread over bottom of one layer, top with second layer.
Dust with powdered sugar and cut into
bars. Store in a tightly-covered container.
Makes 18 bars.

MEXICAN FIESTA COOKIES

1 Cup Butter
½ Cup Sugar
2 Tsp. Vanilla
2 Cups Sifted Flour
¼ Cup Cocoa
1 Tbs. Instant Coffee Powder
½ Tsp. Salt
1 Cup Finely-chopped Nuts
½ Cup Chopped Maraschino
    Cherries, drained
1 Cup Confectioners' Sugar

Beat butter until light; gradually add the sugar. Beat until light and fluffy. Add vanilla and beat to blend well. Sift together the flour, cocoa, coffee powder and salt; gradually add to creamed mixture. Blend in nuts and cherries; chill until easy to handle. Shape dough into 1" balls and place 1" apart on an ungreased baking sheet. Bake in 325°F. oven for 20 min. Remove cookies to cooling racks and, while still warm, roll in confectioners' sugar. Makes about 5 dozen cookies.

BUTTERMILK SNICKERDOODLES

½ Cup Shortening
1 Cup Sugar
2 Eggs, well beaten
2½ Cups Sifted All-purpose Flour
1 Tsp. Baking Powder
½ Tsp. Baking Soda
½ Tsp. Salt
1 Tsp. Ground Cinnamon
½ Tsp. Ground Allspice
½ Tsp. Ground Cloves
¾ Cup Buttermilk
1/3 Cup Seeded Raisins
1/3 Cup Dried Currants
½ Cup Chopped Nuts

Cream shortening and sugar. Add eggs. Mix and sift dry ingredients and add alternately with buttermilk. Stir in fruits and nuts. Pour into greased and floured 2½" muffin pans, filling two thirds full. Bake in preheated moderate oven (375° F.) for about 25 minutes. Makes 24.

PORCUPINES

2 Cups Shelled Pecans
1 Cup Pitted Dates
Flaked Coconut
1 Cup Firmly-packed Dark Brown Sugar
2 Eggs

Grind the pecans and dates with fine blade. Mix with 2 cups coconut, sugar and eggs. Shape mixture with the fingers into rolls 4 inches long and ½ inch thick. Roll in flaked coconut. Place rolls on lightly greased cookie sheet. Bake in preheated 350°F. oven for 10 to 12 minutes. Makes about 3 dozen.

DATE CHEWS

1¼ Cups Pitted Dates
    (1 - 8 oz. package)
1 Cup Walnuts or Pecans
1 - 3½ Oz. Can Moist Coconut
½ Cup Brown Sugar, firmly packed
1 Egg

Force dates and nuts through food chopper, using coarse blade. Add ½ can coconut, brown sugar and egg; mix well. Shape into 2" long finger-shaped pieces; roll in remaining ½ can coconut. Place on greased cookie sheets and bake in preheated 350°F. oven for 10 to 15 minutes. Makes 2 dozen.

PECAN BONBONS

2 Cups Sifted Flour
¼ Cup Sugar
½ Tsp. Salt
1 Cup Butter or Margarine
2 Tsp. Vanilla
2½ Cups Finely-chopped Pecans
Confectioners' Sugar

Sift flour, sugar and salt into mixing bowl. Blend in butter and vanilla with pastry blender. Add 2 cups of the nuts. Shape dough into ½" balls. Roll in remaining nuts. Place about 1½" apart on greased cookie sheet and bake in 350°F. oven for 15 to 20 minutes. Cool on racks. While warm, roll in confectioners' sugar. Makes 4 dozen.

SALADS

CRUNCHY APPLE SALAD

1 Cup Diced, Unpeeled Apples
1 Cup Diced Bananas
1 Tbs. Lemon Juice
½ Cup Drained Pineapple Tidbits
½ Cup Raisins
½ Cup Coarsely-chopped Pecans
1/3 Cup Mayonnaise or Salad
   Dressing

Place apples, bananas and lemon juice in a bowl and toss. Add pineapple, raisins and pecans. Toss lightly. Add mayonnaise & toss just until mayonnaise is mixed thoroughly. Spoon into individual lettuce cups or into salad dish lined with lettuce leaves. Makes 6 servings.

MAKE-AHEAD CRANBERRY SALAD

1 - 8½ Oz. Can Crushed Pineapple
1 - 1 Lb. Can Whole Cranberry
   Sauce
2 - 3 Oz. Pkgs. Raspberry Flavor
   Gelatin
1 - 8 Oz. Pkg. Cream Cheese
2 Tbs. Salad Dressing
1 Cup Heavy Cream, or 1 Envelope
   Dessert Topping Mix
½ Cup Coarsely-chopped Walnuts
1 Chopped, Peeled Tart Apple

Drain pineapple and cranberry sauce, reserving liquid; add enough water to make 2 cups of liquid. Bring to a boil. Dissolve gelatin in hot liquid. Chill until partially set. Beat softened cream cheese (room temperature) and salad dressing together until fluffy. Gradually beat in gelatin; fold this mixture into the whipped cream or topping mix. Set aside 1½ cups of this mixture for topping. Add drained fruits, nuts and apple to the remaining cheese mixture. Pour into a glass dish, 11½x7-3/8x1½" and refrigerate until surface sets, about 20 minutes. Frost with reserved cheese mixture. Chill several hours, or freeze. If frozen, remove salad to refrigerator 1 hour before serving. Makes 12 servings.

CURRIED CHICKEN SALAD

3 Whole Chicken Breasts, split
   (about 3 Lbs.)
2 Carrots, pared and cut up
2 Stalks Celery, cut up
1 Small Onion, peeled and sliced
6 Whole Black Peppercorns
Salt
1 Bay Leaf
3 Cups Boiling Water
½ Cup Thinly-sliced Celery, cut on
   the diagonal
1½ Cups Diced, Unpared, Tart Apple
½ Cup Coarsely-chopped Green Pepper
2 Tsp. Grated Onion
¾ Cup Mayonnaise or Cooked Salad
   Dressing
3 Tbs. Light Cream
½ to 1 Tsp. Curry Powder, or to
   taste
½ Tsp. White Pepper
Watercress Sprigs

In a 4-quart kettle, combine chicken breasts, carrot, cut-up celery, sliced onion, black peppercorns, 1½ teaspoons of salt, the bay leaf, and 3 cups boiling water. Bring to a boil; reduce heat and simmer, covered, for about 30 minutes, or until the chicken is tender. Remove chicken from broth; cool and then refrigerate until well chilled. Refrigerate the broth for use another time.

Remove and discard skin from chicken. Cut meat from bones, in large pieces. In a large bowl, combine chicken, sliced celery, apple, green pepper, and grated onion. In small bowl, combine mayonnaise, cream, curry powder, ¾ teaspoon of salt and the white pepper; mix well. Add to chicken mixture and toss lightly to combine. Refrigerate until serving time--at least 1 hour. Spoon the chicken salad onto a large platter. Garnish with watercress. Makes 6 to 8 servings.

GOLD COAST FRUIT SALAD

1 Small Fresh Pineapple
2 Cups Strawberries
1 - 1 Lb. 13 Oz. Can Pear Halves
4 Medium Seedless Oranges
1 - 6 Oz. Pkg. Process Gruyere Cheese
1/3 Cup Vegetable Oil
3 Tbs. Lime Juice
2 Tbs. Light Corn Syrup
½ Tsp. Grated Lime Peel
¼ Tsp. Salt
1 Medium Head Boston Lettuce

Pare pineapple; quarter lengthwise; core. Cut fruit into bite-size pieces. Wash the strawberries, hull and cut in half. Drain syrup from pears; slice pears. Pare oranges and section. Cube cheese. Combine the vegetable oil, lime juice, corn syrup, lime peel and salt in a jar with a tight-fitting lid; shake well to mix. Line a large salad bowl with lettuce leaves; break remainder of lettuce into bite-size pieces in center of bowl. Arrange fruits in separate sections around edge of lettuce; pile cheese in center. Pour dressing over all and toss lightly to mix. Makes 8 servings.

LAYERED SEAFOOD SALAD

Lime Layer:
1 - 3 Oz. Pkg. Lime-flavored
    Gelatin
1 Cup Boiling Water
1 - 8 Oz. Carton Dairy Sour Cream
    (1 cup)
½ Cup Mayonnaise or Salad
    Dressing
2 Tbs. Lemon Juice
½ Tsp. Salt
Red Pepper Seasoning (a few drops)
1 Large Cucumber

Dissolve the lime gelatin in boiling water in a medium bowl; stir in sour cream, mayonnaise or salad dressing, lemon juice, salt & red pepper seasoning. Chill 30 minutes, or until consistency of unbeaten egg whites. Cut about 12 thin even slices from cucumber, then trim a sliver from each so it will stand flat around edge of mold. Set aside for garnish. Peel remaining cucumber and trimmings and chop fine; fold into thickened lime gelatin mixture; pour into a 12-cup tube mold. Chill 30 minutes, or until sticky-firm.

Seafood Layer:
2 Envelopes Unflavored Gelatin
1½ Cups Water
2 - 1 Lb. Cans Salmon
1 - 7 Oz. Can Crabmeat
½ Cup Mayonnaise or Salad Dressing
2 Tbs. Lemon Juice
1 Tsp. Salt
¼ Tsp. Ground Pepper
2 Egg Whites
1 Cup Whipping Cream
Red Food Coloring

While the mixture in the mold chills, prepare the seafood layer. Soften gelatin in ½ cup of water in a small saucepan. Heat, stirring constantly, until gelatin dissolves. Remove from heat and stir in remaining 1 cup of water. Drain both cans of salmon; remove bones and flake the meat into a medium bowl. Drain the crabmeat; remove any bony tissue; flake meat and add to the salmon. Combine 1/3 each of the seafood and gelatin mixtures at a time in an electric blender container; cover and process at high speed until smooth; pour into a large bowl. Stir in mayonnaise or salad dressing, lemon juice, salt and pepper.

Beat egg whites until they stand in firm peaks in a small bowl. Beat cream until stiff in a medium bowl. Fold beaten egg whites, then whipped cream, into seafood mixture. Tint salmon color with a few drops of food coloring. Carefully spoon this mixture over the layer in the mold. Chill for several hours, or until firm (overnight is best). When ready to serve, run a sharp knife around top of salad, then dip mold very quickly in and out of a pan of hot water. Cover mold with serving plate; turn upside down and gently lift off mold. Stand reserved cucumber slices, flat edge down, around side of salad. Fill center with a few crisp romaine or curly endive leaves if you wish. Makes 24 servings.

GREEK SALAD

1 Small Head Lettuce
1 Cucumber
2 Ripe Tomatoes
1 Cup Cubed Greek Feta Cheese
12 Greek Black Olives
1 Medium Onion, sliced thin
½ Cup Julienne Beets
6 Anchovy Fillets, cut up
1 Tbs. Capers
½ Cup Olive Oil
Vinegar to taste
1 Tsp. Powdered Mustard
Salt to taste

In a large wooden bowl, put coarsely-torn lettuce, thinly-sliced cucumber, cubed tomatoes, cheese, olives, onion, beets, anchovy fillets and capers. Mix oil, vinegar and mustard with salt to taste and pour over salad. Toss gently so as not to break up cheese cubes. Makes 4 to 6 servings.

STRAWBERRY/AVOCADO RING

2 - 3 Oz. Pkgs. Lemon or Lime
  Flavor Gelatin
1 Tsp. Salt
2 Cups Boiling Water
1¼ Cups Cold Water
3 Tbs. Lemon Juice
2 Ripe Avocados, mashed
¼ Cup Mayonnaise
3 Cups Fresh Strawberries
Honey Dressing (see recipe below)

Dissolve gelatin and salt in boiling water. Add cold water and lemon juice; chill until slightly thickened. Combine avocados and mayonnaise; blend well. Stir into gelatin until thoroughly mixed. Pour into a 4-cup mold or 8 individual ring molds. Chill until firm. Unmold and fill center with strawberries. Serve with honey dressing. Makes 8 servings.

Honey Dressing: Combine ½ cup dairy sour cream, 3 tbs. honey and 1/8 tsp. ground mace.

MACARONI, LOBSTER, AND ARTICHOKE SALAD

2 Cups Elbow Macaroni
1 - 9 Oz. Pkg. Frozen Artichoke Hearts
2 - 5½ Oz. Cans Lobster Meat
1 Tsp. Crumbled Dried Basil
1 Tsp. Salt
½ Tsp. Pepper
½ Cup Lemon French Dressing
½ Cup Mayonnaise
Lettuce
½ Cup Sliced Radishes

Cook and drain macaroni. Cook artichoke hearts according to package directions; drain. Combine macaroni, artichoke hearts and the next 5 ingredients; chill. Add mayonnaise and pile on lettuce bed. Decorate with radish slices. Makes 6 to 8 servings.

SALMON-TUNA MOLD

2 Envelopes Unflavored Gelatin
1 Tbs. Steak Sauce
1¾ Cups Canned Tomato Juice
Water
¾ Cup Mayonnaise
1 Cup Dairy Sour Cream
1 Tsp. Grated Lemon Rind
1/3 Cup Chopped, Stuffed Olives
1 Green Onion, chopped
1½ Cups Diced Celery
1 - 7 Oz. Can Salmon
1 - 7 Oz. Can Tuna
Salt and Pepper
Fresh Dill
Lemon Wedges
Paprika

Mix 1 envelope of the gelatin with the steak sauce and ¾ cup of tomato juice. Heat, stirring to dissolve gelatin. Add remaining tomato juice, and pour into a 1½-quart mold. Chill until firm. In top part of double boiler, soften remaining gelatin in ½ cup water. Dissolve over hot water. Stir in mayonnaise & sour cream. Add lemon rind, olives, onion, celery, salmon and tuna. Season to taste with salt and pepper. Put on top of jellied tomato layer. Chill until firm.

ORIENTAL SALAD

2 - 1 Lb. Cans Bean Sprouts,
   drained
¼ Cup Thin French Dressing
1 Tsp. Soy Sauce
2 Cups Broken Fresh Spinach
1 Small Green Pepper, stemmed,
   seeded and cut into thin rings
1 - 1 Lb. 5 Oz. Can Pineapple
   Chunks
1 - 5 Oz. Can Water Chestnuts,
   drained and sliced
¼ Cup Chopped Peanuts
Curry Dressing (see recipe below)

Place bean sprouts in a medium bowl and
drizzle with French dressing and soy sauce.
Toss to mix. Cover and chill, tossing
several times. Chill for at least an hour
to season and blend flavors. Just before
serving, place spinach in a large shallow
salad bowl. Drain the bean sprouts and
layer with green pepper rings over spinach
in bowl. Drain the syrup from pineapple
chunks into a cup; layer the fruit and water chestnuts over green pepper. Sprinkle
with peanuts. Spoon the dressing over all
and toss lightly with two forks until all
ingredients are well coated. Makes 8 servings

Curry Dressing: Blend ½ cup mayonnaise
or salad dressing, 2 tablespoons of the reserved pineapple syrup, and ¼ teaspoon of
curry powder until smooth in a small bowl;
chill. Makes about ½ cup.

APPLE/CUCUMBER SALAD

2 Cups Diced, Unpeeled Apples
2 Cups Diced, Peeled Cucumbers
½ Tsp. Salt
¼ Cup Lemon Juice
½ Cup Salad Dressing
¼ Cup Chopped Nuts (optional)
Lettuce

Toss the apples and cucumbers with salt;
sprinkle with lemon juice. Mix in salad
dressing and nuts. Serve, chilled, on lettuce. Makes 6 servings.

SESAME ASPARAGUS SALAD

1 - 10 Oz. Pkg. Frozen Cut Asparagus
1 Head Romaine Lettuce, broken
   into pieces
2 Pimientos, diced
1 Green Onion, chopped
¼ Cup Toasted Sesame Seed
¼ Tsp. Cracked Pepper
¼ Tsp. Herb Seasoning
2 Tbs. Lemon Juice
2 Tbs. Salad Oil
Salt to taste

Cook, drain and chill asparagus. Add to
next 3 ingredients. Mix sesame seed, pepper, herb seasoning, lemon juice and oil.
Add to first mixture. Toss. Add salt to
taste. Makes 4 to 6 servings.

CHILI-BEAN SALAD

2 Tsp. Chili Powder
¼ Cup Olive Oil or Vegetable Oil
2 Tbs. Vinegar
2 Tsp. Sugar
¼ Tsp. Salt
2 - 1 Lb. Cans Kidney Beans,
   drained
1 Large Green Pepper, diced (1 cup)
1 Small Bermuda Onion, diced (1 cup)
1 Cup Pitted Ripe Olives, halved
2 Tbs. Catsup
1 Tbs. Mayonnaise or Salad Dressing
1 Small Head Iceberg or Leaf Lettuce
1 - 8 Oz. Pkg. Sliced Process American
   Cheese

Heat chili powder in olive oil or vegetable
oil in small saucepan about 2 minutes to
develop flavor; remove from heat. Stir in
vinegar, sugar, and salt; stir into drained
beans in large bowl. Let stand about 30
minutes to season. Stir in green pepper,
onion, olives, catsup and mayonnaise or
salad dressing; toss lightly to mix. Shred
lettuce coarsely, saving some leafy tops
for garnish. Place in a large salad bowl.
Spoon bean mixture on top; tuck leafy
tops around edge. Quarter cheese slices
and arrange, overlapping in two circles
on top of bean mixture. Makes 6 servings.

FRUIT-COCKTAIL SALAD

1 Envelope Unflavored Gelatin
1 - 1 Lb. 13 Oz. Can Fruit
    Cocktail (about 3½ cups)
1 - 3 Oz. Pkg. Cream Cheese,
    softened
1 Cup Mayonnaise
1 - 3 Oz. Pkg. Cherry, Black Cherry,
    or Raspberry-flavored Gelatin
Salad Greens

Soften unflavored gelatin in ¼ cup cold
water. Drain fruit, reserving syrup. Heat
¾ cup syrup; add gelatin and stir until
gelatin is dissolved. Cool. Beat cream
cheese until fluffy; blend in mayonnaise.
Gradually beat in gelatin mixture.

Dissolve the flavored gelatin in 1 cup of
boiling water. Add 1 cup cold water or
syrup and water. Chill until slightly
thickened. Put half of fruit in loaf pan
(9x5x3"); add 1 cup flavored gelatin
and chill until set. Pour in cheese mixture and chill until set. Top with remaining fruit and gelatin. Chill for
several hours, or until firm. Unmold
on greens and slice to serve. Makes 8
servings.

ORANGE-PINEAPPLE SALAD

1 - 3 Oz. Box Orange, or Orange-
    Pineapple Gelatin
1 Cup Hot Water
1 Cup Crushed Pineapple, undrained
    (about 8½ oz.)
1 Cup Diced Orange Sections
1 - 11 Oz. Can Mandarin Oranges,
    drained (about 1¼ cups)
1 Cup Miniature Marshmallows
1 Cup Dairy Sour Cream
2 Tbs. Mayonnaise
2 Tbs. Grated Cheddar Cheese
Salad Greens

Dissolve gelatin in hot water. Add pineapple and chill until mixture thickens
slightly. Fold in next 3 ingredients. Pour
into an 8" square pan and chill until firm.
Mix the sour cream and mayonnaise and
spread on salad. Sprinkle with Cheddar
cheese. Serve on greens. Makes 6 to 8
servings.

TOMATO-MUSHROOM SALAD

4 Sliced Chilled Tomatoes
Salt and Pepper to taste
2 Tbs. Olive Oil
½ Tsp. Fresh or Dry Crumbled Basil
    or Oregano
8 Large Mushrooms, sliced
1 to 2 Tsp. Fresh Lemon Juice

Arrange tomatoes in overlapping rows on a
serving dish. Sprinkle with salt and pepper,
1 tablespoon of the olive oil, and the basil
or oregano. Arrange mushroom slices on
tomatoes. Sprinkle with remaining tablespoon of olive oil and lemon juice. Makes
4 to 5 servings.

HOT POTATO SALAD
WITH FRANKFURTERS

3 Tbs. Bacon Fat
1½ Tbs. All-purpose Flour
1 Tbs. Sugar
1 Tsp. Salt
1/8 Tsp. Pepper
½ Cup Water
1/3 Cup Vinegar
5 Cups Sliced, Cooked Potatoes
1 Small Onion, minced
Chopped Parsley
8 Frankfurters

Heat fat; add flour, sugar and seasonings.
Stir in water and vinegar. Cook until
slightly thickened. Add potatoes, onion
and parsley. Heat well. Cut several diagonal gashes, ¼" deep, in frankfurters.
Brown lightly in a little fat. Arrange on
salad. Makes 4 servings.

SWEET POTATO SALAD

2½ Lbs. Sweet Potatoes
4 Slices Bacon (3½ oz.)
¼ Cup Chopped Onion
1 Tbs. Flour
½ Cup Water
½ Cup Orange Juice
¼ Cup Lemon Juice
2 Tsp. Sugar
½ Tsp. Salt
¼ Tsp. Grated Orange Rind
1 Cup Diced Cucumber

Scrub the potatoes and boil in jackets until just tender, then peel and cut into ¼" crosswise slices. Cut bacon in half-inch lengths with kitchen shears and saute' with the onion until bacon is delicately browned. Blend in the flour thoroughly. Add the water and fruit juices gradually, then add sugar and salt. Heat to boiling, stirring constantly and cook for 2 minutes until smooth and thickened. Add the orange rind, cucumber and potatoes. Stir gently to coat with sauce. Heat thoroughly and serve at once while still warm directly from skillet. Makes 4 servings.

AVOCADO CUPS
(With Strawberry Filling)

2 Avocados
½ Cup Grapefruit Sections
1 Cup Small Whole Strawberries
1 Tbs. Lemon Juice
1 Tbs. Corn Syrup

Glaze:

2 Tbs. Gelatin
¼ Cup Lemon Juice
1 Tbs. Corn Syrup

Dressing:

¼ Cup Salad Oil
2 Tbs. Corn Syrup
2 Tbs. Lemon Juice
1/8 Tsp. Salt
1 Tsp. Sugar
1 Tsp. Flour
1 Egg, separated

Salad: Cut avocados in half lengthwise. Remove seed. Carefully scoop out each half in as large pieces as possible, preserving shape of shell. Dice avocado, combine with grapefruit and strawberries. Add the lemon juice and syrup, which have been blended together. Fill shells with fruit mixture. Remove gelatin mixture from heat, cool slightly and spoon over fruit. Chill about ½ hour. Just before serving, top with a tablespoon of the cooked dressing. Makes 4 servings.

Glaze: Combine gelatin, lemon juice and syrup. Place over boiling water until gelatin is dissolved. Keep in warm water until ready to use.

Dressing: Combine in top of double boiler the oil, syrup, lemon juice, salt, sugar, flour and yolk of egg. Beat thoroughly. Cook until thick and fluffy, stirring constantly. Fold in stiffly beaten egg white, cook one minute longer, stirring gently. Cool.

RICE SALAD
(Polynesian Style)

1 Cup Uncooked Regular Rice
¼ Lb. Mushrooms
½ Cup Vegetable Oil
¼ Cup Cider Vinegar
2 Tbs. Soy Sauce
½ Tsp. Salt
1 - 11 Oz. Can Mandarin Orange
    Segments, drained
1 Cup Thinly-sliced Celery
1 - 5 Oz. Can Water Chestnuts,
    drained and sliced
2 Tbs. Thinly-sliced Green Onions
Iceberg Lettuce

Cook the rice, using direction on package. Spoon rice into a large bowl. While the rice is cooking, trim mushrooms, wash & dry well; slice lengthwise. Add to the rice after it is cooked. Combine vegetable oil, vinegar, soy sauce and salt in a jar with a tight lid; shake well to mix. Pour over rice mixture; toss lightly to mix. Cover and chill at least an hour to allow flavors to blend. Just before serving, fold in mandarin-orange segments, celery, water chestnuts and green onions. Spoon into a lettuce-lined bowl. Makes 6 servings.

GAZPACHO SALAD BOWL

Salad:

2 Large Tomatoes (1 Lb.)
1 Large Cucumber
1 Medium Green Pepper, sliced
    into rings
½ Cup Sliced Onion, separated
    into rings
Snipped Chives
Croutons (optional)

Dressing:

1/3 Cup Olive Oil or Salad Oil
1/3 Cup Red Wine Vinegar
1 Tbs. Snipped Chives
1 Clove Garlic, crushed
1 Tsp. Salt
1/8 Tsp. Cracked Black Pepper
Liquid Hot-Pepper Seasoning
    (a few drops, or to taste)

Make the dressing first. In a jar with a tight-fitting lid, combine all dressing ingredients; shake vigorously to combine.

Peel tomatoes and slice; cut each slice in half. Score unpared cucumber with a fork; slice thin. In salad bowl or shallow glass serving bowl, combine tomato, cucumber, green pepper, onion and dressing. Toss until vegetables are well coated. Refrigerate, covered, until well-chilled--about 2 hours. Just before serving, toss salad. Sprinkle with chives and croutons. Makes 6 to 8 servings.

LIME AND CHEESE GELATIN SALAD

1 Box (3 ounces) Lime-flavored
    Gelatin
1 Can Pineapple Chunks (one 1 lb. 4½ oz.
    can--about 2½ cups)
12 Whole Blanched Almonds
1 Envelope Unflavored Gelatin
1 Lb. (2 cups) Cream-style Cottage
    Cheese
1 Tbs. Fresh Lemon Juice
¾ Tsp. Salt
1/3 Cup Light Cream
½ Cup Chopped Blanched Almonds

Dissolve the lime gelatin in 1 cup of hot water. Add ½ cup of syrup from pineapple and ½ cup cold water. Chill until slightly thickened. Arrange 12 almonds in bottom of deep 1½ quart mold. Carefully pour in slightly thickened gelatin mixture. Chill overnight, or until very firm.

Drain pineapple and dice enough to make 1 cup. Sprinkle unflavored gelatin on ¼ cup cold water; let stand 5 minutes. Dissolve over hot water. Add to cheese with pineapple and remaining ingredients; mix well. Spoon onto firm gelatin in mold. Chill until firm.

Unmold on plate. If desired, garnish with watercress; serve with mayonnaise seasoned with curry powder. Makes 6 to 8 servings.

VIRGINIA CITY SALAD
(with Snow Dressing)

4 Cups Shredded Green Cabbage
1 Cup Pineapple Tidbits, drained
½ Cup Miniature Marshmallows
½ Cup Slivered Blanched Almonds
Snow Dressing (see recipe below)

Just before serving, combine all ingredients except dressing. Top with Snow Dressing. Makes 6 servings.

Snow Dressing:

½ Cup Sugar
1 Tbs. All-purpose Flour
½ Tsp. Salt
3 Tbs. Boiling Water
¼ Cup Cider Vinegar
Juice of 3 Lemons
4 Egg Whites, stiffly beaten

Mix sugar and flour and salt. Add water, cider vinegar, and lemon juice. Stir until well blended. Fold in the beaten egg whites. Cook over low heat, stirring constantly, until smooth and thick. Chill & serve on top of salad.

JELLIED VEGETABLE RING

1 Envelope Unflavored Gelatin
¼ Cup Cold Water
1½ Cups Boiling Water
3 Tbs. Sugar
¼ Cup Cider Vinegar
1 Tsp. Salt
½ Tsp. Curry Powder
Dash of Pepper
1 Tbs. Minced Onion
1 Cup Celery Strips
¾ Cup Finely-shredded Cabbage
¼ Cup Diced, Cooked Beets
Salad Greens
Mayonnaise or Salad Dressing

Soften the gelatin in cold water for five minutes; then dissolve in boiling water. Add sugar, vinegar, seasonings, and onion. Chill mixture until it is slightly thickened; stir and fold in vegetables.

Pour mixture into a 1-quart ring mold. Chill until firm. Unmold on salad greens and serve with mayonnaise. Makes 4 to 6 servings.

PAPAYA SALAD

½ Cup Lemon Juice
¼ Cup Honey
Pinch of Salt
1 Ripe Medium Papaya (2½ to 3 lb.)
1 Large Seedless Orange
Watercress
Black Olives, Blackberries or Blueberries

Combine the lemon juice, honey and salt. Chill in refrigerator. Peel and slice the papaya; remove seeds. Peel orange and section. Arrange alternate slices of papaya and orange wedges in fan shape arrangement on a salad plate. Place a small bunch of crisp cress at the small end and garnish with black olives, blackberries or blueberries. Drizzle with chilled lemon-honey dressing and serve immediately. Makes 4 to 5 servings. Do not eat papaya seeds.

CHILEAN SALAD
(A South American Favorite)

2 Cups Diced Cold Veal, Lamb
  or Chicken
2 Hard-cooked Eggs,
  sliced
1 Tsp. Onion Juice
Mint Leaves (a few), minced
2 Heads Lettuce, shredded
2 Tbs. Chopped Parsley
French Dressing

Wash mint leaves and mince; rinse lettuce and shred. Wash parsley and chop. Combine all ingredients in a bowl and chill thoroughly. When ready to serve, remove from refrigerator and add French dressing to taste. Toss until well mixed and serve on crisp lettuce leaves. Makes 6 servings.

SHRIMP-AND-CHEESE
MACARONI LOAF

1 Envelope Unflavored Gelatin
1¼ Cups Milk
1½ Cups Shredded American Cheese
1 Tbs. Grated Onion
2 - 5 Oz. Cans Shrimp, deveined
½ Cup Minced Celery
2/3 Cup Elbow Macaroni, cooked
1 Tsp. Sweet Garden Relish
1 Pimiento, chopped
½ Cup Mayonnaise
½ Tsp. Salt
Dash of Cayenne
Curry Mayonnaise (see below)

Sprinkle gelatin over milk in top part of double boiler; let stand for 5 minutes. Scald over boiling water, stirring until the gelatin is dissolved. Stir in cheese & onion. Cool, then chill until slightly thickened.

Cut shrimp into halves lengthwise; add the shrimp and remaining ingredients, except mayonnaise, to gelatin mixture. Turn into an oiled 3½-cup fish mold or loaf pan (9x5x3"). Chill until firm. Unmold and garnish with salad greens, tomatoes and cucumbers, if desired. Serve with mayonnaise to which a little curry powder has been added. Makes 6 servings.

TUNA, RICE AND PINEAPPLE SALAD

1 - 6½ Oz. Can White-meat Tuna
  (flaked)
1 - 9 Oz. Can Pineapple Tidbits,
  drained
2 Cups Cold Cooked Rice
¾ Cup Thinly Sliced Celery
1/3 Cup Sliced Stuffed Olives
¼ Cup Minced Green Pepper
Salt
½ Cup Mayonnaise
Salad Greens

Combine tuna, pineapple, rice, celery,
olives and green pepper. Chill. Add
salt to taste and then add mayonnaise.
Mix lightly. Serve on greens. Makes
4 servings.

BING CHERRY MOLD

2 - 3 Oz. Pkgs. Cherry or
  Black Cherry-flavored
  Gelatin
2 Cups Hot Water
1 Cup Cold Water
2 Tsp. Lemon Juice
2 Tbs. Cooking Sherry
1 Cup Dairy Sour Cream
2 Cups Pitted, Halved Fresh
  Bing Cherries
¼ Cup Chopped, Blanched
  Almonds, toasted

Dissolve the gelatin in hot water; add cold
water and lemon juice. To 1 cup of gelatin mixture, add the cooking sherry. Pour
into a 2-quart mold and chill until set.

Chill remaining gelatin until partially set,
then whip until fluffy. Fold in sour cream,
cherries and almonds. Pour on top of the
gelatin layer in the mold. Chill until firm,
about 5 hours, or overnight.

Unmold onto a chilled platter. Circle with
fresh Bing cherries, sliced pineapple, romaine.
Pass bowl of sour cream mixed with mayonnaise and sprinkled with toasted almonds.
Makes 10 to 12 servings.

GREEN BEAN SALAD

1½ to 2 Lbs. Fresh Green Beans
  (or 3 - 9 Oz. Pkgs. Frozen Cut
  Green Beans)
Boiling Salted Water
½ Cup Salad Oil
¼ Cup Tomato-based Chili Sauce
½ Tsp. Dry Mustard
½ Tsp. Savory or Rosemary Leaves
¼ Tsp. Salt
1/8 Tsp. Pepper
1 Clove Garlic, minced or mashed
Lettuce Leaves
½ Medium Onion, cut into very
  thin slices
¼ Cup Wine Vinegar

Wash and cut fresh green beans. Cook in
boiling water until just tender-crisp. Drain
immediately; rinse in cold water. Drain
again and put into a bowl. Combine the
oil, chili sauce, mustard, savory, salt, pepper and garlic in a blender jar and process
until well blended. Pour dressing over the
beans. Cover and refrigerate at least four
hours, or overnight. At serving time, lift
the beans out of the marinade with a slotted spoon and arrange with lettuce in a
serving dish. Cut the onion in very thin
slices, separate into rings and distribute
over the beans. Blend the vinegar into
the remaining marinade, drizzle some over
the beans, and serve the rest at the table.
Makes 6 servings.

SALMAGUNDI SALAD

1½ Cups Diced, Cooked Lamb
½ Cup Diced, Cooked Potato
½ Cup Diced, Cooked Carrots
½ Cup Diced, Cooked Peas or
  Green Beans
¼ Cup French Dressing
2 Sweet Pickles, chopped
1 Hard-cooked Egg, chopped
½ Cup Mayonnaise
Salad Greens

Marinate meat & vegetables in French dressing for 30 minutes. Add remaining ingredients except for greens and mix lightly.
Serve on cold crisp greens. Makes 4 servings.

FRESH BLUEBERRY AND LIME MOLD

2 Envelopes Unflavored Gelatin
1 Cup Cold Water
1½ Cups Hot Water
½ Cup Sugar
¼ Tsp. Salt
½ Cup Fresh Lime Juice
3 Cups Fresh Blueberries, washed
Salad Greens
Mayonnaise

Soften gelatin in cold water. Let stand for 5 minutes. Add hot water, sugar and salt and mix well to dissolve gelatin. Blend in lime juice. Chill until mixture is about as thick as fresh egg whites. Fold in blueberries. Turn into a 5-cup mold and chill until firm. Turn out onto serving plate and garnish with salad greens. Serve with mayonnaise. Makes 6 to 8 servings.

MOLDED GUACAMOLE SALAD

1 Envelope Unflavored Gelatin
5 Medium Tomatoes
2 Ripe Avocados (about 1½ Lbs.)
2 Tbs. White Vinegar
¼ Cup Finely-chopped Onion
2 Tbs. Finely-chopped Green Chili Pepper
1 Tsp. Salt
Oil and Vinegar Dressing

Sprinkle gelatin over ½ cup cold water in a small bowl; let stand 5 minutes to soften. Set bowl in about 1" of boiling water in pan and stir gelatin until dissolved. Peel 1 tomato, slice into a medium bowl and mash with a fork. Cut avocados in half; remove peel and pits and discard. Slice into tomato; mash avocado and tomato until well blended. Add vinegar, onion, chili pepper and salt. Mix in dissolved gelatin until well combined. Turn mixture into a 1-quart bowl and refrigerate until firm--about 4 hours. Unmold onto a serving plate. Slice remaining tomatoes and arrange around guacamole mold. Drizzle tomatoes with about 2 tablespoons of dressing. Makes 8 servings.

COTTAGE CHEESE RING with BANANA DRESSING

2 Envelopes Unflavored Gelatin
½ Cup Cold Water
3 Cups Creamed Cottage Cheese
1½ Cups Mayonnaise
2 Tbs. Lemon Juice
2 Tbs. Sugar
Salt to taste

Sprinkle gelatin on cold water; dissolve over hot water. Cool slightly. Mix cottage cheese and mayonnaise. Stir in dissolved gelatin & mix thoroughly. Add lemon juice, sugar and salt; blend gently but thoroughly. Turn into an oiled 5-cup ring mold. Chill until firm. Fill center of ring with mixed fresh fruit and serve with Banana Dressing. Makes 8 servings.

Banana Dressing:
2 Fully-ripe Bananas
¼ Cup Mayonnaise
¼ Cup Whipping Cream, whipped

Mash the bananas and add the mayonnaise. Whip the cream and fold in. Or put the bananas, mayonnaise and whipping cream in an electric blender and blend until smooth.

CHICKEN-RICE SALAD with CASHEWS

3 Cups Cooked Rice
2 Cups Coarsely-diced Cooked Chicken
½ Cup Diced Celery
2 Green Onions, chopped
1 Tbs. Fresh Lemon Juice
½ Cup Chopped, Salted Cashew Nuts
¾ Cup Salad Dressing or Mayonnaise
Salt and Pepper
Salad Greens

Combine rice, chicken, celery, onions, lemon juice and nuts. Add salad dressing and mix lightly. Season to taste with salt and pepper. Chill and serve on salad greens. Makes 4 servings.

MOLDED FISH

6 Medium Fresh-Water Trout
2 Chicken Bouillon Cubes
2 Cups Hot Water
1 Tbs. Lemon Juice
1 Envelope Unflavored Gelatin
¼ Cup Cold Water
Lemon Slices
Olives
Sour Cream/Cucumber Sauce
  (see recipe below)

Simmer trout in chicken broth made by
dissolving bouillon cubes in hot water &
adding lemon juice. Remove fish to a
deep serving platter; let stand until cool.
Soften gelatin in cold water. Add to hot
broth in saucepan and stir until dissolved.
Chill until gelatin starts to thicken. Spoon
half of gelatin over fish; chill until firm.
Garnish with lemon slices and olives.
Spoon remaining gelatin over this; chill.
Serve with sauce. Makes 4 to 6 servings.

Sauce:
¾ Cup Dairy Sour Cream
¼ Tsp. Prepared Mustard
½ Tsp. Salt
1 Tsp. Grated Onion
1 Tsp. Chopped Parsley
½ Cup Chopped Cucumber
Juice of ½ Lemon

Combine all ingredients and mix well.
Chill. Makes about ¾ cup.

GERMAN CABBAGE SLAW

2 Cups Shredded Cabbage
2 Tbs. Chopped Parsley
1 Tbs. Chopped Onion
2 Slices Bacon, diced
2 Tbs. Vinegar
½ Tsp. Salt
½ Cup Salad Dressing

Cook diced bacon until crisp. Add the
vinegar and salt. Stir well and add to
salad dressing. Stir at once into cabbage,
parsley and onion. Makes 3 servings.

SHRIMP ASPIC

3 - 14 Oz. Cans Chicken Broth
3 Envelopes Unflavored Gelatin
2 - 1 Lb. Pkgs. Frozen Deveined
  Shelled Shrimp
Watercress
Pitted Ripe Olives, slivered
1 Cup Mayonnaise or Salad Dressing
2 Tbs. Lemon Juice
1 Tsp. Grated Onion
3 Hard-cooked Eggs, shelled and
  coarsely chopped
½ Cup Diced Celery

Skim fat from chicken broth. Soften the
gelatin in chicken broth about 5 minutes
in a large saucepan. Heat, stirring constantly, until gelatin dissolves. Pour into
a medium bowl; cool. Cook the shrimp,
following directions on package; drain &
set aside. Set aside 6 shrimp for decoration; cut remainder into bite-size pieces &
place in a large bowl; cover and chill.

Pour ½ cup of the cooled gelatin mixture
into an 8" square pan; chill. Pour ½ cup
of the remaining gelatin mixture into a
9x5x3" loaf pan. Chill until sticky-firm.
Arrange reserved whole shrimp, watercress
sprigs and olives on the aspic in loaf pan
to make a pleasing design. Spoon ½ cup
of the remaining gelatin mixture carefully
over the design, a little at a time, chilling
briefly after each addition. Then chill
completed design layer till it is sticky-firm.
Stir mayonnaise or salad dressing and lemon
juice into remaining gelatin mixture. Place
bowl in a pan of ice and water to speed
setting. Chill, stirring several times, until
as thick as unbeaten egg white. Fold in
onion, chopped eggs, shrimp and celery.
Pour carefully over sticky-firm aspic layer
in loaf pan. Chill about 4 hours, or until
firm. Chilling overnight is really the best.
Just before serving, loosen salad around
edges with a knife; dip pan very quickly
in and out of hot water. Cover pan with
serving plate, turn upside down and gently
lift off pan. Cut small triangles from firm
aspic in square pan. Arrange as decorative
border around salad. Chill until serving
time. To serve, cut salad into 6 slices;
garnish each serving with some of the
aspic triangles. Makes 6 servings

BOSTON BEANS IN GELATIN

1 Cup Tomato Juice
1 - 3 Oz. Pkg. Lemon-flavor
   Gelatin
1/3 Cup Catsup
3 Tbs. Lemon Juice
1 Tsp. Prepared Mustard
½ Tsp. Salt
1 - 1 Lb. Can Baked Beans
   (in tomato sauce)
½ Cup Diced Celery
¼ Cup Drained Sweet-Pickle Relish
Small Romaine Leaves

Heat tomato juice to boiling in a small saucepan; pour over gelatin in a medium bowl and
stir until gelatin dissolves. Stir in catsup,
lemon juice, mustard and salt. Chill for 30
minutes, or until as thick as unbeaten egg
white. Fold in baked beans, celery and pickle
relish; spoon into a 5-cup ring mold. Chill
several hours, or until mold is firm (overnight is best). Unmold onto serving plate;
carefully lift off mold. Stand romaine
leaves in center of ring. Makes 6 servings.

CUCUMBER JELLY SALAD

1 - 3 Oz. Pkg. Lemon-flavored
   Gelatin
Hot Water
½ Tsp. Celery Salt
½ Tsp. Onion Salt
1 Tsp. Prepared Horseradish
2 Tbs. White Vinegar
2 to 3 Cucumbers
Chopped Mint or Parsley

Dissolve gelatin in 1 cup of hot water; add
seasonings and vinegar. Chill until mixture
begins to set. In the meantime, peel the
cucumbers and cut into halves lengthwise.
Discard seeds. Force cucumbers through
a food grinder or shred fine (2 large cucumbers make about 1 cup shredded).
When gelatin is partially set, stir in the
cucumbers and some chopped mint. Pour
the mixture into a shallow dish or 8-inch
square pan and chill until firm. To serve,
cut into cubes and arrange on greens.
Makes 6 servings.

TOMATO SALAD
(Salade de Tomates)

4 to 6 Very Ripe Tomatoes
2 Heads Endive
1 Tbs. Chopped Parsley
1 Tbs. Chopped Chives
1 Tbs. Chopped Fresh Basil
3 Tbs. Olive Oil
1 Tbs. Wine Vinegar
Salt and Pepper to taste

Plunge tomatoes into boiling water for a
second and then let them cool. Peel and
cut into very thin slices. Arrange leaves
of endive around edge of serving dish; add
tomatoes and sprinkle with chopped herbs.
Top with dressing made of the oil, vinegar
and salt and freshly-ground black pepper
to taste. Makes 6 servings.

WHITE BEAN AND TUNA SALAD
(Southern European)

2 - 1 Lb. 4 Oz. Cans Cannelini, or
   1 Lb. Dried White Beans
1 Onion, stuck with 2 cloves and
   1 bay leaf (if using dried beans)
2 - 7 Oz. Cans White-meat Tuna Fish
2/3 Cup Finely-chopped Scallions
½ Cup Finely-chopped Parsley
1 Clove Garlic, finely minced
½ Cup Olive Oil (approximate)
Vinegar or Fresh Lemon Juice
Salt and Pepper

Open and drain the canned beans, or soak
and prepare the packaged beans with onion and bay leaf and cook until tender;
cool. Combine with coarsely-shredded
tuna fish and other seasonings and dress
to suit your taste with olive oil, vinegar,
and salt and pepper. Chill before serving.
This may be prepared while the beans
are hot and eaten hot, although it is best
when served cold for an appetizer or a
luncheon salad. Makes 6 salad servings.

Note: Cannelini are long white beans
which may be found canned or dried.
If you do not find them in your locality,
substitute white pea beans or small dried
Limas.

LIVERWURST AND SALAMI SALAD

2 Cups Diced, Cooked Potatoes
3 Hard-cooked Eggs, diced
1 Cup Diced Celery
1 Tbs. Minced Onion
½ Cup Cubed, Hard Salami
½ Cup Cubed Liverwurst
½ Cup Cubed Sharp Cheddar Cheese
1 Cup Shredded Cabbage
¼ Cup Olive Oil
Salt and Pepper to taste
½ Cup Mayonnaise
Salad Greens
Paprika

Mix first 8 ingredients. Add olive oil, and salt and pepper to taste. Mix lightly but well. Add mayonnaise. Serve salad on greens with a sprinkling of paprika. Makes 4 servings.

BEAN SPROUT SALAD

¼ Cup Pine Nuts
1 Cup Carrots, shredded
½ Cup Sweet Red Pepper, shredded
2 Scallions, shredded (use both white and green parts)
2 Cups Bean Sprouts

Dressing:
2 Tbs. Wine Vinegar
1 Tbs. Chenkong Vinegar
1 Tbs. Rice Vinegar
1 Tbs. Chinese Red Vinegar
2 Tbs. Light Soy Sauce
½ Tbs. Sesame-seed Oil
3 Tbs. Peanut Oil
¼ Tsp. Pepper, freshly ground

Roast the pine nuts and cool. Shred all vegetables, with the exception of the bean sprouts. Refrigerate until ready to use. Mix all dressing ingredients together in a bowl. Just before serving salad, toss dressing and vegetables together until well mixed. Serve at once. Makes 4 servings.

PINK DAWN SALAD

1 Cup Rice
1 Tsp. Salt
4 Hard-boiled Eggs
4 Small, Ripe Tomatoes
1 Tbs. Olive Oil
1 Tbs. Lemon Juice
1 Pkg. Frozen Shrimp or Prawns
3 Bananas
2 Tbs. Tomato Paste
2 Tbs. Mayonnaise
Paprika

Cook the rice in boiling salted water until tender, then drain it and hold it under runnig water. Spread it on a tray to dry and cool. Shell the hard-boiled eggs and cut in half. Skin the tomatoes and slice them. Mix the oil and lemon juice and toss the shrimp in this dressing. Peel the bananas and cut into chunks.

If possible, serve this salad on a green dish. Put the rice in the center and arrange the shrimp, bananas and eggs around it. Place the tomatoes around these, then make a small hollow in the center of the rice and in it place a bowl filled with a mixture of tomato paste and mayonnaise. Sprinkle the rice with paprika.

TEA GARDEN SALAD

1 - 3 Oz. Pkg. Orange Gelatin
1 Cup Hot, Black Tea
1 - 11 Oz. Can Mandarin Oranges
1 - 9 Oz. Can Crushed Pineapple
1 - 5 Oz. Can Water Chestnuts, sliced

Dissolve gelatin in hot tea. Drain & reserve juice from oranges & pineapple. Add 1 cup of reserved juice to gelatin. Add orange juice to equal 1 cup, if needed. Stir well. Chill until gelatin begins to thicken. Add water chestnuts, pineapple and orange sections; spoon into well-oiled molds. Refrigerate until set. Makes 8 servings.

MOLDED HAM SALAD

1 Envelope Unflavored Gelatin
1/3 Cup Cold Water
2 Egg Yolks
¾ Tsp. Salt
Dash of Cayenne
1 Tsp. Powdered Mustard
1 Can Condensed Consomme'
1 Cup Ground, Cooked Ham
1 Slice of Onion, minced
¼ Cup Mayonnaise
¼ Cup Heavy Cream, whipped
Lettuce

Soften the gelatin in cold water. Mix egg
yolks, salt, cayenne and mustard in the
top of a double boiler. Beat mixture until thick and lemon-colored. Add consomme' and cook, stirring, over boiling
water until mixture thickens enough to
coat a metal spoon. Add gelatin and stir
until dissolved. Cool. Add ham, onion,
mayonnaise and cream. Pour into a 1
quart mold and chill until firm. Unmold
on lettuce. Makes 4 servings.

BRAZILIAN SALAD

½ Lb. Skinned Tomatoes
1 Celery Heart
4 Oz. Pineapple Pieces
1 Lettuce Heart
Juice of 1 Lemon
2 Tsp. Cream
Cayenne Pepper

Slice the tomatoes, cut up the celery heart
and mix together with the pineapple pieces.
Use fresh pineapple, if possible; however,
well-drained canned pineapple may be used.
Shred the lettuce and mix this with the
other ingredients, reserving some pineapple
for decorating the salad. Combine the
lemon juice, cream and some cayenne pepper and pour over the salad in a salad bowl.

CUCUMBER AND BEET SALAD

4 Raw Beets (1 Lb.)
3 Tbs. Chopped Onion
Dash of Pepper
1 Tsp. Salt
1½ Tsp. Sugar
2 Tbs. Salad Oil
2 Tbs. Vinegar
2 - 5" Cucumbers, chilled

Wash beets thoroughly and peel. Grate
coarsely into a bowl. Add onion, seasonings, sugar, oil and vinegar; mix. Cover
and chill until ready to serve. Cut the
cucumbers in half lengthwise with a knife,
cut around the edge of the cucumber,
loosening the center part from the skin.
Scoop out center, as close to the skin as
possible, leaving a thin shell. Dice the
fleshy portion and combine with the beet
mixture. Blend quickly, then heap into
the cucumber shells. Serve immediately.
This may be prepared ahead of time and
then combined quickly just before serving.
Makes 4 servings.

SAVORY SHRIMP MOLD

2 Envelopes Unflavored Gelatin
½ Cup Cold Water
1 Cup Boiling Water
2 Bouillon Cubes
¼ Cup Mayonnaise
1 Tsp. Horseradish
1 Tsp. Instant Minced Onion
1 Tbs. Minced Parsley
2 Tbs. Fresh Lime or Lemon Juice
Dash of Worcestershire
Dash of Hot Pepper Sauce
1 Lb. Shrimp, cooked, peeled,
  cleaned and diced
½ Cup Heavy Cream, whipped
Seasoned Salt and Pepper to taste
Salad Greens

Soften gelatin in cold water; add boiling
water and bouillon cubes. Stir until the
gelatin and cubes are dissolved. Set in
refrigerator to chill until slightly thickened. Fold in remaining ingredients, except greens. Pour into 1-quart mold.
Chill until firm. Unmold on greens.
Makes 6 servings.

PINEAPPLE SALAD

1 Egg
2 Tbs. Lemon Juice
2 Tbs. Granulated Sugar
Pinch of Salt
4 Small, Fresh Pineapples
½ Cup Heavy Cream, whipped
1 Cup Miniature Marshmallows
1 Cup Diced Oranges
1 Cup Tokay or Seedless Grapes
1 Cup Sliced Bananas
8 Maraschino Cherries
½ Cup Slivered, Toasted Almonds
1 Cup Orange Sections

In double boiler, beat egg with fork; stir in lemon juice, sugar and salt. Cook over hot water, stirring constantly, for 5 minutes, or until thickened. Remove from heat and cool. Cut crown from each pineapple. Cut off upper third of each pineapple. Remove rind and eyes from these pieces, cut each into ½" slices and core with a small biscuit cutter. Cut into bite-size chunks.

Using a long, sharp knife, cut almost to bottom of pineapple, ½" in from edge, and cut all around. Lift out cylinder and cut into bite-size chunks. Be sure to remove core. Cut a saw-tooth edge around top of each pineapple shell. Wrap each in foil and refrigerate. Fold whipped cream, marshmallows, 1 cup pineapple chunks, diced oranges, grapes, bananas, and cherries into cooled egg mixture. Refrigerate. It is best if this much is done the day before.

About 20 minutes before serving, fold the almonds into the fruit mixture, then spoon into the pineapple shells. Garnish with the orange sections. Makes 4 servings.

MIXED BEAN SALAD

1 - 15 Oz. Can Red Kidney Beans, drained (about 2 cups)
1½ Cups Baby Lima Beans, cooked
½ Bermuda Onion, separated into rings
½ Cup Sliced Radishes
1 Cup Cucumber Slices
1 Tbs. Tarragon Vinegar
¼ Cup Salad Oil
½ Tsp. Salt
½ Tsp. Powdered Mustard
Lettuce

Combine all ingredients, except lettuce. Mix well and chill. When ready to serve, spoon into bowl lined with lettuce leaves. Makes 8 servings.

HAM MOUSSE

1 Tbs. Unflavored Gelatin
¼ Cup Cold Water
2 Egg Yolks, slightly beaten
½ Tsp. Salt
1 Tsp. Dry Mustard
1 Cup Chicken Consomme' or Bouillon
1 Cup Milk
1 Tbs. Grated Onion
1 Tsp. Prepared Horseradish
¼ Cup Finely-diced Green Pepper
2 Tbs. Finely-cut Pimiento, drained
½ Tsp. Paprika
2 Cups Ground Cooked Ham
½ Cup Heavy Cream, whipped
Green Pepper Rings
Small Celery Hearts

Soften gelatin in water. Combine egg yolks, salt and mustard in top of double boiler. Stir in consomme' and milk. Cook, stirring, over boiling water for 5 to 6 minutes, until slightly thickened. Remove from hot water. Add gelatin. Stir until dissolved. Fold in onion, horseradish, green pepper, pimiento, paprika and ham. Chill until mixture begins to thicken. Fold in cream. Pour into a 1½-quart mold. Chill overnight or until firm. Unmold on chilled salad platter. Garnish with green pepper rings, small celery hearts, and, if you like, lettuce-leaf cups containing pickle relish. Makes 6 servings.

HAWAIIAN SPINACH SALAD

3 Oz. Fresh Spinach
2 Cups Coarsely-shredded Red
  Cabbage
1 Medium Avocado, peeled and
  sliced
2 Hard-cooked Eggs, cut into
  wedges
Cherry Tomatoes
Vinaigrette Dressing (your own
  recipe)

Toss spinach leaves with shredded cabbage. Mound vegetables on a salad plate and surround alternately with avocado slices and egg wedges. Top with cherry tomatoes & your favorite vinaigrette dressing and serve. Makes 4 servings.

CHEF'S SALAD--
MEXICAN STYLE

6 Cups Torn Lettuce
1 Cup Shredded Carrot (2 carrots)
1 Cup Chopped Celery (2 celery
  stalks)
1 Cup Cooked Chicken, cut in
  julienne strips
1 Cup Fully-cooked Ham, cut in
  julienne strips
2 Tomatoes, chopped
3 Tbs. Sliced Green Onions, with
  tops

Sauce:
2 Cups Shredded Sharp American
  Cheese (8 oz.)
2/3 Cup Milk
3 Tbs. Chopped, Seeded Canned
  Green Chili Peppers
3 Tbs. Sliced, Pitted Ripe Olives
2 Cups Corn Chips

In a large salad bowl, combine lettuce, carrot, and celery. Arrange chicken, ham, tomatoes, and green onion on top. In a heavy saucepan, combine cheese and milk. Cook and stir over low heat until cheese is melted and mixture is smooth. Stir in the chilies and olives. Just before serving, pour sauce over salad. Toss lightly. Pass corn chips to sprinkle on top. Makes 6 servings.

MOLDED AVOCADO-
TURKEY SALAD

Avocado Layer:
1 - 3 Oz. Pkg. Lemon-lime Flavor
  Gelatin
1 Cup Hot Water
¾ Cup Cold Water
3 Tbs. Lemon Juice
2 Drops Liquid Red Pepper
  Seasoning
1 Avocado, halved, pitted, peeled
  and diced

Turkey Layer:
1 Envelope Unflavored Gelatin
1 Envelope Instant Chicken Broth
  or 1 Chicken Bouillon Cube
½ Tsp. Salt
½ Tsp. Dillweed
5 Drops Liquid Red Pepper Seasoning
1½ Cups Water
½ Cup Mayonnaise or Salad Dressing
2 Cups Diced Cold Roast Turkey
½ Cup Thinly-sliced Celery
¼ Cup Chopped Walnuts

Make the avocado layer. Dissolve lemon-lime gelatin in hot water in a medium bowl. Stir in cold water, lemon juice and liquid red pepper seasoning. Chill 1 hour, or just until as thick as unbeaten egg white; fold in diced avocado. Pour into an 8-cup tube mold. Chill for 30 minutes, or just until sticky-firm. While avocado layer chills, make the turkey layer. Soften gelatin with chicken broth or bouillon cube, salt, dillweed and liquid red pepper seasoning in water in a medium saucepan. Heat, stirring constantly, just until gelatin and bouillon cube, if using, dissolve. Remove from the heat. Beat in mayonnaise or salad dressing until smooth; fold in turkey, celery and walnuts. Spoon over avocado layer. Chill at least 3 hours, or until firm (or chill overnight). Unmold onto a large serving plate; lift mold off carefully. Garnish center with a few salad greens. Makes 8 servings.

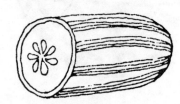

CAESAR SALAD

1 Garlic Clove, crushed
¾ Cup Olive Oil
2 Cups ¼" Bread Cubes, no crusts
2 Large Heads Romaine Lettuce
Black Pepper, freshly ground
½ Tsp. Salt
2 Eggs, soft-cooked for 1 minute
3 Tbs. Fresh Lemon Juice
½ Cup Grated Parmesan Cheese

Mix garlic with oil and let stand overnight. Heat ¼ cup of the oil and saute' bread cubes until golden on all sides. Drain and set aside. Clean and trim romaine. Wash and break into bite-size pieces. Grind the black pepper. Add salt and remaining olive oil. Toss well to coat romaine. Place shelled eggs in center of salad. Add lemon juice and toss until salad greens are coated with creamy dressing. Toss with Parmesan cheese and croutons. Serve at once. Makes 6 to 8 servings.

SUPPER SALAD PLATE

2 Nectarines, peeled (or use
   peaches or plums) and sliced
2 Cups Cantaloupe Balls (or use
   honeydew or watermelon)
1 Avocado, pared and sliced
1 Medium cucumber, cut into spears
1 Tomato, cut in wedges, or 1 cup
   cherry tomatoes
12 Whole Radishes, or seedless green
   grapes
1 Small Red Onion, thinly sliced, or
   8 scallions, trimmed
1 Green Pepper, seeded and cut in
   strips
½ Lb. Cooked Chicken, Turkey or
   Ham, thinly sliced
½ Lb. Swiss, American or Muenster
   Cheese, sliced
Creamy Curry Dressing (see
   recipe below)

Arrange fruits, vegetables, sliced meats and cheese on a large platter. Serve with curry dressing and slices of whole grain bread. Makes 4 servings.

Creamy Curry Dressing:
½ Cup Sour Cream
½ Cup Mayonnaise
1 Tbs. Honey
¼ to ½ Tsp. Curry Powder
1/8 Tsp. Salt

Stir all ingredients until smooth in a small bowl.

FROZEN FRUIT SALAD
in PINEAPPLE BOATS

1 - 8 Oz. Pkg. Cream Cheese,
   softened
½ Cup Mayonnaise or Salad
   Dressing
2 Tbs. Confectioners' Sugar
1 Tbs. Lime Juice
1 Cup Tiny Marshmallows
1 Cup Orange Sections
1 Cup Fresh Peach Slices
½ Cup Halved Green Grapes
½ Cup Chopped Toasted
   Slivered Almonds
¼ Cup Sliced Maraschino Cherries
1 Cup Whipping Cream
3 Small Ripe Pineapples

Beat the cream cheese with mayonnaise or salad dressing, confectioners' sugar & lime juice until smooth (use large bowl). Stir in marshmallows, orange sections, peach slices, grapes, almonds and cherries. Beat cream until stiff; fold into cheese-fruit mixture. Pour into a shallow dish, 8x8x2". Cover and freeze for several hours, or until firm.

Halve each pineapple lengthwise, cutting through the leafy crown. Cut out the core, then cut fruit from rind of each half in one piece; lift out. Slice enough of the fruit crosswise to make 42 thin strips; stand 7, overlapping, in each shell; chill. (Any remaining fruit may be used for another meal.) Remove the fruit salad from the freezer 15 minutes before serving and let stand at room temperature to soften, then cut into 1" cubes. Pile into pineapple boats. Makes 6 servings.

SALMON SALAD

1 - 6 Oz. Pkg. Curry-flavor Rice Mix
Butter or Margarine
Water
1 - 1 Lb. Can Salmon
1 Cup Diced Celery
¼ Cup Sliced Stuffed Olives
2 Tsp. Grated Lemon Peel
¼ Cup Cream, for whipping
½ Cup Mayonnaise or Salad Dressing
Iceberg Lettuce

Prepare rice mix with butter or margarine
and water, following directions on the
package. Place in a large bowl; cool, then
cover and refrigerate for about an hour.
While rice chills, drain liquid from salmon;
remove skin and bones. Flake salmon;
fold into rice with celery, olives and lemon
peel. Beat cream until stiff in a small bowl;
fold in mayonnaise or salad dressing. Fold
into salmon mixture. Place lettuce leaves
on serving plates to form cups; spoon the
salmon mixture into lettuce cups. Garnish
with sliced olives. Makes 6 servings.

SUMMER SALAD

2 Cups Finely-sliced Raw Spinach
1½ Cups Sliced, Peeled Cucumbers
1/3 Cup Sliced Green Onions, including
   some of the tops
½ Cup Sliced Radishes
2 Cups Creamed Cottage Cheese
   (1 pint)
1 Cup Commercial Sour Cream
2 Tsp. Lemon Juice
½ Tsp. Salt
Freshly-ground Pepper
Parsley and Paprika for garnish

In a bowl, combine sliced spinach, sliced
cucumbers, onions and radishes. Toss
together lightly. Arrange on four individual salad plates or in wooden salad
bowls. In center of each serving, place a
mound of cottage cheese. Blend together
sour cream, lemon juice, salt and pepper
and pour over the salads. Sprinkle top
of each salad with a little paprika and
chopped parsley, if desired. Makes 4
servings.

CRABMEAT SALAD with MELON BALLS

1 Honeydew Melon
2 - 6½ Oz. Cans King Crabmeat,
   drained
1½ Cups Thinly-sliced Celery
2 Tbs. Snipped Parsley
½ Lb. Baked or Boiled Ham Slices
¼ Cup Mayonnaise or Salad Dressing
2 Tbs. Lemon Juice
1 Tsp. Salt
¼ Tsp. Pepper
2 - 10 Oz. Pkgs. Frozen Melon Balls

Early in the day, cut off top of honeydew
melon ¼" down. With a melon baller,
make balls from seeded melon meat. With
a sharp knife, cut saw-toothed edge around
top of melon. Refrigerate melon and melon
balls, covered. Put frozen melon balls into
refrigerator to thaw. Into a large bowl,
flake the crabmeat, reserving a few pieces
for a garnish. Add celery, parsley and ham
slices (snipped into long strips) to the crabmeat; refrigerate. In a small bowl, blend
the mayonnaise, lemon juice, salt and pepper; refrigerate. About 5 minutes before
serving, pour the mayonnaise mixture over
the crabmeat mixture; toss with a fork.
Pile lightly in the melon shell; garnish with
reserved crabmeat pieces. Arrange the
melon shell on a serving platter; surround
with melon balls. Makes 10 servings.

GINGER-ALE FRUIT MOLD

1 - 3 Oz. Pkg. Lemon-flavored Gelatin
2 Cups Ginger Ale
2 Cups Diced Fruit (orange, pear, banana,
   cherries, apple), drained
¼ Cup Chopped Nuts
1 Tbs. Chopped Candied Gingerroot
Salad Greens
Mayonnaise

Dissolve gelatin in 1 cup hot ginger ale and
cool. Add 1 cup cold ginger ale. Chill until partially set; then stir in fruit, nuts, and
gingerroot. Pour into a 1-quart mold and
chill until firm. Unmold on salad greens &
serve with mayonnaise. Makes 4 servings.

CARROT-COCONUT SALAD

1 Cup Flaked Coconut
1½ Cups Shredded Raw Carrots
¼ Cup Seedless Raisins
2 Tbs. Fresh Lemon Juice
1 - 11 Oz. Can Mandarin Oranges,
    drained
1/3 Cup Mayonnaise
Salt to taste
Salad Greens

Mix all ingredients except greens. Chill
and serve on a bed of salad greens.
Makes 4 to 6 servings.

MOLDED CHICKEN SALAD

2 Envelopes Unflavored Gelatin
1 Tbs. Sugar
1 Tsp. Curry Powder
3½ Cups Canned Chicken Broth
2 Tbs. Lemon Juice
1/3 Cup Chutney (bottled), finely
    chopped
4 Cups Diced, Cooked Chicken
1 Cup Chopped Celery

Soften gelatin with sugar and curry powder
in 1 cup of the chicken broth in a medium
saucepan. Heat, stirring constantly, just until the gelatin is dissolved; remove from the
heat. Stir in remaining 2½ cups of broth.

Measure ½ cup of the gelatin mixture into
a small bowl and set aside to use later.
Stir lemon juice into remaining gelatin in
the saucepan. Chill about 50 minutes, or
until as thick as unbeaten egg white. Stir
chutney into gelatin in small bowl; pour
into a 6-cup mold and chill about 30 min.,
or just until sticky-firm. Fold chicken and
celery into the thickened gelatin in the
saucepan. Spoon mixture over the chutney
layer in mold. Chill several hours, or overnight.

To unmold, run tip of a thin-bladed knife
around top of mold. Dip mold very
quickly in and out of a pan of hot water.
Cover mold with serving plate; invert and
gently lift off mold. Garnish as desired.
Makes 6 servings.

GERMAN POTATO SALAD

¾ Cup Diced Bacon
1 Cup Chopped Celery
1 Cup Chopped Onion
3 Tbs. Flour
1-1/3 Cups Water
2/3 Cup Cider Vinegar
2/3 Cup Sugar
3 Tsp. Salt
½ Tsp. Pepper
8 Cups Cubed, Cooked Potatoes
    (about 8 medium)
1 Cup Sliced Radishes
½ Cup Chopped Dill Pickle (optional)

Cook bacon in large skillet; drain off fat.
Measure fat and return ¼ cup to skillet.
Add celery and onion and cook 1 minute;
blend in flour. Stir in water and vinegar;
cook, stirring constantly, until mixture is
thick and bubbly. Stir in sugar, salt and
pepper. Pour mixture over potatoes and
bacon in a greased 3-quart casserole; mix
lightly. Cover and bake in 350°F. oven
for 30 minutes. Remove from oven. Stir
in radishes and dill pickle. Serve at once.
Makes 10 to 12 servings.

THREE-BEAN SALAD

4 Oz. Italian-style Salad Dressing
1 Tbs. Worcestershire Sauce
¾ Cup Sweet Pickle Relish,
    drained
1 - 1 Lb. Can Cut Wax Beans,
    drained
1 - 1 Lb. Can Cut Green Beans,
    drained
1 - 15 Oz. Can Kidney Beans,
    drained
½ Cup Sliced Red Onion
1 Quart Salad Greens

In a large bowl, combine salad dressing,
Worcestershire sauce, pickle relish and all
of the beans; toss lightly to combine.
Refrigerate, covered, until well chilled--
about 4 hours. Just before serving, add
onion and salad greens. Toss to combine.
Turn into salad bowl. Makes 8 servings.

MISCELLANEOUS

CRANBERRY PUNCH

2 Pints Cranberry Juice Cocktail
½ Cup Fresh Orange Juice
2/3 Cup Fresh Lemon Juice
2 Cups Boiling Water
5 Tea Bags
¼ Tsp. Cinnamon
¼ Tsp. Nutmeg
¾ Cup Sugar
2½ Cups Water
Orange Slices
Whole Cloves

Pour the boiling water over the tea bags
and spices. Cover and steep for 5 minutes.
Remove the tea bags. Stir in the sugar;
cool. Add 2½ cups water, cranberry juice,
orange juice and lemon juice and chill.
Garnish with orange slices stuck with cloves.
Makes 2½ quarts.

FRUIT KEBABS

3 Large Firm Ripe Pears
3 Large Firm Ripe Apricots
3 Medium Apples
3 Medium, Firm Ripe Bananas
½ Cup Butter or Margarine
2 Tbs. Brown Sugar
1 Tbs. Honey
2 Tsp. Lemon Juice
1 Tsp. Ground Ginger
¾ Tsp. Ground Cinnamon
½ Tsp. Ground Mace

Pare pears, quarter and core. Peel apricots,
pit and quarter. Quarter apples and core;
cut each piece of fruit in half. Peel the
bananas; cut each crosswise into 6 pieces.
Thread all fruits, dividing evenly, onto six
long skewers. Place on rack in broiler pan.

Melt the butter or margarine in a small
saucepan; stir in brown sugar, honey, lemon
juice and spices. Brush part of mixture
over fruits. Broil, 4 to 6 inches from heat,
turning and brushing several times with remaining honey mixture, for 10 minutes, or
until lightly glazed. Serve hot with baked
ham or chicken or veal curry.

DIVINITY

2-1/3 Cups Sugar
½ Cup Water
2/3 Cup Light Corn Syrup
¼ Tsp. Salt
2 Egg Whites, stiffly beaten
1 Tsp. Vanilla Extract

In saucepan mix sugar, water, corn syrup,
and salt. Bring to a boil and cook, stirring, until sugar is dissolved. Continue
cooking, without stirring, until a small
amount of mixture forms a very hard ball
when dropped into very cold water (cook
to 266°F. on candy thermometer). Wipe
away any crystals that form on side of
pan with a damp cloth wrapped around a
fork. Gradually pour mixture over beaten
egg whites, beating constantly. Continue
beating until candy is very stiff and mixture will hold its shape when dropped
from a spoon. Stir in vanilla. Pour into
a buttered 8" square pan. Let stand until
firm. Cut into squares. Or drop mixture
by tablespoonfuls onto wax paper and
let stand until firm. Makes about 1¼
pounds, or 16 pieces. For a variation,
the dropped candy may be topped with
half of a nut, or a piece of candied
cherry. If desired, sprinkle candy in
pan with chopped nuts, chocolate shot,
or flaked coconut.

ZESTY FRENCH DRESSING

½ Cup Finely-chopped Onion
1 Clove Garlic, finely chopped
¼ Cup Sugar
1 Cup Red-wine Vinegar
1 Cup Olive Oil
1 Cup Catsup
2 Tsp. Salt
1 Tsp. Dry Mustard
1 Tsp. Paprika
1 Tsp. Dried Oregano Leaves

Combine all ingredients in jar with tight-
fitting lid; shake to mix well. Refrigerate,
covered, for at least 2 hours to blend the
flavors. Strain to remove onion and garlic. Shake well just before using. Makes
2¾ cups.

CHEESE-MUSHROOM CANAPES

1 Tbs. Butter
1 Drop Tabasco Sauce
1 Tbs. Flour
2 Tbs. Cream
1 - 3 Oz. Can Chopped Broiled
  Mushrooms
2 Oz. Processed Cheese, grated
  (about 4 tablespoons)
36 Narrow Toast Fingers

Place butter and tabasco in saucepan over
low heat. Stir in flour until smooth. Add
cream and broth drained from mushrooms.
Bring to boiling point, stirring constantly.
Add cheese. Continue stirring until cheese
melts. Remove from heat. Chop mushrooms very fine. Add to cheese mixture.
Spread on toast fingers. Heat thoroughly
under broiler just before serving. Makes
1 cup of spread--about 36 small canapes.

PLUM MINCEMEAT

4 Lbs. Prune Plums
5 Medium Apples
½ Cup Cider Vinegar
Juice and Grated Rind of 1 Orange
Juice and Grated Rind of 1 Lemon
4½ Cups Light Brown Sugar
½ Lb. Dried Currants, rinsed and
  drained
½ Lb. Raisins
1 Lb. Ready-cut Mixed Peels
1½ Tsp. Salt
½ Tsp. Ground Allspice
1 Tsp. Ground Nutmeg
1 Tsp. Ground Cloves

Wash prune-plums, pit and cut into coarse
pieces. Peel and grate apples; add to prune-
plums along with vinegar, juices, and grated
rinds of orange and lemon. Bring to boil,
then simmer, stirring occasionally, until
fruit is just tender, about 30 minutes.

Add remaining ingredients and cook slowly
until fairly thick, about 1 hour. Stir frequently to prevent scorching. Pour into
hot sterilized jars; seal at once. Store in
a cool, dry place. Makes about 6 pints.

SPICED CANTALOUPE

4 Cantaloupe
2 Tsp. Powdered Alum
2 Cups White Vinegar
4 Cups Sugar
4 Cinnamon Sticks
1 Tbs. Whole Cloves
1 Tbs. Allspice

Peel melons; cut into halves and remove
seeds and fiber. Cut into one-half inch
cubes. Mix 3 quarts of water with the
alum and add melon. Let stand overnight.
Drain the melon. In a preserving kettle
mix vinegar, sugar, 1 cup of water and
the spices tied in a cheesecloth bag. Add
the melon; cover and boil for 15 minutes.
Pack melon into hot sterilized jars.

HONEY PUFF PANCAKE

1 Cup Milk
6 Eggs
3 Tbs. Honey
1 - 3 Oz. Pkg. Cream Cheese,
  softened
1 Cup All-purpose Flour
½ Tsp. Salt
½ Tsp. Baking Powder
3 Tbs. Butter or Margarine
Powdered Sugar
Jelly
Lemon Wedges

Preheat oven to 400°F. Measure the flour.
In blender, place milk, eggs, honey, cream
cheese, flour, salt and baking powder. Let
stand while preparing skillet. Grease a 10"
ovenproof skillet with 1 tablespoon of margarine. Add remaining 2 tablespoons of
margarine to the skillet; heat in 400°F. oven
just until margarine sizzles, about 2 minutes.
While skillet is in oven, blend ingredients at
high speed for 1 minute; scrape sides of the
blender and blend at high speed for 1 minute or until smooth. Remove skillet from
oven; immediately pour batter into hot skillet. Bake at 400°F. for 20 to 25 minutes,
or until puffed and dark golden brown.
Serve immediately with a sprinkling of
powdered sugar, a spoonful of jelly and a
lemon wedge. Makes 6 servings.

GLACE' NUT PATTIES

3 Cups Nutmeats
2 Cups Granulated Sugar
1 Cup Firmly-packed Light
  Brown Sugar
½ Cup Light Corn Syrup
½ Cup Water
¼ Tsp. Salt
¼ Cup Butter

Break half of nuts into small pieces; leave the rest whole. Spread out in tins to heat in slow oven. Combine white and brown sugars, syrup and water in saucepan; cook, stirring constantly, until sugar is dissolved. Continue cooking to the crack stage (300° F.), or until a little tried in cold water is brittle. Use very low heat toward the end of cooking to prevent darkening of syrup; stir only enough to prevent scorching. When done, remove from heat. Add salt, butter and warm nuts; stir only enough to mix. Do not scrape sides of pan. Spoon candy out in small amounts onto a buttered enamel tabletop. When candy is cold, tap table lightly to help loosen patties; remove with spatula. Keep in a tightly covered tin. Makes about 3 doz., depending upon size.

CLAM BITES

1 Egg, separated
1 - 10½ Oz. Can Minced Clams
1 Tsp. Melted Butter
½ Cup All-purpose Flour
Salt and Pepper

Beat egg yolk until light. Drain clams, reserving liquid. Stir into egg yolk the butter, flour, ¼ teaspoon salt, and ¼ cup clam liquid. Add milk, if necessary, to make ¼ cup. Fold in stiffly beaten egg white. Add clams and let stand for at least 1 hour at room temperature. Drop by teaspoons into hot deep fat (375°F. on a frying thermometer) and fry until golden brown, 5 to 6 minutes. Drain on absorbent paper. Sprinkle with salt and pepper and serve hot on toothpicks. Fry these at the last minute before serving. Makes about 2 dozen.

SPUN APPLE SLICES

1 Cup All-purpose Flour
1 Egg, lightly beaten
½ Cup, plus 2 Tbs. Cold Water
2 Medium-size Firm Apples
3 Cups Peanut Oil + 1 Tbs.
1 Cup Sugar
¼ Cup Cold Water
1 Tbs. Black Sesame Seeds

Pour the flour into a fairly large bowl. Combine the cold water with the beaten egg and add to the flour, stirring constantly with a large spoon. Stir until you have formed a smooth batter.

Cut the apples into quarters. Peel and cut away the cores. Cut the quarters into eighths. Lightly grease a large serving plate with oil. Fill a large bowl with one quart of water plus a dozen ice cubes.

In a 2 to 3-quart saucepan, heat the 3 cups of oil until it reaches 375°F. on deep-frying thermometer. In a 12" wok or 10" skillet, heat 1 tablespoon of oil with the sugar and water. Bring the sugar and water to a boil over high heat, stirring only until the sugar dissolves. Cook this mixture briskly without stirring until the syrup registers 300°F. on a candy thermometer or reaches the hard-crack stage. Stir in the sesame seeds and turn the heat down to its lowest point.

Drop 8 of the apple wedges into the batter, stirring them to coat them thoroughly. With a slotted spoon, transfer the apple wedges to the heated oil and deep-fry them for 1 min., or until they turn light amber. Immediately lift them out of the oil and put them into the skillet of hot syrup. Stir the wedges to coat them thoroughly with syrup, then, using the slotted spoon or tongs, drop them one at a time into the bowl of ice water. The syrup coating will harden instantly and enclose each piece of apple in a clear, brilliant glaze. Transfer the finished spun apples to the greased serving plate and make the second batch of apple slices. Serve as soon as possible so that the candy glaze will not have a chance to soften. Makes 16 apple slices.

COCKTAIL MACADAMIAS

1 - 7 Oz. Jar Macadamia Nuts
2 Tbs. Butter or Margarine, melted
½ Tsp. Seasoned Salt
¼ Tsp. Liquid Hot-pepper Seasoning
¼ Tsp. Paprika
¼ Tsp. Garlic Salt

Preheat oven to 375°F. In a shallow baking pan, toss nuts with butter, seasoned salt, hot-pepper seasoning, and paprika. Bake 10 minutes. Drain nuts on paper towels. Sprinkle with garlic salt and serve slightly warm. Makes 1¼ cups.

CHEESE-AND-TOMATO FONDUE

1 Clove Garlic, split
1 Lb. Natural Swiss Cheese, grated
1¼ Cups Dry White Wine
1 - 8 Oz. Can Tomato Sauce
Dash of Salt
Dash of Pepper
2 Tbs. Cornstarch
1 Long Loaf French or Italian Bread

Use a fondue pot, deep baking dish with glazed interior, flameproof glass saucepan or crockery utensil. Do not use a metal pan.

Rub bottom and side of fondue pot with cut sides of garlic. Place cheese, 1 cup of wine, the tomato sauce, salt and pepper in the pot. Cook over medium heat, stirring constantly, just until cheese melts. Remove from heat. Do not cook longer, even though cheese and wine are not blended. In a small bowl, make a smooth paste of cornstarch and remaining wine. With a wire whisk, mix the cornstarch mixture into the cheese mixture. Return to medium heat; cook, stirring constantly 2 to 3 minutes, or until fondue is creamy and as thick as medium white sauce.

To serve: Set fondue over low flame or candle warmer. Cut bread into 1'' cubes for dipping into fondue. Makes 12 servings.

CHICKEN SPREAD

1 - 3 Oz. Pkg. Cream Cheese, softened
½ Tsp. Celery Salt
½ Tsp. Onion Salt
1 Tsp. Seasoned Salt
1 Tsp. Worcestershire
Dash of Tabasco
1/3 Cup Commercial Sour Cream
¼ Cup Finely-chopped Toasted Almonds
1 Cup Finely-chopped Cooked Chicken
1 - 3 Oz. Can Mushrooms, drained and finely chopped
Snipped Parsley

In a bowl, blend cream cheese, celery salt, onion salt, seasoned salt, Worcestershire, Tabasco and sour cream. Stir in almonds, chicken and mushrooms. Pile into serving dish and refrigerate for several hours before serving. When ready to serve, sprinkle parsley over top of spread. Serve with your favorite crackers. Makes about 2 cups.

MULLED CIDER

4 Qts. Bottled Cider or Apple Juice
2 Cups Orange Juice
6 Tbs. Brown Sugar
¾ Tsp. Bitters
2 Tsp. Whole Cloves
6 Cinnamon Sticks
2 Tsp. Whole Allspice
¼ Tsp. Nutmeg
6 Pints Lime Sherbet
8 Thin Orange Slices, with peel left on

In a large kettle, combine cider and orange juice. Stir in brown sugar, bitters, cloves, cinnamon sticks, allspice and nutmeg. Simmer, uncovered, over low heat for 30 min., then cool and refrigerate until the next day. With a small ice-cream scoop or spoon, make 32 balls of lime sherbet. Store on a foil-covered cookie sheet in the freezer. About 30 minutes before serving, strain the cider mixture and reheat. Just before serving, pour into punch bowl; garnish with orange slices. Arrange on serving table with punch cups. Place a sherbet ball in each cup and ladle hot punch over it. Makes 32 servings.

MEXICAN PANCAKES

3 Cups Sifted Flour
1 Tbs. Sugar
1 Tsp. Baking Powder
1 Tsp. Salt
4 Eggs
1 Cup Milk
¼ Cup Melted Butter
Water
Oil, for frying

Sift flour, sugar, baking powder, and salt together. Break eggs into this mixture. Add 1 cup of milk and the melted butter and beat the mixture, adding as much water as is necessary to make a dough that is easily handled. Knead the dough well and form into small balls. Cover the balls with a cloth and leave for 20 minutes. Sprinkle some flour on a board and roll out each ball into a very thin round pancake. After letting these stand for an additional 5 minutes, fry them in deep, hot oil until they are golden brown, crisp and flaky. Drain on absorbent paper and dip into a mixture of sugar and cinnamon, or serve covered with thin honey. In Mexico these are often served, broken up in a bowl, topped with a syrup of brown sugar and cinnamon.

SWEET-TART ORANGE SLICES

8 Whole Medium Oranges, unpeeled
5 Cups Sugar
3 Cups Water
1¼ Cups Vinegar
24 Whole Cloves
2 Sticks Cinnamon

Select oranges with unblemished skins. Simmer whole oranges in enough water to cover, until tender, about 20 minutes. Drain, cool and slice fairly thin. Combine sugar, water, vinegar and spices. Bring to a boil. Add the orange slices and simmer for 20 minutes; remove cinnamon sticks. Spoon orange slices into 6 hot pint jars. Pour on cooking liquid to cover. Place 2 or 3 cloves from liquid in each jar. Seal and refrigerate. Makes 6 pints.

PICKLED CABBAGE

5 Lbs. Cabbage
6 Medium Onions
3 Green Peppers
½ Cup Salt
¾ Cup Mustard Seeds
2 Tbs. Celery Seeds
4 Cups Sugar
Vinegar

Using a chopping bowl or food processor, chop cabbage, onions and peppers very fine. Do not grind. Stir in salt and let stand for 24 hours. Drain well. Add the mustard seeds, celery seeds and sugar and mix well. Cover with vinegar. Pack in sterilized pint jars and cover. Keep in a cool place. Makes about 9 pints.

HAZELNUT CANDY

1 Cup Butter or Margarine
1-1/3 Cups Sugar
1 Tbs. Light Corn Syrup
3 Tbs. Water
1 Cup Coarsely-chopped Hazelnuts, toasted
4 - 4½ Oz. Bars Milk Chocolate, melted
1 Cup Finely-chopped Hazelnuts, toasted

Melt the butter or margarine in a large saucepan. Add sugar, syrup and water. Cook, stirring occasionally until a little dropped into cold water hardens and cracks (300°F. on candy thermometer). Remove at once from heat. Stir in coarsely chopped nuts. Spread in ungreased pan measuring about 13x9x2". Let cool completely.

Turn out on waxed paper. Spread top with half of the chocolate. Sprinkle with half the finely chopped nuts. Cover with waxed paper and invert. Spread the other side with remaining chocolate. Sprinkle with remaining finely chopped nuts. Let stand until chocolate is firm. Chill if necessary. Break into pieces. Makes about 1½ pounds, or 24 or more pieces.

PEANUT BUTTER BALLS

1 Cup Peanut Butter
¼ Cup Butter
2 Tbs. Cream
Pinch of Salt
1 Tsp. Vanilla
1 Cup Confectioners' Sugar
½ Cup Finely-chopped Dates
½ Cup Finely-chopped Walnuts

Mix all ingredients and shape into round balls. Make a thin icing of confectioners' sugar and a little milk; roll balls in it and then in chopped peanuts. Set on waxed paper until icing hardens.

ZIPPY CORN RELISH

2 - 12 Oz. Cans Whole-kernel Corn,
    drained
1 Tsp. Sugar
½ Tsp. Salt
¼ Tsp. Paprika
¾ Cup Vegetable Oil
¼ Cup Cider Vinegar
1 Tbs. Prepared Horseradish
1½ Tsp. Worcestershire Sauce
2 Drops Liquid Red Pepper
    Seasoning

Combine all ingredients, except corn, in a jar with a tight-fitting lid; shake well to mix. Pour over corn in a medium bowl; toss lightly to mix. Cover and chill for several hours, or overnight, to season and blend flavors. When serving, spoon relish into serving dish with as little dressing as possible. Makes about 4 cups of relish.

SEA FOAM CANDY

1¾ Cups Light Brown Sugar,
    firmly packed
¾ Cup Sugar
½ Cup Hot Water
¼ Cup Light Corn Syrup
¼ Tsp. Salt
2 Egg Whites
1 Tsp. Vanilla
½ Cup Broken Walnuts

Combine sugars, water, corn syrup and salt in a 2-quart heavy saucepan. Cook, stirring constantly, until sugars dissolve and mixture reaches a boil. If sugar crystals form on sides of pan, wipe them off. Continue cooking, without stirring, at a fairly low boil to the hard ball stage (260°F. on a candy thermometer). Remove from heat.

At once beat egg whites until stiff. Pour the hot syrup in a thin stream over egg whites, beating constantly with electric mixer on high speed. Add vanilla; continue beating until candy forms soft peaks and starts to lose its gloss, about 10 minutes. Stir in nuts. Drop rounded teaspoonfuls onto waxed paper, swirling candy to make peaks. Makes 30 to 36 pieces, or about 1 lb.

OVEN CARAMEL CORN

3¾ Quarts of Popped Corn (about
    15 cups)
1 Cup Brown Sugar (packed)
½ Cup Butter or Margarine
¼ Cup Light Corn Syrup
½ Tsp. Salt
½ Tsp. Soda

Divide popped corn into 2 ungreased baking pans, 13x9x2". Heat sugar, margarine, corn syrup and salt, stirring occasionally, until bubbly around the edges. Continue cooking over medium heat for 5 minutes. Remove the syrup from the heat and stir in the soda until foamy. Pour over the popped corn, stirring until corn is well coated. Bake in a preheated 200°F. oven for 1 hour, stirring every 15 minutes.

PATE DE FOIE GRAS

2 Lbs. Chicken or Veal Livers
1 Lb. Fresh Pork
2 Onions
1 Slice Bacon
4 Eggs
Salt Pork
¼ Tsp. Nutmeg
¼ Tsp. Allspice
¼ Tsp. Salt
1/8 Tsp. Pepper

Chop onions and cook with diced bacon.
Put liver and pork through the finest blade
on grinder. Add seasonings, yolk of egg &
stiffly-beaten egg whites. Mix all well. Line
a mold with minced lean salt pork. Put in
mixture and cover with lard. Bake in moderate oven for 2 hours. Cool and take out
of mold. Serve in thin slices.

TUTTI-FRUTTI POPCORN BALLS

10 Cups Freshly-popped Corn
1 - 6 Oz. Can Pecans
1 - 4 Oz. Jar Candied Red Cherries,
   halved
1 - 1 Lb. Pkg. Confectioners' Sugar,
   sifted
2/3 Cup Light Corn Syrup
2 Tbs. Water
Red Food Coloring
16 Large Marshmallows (¼ Lb.)
¾ Tsp. Peppermint Extract

Mix popcorn, pecans and cherries in two
buttered jelly-roll pans. Combine about 1
cup of the confectioners' sugar, corn syrup
and water in a medium-size saucepan. Heat
slowly, stirring constantly, until sugar dissolves. Stir in a few drops of food coloring
to tint light pink. Stir in remaining confectioners' sugar slowly and heat, stirring constantly, to boiling. Stir in marshmallows
until melted. Remove mixture from heat.
Stir in peppermint extract. Pour half of
the syrup over popcorn mixture in each
pan. Toss until evenly coated. Cool until easy to handle, then shape into 1½"
balls. Let stand on wax paper until firm.
Store in a tightly-covered container.

CARROT NIBBLERS

1 Lb. Carrots
3 Tbs. Salad Oil
3 Cloves Garlic, minced
1 Tbs. Coarsely-chopped Onion
¼ Cup Vinegar
1½ Tsp. Salt
½ Tsp. Dry Mustard
1 Tbs. Whole Pickling Spices
1/8 Tsp. Pepper
1 Onion, thinly sliced

On the day before the nibblers are needed,
cut pared, whole carrots into lengthwise ¼"
thick slices. Then cut into strips 3" long
and 3/8" wide. In salad oil, in a skillet,
saute' garlic and chopped onion until almost
tender, about 5 minutes. Stir in vinegar,
salt, mustard, spices (tied in cheesecloth),
pepper and carrots. Simmer, covered, for
5 minutes. Carrots should still be very
crunchy and crisp. Remove cheesecloth
with spices. Transfer carrot mixture to a
shallow dish; top with a layer of onion
slices. Cover and refrigerate until needed,
basting occasionally. Serve cold. Makes
8 to 12 servings.

SPICED APPLE RELISH

12 Medium Apples, peeled and
   cored
3 Quarts Water
3 Tbs. Vinegar
1 Cup Sugar
½ Cup Light Corn Syrup
1 Cup Vinegar
2/3 Cup Water
2 Tsp. Whole Cloves
1½ Sticks Cinnamon

Cut apples into eighths and cover with water
and vinegar. Combine all other ingredients
in kettle; bring slowly to a boil. Add well-
drained apples; cover and boil for 3 minutes,
stirring occasionally. Pack apples in hot jars
and cover with liquid; adjust lids. Process
in boiling water bath (212°F.) for 15 min.
Remove jars from canner and complete the
seals unless closures are self-sealing type.
Makes 4 pints.

CRANBERRY-FIG JAM

3 Cups Dried Figs
3 Cups Water
Grated Rind of 1 Orange
4 Cups Cranberries
3 Cups Sugar
¼ Tsp. Salt

Wash figs and remove the hard stem ends.
Put through a food chopper, using medium
blade. Add water and boil for 30 minutes,
stirring frequently. Add rinds, cranberries,
sugar and salt and boil for another 30 min.
Stir often to prevent burning. Pour into
hot sterilized glasses and seal. Makes six
½-pint jars.

APPLE APPETIZER

1 Cup Creamed Cottage Cheese
1 - 2¼ Oz. Can Deviled Ham
1 Tsp. Grated Onion
2 Tbs. Chopped Black Olives
1 Tbs. Minced Pimiento
2 Tsp. Dry Sherry
3 Unpeeled Red Eating Apples,
   cut into wedges and sprinkled
   with lemon juice

Combine all ingredients, except apples, and
mix well. Pile in small bowl and surround
with apple wedges. Use apple wedges to
dip into mixture. Makes about 1½ cups.

PINEAPPLE-ORANGE COOLER

1 - 6 Oz. Can Frozen Concentrated
   Pineapple Juice
Water
½ Pint Orange Sherbet

Combine frozen concentrated pineapple
juice with water, following label directions.
Use an electric blender container. Add
orange sherbet, cover and whirl in blender
for ½ minute, or until frothy. Pour into
small glasses or cups and top with more
sherbet and a sprig of fresh mint. Makes
6 servings.

CANTALOUPE PICKLES

2 Large Cantaloupes
3 Cups Sugar
1 Lemon, sliced thin
1 Tbs. Whole Cloves
1 Tbs. Whole Allspice
6 - 1" Sticks Cinnamon
1 Tsp. Salt
1½ Cups Cider Vinegar
1½ Cups Water

Quarter, seed and pare the cantaloupes; cut
meat into 1" cubes. You should have about
8 cups. Combine cantaloupe with remaining
ingredients in a kettle; heat to boiling. Simmer, stirring often from bottom of kettle,
for 45 minutes, or until melon is translucent
and syrup is slightly thickened. Ladle into
hot sterilized jars; fill with remaining hot
syrup. Seal, following manufacturer's directions. Let jars cool; label and store in a
cool dry place. Makes 3 pints.

SPARERIB APPETIZERS

2½ Lbs. Fresh Spareribs
1 Slice Onion
¾ Cup Sugar
2 Tbs. Cornstarch
½ Tsp. Curry Powder
1/8 Tsp. Ground Cloves
¾ Cup Water
1/3 Cup Cider Vinegar
2 Tbs. Soy Sauce
1 Garlic Clove, crushed

Have butcher crack spareribs into 2-inch
long pieces. When ready to cook, cut
apart and separate into ribs; place in a
kettle with onion and water to cover.
Cover and simmer for 50 minutes, or until meat is tender but still clings to bones.
Drain and chill. When ready to finish
cooking, mix the sugar, cornstarch, curry
powder and cloves in a small saucepan;
stir in remaining ingredients. Cook, stirring constantly, until sauce thickens and
boils 3 minutes. Place ribs on a rack in
a large pan; brush with part of the sauce.
Bake in 350°F. oven for 45 minutes,
turning and brushing several times with
the remaining sauce. Makes 6 servings.

HOT CHOCOLATE
(Guatemalan Style)

2 Oz. Unsweetened Chocolate (2 squares)
2 Tbs. Water
½ Cup Sugar
1 Tbs. Cornstarch
2 Cups Freshly-brewed Strong Black
    Coffee
1½ Tsp. Ground Cinnamon
½ Tsp. Vanilla Extract
1/8 Tsp. Salt
3 Cups Hot Milk

Grate the chocolate into the top part of a double boiler over boiling water. Add the 2 tablespoons of water and mix the chocolate and water into a smooth paste. Add sugar mixed with cornstarch. Gradually stir in the coffee. Beat until smooth. Cook for about 5 minutes, stirring occasionally. Stir in cinnamon, vanilla, salt and milk. Blend thoroughly. Cook mixture for about 20 minutes, stirring occasionally. Before serving, beat with rotary beater until frothy. Makes about 6 cups, or 6 to 8 servings.

OLD-FASHIONED CANDIED FRUIT ROLL

½ Lb. Seedless Raisins
¼ Lb. Dried Figs
¼ Lb. Dried Apricots
½ Lb. Dates
¼ Lb. Candied Pineapple
½ Lb. Moist Coconut
½ Lb. Pecans or Walnuts
3 Tbs. Butter, melted
2 Cups Sugar
¾ Cup Water
3 Tbs. Vinegar

Choose fresh dried fruits when making this confection. Wash raisins, figs, and apricots and shake in a cloth to remove excess moisture. Remove seeds from dates and combine with washed fruits, pineapple and coconut. Put fruit-coconut mixture through a food grinder, using the coarse blade.

Combine ground mixture with coarsely chopped nuts and spread out on a flat pan which has been spread with the melted butter. Put sugar, water and vinegar into a saucepan; mix well and wipe down sugar from sides of pan before heating. Cook without stirring to the soft ball stage (234°F.). Remove from heat and pour over the fruit. Do not scrape any syrup out of the pan. Let cool, then knead the mixture until well mixed. Form into two rolls about 2 inches in diameter. Wrap in waxed paper or a dampened, clean cloth and place in refrigerator for about 3 hours or until it slices well. If it is to be served later on or packed for gifts, wrap in several layers of heavy waxed paper or moisture-proof cellophane and store in a tightly-covered box and keep in a cool place. Cut into ¼ inch slices to serve. Makes 3½ pounds.

AVOCADO HORS D' OEUVRES

3 Green Onions
3 Large, Ripe Avocados
¼ Cup Fresh Lemon Juice
Tabasco Sauce, to taste (3 or
    more dashes)
1 Tsp. Salt
¾ Tsp. Ground Coriander
½ Lb. Salted Cashews, chopped
    (about 2 cups before chopping)
1/3 Lb. Monterey Jack Cheese,
    shredded
½ Cup All-purpose Flour
1½ Cups Fine Dry White Bread
    Crumbs
Peanut Oil, for deep frying

Mince both green and white portions of the green onions and drop into a stainless steel bowl. Peel and seed avocados and add to green onions. Immediately add the lemon juice, Tabasco, salt and coriander. Mash with a fork until mixture is well combined. Stir in the chopped cashews and shredded cheese. Roll small balls (about 1 tbs. each) of avocado mixture lightly in flour, then coat well with bread crumbs. Pour oil into a heavy pan to depth of several inches; bring to a temperature of 350°F. on deep-frying thermometer. Fry the avocado balls until crisp and deep golden brown, about 2 min. Drain and serve while still hot. Makes approximately 60 hors d'oeuvres.

HUSH PUPPIES

2 Cups Ground Cornmeal
1½ Tsp. Salt
1 Tsp. Sugar
2 Tsp. Baking Powder
1 Tbs. Instant Minced Onion
2 Eggs, beaten
½ Cup Milk
Fat for Frying

Mix first 5 ingredients. Add eggs and milk and mix well. Shape into balls the size of a large walnut. Fry in hot deep fat (375°F. on a frying thermometer) until well browned and done, turning once. Drain on absorbent paper. Makes 4 servings.

BAKED BANANAS

5 Medium-size Green-tipped Bananas
3 Tbs. Lemon Juice
1½ Cups Crushed Cornflakes
   (approximately)

Peel the bananas; roll first in lemon juice and then in the crushed cornflakes. They should be well coated. Lay in a buttered baking pan and bake 20 to 25 minutes in a moderate oven (350°F.) until outside is brown and crisp and banana is soft. Serve hot, plain or with your favorite sauce. Makes 5 servings.

CHOCOLATE CANDY

2 - 6 Oz. Pkgs. Semi-sweet
   Chocolate Pieces
½ Cup Dairy Sour Cream
¾ Cup Confectioners' Sugar
¼ Tsp. Salt
2 Cups Finely-crushed Vanilla Wafer
   Crumbs
½ Cup Broken Walnuts

Melt semi-sweet chocolate pieces over hot (not boiling) water. Remove from water and stir in sour cream, confectioners' sugar and salt. Blend in vanilla wafer crumbs. Spread in a foil-lined 8" square pan. Press walnuts into surface. Chill until firm. Cut into 1" squares. Makes 64 pieces.

BOURBON BALLS

1 - 6 Oz. Pkg. Semisweet Chocolate
   Pieces
3 Tbs. Light Corn Syrup
¼ Cup Bourbon
½ Cup Sugar
1¼ Cups Crushed Vanilla Wafer
   Cookies (about 36)
1 Cup Finely-chopped Pecans
1 - 4 Oz. Container Chocolate
   Decorating Sprinkles

Melt the chocolate pieces in the top of a double boiler over simmering water. Remove from heat. Blend in corn syrup & bourbon. Stir in sugar, vanilla wafer cookies and pecans until well combined. Roll mixture, a rounded teaspoonful at a time, into balls between palms of hands. Roll balls in chocolate sprinkles to coat generously, pressing firmly as you roll them. Place in a jelly-roll pan; cover & chill for several hours. Makes about 3 dozen.

PINEAPPLE-CHEESE BALL

2 - 8 Oz. Pkgs. Cream Cheese,
   softened
1 - 8½ Oz. Can Crushed Pineapple,
   drained
2 Cups Chopped Pecans
¼ Cup Finely-chopped Green Pepper
2 Tbs. Finely-chopped Onion
1 Tbs. Seasoned Salt
Canned Pineapple Slices
Maraschino Cherries
Parsley Sprigs
Assorted Crackers

In a medium bowl, with a fork, beat the cream cheese until smooth. Gradually stir in the crushed pineapple, 1 cup pecans, green pepper, onion and salt.

Shape this into a ball. Roll in remaining nuts. Wrap in plastic film or foil. Refrigerate until well chilled, preferable overnight. To serve: Place cheese ball on a serving board. If desired, garnish with pineapple slices, cherries, and parsley. Surround with crackers. Let guests help themselves. Makes about 40 appetizer servings.

GOLDEN JAM

2 Large Oranges
6 Cups Diced Rhubarb
3 Cups Ground Raw Carrots
3 Cups Light Corn Syrup
2 Cups Sugar

Remove seeds and grind oranges. Combine with remaining ingredients and let stand overnight. Bring to a boil and cook slowly until rhubarb is transparent and mixture is thickened. Pour into hot sterilized jars & seal. Makes ten half-pint jars.

FROZEN STRAWBERRY DRINK

1 - 10 Oz. Pkg. Sliced, Frozen
  Strawberries
1 Quart Milk
1 Pint Strawberry Ice Cream
1 Tsp. Grated Lemon Peel

Let strawberries thaw. Combine all ingredients in a chilled bowl. Beat with rotary beater, or combine half the ingredients at a time in electric mixer and beat at high speed for 1 minute. Pour into chilled tall glasses. Makes 8 servings.

MAPLE BUCKWHEAT CAKES

½ Cup Maple Sugar, crumbled
1 Egg, beaten
1 Cup Dairy Sour Cream
½ Cup Water
1 Cup Buckwheat Flour
1 Tsp. Baking Soda
½ Tsp. Baking Powder
½ Tsp. Salt

Beat together maple sugar, egg, sour cream and water until mixture is smooth. Sift together buckwheat flour, soda, baking powder and salt. Combine mixture and beat quickly until smooth. Batter will be very thick. Drop by spoonful onto hot griddle. Leave space between the cakes since they spread in cooking. Makes about sixteen 4" cakes.

GLAZED STUFFED SHRIMP

12 Cleaned, Cooked Small Shrimp
2 Tbs. Lemon Juice
2 Tbs. Catsup
Dash of Red Pepper Seasoning
1/8 Tsp. Worcestershire Sauce

Filling:
3 Tbs. Finely-chopped Celery
1 Tbs. Chili Sauce
4 Drops Fresh Onion Juice
4 Drops Worcestershire Sauce

Gelatin Coating:
2 Tsp. Plain Gelatin
2 Tbs. Water
1 Tbs. Lemon Juice
Dash of Salt

Marinate the shrimp for 2 hours or longer in a marinade made of the lemon juice, catsup, red pepper seasoning and Worcestershire sauce. Toss to coat well. Stick a toothpick through shrimp to help hold it in a rounded form. Place on a sheet of waxed paper. Combine the filling ingredients and fill the cavity made by curve of shrimp.

Combine gelatin and water and let stand 5 minutes. Melt over hot water. Add the lemon juice and salt. Pour about ½ teaspoonful over each shrimp, using half of the mixture. Place in refrigerator to set. Remove shrimp from refrigerator, turn each one over and drip remaining gelatin mixture on other side. Cover and return to refrigerator to set. Serve cold on the end of a toothpick. Do not keep overnight as shrimp are very perishable. Makes 12.

SAN BERNARDINO LEMON-AND-CREAM DRESSING

Juice of ½ Lemon
1 Cup Mayonnaise
2 Tbs. Heavy Cream
1 Tsp. Grated Lemon Peel

Add lemon juice to mayonnaise. Fold in whipped cream and peel. Makes about 1¼ cups mayonnaise. Especially good on fruit and vegetable combinations.

YEAST WAFFLES

2 Cups Milk
1 Pkg. Active Dry Yeast
½ Cup Warm Water (110 to
    115°F.)
1/3 Cup Melted Butter
1 Tsp. Salt
1 Tsp. Sugar
3 Cups Sifted All-purpose Flour
2 Eggs, slightly beaten
½ Tsp. Baking Soda

Scald milk; cool to lukewarm. Sprinkle
yeast on warm water in large bowl; stir to
dissolve. Add milk, butter, salt, sugar and
flour to yeast; mix thoroughly with rotary
or electric mixer until batter is smooth.
Cover and let stand at room temperature
overnight. When ready to bake, add eggs
and baking soda. Beat well. Bake on preheated waffle iron. Makes 6 to 8 waffles.

NUTMEG SAUCE

1 Tbs. Flour
1 Cup Sugar
2 Cups Boiling Water
1 Tbs. Butter
½ Tsp. Grated Nutmeg
1/8 Tsp. Salt

Mix sugar, flour and salt; add boiling water
gradually, stirring constantly. Add the butter and cook for 5 minutes. Remove from
heat and stir in the nutmeg. Serve over your
favorite plain cake or pudding.

PAPAYA COCKTAIL

1 Medium Grapefruit
2¼ Cups Finely Diced Papaya
Pinch of Salt
2 Tbs. Sugar
1 Tbs. Lemon Juice
Strawberries or Cherries for Garnish

Squeeze the grapefruit and remove seeds.
Do not strain juice. Add the next four
ingredients and mix. Chill thoroughly.
To serve, pour into narrow glasses and
top with a strawberry or cherry. Makes
2 cups. Do not eat the papaya seeds.

HOT CRAB-MEAT BALLS

2½ Tbs. Butter or Margarine
3 Tbs. Flour
½ Cup Consomme' or Chicken
    Stock
½ Tsp. Salt
¼ Tsp. White Pepper
½ Cup Heavy Cream
2 Cups Crab Meat
½ Tsp. Finely-cut Tarragon
2 Tsp. Finely-cut Parsley
1 - 3 Oz. Can Chopped Broiled
    Mushrooms
2 Tbs. Butter or Margarine

Melt 2½ tablespoons butter or margarine in
a saucepan. Stir in flour and mix until
smooth and golden. Stir in consomme' or
chicken stock and boil for 1 or 2 minutes.
Add salt and pepper; stir in cream slowly.
Remove from heat. Flake the crab meat
lightly with a fork. Remove all fibers. Add
crab, tarragon, parsley and mushrooms to
cream sauce. Mix. Spread on platter to
cool. Form crab mixture into small balls.
Refrigerate or freeze. At cocktail time,
saute' lightly in hot butter or margarine.
Use a chafing dish to keep the crab meat
balls hot. Serve each on wooden pick.
Makes about 30 balls.

MEXICAN SPICED NUTS

1 Egg White
½ Cup Sugar
1 Tbs. Instant Coffee Powder
¼ Tsp. Salt
¼ Tsp. Ground Cinnamon
2 Cups Mixed Shelled Nuts
    (walnuts, pecans, Brazil nuts,
    filberts, blanched almonds,
    Macadamia nuts or peanuts)

Beat the egg white until it is foamy. Blend
in sugar, instant coffee, salt and cinnamon.
Stir in nuts and coat well. Lift out, a few
at a time, with a fork (hold over the bowl
to drain). Place, without touching one another, on buttered cookie sheet. Toast in
325°F. oven for about 20 minutes, or until
golden. Cool and store in an airtight
container. Makes 2 cups.

CHEESED POTATO CHIPS

1 - 4 Oz. Pkg. Potato Chips
½ Cup Grated Cheese
1 Tbs. Poppy Seeds
½ Tsp. Thyme

Preheat oven to 350°F. Spread the potato chips on baking sheets. Sprinkle with the cheese, then with poppy seeds and thyme. Heat 5 to 8 minutes, or until cheese is melting. Serve hot. Makes 6 servings. Vary the cheese for new flavors; use crumbled bleu cheese and finely diced olives together.

SPICED ORANGE PEEL

1 Quart Orange Peel, cut into
  ½x2" strips
1¾ Cups Sugar
1/3 Cup Vinegar
1 Tbs. Whole Cloves
3 Sticks Cinnamon

Cover the orange peel with water and let stand in refrigerator overnight. Drain well and put in a kettle; cover with water. Bring to a boil; drain and again cover with water. Bring to a boil again and then drain. Cover with water and bring to a boil for a third time; simmer for 10 minutes, or until tender. Drain. Put peel and remaining ingredients in kettle and simmer for 5 min. to form a thick syrup; stir frequently. Pour into hot sterilized ½-pint jars and seal. Makes about three ½-pint jars.

SQUASH PANCAKES

2½ Lbs. Yellow Summer Squash
3 Eggs, beaten
1 Cup All-purpose Flour
½ Cup Milk
2 Tsp. Salt
¼ Tsp. White Pepper
2 Tbs. Grated Onion
Vegetable Oil, for frying

Grate uncooked squash. Beat in remaining ingredients, except oil. Drop by tablespoon into a little hot oil in skillet. Brown on both sides and serve hot. Makes 4 to 6 servings.

TOASTED FILBERT KISSES

3 Egg Whites
1/8 Tsp. Salt
1 Cup Sugar
1 Tsp. Grated Lemon Rind
½ Tsp. Ground Cinnamon
1 Cup Toasted and Ground Filberts

Beat egg whites until foamy. Add salt and beat until whites begin to hold their shape. Gradually add sugar and beat until stiff but not dry. Fold in lemon rind, cinnamon and nuts. Drop by teaspoonfuls onto a greased cookie sheet and bake in a very slow oven (275°F.) for 20 to 25 minutes. Be sure to preheat oven. Makes 6 dozen.

To toast filberts: Spread nuts in shallow baking pan containing 1 teaspoon melted butter. Brown in hot oven (400°F.), stirring every 5 minutes. Turn out on brown paper to cool.

POTATO PANCAKES

4 Large Potatoes, pared
  (about 2 lbs.)
¼ Cup Grated Onion
2 Eggs, slightly beaten
2 Tbs. Flour
¾ Tsp. Salt
Dash of Nutmeg
Dash of Pepper
Salad Oil or Shortening for
  frying
Chilled Applesauce or Sour Cream

On medium grater, grate potatoes. Drain very well; pat dry with dish towel. Measure 3 cups. In large bowl, combine grated potato with onion, eggs, flour, salt, nutmeg & pepper. In large, heavy skillet, slowly heat oil, 1/8" deep, until very hot but not smoking. For each pancake, drop 2 tablespoons potato mixture at a time into hot fat. With spatula, flatten against bottom of skillet, to make a pancake 4 inches in diameter. Fry 2 or 3 minutes on each side, or until golden brown. Drain well on paper towels. Serve hot with applesauce or sour cream. Makes 12.

CITRUS REFRESHER

1 Cup Sugar
1 Tsp. Whole Cloves
Dash of Salt
1 - 2" Piece Cinnamon Stick
¾ Cup Lemon Juice
2 Cups Orange Juice
1 Pint Orange Sherbet
3 - 10 Oz. Bottles Carbonated
   Lemon Drink or Ginger Ale,
   well-chilled
Maraschino Cherries, with stems
Mint Sprigs

In a medium saucepan, combine sugar, 2 cups water, cloves and salt. Bring to boiling, stirring to dissolve sugar. Reduce the heat and simmer for 10 minutes. Add cinnamon stick and cool.

Combine lemon juice and orange juice with the cooled syrup; mix well and refrigerate until very cold--several hours. To serve, pour 1 cup juice into each of four tall glasses; add 1 large spoonful of sherbet and fill glass with carbonated drink. Stir. Garnish with cherry and a mint sprig. Makes 4 servings.

MEXICAN ORANGE CANDY

1 Cup Sugar
¼ Cup Boiling Water
2 Cups Sugar
Pinch of Salt
1 Cup Evaporated Milk
1 Tsp. Grated Orange Rind
1 Cup Chopped Nuts

Caramelize 1 cup of sugar to an amber color. Add boiling water and boil, stirring occasionally until caramel is entirely dissolved. Add the 2 cups of sugar, salt, and milk, and cook to a soft ball stage (236°F.). Just before candy is done, add orange rind. Remove from heat and cool. Beat until candy begins to stiffen, then stir in nuts and drop by teaspoonfuls onto buttered waxed paper. Makes 1¾ pounds.

MOLASSES FUDGE

1 Cup Granulated Sugar
1 Cup Brown Sugar
½ Cup Cream
¼ Cup Molasses
¼ Cup Melted Butter
2 Oz. Unsweetened Chocolate,
   grated
1½ Tsp. Vanilla

Combine sugar, brown sugar, cream, molasses and butter. Bring to a boil and boil for two minutes. Add chocolate. Boil 5 minutes longer, stirring until well blended and then, only enough to prevent burning. Remove from the heat; add vanilla and stir until mixture is creamy. Turn into a buttered pan & chill. Cut into squares.

GINGER TOMATO CONSERVE

1¼ Lbs. Small Yellow or Red
   Tomatoes
2¾ Cups Sugar
Grated Rind of 1 Lemon
1 Tbs. Chopped, Candied Gingerroot,
   or 1 Piece of Whole, Dried
   Gingerroot
1 Tsp. Whole Cloves
1 Tbs. Fresh Lemon Juice

Core tomatoes and prick several times with a fork. Heat tomatoes and sugar slowly with lemon rind, gingerroot, and cloves until sugar dissolves. Bring to a boil and simmer, uncovered, for 20 minutes, or until thick. Add lemon juice and pour into 3 hot sterilized 6 oz. glasses. Seal with paraffin.

BEEF-AND-CHEESE DIP

1½ Lbs. Lean Ground Beef
2 Lbs. Pasteurized Process American
   Cheese
2 Onions, peeled and grated
6 or 7 Hot Peppers, minced
2 Large Tomatoes, peeled
   and finely chopped

Cook beef in skillet until meat is no longer pink. Drain off fat. Put meat into an electric cooker. Cut cheese into small pieces; put into cooker with remaining ingredients. Stir well. Cover and cook on high for 1 hour, or until cheese is melted and mixture is blended. Serve with crackers, corn chips or potato chips. Makes about 1½ quarts of dip.

HARD SAUCE

1/3 Cup Butter
1 Cup Powdered Sugar
¼ Tsp. Lemon Extract
1 Tsp. Vanilla Extract

Cream butter; add sugar gradually and then the flavoring gradually. Continue creaming until smooth and fluffy. Chill. This may also be flavored with strong coffee, caramel or crushed fruit instead of the lemon and vanilla extracts. Brown sugar or grated maple sugar, instead of powdered sugar, also makes a delicious sauce.

GUMDROP CANDIES

1 Can Sweetened Condensed Milk
¼ Tsp. Salt
½ Cup Nuts, chopped
3 Cups Cornflakes
1 Cup Cut Gumdrops (heaping cup)
Flavoring (lemon or vanilla)
Coconut

Pour contents of milk can into top of a double boiler. Add salt, cook until thickened. Add cornflakes, finely crushed (measure before crushing). Add gumdrops, nuts and flavoring. Take out by teaspoonful & roll in coconut. Let stand on wax paper until firm.

TOMATO, PEPPER AND CELERY RELISH

3 Medium Tomatoes
1 Green Pepper, minced
1/3 Cup Diced Celery
1 Small Onion, minced
1½ Tsp. Salt
2 Tbs. Vinegar
2 Tbs. Sugar
½ Cup Cold Water
1/8 Tsp. Pepper

Peel and dice tomatoes. Combine with remaining ingredients. Chill for several hours. Drain. Makes about 2 cups.

PEANUT-BUTTER APPLE STICKS

1 Egg
¾ Cup Firmly-packed Light Brown Sugar
¼ Cup Milk
1 Tsp. Vanilla Extract
½ Cup Peanut Butter
¾ Cup Sifted All-purpose Flour
1 Tsp. Baking Powder
½ Tsp. Ground Cinnamon
¼ Tsp. Salt
1 Cup Chopped, Peeled Raw Apples
Sifted Confectioners' Sugar

Beat egg until light. Gradually beat in the brown sugar. Add milk, vanilla and peanut butter and mix well. Fold in sifted flour, baking powder, cinnamon and salt. Add the chopped apple. Spread batter in a greased 8x8x2'' pan and bake at 350°F. for 30 to 35 minutes. Cool for 5 minutes. Cut into 24 pieces. Roll in confectioners' sugar. Makes 24 sticks.

PICKLED PEACHES

8 Lbs. Firm Ripe Peaches
Whole Cloves
2 Qts. Cider Vinegar
8 Cinnamon Sticks
9 Cups Sugar (4 Lbs.)

Wash peaches and peel. Stud each with 2 whole cloves. Put vinegar, cinnamon and sugar into kettle, bring to a boil and boil for 10 minutes, or until syrup is fairly thick. Add peaches and simmer gently until tender. Let stand in syrup overnight. The next day lift out peaches and pack in hot sterilized jars. Boil syrup rapidly until thickened and pour over peaches in jars. Seal. Let stand for several weeks to develop flavor before using. Makes about 32 peaches.

CURRIED CRAB SPREAD

1 Cup Crabmeat (fresh, frozen
   or canned)
2 Tbs. Fresh Minced Parsley
1 Tbs. Finely-minced Onion
3 Tbs. Mayonnaise
¼ Tsp. Curry Powder
1 Tbs. Lemon Juice

Combine the crabmeat with the parsley, onion, mayonnaise, curry powder and lemon juice in a bowl; chill for 15 min. Makes about 1¼ cups of spread. Serve with shredded wheat wafers or Melba toast.

You can use 2 tablespoons of dried parsley and 1 tablespoon of instant minced onion if you prefer. In this case, cover the mixture and refrigerate it for at least 1 hour to allow flavors to mellow.

MAPLE SYRUP FUDGE

1 Cup Maple Syrup
2 Cups Sugar
2 Tbs. Butter
½ Cup Cream
1 Cup Chopped Walnuts

Combine all ingredients, except nuts, in a saucepan. Stir over heat until sugar is dissolved. Boil gently, without stirring, to the soft ball stage (238°F.) on the candy thermometer. Cool to lukewarm and beat until the color changes and the candy begins to set. Stir in the chopped nuts and turn into a buttered pan. When firm, cut into squares.

WELSH RABBIT

1 Tsp. Worcestershire
½ Tsp. Powdered Mustard
Dash of Paprika
½ Cup Ale
1 Lb. Natural Sharp Cheddar
   Cheese, shredded

Combine Worcestershire, mustard and paprika in a skillet. Add ale and let stand over very low heat until ale is heated through. Stir in cheese and continue to stir until cheese has melted. Do not overheat. Serve immediately over hot toast on heated plates. Makes 4 to 6 servings.

CHOCOLATE NUT WAFFLES

2 Cups Pancake Mix
2 Cups Chocolate Milk (purchased)
1/3 Cup Melted Shortening
2 Eggs
½ Cup Chopped Nuts
1½ Pints Vanilla Ice Cream
Chocolate Syrup

Combine pancake mix, chocolate milk, shortening and eggs in mixing bowl. Beat with rotary beater until fairly smooth. Stir in nuts. Bake in hot waffle iron until steam stops. Serve hot with vanilla ice cream and chocolate syrup. Makes 5 servings.

BUTTERSCOTCH SAUCE

3 Lbs. Light Brown Sugar (6¾ cups)
3 Cups Corn Syrup
1 Cup Butter or Margarine
¾ Tsp. Salt
3 Cups Evaporated Milk
   (undiluted)
1 Tbs. Vanilla Extract

In a heavy kettle, combine light brown sugar, corn syrup, butter or margarine, and salt. Bring to a full boil, stirring until the sugar is dissolved. Add the milk and vanilla. Serve warm or cold. Makes about 10½ cups, or enough sauce for 50 servings.

ALMOND SHRIMP APPETIZERS

½ Cup Butter or Margarine
3 Garlic Cloves, minced or mashed
½ Cup Sliced Almonds
2 Lbs. Medium Shrimp, shelled,
   cleaned and deveined
½ Cup Chopped Parsley
Lemon Wedges

Melt the butter in a frying pan. Add the garlic and almonds and stir over medium heat until almonds are lightly toasted. Add the shrimp and keep turning until meat is opaque. Cook and turn for about 5 minutes. Stir in parsley. Transfer to a serving dish or warming tray. Serve with lemon wedges. Makes 8 servings.

SPANISH CHOCOLATE DRINK

2 Oz. Unsweetened Chocolate
   (2 squares)
2 Cups Milk
½ Cup Sugar
1 Tsp. Vanilla Extract
1/8 Tsp. Ground Cloves
1 Egg

In top part of double boiler, over hot water, melt together chocolate and milk. Beat with a rotary beater until blended. Stir in sugar, vanilla and cloves. Beat egg until frothy in pitcher in which chocolate will be served. Pour chocolate over egg and beat again to a froth. Serve at once. Makes about 3½ cups or 4 servings.

COCONUT-PECAN BALLS

2 Boxes Confectioners' Sugar
1 Can Coconut
1 Cube of Margarine (½ cup)
2 Pkgs. Chocolate Chips
4 Cups Pecans
1 Can Sweetened Condensed Milk
½ Bar Paraffin Wax

Mix powdered sugar, pecans and coconut together. Add milk and margarine. Work all ingredients together and shape into balls or into long rolls. Put into refrigerator to harden. Melt chocolate chips and wax in double boiler. Leave on low heat and dip each piece of candy in the chocolate mixture. Drain on waxed paper.

APRICOT-COCONUT CANDY

8 Oz. Dried Apricots (1 cup)
1 Cup Shredded Coconut
¾ Cup Pistachio Nuts
1 Tsp. Grated Lemon Peel
1 Tsp. Lemon Juice
1 Tbs. Orange Juice
2 Tbs. Confectioners' Sugar
Granulated Sugar

Steam apricots in the top part of double boiler over boiling water for 10 minutes. Put apricots, coconut, nuts and peel through food grinder together twice, using a fine blade. Add juices and confectioners' sugar. Stir well. Shape into small balls. Roll in granulated sugar. Let dry several hours before using or storing in airtight container. Makes approximately 2 dozen balls. If desired, these may be dipped in chocolate coating. Let dry on waxed paper until chocolate is cold and firm.

MAIN DISHES

CAKES - BREADS

DESSERTS

COOKIES

SALADS

MISCELLANEOUS